A Companion to the Study
of St. Anselm

A Companion to the Study of St. Anselm

by Jasper Hopkins

UNIVERSITY OF MINNESOTA PRESS · Minneapolis

Printed in the United States of America
at Lund Press, Minneapolis
Published in the United Kingdom and India by the Oxford University
Press, London and Delhi, and in Canada
by the Copp Clark Publishing Co. Limited, Toronto

Library of Congress Catalog Card Number: 72-79097

ISBN 0-8166-0657-9

The *Philosophical Fragments* has been translated from
*Ein neues unvollendetes Werk des hl. Anselm von
Canterbury*, edited by Pater Franciscus Salesius
Schmitt (*Beiträge zur Geschichte der Philosophie
und Theologie des Mittelalters*, 33/3. Founded by
Clemens Baeumker). Münster (Westfalen):
Aschendorff Press, 1936.

To Herbert W. Richardson and to F. S. Schmitt, whose death while this book was in press is a loss to all students and scholars of medieval thought

Preface

Interest in the life and thought of Anselm of Canterbury (1033–1109) has burgeoned so rapidly since World War II that we might appropriately speak of a renascence. The occasion for this renascence was the appearance of F. S. Schmitt's critical Latin edition of Anselm's complete works, which was published in five volumes between 1938 and 1951. (A sixth volume, an index, was published in 1961.) In recent years not only have Anselm's major treatises been translated into English but so also have the two documentary sources of his life written by Eadmer, monk of Canterbury.[1] Moreover, D. P. Henry has been able to make sense out of *De Grammatico* and has gone on to scrutinize the main aspects of Anselm's logic. R. W. Southern has written a discerning biography which touches upon theological as well as political and ecclesiastical developments. And a number of individual studies have been produced dealing with such topics as the ontological argument, the theory of the atonement, and the symbolism of the sacraments. Still more currently, we may now look forward to a series of *Analecta Anselmiana* under the editorship of F. S. Schmitt et al.

Given this renewal of scholarship, the time has now come for a companion to the study of St. Anselm — envisioned primarily as a handbook for students. This work treats systematically and critically the major philosophical and theological themes taken up by this most important

1. See the bibliography for a list of some of these recent works.

intellectual figure in the late eleventh- and early twelfth-century Latin Church. In preparing this volume, I have drawn upon, and entered into discussion with, already existing studies of particular topics in Anselm's writings. At the same time, I have sought to give a unified interpretation of the interrelationship of these topics and, furthermore, to exhibit the close affinity between philosophy and theology as it existed in the period between Augustine and Aquinas. To this end, I have treated not only the more philosophical issues of truth, freedom, and evil, but also the specifically theological themes of trinity, incarnation, and redemption. It is not precisely true that for Anselm philosophy is conceived generally as a mere handmaid of theology (*ancilla theologiae*). But it is true that as monk of Bec and archbishop of Canterbury his own concern with philosophy was primarily for the sake of theology. Indeed, a clear distinction between these two disciplines had to await the articulation of Thomas Aquinas in the thirteenth century.

Chapter I deals with the character of Anselm's works, their ordering, and their historical sources. In the short section on chronology I have summarized the conclusions and underlying textual evidence originally presented by F. S. Schmitt in the *Revue Bénédictine*. Although Schmitt's ordering of the Anselm corpus is incontrovertible, many American students, even at the graduate level, are not sufficiently versed in German to have ready access to Schmitt's arguments. Chapter II deals with the broad topic of faith and reason and contends with the question of whether or not Anselm addressed the ontological argument to believers only — whether, for that matter, he even thought of himself as proving the existence of God. Chapter III takes up the structure of the ontological argument, discussing Anselm's conception of necessity and taking exception to a contemporary defense of the argument's soundness. Chapter IV sets forth the doctrine of the Trinity and shows how Anselm followed Augustine by distinguishing between relational and substantial predicates in order to make plausible the notion that God is three persons in one nature. Chapter V examines Anselm's conviction that the human will has remained free even though human nature has fallen. In this same chapter Anselm's theory of language, concept of truth, and doctrine of not-being are explored. Chapter VI clarifies and criticizes Anselm's teachings in regard to atonement and original sin. Anselm views the death of Christ as restoring honor to God on man's behalf. The *Cur Deus Homo*, accordingly, expounds a theory of atonement which makes full sense only in the light of the orthodox dogma that Jesus was the God-man, two natures in one person. The first appendix adds a translation of the *Philosophical Fragments*,[2] whose subject matter possibly was meant by Anselm to be included in the curriculum of the *trivium*. Among other things these fragments deal, incompletely, with the "logic" of the Latin verb *facere*, the concept of possibility, and the divisions of causation. The second appendix discusses briefly Anselm's methods of arguing, inasmuch as these were typical of the early Middle Ages.

For different reasons I owe special acknowledgment to Herbert Richardson and F. S. Schmitt. The former first interested me in Anselm and in the project of rendering into English Anselm's remaining untranslated major treatises. These translations appeared in two volumes in 1967 and 1970. Intense study of the Latin texts with Herbert Richardson fostered a familiarity with Anselm that undergirds the present book. In last analysis, therefore, this book could not have been written without the initiative and genius of my earlier collaborator and continuing friend, whom I have repeatedly consulted. To F. S. Schmitt I am indebted for having laid the foundation for all Anselm scholarship. His reliable textual, historical, and critical studies constitute a monumental achievement in demarcating and illuminating the mind of Anselm. Without question Father Schmitt is the leading international authority on Anselm. I have profited by the opportunity to talk and to correspond with him.

To the National Endowment for the Humanities I am grateful for a research fellowship to work in Munich during 1967–68, at which time I wrote the first draft of this manuscript.

Jasper Hopkins

December 1971

2. Portions of these fragments have also been translated by D. P. Henry, *The Logic of Saint Anselm* (Oxford, 1967), pp. 121–133, 158–161.

Anselm's Works

Abbreviations

M	*Monologion* (Soliloquy)
P	*Proslogion* (An Address)
DG	*De Grammatico* (On the Word *Grammaticus*)
DV	*De Veritate* (Concerning Truth)
DL	*De Libertate Arbitrii* (On Freedom of Choice)
DCD	*De Casu Diaboli* (On the Fall of Satan (the Devil))
DIV	*Epistola de Incarnatione Verbi* (On the Incarnation of the Word)
CDH	*Cur Deus Homo* (Why God Became Man)
DCV	*De Conceptu Virginali et de Originali Peccato* (On the Virgin Conception and Original Sin)
DP	*De Processione Spiritus Sancti* (On the Procession of the Holy Spirit)
	Epistola de Sacrificio Azimi et Fermentati (The Sacrifice of Leavened and Unleavened Bread)
	Epistola de Sacramentis Ecclesiae (The Sacraments of the Church)
DC	*De Concordia Praescientiae et Praedestinationis et Gratiae Dei cum Libero Arbitrio* (On the Harmony

NOTE: For a list of English translations of Anselm's works, see the bibliography.

of the Foreknowledge, the Predestination, and the Grace of God with Free Choice)

Meditatio ad Concitandum Timorem (Meditation for Arousing Dread)

Deploratio Virginitatis Male Amissae (Lament for Virginity Evilly Lost)

Meditatio Redemptionis Humanae (Meditation on Human Redemption)

PF *Ein neues unvollendetes Werk des hl. Anselm von Canterbury* (Philosophical Fragments)

Orationes (Prayers)

Ep. *Epistola, -ae* (Letter-s)

Other Works
(For full citation see the bibliography)

DT Augustine's *De Trinitate* (On the Trinity). E.g., DT 7.4.7 indicates Book 7, Chapter 4, Section 7

ST Thomas's *Summa Theologica* (Compendium of Theology)

PL *Patrologia Latina* (ed. J. P. Migne) *

CCSL *Corpus Christianorum.* Series Latina

AA *Analecta Anselmiana* (ed. F. S. Schmitt)

SB *Spicilegium Beccense I*

HSD *L'homme et son destin*

S *Sancti Anselmi Opera Omnia* (ed. F. S. Schmitt). E.g., S I, 237:7 indicates Volume 1, page 237, line 7.

SR *Sola ratione* (ed. H. Kohlenberger)

* For convenience, references to Augustine's Latin texts are to PL. Attention is called to the texts in CCSL and CSEL (*Corpus Scriptorum Ecclesiasticorum Latinorum*).

Table of Contents

Chapter I   Basic Writings and Sources   3

Chapter II   Faith and Reason   38

Chapter III   Ontological Argument   67

Chapter IV   Doctrine of the Trinity   90

Chapter V   Doctrine of Man, Freedom, and Evil   122

Chapter VI   Christology and Soteriology   187

Appendix I   Anselm's Philosophical Fragments   215

Appendix II   Anselm's Methods of Arguing   246

English Translations of Anselm's Works   257

Abbreviations   259

Bibliography   260

Index   279

A Companion to the Study
of St. Anselm

Chapter I

Basic Writings

and Sources

ANSELM'S WORKS

Systematic character. The systematic unfolding and almost total internal consistency of the writings of Anselm of Canterbury have long evoked amazement. The straightforward definitions of "truth," "justice," and "freedom," for instance, as set forth in the early dialogues *De Veritate* and *De Libertate*, are carried through subsequent treatises with perfect harmony — to the point where the latest work, *De Concordia*, explicitly utilizes these same definitions of "justice" and "freedom," while not conflicting with the doctrine of truth. Unlike Augustine, Anselm had no need to write *retractationes* (reconsiderations); the working out of his doctrines is not subject to that kind of historical development which makes a distinction between *early* and *late* important. Anselm's genius lay in his ability to formulate and deal intensively with a particular problem without losing sight of the direction in which his proposed solution would lead. Thus, although he does not discuss the relevance of grace to free choice in *De Libertate*, he recognizes that he owes the reader such a discussion, thereby implying that he has already begun to contemplate this relationship.[1] And again, although the immediate occasion of the *Cur Deus Homo* is to demonstrate why man's salvation rationally necessitates the divine incarnation, Anselm is aware that he must take up else-

1. S I, 173:10–15.

where, and more extensively, the issue of original sin and infant baptism, as a supplement to the main arguments of the *Cur Deus Homo*. (This he does in *De Conceptu*.) No less striking is the fact that he works with only a handful of examples, introducing them wherever his arguments intersect at the same point.[2] This use of standard examples further manifests the systematic coherence between one work and another.

The unity of Anselm's works may perhaps be accounted for by two factors: the mature age at which he began to write; and the limited number and the concentrated scope of his writings. When he composed the *Monologion* he was already forty-three years old. By that time he had spent seventeen years studying at Bec, four of them with Lanfranc, who is credited with having revived the *trivium* and *quadrivium*.[3] By contrast with Augustine, Anselm wrote only a modest number of *opera*: nineteen prayers, three meditations, five dialogues, and six discourses (though nearly four hundred letters). By limiting his philosophical and theological doctrines to eleven major works (the *Monologion* and the *Cur Deus Homo* being the longest), he was able to interlace his ideas from book to book. Thus, *De Processione* overlaps with *De Incarnatione*; *De Incarnatione* with *De Conceptu*; and *De Conceptu* with the *Cur Deus Homo*. Far from being incidental, this overlapping serves a purpose. In some cases Anselm is giving new arguments for, and explanations of, the same doctrine. The *Monologion*, *De Incarnatione*, and *De Processione* all deal to a greater or lesser extent with the doctrine of the Trinity. And *Cur Deus Homo* I, 16–18, expands on the topic of men replacing fallen angels — as dealt with in *De Casu Diaboli* 5. *De Casu Diaboli* takes up anew, and at length, the question of what is meant by "nothing" — a question treated preliminarily in *Monologion* 8. And both *De Conceptu* 5 and *De Concordia* I, 7, repeat the conclusions about the word "nothing" and its meanings. In other cases, Anselm must appeal to previously established notions which are presupposed by an argument immediately underway. God's impassibility, established in *Monologion* 25, is presupposed by the discussion of *Cur Deus Homo* I, 8. And the idea that the

2. Such examples are as follows: the rich man in relation to the poor man (M 8; DL 2); the master-servant example (M 3; DP 2); the blind man illustration (DCD 11; DCV 5); various illustrations of the role of "ought" and "can" (DV 8; CDH II, 17); the case of delivering a beating (DV 8; CDH I, 7).

3. "We may acquit Ordericus of undue enthusiasm, when, in a long and celebrated passage, he speaks of the school of Bec, which made of all its monks philosophers." D. Knowles, *The Monastic Order in England* (Cambridge, 1949), p. 97.

good angels must not have been advantaged by the fall of the evil angels, expounded in *De Casu Diaboli* 25, is only alluded to in *Cur Deus Homo* I, 17. In still other cases, Anselm anticipates himself from one work to another. In *Proslogion* 9 we find him already puzzling over the question of how a fully just God can spare the wicked — the problem of the later *Cur Deus Homo*.[4]

Although a distinction between the early and the later Plato, for example, is crucial to discussing his theory of Forms, no such distinction, we have said, helps to understand a single one of Anselm's doctrines.[5] In overlapping works Anselm reaffirms rather than changes his views. What does change, however, is his style and, to some extent, his method. His first argumentative writings, the *Monologion* and the *Proslogion*, were regarded as meditations. In fact, the original title for the *Monologion* was "An Example of Meditating about the Rational Basis of Faith" (*Exemplum meditandi de ratione fidei*); and the intonations and prayers of the *Proslogion* are reminiscent of Augustine's importunings in the *Confessions*. By contrast, the subsequent dialogues — *De Grammatico*, *De Veritate*, *De Libertate*, *De Casu Diaboli*, *Cur Deus Homo* — do not represent arguments set forth in the aura of prayer, although like the *Proslogion* they are intended to aid students grappling with the difficulties that inevitably confront those who insist on reasons for their faith. The *Cur Deus Homo* must be considered an exception to the other dialogues inasmuch as its interlocutor, Boso, is a real rather than an imaginary person (the *discipulus*) and its purpose is to answer real rather than hypothetical opponents. On the other hand, *De Grammatico* is an exception because it serves purely as a philosophical manual providing training in dialectic and having no ostensible connection with theology.

4. The *Meditation on Human Redemption* (1099) serves as a summary of the central argument of the *Cur Deus Homo*.

5. See F. S. Schmitt, "Zur Chronologie der Werke des hl. Anselm von Canterbury," *Revue Bénédictine*, 44 (1932), 322–350. Schmitt orders Anselm's major works as follows: *Monologion*, completed in the second half of 1076. *Proslogion*, probably written about 1077–78. The controversy with Gaunilo occurred the next year or so. *De Grammatico*, *De Veritate*, and *De Libertate*, probably written between 1080 and 1085. *De Casu Diaboli*, probably completed sometime between 1085 and 1090. *Epistola de Incarnatione Verbi*, the first recension was finished before September 1092. The final recension was published about the beginning of 1094. *Cur Deus Homo*, begun between 1094 and 1097; completed in the summer of 1098. *De Conceptu Virginali et Originali Peccato*, written between the summer of 1099 and the summer of 1100. *De Processione Spiritus Sancti*, completed in summer 1102. *Epistola de Sacrificio Azimi et Fermentati* and *De Sacramentis Ecclesiae*, written about 1106–7. *De Concordia*, written about 1107–8.

Anselm is clear about his purpose in utilizing the dialogue format: "Since topics investigated by means of question and answer are more acceptable because more clear — especially to those who are slower in following, but also to many others as well — I shall take that discussant who presses me more insistently than the others, so that in this way Boso may ask and Anselm answer" (CDH I, 1. S II, 48:11–15). Anselm's dialogues differ from Plato's by making no mention of historical setting, and by otherwise furnishing no mask of having actually occurred as recorded. Indeed, Anselm's works taken collectively exhibit no sense of history. Even when he approaches a characteristically historical issue such as the incarnation, he approaches it ahistorically, educing considerations "apart from Christ" (*remoto Christo*) appealing to "rational necessity" (*rationibus necessariis*). In later life Anselm drops the dialogue format altogether, preferring a direct confrontation with Roscelin or the Greeks or whatever other opponents he is facing. These later treatises also become more hermeneutical. Anselm involves himself to a greater degree in the task of interpreting Scriptural texts, in order to show that they do not conflict with what reason teaches. To take one example, he hastens in *De Conceptu* 14 to render the "real meaning" of Psalms 51:5 ("I was begotten in iniquity, and in sin did my mother conceive me"), so that no one by appealing to Scripture may fault his sustained argument regarding original sin. His earlier dialogues *De Veritate*, *De Libertate*, and *De Casu Diaboli* had indeed touched upon this kind of exegesis. He even describes these dialogues as "pertaining to the study of sacred Scripture" (S I, 173:2). Yet they only sporadically take up questions of Scriptural interpretation and instead primarily concentrate on furnishing non-Scriptural justifications for views believed to be stated in Scripture. The later treatises, on the other hand, not only are more occupied with explicating biblical passages but also make use of biblical teachings in the course of completing the various lacunae in an extended line of reasoning. A prime example of this is found in *De Processione* 1: (1) "We must therefore conclude with absolute and irrefutable necessity that if the above-mentioned things are true (things which we believe the same as do the Greeks), then either the Son exists from the Holy Spirit or the Holy Spirit exists from the Son." (This is a "mixed" premise depending in part on reason and in part on authority.) (2) "But that the Son does not exist from the Holy Spirit is known clearly from the Catholic faith. For God only exists from God either by being begotten (as is the Son) or by proceeding (as does the Holy Spirit)." (The rejection of one of the alternatives specified in the disjunction cannot be done by reasoning alone, and hence must be accomplished by the introduction of a proposition whose truth is established by defined faith.) [6](3) "And so it follows by an irrefutable argument that the Holy Spirit exists from the Son." (The conclusion follows from the form of the argument.)

Another example is the argument in *De Conceptu* 3, posed against those who maintain that original sin is not really a sin. For were it not a sin, notes Anselm, "It would immediately follow that an infant, who has only original sin, is free from sin; and then the Son of the Virgin would not be the only man who was without sin both in His mother's womb and at His birth. If this were the case, then either those infants who have only original sin and die without baptism would not be condemned, or else they would be condemned without sin. *But we believe (accipimus) neither of these alternatives.* So we must conclude that every sin is injustice and that since original sin is an unconditional sin, it is also injustice" (S II, 142:26–31). The more universal appeal to Scripture which characterizes the later works represents a change in method, then, as well as a change in style. In a general way, the later works are more doctrinal, the earlier more philosophical. In the period at Bec, Anselm dealt with the proof of God's existence, the nature of evil, the definition of "freedom," the two truths of propositions, the theory of paronymy, the theory of sight, and the meaning of special terms like "ought." To see this contrast between the philosophical and the doctrinal more fully, one need only compare the *Monologion* with *De Processione*. Both concern the Trinity. But the former more than the latter moves by reason alone (*ratione sola*) and without appeal to Scripture. The *Cur Deus Homo*, a middle work, combines earlier discussions of "ought to" and "able to" with its own analysis of "necessary to" — and enlists these to

6. Note the following argument in DP 2: "Now, the Holy Spirit can only have existence in one of two ways: (1) either from another (as is the case with the Son), or (2) from no one (as is the case with the Father). But if He exists from no one, then He exists just as the Father exists, and an alternative follows: Either (a) each one exists through Himself in such a way that neither has anything from the other; and then there are two gods, namely, the Father and the Holy Spirit. Or (b) since they are one God, and if each one exists from no one, then we are unable to find anything in the Christian faith to differentiate them from each other. But then the Father and the Holy Spirit would be one-and-the same; i.e., they would both be one person. *But true faith abhors both of these alternatives;* therefore, it is false that the Holy Spirit exists from no one." S II, 187:33–188:5 (my italics).

answer the theological question of whether Jesus was able to avoid death. *De Concordia* concentrates on the topic of freedom and foreknowledge, but unlike *De Libertate* and *De Casu Diaboli* it introjects the theological consideration of grace. (Some of the more philosophical parts of *De Concordia* were first composed during Anselm's early period.) Moreover, a further change in method has its beginnings in *De Concordia*, where Anselm advances three systematic questions to be answered by combined appeals to reason, Scripture, experience, and considerations of language. Here in a primitive way he foreshadows the sophisticated method of presentation crystallized a century later in the *Summa Theologica* of Aquinas.

Anselm seems to imitate Boethius's theological tractates by citing no authorities. R. W. Southern rightly asserts that this lack of overt quotation by Anselm "sets him apart from all his contemporaries, except those who came under his immediate influence, and from the main line of development of medieval scholastic thought." [7] But although extensive references to Augustine and the earlier Fathers are no doubt the rule during the period up to Anselm (and even later), the case of Boethius indicates that Anselm is not without precedent. For the author of the tractates, like his eleventh-century successor, probes the doctrine of the Trinity using reason alone, without appealing to the authority of Scripture; nonetheless, he acknowledges Scripture's authority and at the same time expresses indebtedness to Augustine as Anselm does in the preface to the *Monologion*. One should not infer that Anselm's decision against the marshaling of authorities stems from a detailed ignorance of these works. No doubt he was more interested in pursuing arguments and in defending dogmas than in conducting extensive historical research. But like all scholars at Bec he was versed in the doctrines of the Fathers. Moreover, his intimate acquaintance with Augustine and Boethius is obvious even in the absence of a list of overt references to them. In the *Monologion* preface he expresses apprehension lest he be considered to be setting forth new (and false) ideas. He there betrays hesitancy at publishing a work which minimizes recourse to authorities; and his explicit reference to Augustine, as well as his request that the preface be copied with the *Monologion*, must be understood as an attempt to anticipate suspicions. When we remember Augustine's unfocused treatment of sundry topics

---

7. *Saint Anselm and His Biographer* (Cambridge, 1963), p. 52.

and his interruptive — even distractive — use of Scriptural quotations, we may be more appreciative that Anselm here stands with Boethius.[8]

Chronology of writing. The chronological ordering of Anselm's works is based upon both internal and external considerations; for not only does Anselm specifically refer from one work to another, but Eadmer, his contemporary and biographer, furnishes information regarding when and where a number of these works were written.[9] A survey of Anselm's major writings reveals the following: (1) The *Proslogion* preface refers to the *Monologion* as previously written. (2) The preface to the three dialogues *De Veritate*, *De Libertate*, and *De Casu Diaboli* asks that they be arranged in that order, but says nothing about the actual sequence of composition. (3) *De Veritate* 1 repeats the argument about the eternal nature of truth which is advanced in the *Monologion*, and mentions the *Monologion* by name. (4) *Cur Deus Homo* II, 9, indicates that *De Incarnatione* has already been written. (5) *De Conceptu* is subsequent to the *Monologion, Proslogion, De Veritate, De Casu Diaboli, Cur Deus Homo* — all of which are therein named. *De Conceptu* is the sequel to the *Cur Deus Homo*, and gives another reason for how God could assume from the sinful mass a nature which had no sin. (6) *De Processione* 9 mentions *De Incarnatione* and the death of Pope Urban II (1099). (7) The preface to the *Cur Deus Homo* states that this book was begun when Anselm was already archbishop and completed while he was an exile in Capua, Italy (1098). (8) *De Incarnatione*, cast in the form of a letter to Pope Urban II, was begun at Bec and completed in England. The content of Chapter 1 implies that the completion came not long after Anselm was made archbishop.

These pieces of information, taken alone, furnish only incomplete guidelines for the ordering of Anselm's works. Yet from these facts it seems clear that the *Monologion* and the *Proslogion* are the earliest systematic works and that *De Veritate*, *De Libertate*, and *De Casu Diaboli*

8. We may remember too that in our own day Paul Tillich's *Systematic Theology* has no footnotes. Yet no one would think of denying his extensive historical knowledge. Anselm is self-consciously adopting a terse style. Note his statement to this effect in the *Monologion* preface. S I, 7:8–11.
   In Ep. 83 Anselm indicates that his views in the *Monologion* have been misunderstood.

9. This section on chronology summarizes the conclusions of F. S. Schmitt, whose investigations into the dating of Anselm's works cannot be challenged. See n. 5 above.

come next — assuming they were composed at different times during roughly the same period (*tres tractates . . . feci diversis temporibus*). Following these dialogues are *De Incarnatione, Cur Deus Homo* (1098), *De Conceptu*, and *De Concordia*. We know that *De Processione* was written after 1099 — i.e., after Pope Urban's death, and therefore after the *Cur Deus Homo* — but we do not learn how long afterward.

Anselm's letters cast some, but not much, light on the question of chronology. Four of them have noticeable bearing. (1) An exchange of correspondence with Hildebert, bishop of Le Mans, finds Hildebert thanking Anselm for having sent a copy of *De Processione* (Ep. 240).[10] The letter seems to have been composed sometime between April and December of 1102. (2) From two versions of *Epistola* 97 one can surmise something about the possible date of *De Casu Diaboli*. To the first version is appended a special treatise discussing the word "evil" and whether it is a name. Since this treatise was written "recently" (*nuper*), and since by implication it is complete in itself, one may infer that *De Casu Diaboli* had not yet been composed. However, in the second recension the essay is no longer appended. One plausible hypothesis for this omission is that *De Casu Diaboli* was now finished, rendering the shorter essay superfluous. If this second recension can be dated around 1092–93, as Schmitt suggests, then there would be at least some reason for fixing that as the extreme date of composition for the dialogue. (3) With *Epistola* 72 to Lanfranc (then in Canterbury) Anselm sends a copy of the *Monologion*. In a subsequent letter (Ep. 77) he defends himself against objections which Lanfranc had raised to this work. It is not unlikely that this letter was dispatched to Canterbury along with numbers 78 and 79. And *Epistola* 78 contains Anselm's congratulations to Gundulf on his consecration as bishop of Rochester, an event occurring in March 1077. If, then, Anselm's reply to Lanfranc was drafted in the early spring of 1077, it is probable that the *Monologion* had been completed and sent off before the end of 1076. (4) *Epistola* 109 to Hugh, archbishop of Lyons, requests that the *Monoloquium de ratione fidei* and the *Alloquium de ratione fidei*, sent earlier, have their titles changed to simply *Monologion* and *Proslogion*. Anselm intimates that he has no other works available but

10. Ep. 239 from Hildebert requests that the sermon he heard Anselm deliver at the Council of Bari be set down in a tractate and that Anselm argue against the Greeks using authorities accepted by both the Greeks and the Latins. And Ep. 241 is Anselm's reply to 240 stating that he will send some of his other works which Hildebert has not seen.

expresses the hope that some will be forthcoming.[11] The *Monologion* and the *Proslogion* thus seem to be the earliest systematic writings.

With these gleanings from Anselm himself in mind, we may turn to Eadmer for his account of the basic works. Eadmer lists the works composed at Bec without mentioning the time of their composition. He implies that all of Anselm's works at Bec were written during the time of his priorship (1063–78), and that during the next fifteen years as abbot (1078–93), Anselm wrote no major discourses. These first works Eadmer lists as *De Veritate, De Libertate, De Casu Diaboli, De Grammatico, Monologion*, and *Proslogion* — in this order, though nowhere does he state that this order corresponds to the chronology of actual production. Morever, we are told that as archbishop (1093–1109), Anselm produced *De Incarnatione*, the *Cur Deus Homo, De Conceptu, De Processione*, and *De Concordia*, respectively. As has already been mentioned, *De Incarnatione* was addressed to Pope Urban II and was later used by the pope at the Council of Bari (October 1098). *De Conceptu*, together with the *Meditatio Redemptionis Humanae*, was written in exile at Lyons (1099–1100). Regarding *De Processione*, it is impossible to discern from Eadmer any information, for neither in *Vita Anselmi* nor in *Historia Novorum* does he mention this work by name. Finally, Eadmer mentions that *De Concordia* was written sometime during Anselm's recurrent illness at the Abbey of St. Edmund's (1107–8).

A comparison of Eadmer's and Anselm's statements indicates that Eadmer's ordering of the works written at Bec cannot be correct. The *Monologion* could not have been written after *De Veritate*, simply because *De Veritate* refers to the *Monologion* as completed, and because there are no signs of this being a later insertion. One may infer either that Eadmer did not know the true order of these works or that he did not intend to put them down in such order.[12] The latter alternative must be affirmed, since Eadmer must have read Anselm's works, and thus must have known the striking cross-reference in *De Veritate*. As for Eadmer's implication that Anselm wrote no works while abbot, we have already

11. "If you have act in accordance with our request [to change the titles], I wish to repay this to Your Paternity — so that if God grants me to write those things which I desire to write, I will not deprive you of seeing them, since I think that they will be no less acceptable than the earlier writings." S III, 242.

12. Eadmer tells us that Anselm read a copy of the biography while it was still in progress and made corrections to it. But presumably the list of writings at Bec was not "proofread."

seen that there is reason to date *De Casu Diaboli* sometime during the last part of Anselm's tenure as abbot. And if *De Veritate, De Libertate*, and *De Grammatico* were of the same period, then they too were worked out after Anselm was promoted from prior to abbot. Schmitt suggests that Eadmer was not well informed about Anselm's order of writing during the period at Bec; for although he had met Anselm briefly in 1079, he had no detailed and firsthand acquaintance with his activities before Anselm's arrival in England in 1092. Hence we must distinguish Eadmer's reliability during the Canterbury period from his reliability during the earlier period.[13] And in fact Eadmer's order of reference to works of the Canterbury period harmonizes with what we learn from internal evidence and the letters.

Even if exact dating of all the works is impossible, still we know what we need to about the development of Anselm's thinking and about the interrelationship of his ideas — a fact which renders more precise dating unnecessary (from this point of view). As for the *Philosophical Fragments*, no accurate dating is possible, except to say that it was the collective product of Anselm's thought beginning from the period of his first dialogues. The composite drawn together by Schmitt was not written at one time — even though in the *Cur Deus Homo* Anselm did witness his intention to write an entirely separate treatise: "I see another reason why at present we can scarcely if at all deal fully with the issue at hand. For in order to do so it is necessary to treat the notions of ability, necessity, will — together with other inter-related notions. And so the development of these topics requires a separate treatise — one which though difficult to write is nonetheless worth the trouble. For knowledge of these topics clears up certain problems produced by ignorance" (CDH I, 1. S II, 49: 7-13). The topics mentioned here — ability, necessity, and will — constitute the passages collected by Schmitt under the title *Ein neues unvollendetes Werk des hl. Anselm von Canterbury*. We should not suppose that the whole composition of these philosophical fragments must be subsequent to that of the *Cur Deus Homo* in the way the writing of *De Conceptu* is. The longest section — the section on *facere* — exhibits that pronounced interest in dialectic which characterizes *De Grammatico*, and may indeed have been written about the same time.[14]

13. Schmitt, "Zur Chronologie der Werke," p. 327.

14. The dialogue format also suggests that PF was not one of Anselm's later works. Schmitt reasons that at least the "Exordium" was written after CDH, for it ex-

Aside from these fragments, there are no incomplete or lost works of Anselm's, since copies do exist of every major treatise known to have been written by him. However, the problem of lost recensions of existing works is somewhat different. In the preface to the three dialogues *De Veritate, De Libertate,* and *De Casu Diaboli,* as well as in the preface to the *Cur Deus Homo* and in the first chapter of *De Incarnatione,* Anselm is disturbed because students had prematurely transcribed these texts. With regard to the other works, manuscript evidence enables the determination of a number of revisions for the *Monologion, De Sacrificio Azimi,* and *De Concordia.* In general, later recensions of the same work may add new material, but actual corrections of earlier versions are few. After reading a draft of the *Monologion,* Lanfranc sent off suggestions for correction. Although this letter has never been found, we do have Anselm's reply (Ep. 77) defending himself for not having cited authorities. There is no indication that he was moved by Lanfranc's criticisms, for his subsequent improvements on the draft are of only incidental and linguistic importance.

We may also attribute the differences in the versions of *De Incarnatione* to students' having copied unfinished forms of it.[15] The same holds true of *De Concordia,* where the earliest drafts contain parts of *De Libertate,* as well as a projected section of *De Veritate.* One may conjecture that copies were made, unsanctioned by Anselm, before he had settled on *De Veritate* as an independent work.[16] Changes from one recension of a specific work to another are not all Anselm's — copyists having been

presses dissatisfaction with a solution which is found in CDH, as can be seen in the two examples which follow. CDH II, 17: "Whenever God is said not to be able, an ability is not denied Him but an insuperable power and strength are signified." PF 24:22–25: "If you answer that this impossibility and necessity signify in God an insuperable strength, then I ask: why should this strength be designated by names signifying weakness?" Presumably, had Anselm written CDH after this section of PF, he would have raised against himself the same objection as in PF.

15. See F. S. Schmitt, "Cinq recensions de l'*Epistola de Incarnatione Verbi* de S. Anselme de Cantorbéry," *Revue Bénédictine,* 51 (1939), 275–287. Note also R. W. Southern, "St. Anselm and His English Pupils," *Mediaeval and Renaissance Studies,* 1 (1941–43), 34: "It is interesting to see the change from the rather personal and interrogative form of the first version to the more dogmatic statement in the final one; but more important is the substitution of the phrase *nequit intelligi* for the weak *magis impossibile est,* and the further alteration which this entailed." Note that while Southern thinks there are only three recensions of DIV, Schmitt claims five.

16. F. S. Schmitt, "Eine frühe Rezension des Werkes *de Concordia* des hl. Anselm von Canterbury," *Revue Bénédictine,* 48 (1936), 41–70.

13

inclined to make minor emendations themselves. Some of the differences in *De Sacrificio Azimi*, for instance, can be explained on this basis.[17]

The Libellus. Without Anselm's approval the first recension of the *Cur Deus Homo* was transcribed and circulated before he had finished it. In 1933 E. Druwé published a text purporting to be this missing first version.[18] One of the striking features of the *Libellus*, as Druwé calls it, is its remarkable difference from the final version of the *Cur Deus Homo*. For, unlike the close similarity between Anselm's recensions of other works, the *Libellus* shows a more purely theological, and less apologetical, tone than the *Cur Deus Homo*. The *Libellus* is a speculative "meditation" on the fittingness of the incarnation, claims Druwé, whereas the *Cur Deus Homo* is a dialogue aimed at leading unbelievers to recognize the truth of the incarnation. That is, the *Cur Deus Homo* by contrast with the *Libellus* places more emphasis upon merely rational presuppositions.

The differences, Druwé thinks, can be accounted for not only on the basis of untimely transcription but also as a result of the long period from the time Anselm began the *Cur Deus Homo* in England until he finished it in Capua — time enough for reconsidering and restructuring. Selected titles from the forty chapters of the *Libellus* indicate what type of topics Anselm treated: That the Son alone ought to have been incarnated; The ways in which God was able to make a man; What He assumed from the Virgin Mother; That the Son of God and of the Virgin was unable to sin; On human free choice; Whether Satan foreknew that he was going to fall and to be punished; That angelic nature was to be restored from the number of men rather than from the number of angels; That in the beginning the Heavenly City was not completed by the number of angels but was to be completed by the number of elect men; and, That God is the Supreme Good. These subjects constitute some of the issues dealt with in the *Cur Deus Homo*, but they also overlap with sections of *De Conceptu* and *De Concordia* (later than the *Cur Deus Homo*), and with *De Casu Diaboli* (earlier than the *Cur Deus Homo*). This similarity of content, together with a likeness of style, led Druwé to consider the *Libellus* genuinely Anselmian.

17. F. S. Schmitt, "Eine dreifache Gestalt der 'Epistola de Sacrificio azimi et fermentati' des hl. Anselm von Canterbury," *Revue Bénédictine*, 47 (1935), 216–225.
18. *Libri Sancti Anselmi "Cur Deus Homo" prima forma inedita* (Rome, 1933).

Unfortunately, however, countervailing reasons force the conclusion that the *Libellus* is spurious. These reasons have been adequately given by J. Rivière: (1) The *Libellus* is not mentioned in the catalogue of Anselm's works. (2) The content of the *Libellus* is significantly inferior to that of the *Cur Deus Homo*. (3) The *Libellus* utilizes works which postdate the *Cur Deus Homo*. (4) The *Libellus* is literarily superior to the *Cur Deus Homo*.[19] Of these reasons, the first and the third are by themselves untelling; the second and the fourth, however, are decisive. Druwé is certainly right when in answering Rivière he notes that not all recensions of Anselm's works are listed in ancient manuscript catalogues — and in particular that the uncontested first recension of *De Incarnatione* is not explicitly listed.[20] Furthermore, the fact that the *Libellus* utilizes parts of *De Concordia* and *De Conceptu* is of no consequence. We already know that a segment of *De Concordia* was on hand twenty years before its actual publication, and that parts of the argument appearing in *De Conceptu* were already in Anselm's mind when he drafted the *Cur Deus Homo*. Moreover, Anselm's way of theologizing was to repeat interconnecting themes and examples from book to book. Thus Druwé is aware that *Cur Deus Homo* II, 1, is a repetition of *Monologion* 68–69, and that *De Incarnatione* 10 is an anticipation of *Cur Deus Homo* II, 9.[21]

Nonetheless, the *Libellus* cannot be considered Anselm's. Rivière has shown that the Latin syntax of the *Libellus* is *superior* to that of the *Cur Deus Homo* and other Anselmian works. It is implausible that in Anselm's polished and final version of a text, he should have written with less of an eye to grammar and style than in his earlier draft. Moreover, the content of the *Libellus* is intellectually inferior — in organization, in depth of sustained argument — to that of the *Cur Deus Homo*. From these observations alone the *Libellus* begins to look like a disquisition compiled by a later writer who had Anselm's treatises before him. Moreover, Anselm stated explicitly that the first parts (*primae partes*) of the *Cur Deus Homo* were prematurely transcribed. Yet the *Libellus* contains

19. "Un premier jet du 'Cur Deus homo'?" *Revue des sciences religieuses* (July 1934), 1–41. Note Druwé's reply, "La première rédaction du 'Cur Deus homo' de saint Anselme," *Revue d'histoire ecclésiastique*, 31 (1935), 501–540. And Rivière's counter, "La question du 'Cur Deus homo,'" *Revue des sciences religieuses*, 16 (1936), 1–32. See also F. S. Schmitt, "Zur Entstehungsgeschichte von Anselms 'Cur Deus homo,'" *Theologische Revue*, 34 (1935), 217–224.

20. "La première rédaction," p. 524.

21. *Ibid.*, p. 531.

sections from the middle and later parts—confirming the view that its author already had the completed *Cur Deus Homo* in front of him.[22] In last analysis, to suppose that the *Libellus* is the first version of the *Cur Deus Homo* goes against all other comparisons between earlier and later recensions of Anselm texts. For in other cases, the variances are not extensive and many sentences remain the same. But not a single sentence from the *Libellus* "recurs" in the *Cur Deus Homo*.[23]

We have noted the systematic character and self-consistency of Anselm's major treatises. His simple techniques of method serve well the clarity of his arguments. Banishing lavishness and profuseness, he expresses himself with a conciseness which seeks to induce rather than seduce understanding. His way of thinking mirrored, as it were, his way of living. For he seemed most content in the worldly unadornment of the monastery—whether in Bec or on the mountaintop in Capua where he finished the *Cur Deus Homo*. And the fervent steadfastness with which he gave himself to daily duties parallels the unfailing vigor with which he originated and doggedly developed a nexus of arguments.

THE QUESTION OF
SOURCES AND PUPILS

Augustine. Uncontestably, Augustine is the major source upon whom Anselm draws. Although mentioned by name only six times,[24] his influence is preponderant. Even where Anselm does not cite him directly, he appropriates examples, poses problems in exactly the same way, and borrows arguments without acknowledgment. In this respect, Anselm is at one with the age in which he lived—an age which heralded Augus-

22. E.g., *Libellus* 19: "That an unchanging reason opposes the restoration of the [evil] angels." This is the topic of CDH II, 21 ("That it is impossible for the Devil to be reconciled"). And *Libellus* 6 ("The ways in which God was able to make a man") is the topic dealt with in CDH II, 8.

23. Schmitt, "Entstehungsgeschichte," p. 223. I do not discuss A. Combes's *Un inédit de saint Anselme? Le traité 'De unitate divinae essentiae et pluralitate creaturarum' d'après Jean de Ripa (Etudes de philosophie médiévale* 34), Paris, 1944. Flourishing about 1360, John of Ripa comments on the *De Unitate*, which he attributes to Anselm. Combes treats the problem of Anselmic authenticity fairly—conceding that the favorable evidence is not decisive. But he does not see that, in fact, the total evidence is decisive against authenticity.

24. M preface (S I, 8); DIV 6, 16 (S II, 20, 35); Eps. 78, 83, 204. These six times are all with reference to DT.

tine as the greatest of the Church Fathers, prided itself in mastering his thought, and sought to pass on the rich theological tradition which had emerged from his dogmatics. In such an era Peter Lombard could write the *Books of Sentences* (about 1150) and feel it justifiable to take ninety per cent of his patristic quotations from Augustine. Lanfranc could urge Anselm to make his indebtedness to Augustine more explicit in the *Monologion*. And Gaunilo could find it useful to invoke Augustine's authority when disagreeing with the *Proslogion* argument.

In *De Veritate* I Anselm repeats his well-known argument for the eternal nature of truth:

Let anyone who can, try to conceive of when the following proposition began to be true, or was ever not true, namely, that something was going to exist. Or let him try to conceive of when the following proposition will cease being true, namely, that something has existed in the past. Now if neither of these things can be conceived, and if neither proposition can be true unless there is truth, then it is impossible even to conceive that truth has a beginning or an end. Finally, suppose that truth had had a beginning, or suppose that it would at some time come to an end: then even before truth had begun to be, it would have been true that there was no truth; and even after truth had come to an end, it would still be true that truth had come to an end. But since these statements could not be true unless there was truth, there would have to have been truth before truth came to be, and there would still have to be truth after truth had ceased to be. But these conclusions are preposterous. Therefore . . . truth cannot be confined by any beginning or end.

Augustine had already advanced this argument in the *Soliloquies*,[25] and had extended it to cover the notion of degrees of reality (being): "Truth does not exist in mortal things. But since it must exist somewhere, there are immortal things. Now nothing is true in which truth does not exist. Therefore, only immortal things are true. A false tree is not a tree; a false log is not a log; false silver is not silver; and in general, whatever is false does not exist. But whatever is not true is false. Hence, only immortal things are rightly said to exist." [26] Since truth is ultimately identifiable with God—the Supreme Being—only He truly exists; all else exists in a less real way. This is precisely Anselm's notion in the *Monologion* and the *Proslogion*—a notion which (although not pronouncedly

25. 2.2.2 (PL 32:886). Cf. 2.15.28 (PL 32:898). N.B. Thomas's objection to this argument, ST 1st, 16, 7.
26. *Soliloquies* 1.15.29 (PL 32:884).

recurrent in his other works) all his systematic writings presuppose. In the *Monologion* he states without hesitancy: "It is clear that some natures exist more than others or less than others" (Ch. 31. S I, 49:20–21). And, reminiscent of Augustine's *Expositions of the Psalms* (134.4), he goes so far as to declare that God alone really exists. All other things, he tells us, are in a sense nonexistent — in that they come from nothing, are not the source of their own existence, and would return to nothing unless sustained by God (M 28). According to this line of thinking the following argument becomes plausible:

From some substance which lives, perceives, and reasons let us imaginatively (*cogitatione*) remove first what is rational, next what is sensible, then what is vital, and finally the remaining bare existence. Now, who would not understand that this substance, thus destroyed step by step, is gradually reduced to less and less existence — and, in the end, to non-existence? Yet those characteristics which when removed one at a time reduce an essence [a being] to less and less existence increase its existence more and more when added to it again in reverse order. Therefore, it is clear that a living substance exists more than does a non-living one, that a sentient substance exists more than does a non-sentient one, and that a rational substance exists more than does a non-rational one. So without doubt every essence [every being] exists more and is more excellent to the extent that it is more like that Essence which exists supremely and is supremely excellent (M 31).

Adherence to the degrees-of-reality principle places Anselm squarely in the Augustinian tradition, for Anselm like Augustine assumes that the more perfect a thing is the more real it is.[27] And in accordance with this tradition he develops in *Proslogion* 2 and 3 his argument that God truly exists (*quod vere sit Deus*). Thus, the assertion that God exists so truly that He cannot be thought not to exist (*quod utique sic vere est, ut nec cogitari possit non esse*) embodies not simply the claim that God really exists; it is in addition a statement about the supremacy of God's reality.[28] The hierarchical conception of reality in terms of which God is understood as the supremely real being (*summa veritas; essentia quae summe est*) makes it possible for Anselm to believe with Augustine that if some-

27. Cf. M 31 with Augustine, *Free Choice* 2.6.13 (PL 32:1248). Note M 3 (S I, 16: 20–23) and M 35 (S I, 54:1).

28. One may agree with A. Stolz's point here without agreeing with his conclusion that the *Proslogion* does not attempt to prove the existence of God. See his " 'Vere esse' im Proslogion des hl. Anselm," *Scholastik*, 9 (1934), 400–409.

thing is mutable, it does not truly exist; and, contrapositively, if something truly exists, it is not mutable.[29]

The language of *vere esse* in the *Proslogion* argument coincides with Augustinianism. Indeed, Anselm's description of God as "something than which nothing greater can be thought" (*aliquid quo maius nihil cogitari potest*) is not foreign to Augustine. In *Confessions* 7.4.6 Augustine remarks of God: no one "ever has been or ever will be able to conceive of something which is better (*melius*) than You, who are the supreme and perfect good." [30] And in *Catholic and Manichean Ways of Life* 2.11.24 he affirms that God "must be understood or believed to be the absolutely supreme good, than which nothing better (*melius*) can exist or be thought." [31] When we remember that for Anselm "greater" (*maius*) means — when applied to God — "better" (*melius*) or "more worthy" (*dignius*), we realize that there is no difference between his statement and Augustine's. What is unique in the history of thought is not this definitional premise from which the ontological argument moves, but rather the formulation of the argument as a whole. In a broad sense, the premise is a part of early Christian theology as a whole. But the argument utilizing this premise occurred to Anselm and not to Augustine, and is a tribute to his brilliance irrespective of whether the proof is actually sound.

The degrees-of-reality principle easily gives rise to the notion that every being insofar as it exists, is good, and that evil is a form of not-being. For "just as every good and only good comes from the highest good, so every being and only being comes from the highest being. Moreover, since the highest good is the highest being, it follows that every good is a being, and every being is a good. Therefore just as nothing and not-being are not beings, so they are also not good. And thus, nothing and not-being are not from God, from whom come only being and good" (DCD 1). This very way of viewing being in relation to

29. *On the Gospel of John* 38.10 (PL 35:1680). Cf. also *Nature of the Good* 19 (PL 42:557); *Catholic and Manichean Ways of Life* 2.1.1 (PL 32:1345); DT 8.1.2 (PL 42:947–948).

30. "Neque enim ulla anima umquam potuit poterivte cogitare aliquid, quod sit te melius, qui summum et optimum bonum es." PL 32:735.

31. "Summum bonum omnino, et quo esse aut cogitari melius nihil possit, aut intelligendus, aut credendus Deus est. . . ." PL 32:1355. Note also *Christian Doctrine* 1.7.7 (PL 34:22); Boethius, *Consolation of Philosophy* 3.10 (PL 63:765); *Free Choice* 3.2.5 (PL 32:1273); DT 5.8.9.

goodness is also present in Augustine's *Enchiridion* 12 and *Nature of the Good* 20. In these two passages Augustine crystallized for the Middle Ages a standard argument — whose rudiments are as old as Plotinus — for regarding evil as a privation, i.e., as a kind of not-being. And this common argument appears in Anselm in *De Casu Diaboli* 10, where the student alludes to it by way of concession: "There are certain arguments which prove that evil is nothing. For example, I might say that evil is only corruption, or defect, which has no being except as it is in some being. The greater the corruption, the more it reduces towards nothing the being it is in; and if the being it is in becomes absolutely nothing, we find that its corruption, or defect, is nothing also. So it can be proved by this argument that evil is nothing, and there may be other arguments to the same effect." Anselm does not repudiate this argument but rather presupposes it (or at least its conclusion) throughout the remaining discussion. It is unlikely that he would have known the argument without also knowing that it comes through Augustine.

Anselm has also followed Augustine in maintaining that truth in all things is ultimately one Truth because if something is true, it can only be so by virtue of its accordance with an eternal Truth.[32] By identifying this eternal Truth with God (M 16), Anselm is able to contend (in reverse fashion) that when God creates something, He implicitly confers on it a kind of truth. For when He creates, He creates in accordance with a model, or exemplar, in His mind.[33] Insofar as all beings correspond to a pattern in the Divine Mind, they may be said to be true. And since all created things necessarily so accord, there is truth in the essence of all things (DV 7). These things exist in themselves, in the human mind's knowledge of them, and in the mind of God. In themselves they exist more truly, or really, than in the human mind's knowledge of them, but less truly than in the mind of God (M 36). Such a notion of exemplarism, like the accompanying theory of reality, owes its impetus to Augustine. In *Eighty-Three Different Questions* Augustine contends that certain archetypal ideas, forms, or reasons exist unchangeably in the Divine Mind.[34] This is exactly the view which Anselm takes over

---

32. Cf. DV 13 with Augustine's *Free Choice* 2.12.34 (PL 32:1259). Both Augustine and Anselm say *secundum illam* [i.e., *veritatem*].

33. ". . . quasi exemplum, sive aptius dicitur forma, vel similitudo, aut regula." M 9. Note also M 34, where Anselm indicates that created things exist in the mind of God before, during, and after their existence in time. S I, 53:22–24.

34. "Sunt namque ideae principales formae quaedam, vel rationes rerum stabiles atque

and develops in his *Monologion* and *De Veritate*. But not content merely to repeat Augustine, he seeks to work out an entire theory of truth — of which the doctrine of exemplarism forms only a small part.

Though Augustine adopted the doctrine of exemplarism from Plotinus, his theory of vision stems from Platonism. Plato had maintained at *Sophist* 266c and *Timaeus* 46a that sight results when a ray streams out from the eye and meets with light coming from an object. And Augustine was to say in Book 12 of his *Literal Commentary on Genesis* that "light . . . is emitted through the eyes and goes forth in the rays of the eyes in order that visible objects may be seen." [35] Because this had become a common theory, Anselm, who certainly knew of it directly from Augustine, was not hesitant to invoke it in *De Libertate* 7, where he refers to "the ray which passes through the eyes by means of which we sense light and the objects in the light." He also subscribes to the other major feature of the Augustinian theory of vision — viz., that the faculty of sense, in its normal functioning, is not responsible for an individual's perceptual errors. [36] If a straight stick looks broken when half of it is thrust into water, the fault cannot be attributed to our eyes, which report what in fact appears. Rather, if we are deceived, the blame must rest upon the faculty of judgment (*iudicium*), which wrongly infers that such a stick is broken because it looks broken. That is,

truth or falsity is not in our senses, but in our belief about them. The outer sense does not report lies to the inner sense, but the latter deceives itself. This is sometimes easy to realize, other times difficult. For when a boy is afraid of the statue of a dragon posed as if to eat him up, we easily recognize that the sight of the dragon doesn't cause his fear (for the boy's sight reports to him nothing more than an older person's sight reports to him); rather, it is caused by his childish inner sense, which does not yet know well enough how to distinguish between a real thing and its likeness (DV 6).

Anselm's mention of an inner sense (*sensus interior*) in contrast to an outer sense (*sensus exterior*) is taken from Book 2 of Augustine's *Free*

incommutabiles, quae ipsae formatae non sunt, ac per hoc aeternae ac semper eodem modo sese habentes, quae in divina intelligentia continentur." 46.2 (PL 40:30). Note also *On the Gospel of John* 1.17 (PL 35:1387). Cf. *Literal Commentary on Genesis* 5.14.31 (PL 34:332).

35. 12.16.32 (PL 34:466). Cf. 4.34.54 (PL 34:320); 7.13.20 (PL 34:362). Note DT 9.3.3 (PL 42:962–963); *Greatness of the Soul* 23.43 (PL 32:1060).

36. Cf. Augustine, *True Religion* 33.62 (PL 34:149–150); *Against the Academicians* 3.11.26 (PL 32:947).

Choice. The inner sense, according to Augustine, is that faculty (common to animals and man) which "interprets" the information transmitted from the outer senses. This faculty has three functions: it *organizes* the data from the five senses into a coherent percept; it accounts for the *awareness* that one is at a given moment perceiving; it *judges* that the object perceived is harmful or helpful, friendly or unfriendly, pleasant or unpleasant, according to the *memory* of past experiences. Anselm distinguishes the inner from the outer sense in order to explain the possibility of perceptual error and to maintain that God has not created man with a sensory apparatus which intrinsically conduces to error. This very theological consideration also had led Augustine to oppose those who saw evil and falsehood as inherent in created beings.

In *Monologion* 10 Anselm distinguishes uttering a word, thinking the word silently, and imagining or conceiving the thing which the word signifies. For instance, one may utter the word "man," think it to himself, or imagine a man, or conceive of him apart from an image. Whereas the uttering and the thinking of a word are relative to a given language (Latin, Greek, French, etc.), Anselm contends that concepts "are natural and are the same among all nations" (*naturalia sunt et apud omnes gentes sunt eadem*). This distinction between the natural concept and the conventional word which represents the concept is taken from Augustine's *On the Trinity*.[37] Here Augustine notes that concepts of physical objects are all derived from experience. "For no one can at all conceive of (imagine) a color or a shape which he has never seen, nor a sound which he has never heard, nor a flavor he has never tasted, nor an odor he has never smelled, nor the feel of an object which he has never touched."[38] In *Monologion* 11 Anselm adheres to this same view, while pointing out that the mind has the ability to compound new forms by imaginatively putting together in novel ways forms which it has once perceived. Yet even this feature of perception had not gone unmentioned by Augustine (Ep. 7).

Another striking point of comparison between Anselm and Augustine occurs in *De Casu Diaboli*, which begins with the Apostle's question: "What do you have that you have not received?" (I Cor. 4:7). The question implies that the very existence of men, as well as every natural en-

---

37. E.g., 14.7.10; 15.10.19; 15.14.24; 15.21.40. N.B. Sermon 225.3.3. Anselm's distinctions do not parallel exactly those made by Augustine in DT 9.10.15.

38. DT 11.8.14 (PL 42:995).

dowment and ability, comes from the Creator. Yet if men and angels received a perfect will for uprightness, how could Satan and Adam have sinned? Moreover, as the student remarks,

it is evident that the angel who remained upright in the truth persevered because he had perseverance; moreover, he had perseverance because he received it, and he received it because God gave it. It follows, then, that the angel who did not "remain upright in the truth" (John 8:44) did not persevere because he did not have perseverance; moreover, he did not have perseverance because he did not receive it, and he did not receive it because God did not give it. So if you can, I want you to show me Satan's blame in not persevering when God did not grant him perseverance and when he could have nothing without God's giving it (DCD 2).

Anselm proceeds to explain how the gift of perseverance was to be God's reward to Satan and Adam had they merited it by willing the uprightness with which they were created. Even though the very ability to keep uprightness (*rectitudo*) comes from God, the use of this ability is the individual's and not God's. Accordingly, when Satan and Adam chose to sin, they failed to exercise the ability which they had for keeping uprightness — a failure which resulted in the deprivation of uprightness. So the first man and the apostate angel forfeited the gift of perseverance by casting away the initial gift of uprightness. Therefore, they did not have perseverance because they did not receive it; and they did not receive it, *not* because it was not given, or offered, but because they did not accept it.

In *The Spirit and the Letter* Augustine also puzzles over whether the will by which we believe is a gift of God. Relating this problem directly to I Corinthians 4:7, he poses Anselm's dilemma: If this will is not received, man may glory in something possessed apart from God; and if this will is received, why are unbelievers without it? [39] And in *Reproof and Grace* he raises against himself exactly the same argument as does Anselm: If Adam did not persevere in uprightness, it was because he did not receive perseverance; and if he did not receive it, how is he to be blamed for not persevering — since he could have nothing from himself? [40] Here appears too the very word *rectitudo*, which plays so important a role in Anselm's dialogues.[41] Furthermore, we find in Augus-

39. 33.57 (PL 44:237–238).

40. 10.26 (PL 44:932).

41. Note also Augustine, *Expositions of the Psalms* 44.17 (PL 36:504).

tine the verdict that Satan could not have foreknown his fall – a topic which coincides with *De Casu Diaboli* 21. Augustine points out [42] that had Satan foreknown he was to fall, he would have been wretched; yet before any sin, he was supposed to be happy – the very argument used by Anselm.

Another belief held by both Anselm and Augustine is that the number of fallen angels is to be compensated for by the elevation of redeemed men to their places. Put forth briefly by Augustine in his *Enchiridion*,[43] the fuller reasoning awaited Anselm's *Cur Deus Homo* I, 16–17. The view that men are to be substituted for fallen angels nowhere occurs in Scripture. Rather, it is the product of rationalistic considerations: Either God foreknew the number of inhabitants intended for the Heavenly City or He did not (cf. Wisd. 11:21). But He must have foreknown this, since He always knows all things, including His own intentions. Assume that in the order of divine decrees the decree to create the angels is logically prior to the decree to create men. Then either the number of angels created was greater than the number in question or it was not greater. But if angels were created in excess of the foreknown number, then the fall of some would be necessary – something theologically impossible to believe. This fall would be necessary not because it was foreknown but because God would be intending it in the course of intending the affixed number. And everything which God intends must come to pass. Since, then, the number of angels could not have been greater than the definite number of rational beings intended for eternal happiness, and since some angels fell (with no possibility of restoration), human beings must have been created to complete the number of rational natures that would occupy a heavenly place.

There can be no doubt that Anselm, as on so many other occasions, draws this notion of replacement from his predecessor. But equally, there can be no doubt that his analysis extends further than the mere germinal thoughts found in Augustine.[44]

In *Free Choice*, Book 3, Augustine argues for the compatibility of divine foreknowledge and human free will in order to demonstrate that a man is responsible for his sins even though God already knows he will

42. 10.27 (PL 44:933).

43. 9.29 (PL 40:246). Also note *Reproof and Grace* 13:39-40.

44. See D. P. Henry, "Numerically Definite Reasoning in the *Cur Deus Homo*," *Dominican Studies*, 6 (1953), 48-55.

commit these sins. For if what is foreknown is thereby certain and if God foreknows that *by my own will* I shall choose to sin, then it is certain that I shall willingly commit the sin. Accordingly, God's foreknowledge renders human freedom all the more steadfast.[45] Exactly the same argument is taken up by Anselm in *De Concordia*:

But you will say to me: "Your reasoning does not do away with the necessity of my sinning or of my not sinning, because God foreknows whether I am going to sin or not to sin; and therefore, if I sin, it is necessary for me to sin, and if I do not sin, it is necessary that I do not sin." To this I reply: You ought not to say merely "God foreknows that I am going to sin" or "God foreknows that I am not going to sin." But you should say "God foreknows that it is without necessity that I am going to sin" or "God foreknows that it is without necessity that I am not going to sin" (I, 1. S II, 246:14–19).

There is every reason to suppose that Anselm self-consciously adapted this argument from Augustine.[46]

Another problem that Augustine explicitly dealt with is, How can we say of Jesus that He was begotten of the Holy Spirit as well as of Mary when He is not to be called the Son of the Holy Spirit, as He is called the Son of Mary? In the *Enchiridion* Augustine answers this question by insisting that being begotten of a thing is not the same as being a son of that thing (hair is begotten of a man but is not a son), and that being the son of someone is not the same as being begotten of him (one may be a son by adoption).[47] In *Monologion* 39 Anselm articulates the same argument, using the same example, though in response to a different issue.

Countless items are said, without qualm, to be begotten from those things to which they owe their existence. We speak this way even in cases where things do not, analogously to a child and its parent, resemble the thing from which they are said to be begotten. For example, we say that hair is begotten from a head and fruit from a tree, even though hair does not resemble a head nor fruit a tree. If, then, many such things are meaningfully said to be begotten, the Word of the Supreme Spirit can fittingly be said to exist from it by being begotten. Indeed, the more perfectly the Word, in existing from the Spirit, resembles the Spirit with the likeness

45. 3.3.8 (PL 32:1275). Note also *On the Gospel of John* 53.4 (PL 35:1776).

46. In *Consolation of Philosophy*, Bk. 5, Boethius also deals with the relationship of freedom and divine foreknowledge. Although he does not use the argument presented above, his own discussion is indebted to Augustine.

47. Ch. 39 (PL 40:252).

as if of offspring to parent, the more fittingly the Word may be said to be begotten.

It is also noteworthy that in *De Processione* Anselm's defense of the *filioque* doctrine — that the Holy Spirit proceeds from the Father *and the Son* — is drawn from Augustine.[48] Moreover, his distinction between relational and substantial terms (apropos of the three persons and the one nature in God) likewise comes from Augustine's *On the Trinity*.[49]

Finally, the principle *credo ut intelligam*, which exhibits the relationship between faith and reason, has a direct impact on Anselm, who adopted it from *On the Trinity* (e.g., 5.2.2) and *Free Choice* (1.2.4). To say the least, it is the basic principle of the *Proslogion*, which Anselm originally entitled "Faith Seeking Understanding" (*Fides Quaerens Intellectum*). Like Augustine, Anselm follows an Old Latin translation of the Septuagint, instead of the Vulgate, when he reads Isaiah 7:9 as "Unless you believe you will not understand" (*nisi credideritis, non intelligetis*). This reading is deliberate, since neither Anselm nor Augustine was unaware of the alternative rendering: "Unless you believe, you will not continue" (see Augustine, *Christian Doctrine* 2.12.17).

To establish the precise number of places where Augustine's influence has modified Anselm's thinking is of no consequence. What is important is to recognize that such influence is there and that it constitutes a major dimension. One cannot ascribe a direct borrowing to every passage where Anselm shares an idea with Augustine. For the same idea may occur to two different people. But where we find an explicit acknowledgment of indebtedness, where the *configuration* of ideas is the same, where the same arguments and examples are used to shore up the same point, where the writings of the one were available to the other — here we may confidently speak of sources and influences. We should not expect Anselm to appropriate Augustine's very words or in every case to cite Augustine's writings by name as he does with *On the Trinity*. Such a criterion for attributing a connection of sources is too rigid. In a theological era still predominantly Augustinian, the monastic schools would have organized, and would have fostered extensive familiarity with, the set of arguments and reasons scattered throughout Augustine's writings.

48. DT 15.17.29; 15.26.47 (PL 42:1081, 1094). *On The Gospel of John* 99.6–8 (PL 35: 1888–90).

49. DT 5.6.7 (PL 42:914–915); DT preface to Bk. 8 (PL 42:947); *On the Gospel of John* 39.4 (PL 35:1683).

Basic Writings and Sources

More interesting than the similarities are the differences between Anselm and Augustine, for here shines forth the former's genius. No mere intellectual scribe, Anselm positions himself against Augustine in a number of areas. He rejects the devil-ransom theory of atonement propagated from *On the Trinity* 13.12–15 and popularized during the early Middle Ages. *Cur Deus Homo* I, 7, begins with an allusion to the common theory (*illud quod dicere solemus*) that God was obliged to deal with Satan justly rather than forcibly since Satan had a claim on man, who delivered himself freely into captivity. This common theory is indeed Augustine's.[50] Yet Anselm rejects it outright: God owes to Satan only the force of punishment, and only the Creator has rights over man. The *Cur Deus Homo* represents a systematic alternative to the view sketched by Augustine and made popular after his lifetime.

Moreover, Anselm's definition of "freedom" is subtly different from Augustine's in that Anselm defines "freedom" exclusively in relation to uprightness of will ("freedom is the ability to keep uprightness of will for its own sake"). And since men always have this ability, they are always free. That is, on Anselm's understanding, even unredeemed men, though they have lost uprightness of will, still have the ability to **keep** uprightness should it be restored to them again. And in this sense they are free (DL 3). Augustine, too, defines "freedom" in terms of having an ability. But for him, unredeemed men are not free *because* they could keep uprightness of will were it restored to them. Rather, they are free in the special, and limited, sense of still being able to do evil (*posse peccare*), even though they are not able to do the good (*non posse non peccare*). Augustine thus tends to define "human freedom" as a neutral power of choice, without making the general object of choice intrinsic to the definition.

Still further, Schmitt has argued, plausibly, that in *Monologion* 1, which borrows from *On the Trinity* 8.3, Anselm intentionally deplatonizes Augustine's discussion of the good. For though Anselm's treatment of the topic follows Augustine's up to a point, it noticeably stops short of repeating three themes: that the notion of the good has been impressed upon the soul; that the good itself can be viewed by the soul; and that all goods *participate* in the one good.[51]

50. See also DT 15.25.44; *Free Choice* 3.10 (PL 32:1286–87); Sermon 27 (PL 38:179).
51. "Anselm und der (Neu-)Platonismus," AA I, p. 48. See the reply by K. Flasch,

It is expedient to postpone discussing differences of substance and emphasis between Anselm and Augustine, for these points will emerge more clearly from a detailed analysis of specific doctrines. Let it suffice here to note that even where Anselm *agrees* with a given Augustinian teaching, the different way in which he develops the teaching preserves his intellectual independence. Most often he picks up from Augustine a problem together with one or two ways of treating it. Then he proceeds to develop the topic more coherently and concentratedly than had Augustine — sometimes educing new considerations, sometimes simply extending his predecessor's line of thought. Thus, as we have seen, he considers the problem of truth within a dialogue which unfolds step by step and which, although beginning with an argument from Augustine and utilizing various other points from him along the way, nonetheless propounds a notion of *rectitudo* that is more comprehensive than anything from Augustine. For this very notion becomes central not only to the theory of truth but also to the doctrine of redemption.

Boethius-Aristotle. If the Augustinian tradition represents a major source for Anselm, then so also does the Aristotelian tradition mediated through Boethius. Boethius's translations of, and commentaries on, Aristotle's *On Interpretation* and *Categories* were available to Anselm. Although never referring to Boethius or mentioning him by name, Anselm does refer explicitly to Aristotle eight times — citing the *Categories* and alluding to *On Interpretation*.[52] The prior and the posterior *Analytics* were not available,[53] but Anselm would have known Boethius's works on the categorical and the hypothetical syllogism. Many of the elementary logical paradigms used by Anselm belong generally to the early Middle Ages and can be found in Boethius.[54] By the eleventh century such paradigms had become a common part of pedagogical tradition and were referred to repeatedly in illustrating points about the notions of truth,

"Der philosophische Ansatz des Anselm von Canterbury im Monologion und sein Verhältnis zum augustinischen Neuplatonismus," AA II, 1–43.

52. S I, 154, 162–165; S II, 125. Of these eight times, all but one occur in DG and are in reference to the *Categories*. The remaining instance is CDH II, 17, where *On Interpretation*, though unnamed, is obviously intended.

53. Boethius's translations of Aristotle's *Analytics*, *Topics*, and *Sophistical Refutations* were lost. Those appearing in PL 64 are not from Boethius but from James of Venice.

54. "A man is not a stone"; "Every man is *grammaticus*"; "When it is day it is not night"; etc.

falsity, and implication. It is not surprising, then, that Anselm should take up the problem of paronymy by posing the question of whether the word *grammaticus* indicates a substance or a quality.[55] Prompted by Aristotle's remarks in *Categories* 2, Anselm develops this problem by utilizing these standard cases.

As *De Grammatico* draws upon Boethius's translation of, and commentary on, Aristotle's *Categories*, so *De Veritate* is influenced by *On Interpretation*. The very definition of a proposition as "a sentence which is either true or false" is ultimately from Aristotle.[56] And Anselm's understanding of a proposition's being true when what it affirms to exist does exist, or when what it denies to exist does not exist (DV 2), draws upon the Aristotelian notion of truth as correspondence.

When speaking of Aristotle's influence on Anselm, we must not regard Boethius as a mere conveyer of Aristotle; for at times Anselm is indebted to Boethius himself. This indebtedness is especially clear with regard to the definition of "eternity." In *Consolation of Philosophy* 5.6 Boethius observes that eternity is "the complete possession — at once and as a whole — of endless life": *Aeternitas igitur est interminabilis vitae tota simul et perfecta possessio* (PL 63:858). And this is precisely Anselm's definition in *Monologion* 24.[57] Since Anselm knew the *Consolation of Philosophy*, he is obviously indebted to Boethius for his definitional formulation. In a broad sense, of course, both Anselm and Boethius are drawing upon Augustine's distinction between eternity and perpetual existence in time. Eternity differs from perpetuity because in the former there are no distinctions of before and after, earlier and later. That is, eternity is eternity precisely because its dimension is altogether nontemporal. Although Anselm in the *Monologion* is reflecting Augustine's viewpoint, he is doing so exactly in terms of its Boethian articulation.

At other times it is not clear how much Anselm owes to Boethius, how much to Augustine, and how much to himself. Boethius's definition of

55. See D. P. Henry, *The De Grammatico of St. Anselm* (South Bend, Ind., 1964). In *The Logic of Saint Anselm*, p. 138, Henry draws attention to the parallel between *to cause to be* (*facere esse*) and *to cause not to be* (*facere non esse*), considered contraries by Anselm in PF, and *necessary to be* (*necesse est esse*) and *necessary not to be* (*necesse est non esse*), called contraries by Boethius.

56. Cf. Boethius, PL 64:313 (Aristotle, DI 17ᵃ 1–4). As for Boethius's commentary on Cicero's *Topics*, L. Steiger points out passages which Anselm seems to have known about. See "Contexe Syllogismos," AA I, p. 119.

57. "Videtur enim eius aeternitas esse interminabilis vita simul perfecte tota existens." S I, 42:18–21.

"person" as "the individual substance of a rational nature" is not foreign
to Anselm, who recognizes that *person* is ascribed only to *individuâ ra-
tionalî naturâ*.[58] But Anselm nowhere expresses the exact Boethian formula. So too, the argument that God's *fore*knowledge of future events
should rather be called *knowledge* of an unchanging present may have
come to Anselm's attention from *Consolation of Philosophy* 5.6 (PL 63:
860) or directly from Augustine. In this case, the only certainty is that
the argument did not originate with Anselm.

Plato. There is no reason to suppose that Anselm could read Greek.
What he knew of Aristotle, he knew through Latin translations and
commentaries, as we have seen. What he learned of Plato, he learned
through whatever references, discussions, or translations were available
in his day. For instance, Boethius refers to Plato's doctrine of remi-
niscence and to his doctrine of eternity, and Augustine's works are
sprinkled with allusions to Platonic and neo-Platonic teachings. Anselm
can be expected to have been aware of these passages as well as generally
to have kept contact with the tradition of neo-Platonism which had
never died out in the schools. There is no evidence to suggest his having read a Latin translation of the *Timaeus*, but there are some considerations of circumstance to be kept in mind. The twelfth-century catalogue
of the library of Bec lists Chalcidius's commentary on Plato and copies
of Cicero's translation of the *Timaeus*. But we cannot be sure that these
copies antedate Anselm. According to J. Sulowski, Chalcidius's commentary was known at Chartres from the time of John Scotus Erigena:
"Chalcidius was not only regarded as an authority by the School of
Chartres, but also his work was a generally accepted handbook of philosophy from which nearly all the medieval thinkers were educated, or
which they knew." [59] If Sulowski is right, then one is not unjustified in
assuming that Chalcidius would have been known in other parts of

58. Cf. Boethius, *The Person and the Two Natures* 3 (PL 64:1343), with M 79 (S
I, 86:7).

59. In *L'homme et son destin* (Paris, 1960), p. 155. Moreover: "Extensive research
has led us to the consideration that the *Commentary* is dependent on Neo-Platonism, in particular on Porphyry's *Commentary on the Timaeus* which Chalcidius
translated with a few minor changes. Confirmation of the Neo-Platonic character
of Chalcidius' *Commentary* is of fundamental importance for the history of the
Middle Ages because we thus settle the question of sources used in the Middle Ages
and solve the problem of (*sic*) on what depended so many authors of those times."
Pp. 154–155.

France as well, since manuscripts typically circulated from school to school.[60] Sulowski's conclusions contrast with certain older views. J. Thompson has remarked, "It is not certain that Plato's *Timaeus* in Chalcidius' Latin version was at Chartres, although Fulbert thought him superior to other thinkers of antiquity." [61] Becker's *Catalogi Bibliothecarum Antiqui*, an eleventh-century catalogue of the library at Chartres, lists no copies of the *Timaeus*. And Manitius's collection of manuscript catalogues, which builds upon Becker's work, shows that the *Timaeus* is listed at Fleury during the eleventh century, though not at Chartres.[62]

In any event, Latin versions of the *Timaeus* were around during Anselm's period. To what extent Anselm might have been familiar with this work will probably always remain unknown; yet it is evident enough that he was not under its influence. The theory of vision mentioned at *Timaeus* 46a reoccurs in *De Libertate* 7. But since the same theory is advanced by Augustine, it is more plausible to attribute Anselm's acquaintance with it to his acknowledged reading of *On the Trinity*. As for the *Monologion* and its doctrine of being, there are those, like Rémusat, who have detected the shadow of Plato's hand here: "Read and re-read the *Timaeus*. The likeness, or rather identity, of the doctrine to Anselm's is striking. Diverse goods imply and manifest the absolute good; and the supreme Good is God. The whole of Platonism revolves around this fundamental idea; and, philosophically, Anselm adds little. His merit was to have set the doctrine within a clear and systematic proof — and, above all, in his own day to have searched for the knowledge of God in the necessary notions of the human mind." [63] But as a rule of thumb

60. "The library of Fleury seems to have received the constant attention of the abbots, and the scribes copied constantly both new and old texts. Abbo, suffering from a lack of books, required each scholar to present two manuscripts to the monastery on entering. . . .Fleury's manuscripts traveled the length of Gaul, and even went to England to be copied, sometimes overstaying the period of their loan, as a letter of Abbo querulously tells us." *The Medieval Library* (Chicago, 1939), p. 230.

61. *Ibid.*, p. 235. Fulbert left Rheims for Chartres, perhaps between 987 and 992, finding only a small library there: "4 manuscripts of Augustine's tracts, a few of Jerome, and single volumes of Prosper, Mamertius Claudius, Cassiodorus, Rhabanus Maurus, Martianus Capella, and Boethius. There were only 4 manuscripts of dialectic — no Porphyry, nothing of Plato, practically nothing of Aristotle."

62. Becker lists this catalogue as unknown in place; Manitius ascribes it to Fleury. Note Thompson: "Two catalogues of the tenth century have been dubiously ascribed to Fleury." In the second catalogue is the *Timaeus*. *The Medieval Library*, pp. 227–228.

63. *Saint Anselme de Cantorbéry* (Paris, 1853), p. 482. Cf. the following: (1) "It is

— and Rémusat himself is aware of this — one should first look to Augustine before maintaining that Anselm had a direct knowledge of Plato. If these same doctrines are present in Augustine, it is more likely that Anselm encountered them there. Only if a strong conceptual or verbal parallel could be found between the *Monologion* and the *Timaeus* — at a place where there is no parallel with Augustine — then and only then might we be justified in designating Plato as a direct source of Anselm's ideas, in the absence of internal citations and of external evidence. But, in fact, no such parallel exists.

Lesser influences. A number of lesser figures have been thought to influence Anselm. Among these is Pope Gregory I (540–604), whose *Moralia* became a handbook of study for the Middle Ages. This hermeneutical commentary on the Book of Job was known to Anselm, for he mentions it in his correspondence with Lanfranc.[64] Gregory's emphasis upon Job's uprightness (*rectitudo*) before God may have suggested the centrality of this concept to Anselm, who defines "justice" as "uprightness of will kept for its own sake" (*rectitudo voluntatis per se servata*). But we cannot be sure — especially when we recall Augustine's use of *rectitudo* in *Reproof and Grace* 10.26, a work which we know to have made a great impact on Anselm. A. Stolz claims that the *Proslogion* is influenced by Gregory's mysticism rather than by Augustine's theory of contemplation. "Individual concepts of Anselm's theory of contemplation . . . can also be found in Augustine. Nevertheless, we must hold to a direct influence from the *Moralia*, because the conceptual and terminological correspondence with Gregory vastly exceeds that with Augustine." [65] But in the next chapter we shall see that Stolz's interpretation

necessary, however, to admit that Anselm knows only the *Timaeus* of Plato, and (again) through the translation and neo-Platonic commentary of Chalcidius. Otherwise he finds Plato only in the citations of Cicero, Boethius, St. Augustine, and perhaps the grammarians. Without doubt, Platonic influence is quite pronounced in *De Veritate*. . . ." Filliatre, *La philosophie de saint Anselme* (Paris, 1920), p. 21.

(2) "Did he know the *Timaeus* of Plato in Chalcidius' translation? Here we know nothing; Anselm did not say a word about this to us." Draeseke, "Sur la question des sources d'Anselme," *Revue de philosophie*, 15 (1909), 644.

(3) "Concerning the *Timaeus*, we would not venture to deny the possibility of admitting that St. Anselm knew it. We do not see, it is true, any reason for admitting a direct influence. Moreover, we do not find it mentioned in Bec's catalogue." Koyré, *L'idée de Dieu dans la philosophie de st. Anselme* (Paris, 1923), p. 107n.

64. Especially Eps. 23 and 25 (S III, 130, 132).

65. "*Das Proslogion* des hl. Anselm," *Revue Bénédictine*, 47 (1935), 346. Further-

of Anselm is tendentious, that it reads the *Proslogion* as a work of mystical theology and is therefore predisposed to find there traces from Gregory. In any case, just as we must not disregard parallels with the *Moralia*, so we must also not ignore discrepancies. In *Cur Deus Homo* II, 21, for instance, Anselm does not employ Gregory's argument that fallen man but not fallen angels should be restored because man was handicapped by having a body.[66] But with Gregory and Augustine he does give weight to that difference whereby man fell being tempted by another, whereas Satan fell through his own wickedness.

As for Lanfranc, his *Dialectic* and *Questions* have been lost, making it impossible to assess the precise role he played on Anselm's development.[67] We know of his reputation as a logician and a dialectician. And "it was Lanfranc who first distinctly described the change in the Eucharistic elements in terms of the Aristotelian categories of substance and accidents."[68] Lanfranc invoked this distinction in the controversy with Berenger, who propounded the logical-grammatical principle that a statement whose subject concept is contradicted by its predicate concept cannot be asserted. "Berenger applied this principle to the words of consecration in the Mass, *Hoc* (indicating the Eucharistic Bread) *est corpus meum*. According to the grammarians of the day pronouns stood for the substance of things considered apart from their accidents. Hence the pronoun *Hoc* indicated the substance of the Bread. But on Lanfranc's view the substance of the Bread ceased to exist as a result of the words of consecration. Thus in the statement *Hoc est corpus meum* the subject of the sentence (the substance of the Bread) would be destroyed by the predicate."[69] Southern sees in this dispute an attempt by Berenger to infer something about the nature of sacramental reality on the basis of linguistic considerations. And he calls attention to the fact that "in a similar way Anselm tried to show that in the sentence 'God does not exist' the necessary implication of the subject is destroyed in the predicate, and therefore this sentence must be invalid and strictly meaning-

more, "if the *Proslogion* is dependent on Gregory in this respect, then of course the very contemplation of which the *Proslogion* speaks must also be Gregorian."

66. Cf. *Moralia* 4.3 (PL 75:642).

67. Note Koyré: "Lanfranc could not have had a profound influence on Anselm's philosophical development. He was an able dialectician but no philosopher at all." *L'idée de Dieu*, p. 101.

68. R. W. Southern, *Saint Anselm and His Biographer*, p. 21.

69. *Ibid.*, p. 24.

less."[70] No doubt, Anselm's interest in Aristotelian logic and dialectic was stimulated by his teacher Lanfranc.

Fredegisus's *Darkness and Nothing* (PL 105) may have been in Anselm's mind as he wrote *De Casu Diaboli*.[71] Flourishing in the ninth century, Fredegisus was taught by Alcuin and in 804 became abbot of St. Martin's in Tours. He seeks to show that the *nothing* from which God created the world was other than absolutely nothing.[72] When Anselm rejects this position, he may or may not be self-consciously arguing against Fredegisus.[73]

With regard to others, there is no evidence from Anselm's works to suggest that he was influenced by anyone else except Cicero and — it has been claimed — Paulus.[74] Schmitt shows that Anselm did not know of Aristotle's formal and final causes and that his notion of efficient, material, and auxiliary causes comes from Cicero's *Topics*. However, Anselm did not know Boethius's criticism of Cicero in his commentary *On Cicero's Topics* (AA I, 44).

Pseudo-Dionysius and John Scotus Erigena. Sometime before 532, works began appearing under the name of Dionysius the Areopagite, a convert to the Gospel preached by St. Paul on Mars Hill in Athens (Acts 17:34). Assumed to be genuine, these writings were to have a widespread effect upon the Middle Ages. They were quoted at the session of bishops in Constantinople in 532 and were translated into Latin by Hilduin of Saint-Denis and retranslated by John Scotus Erigena (810–877). The four treatises of pseudo-Dionysius are strongly neo-Platonic, with an

---

70. *Ibid.*, p. 25.

71. According to Fredegisus "every signification is of what is. But 'nothing' does signify. Therefore, it signifies what is, i.e., an existing thing." PL 105:752.

72. Cf. Filliatre, *La philosophie de saint Anselme*, p. 29.

73. "When we say 'A man is' we specify something, viz., *a man*. When we say 'A man is not' we remove something, viz., *a man*, by negating it." Comparison of this example in *Darkness and Nothing* (PL 105:753) with DCD 11 is inconclusive, since the example goes back at least as far as Boethius (PL 64:424).

74. Ep. 242 from Mathilde, Queen of England, to Anselm quotes from Cicero's *On Old Age* — implying some familiarity on Anselm's part. Moreover, study of Cicero was generally a part of monastic training. D. P. Henry reminds us that Lanfranc lectured on the pseudo-Ciceronian *Rhetorica ad Herennium* (*The Logic of Saint Anselm*, p. 8). Henry also notes the parallels between Anselm's discussion of *facere* in PF and a similar discussion by Paulus. Still, the twelfth-century catalogue of Bec contains no reference to Paulus, as Henry himself acknowledges (*The Logic of Saint Anselm*, pp. 10–11).

emphasis upon the hierarchy of being and mystical theology. It is this philosophical notion of divine being and created being which led some interpreters to view the *Monologion* as partly indebted to this pseudo-nymous author. The same kind of consideration has led others to see Erigena's pantheistic metaphysics as a partial determinant of the *Monologion*'s reasoning. Thus, M. Charlesworth can write: "From Augustine, together with Denys the Areopagite, and perhaps from John Scotus Erigena, St. Anselm derived a general neo-Platonic 'world-view' characterized by a hierarchical conception of reality, where everything is graded or ordered according to different 'degrees of perfection,' and by an 'exemplarism,' according to which created beings in the world derive their being and perfection by way of 'participation' in the Divine ideal or archetype or exemplar." [75]

All that Charlesworth mentions can be found in Augustine without recourse to pseudo-Dionysius and Erigena, but he may have in mind certain passages in the *Monologion* where Anselm speaks with pantheistic leanings, as it were. For example, *Monologion* 14 states: "It is absurd to think that just as what has been created cannot at all exceed the greatness of the creating and sustaining Essence so the creating and sustaining Essence cannot at all exceed the totality of created things. Accordingly, it is clear that this Essence sustains, excels, limits, and pervades all other things. . . . It exists in and through all other things and likewise is that from which, through which, and in which all other things exist." When we remember that no pantheist has ever wanted to identify God completely with the universe, it might seem at first glance as if Anselm were leaning in the direction of Erigena.[76] Yet the fact that Anselm is here alluding to Scripture (Rom. 11:36) constitutes a prima facie ground for *not* interpreting the passage above as indicating other influences. Indeed, there is nothing specific in Anselm's works to confirm the theory that he either borrowed from or wrote under the direction of pseudo-Dionysius or Erigena. Even when he discusses predestination, he does not do so in the context of Erigena's *Divine Predestination*, nor does

75. *St. Anselm's Proslogion*, p. 23.

76. Others who hold that there is either a direct line of influence or at least a spiritual kinship between Dionysius or Erigena, on the one hand, and Anselm, on the other, are the following: G. Leff, *Medieval Thought: St Augustine to Ockham* (Baltimore, 1958), p. 64; Rémusat, *Saint Anselm de Cantorbéry*, p. 485; Filliatre, *La philosophie de saint Anselme*, p. 20; Rousselot, *Etudes sur la philosophie dans le moyen-âge (première partie)* (Paris, 1840), pp. 215–216.

he utilize considerations peculiar to this treatise. (We must remember, too, how often the treatise itself cites Augustine.)

It is true that the Fourth Homily recorded in Migne at PL 158:608 finds Anselm speaking of pseudo-Dionysius. Rémusat makes much of this,[77] but Wilmart was later to prove that all the homilies are spurious.[78] Moreover, the fact that the twelfth-century catalogue of the library at Bec lists the works of pseudo-Dionysius does not itself prove anything, since these books may have been deposited after Anselm's lifetime.[79] By the same token, the catalogue's lack of reference to Erigena provides, by itself, only a presumption against the hypothesis that Anselm during his period at Bec — i.e., before and during the time he wrote the *Monologion* — had read Erigena.[80]

In last analysis, close scrutiny of the *Monologion* as well as of Anselm's other works discloses no unusual conceptual link between Anselm and these two predecessors. Any correspondences with neo-Platonism which the three share do not constitute sufficient grounds for ascribing to Anselm an influence from any other source than from Augustine. And, as we noted, Schmitt argues that to some extent Anselm even deplatonizes Augustine.

Anselm's pupils. Although Anselm never founded a school, his teaching, as well as his writing, was to have its own direct influences. We must remember that his foremost pupil, Anselm of Laon, studied at Bec and that Gilbert Crispin, monk of Bec and later abbot of Westminster, wrote his *Debate between Christian and Jew* with an eye on the *Cur Deus Homo.* Anselm's sayings were anonymously compiled sometime during the period immediately following his death.[81] Schmitt makes us aware that there are really two works which were redacted: *De morum quali-*

77. *Saint Anselme de Cantorbéry*, p. 483.

78. "Les homélies attribuées à saint Anselme," *Archives d'histoire doctrinale et littéraire du moyen âge*, 2 (1927), 5–29.

79. Pseudo-Dionysius is listed at Chartres in the eleventh century. See G. Becker, *Catalogi Bibliothecarum Antiqui* (Bonn, 1885).

80. "All we know is that nothing is opposed to the hypothesis that St. Anselm might well have had contact with *De divisione naturae.* . . . That St. Anselm had written a short treatise [*De Unitate*] intended to state precisely his position on the relations of created plurality to the creating unity, and that in writing this he had more than once touched lightly on great Erigenian themes, is a hypothesis that one cannot reject as impossible." Combes, *Un inédit de saint Anselm?* p. 222. See n. 23 above.

81. These appear uncritically in PL 159 under the title *De Similitudinibus*, and are primarily short edifying statements on such topics as friendship, joy and sorrow,

tate per exemplorum coaptationem, put together by an unknown member of the Canterbury circle (and not identical with the general compiler), and the *Dicta Anselmi* of Alexander. The general redactor conflated these, adding excerpts from Eadmer's *Vita Anselmi* and his *De beatitudine caelestis patriae*.[82] The major part of the work presumably mirrors Anselm's conversations with his associates and pupils. Eadmer himself tells of Anselm's zest for conversation: "If I were to describe him as he discoursed about humility, patience, gentleness, or about this obedience which I have just shortly touched on, or about any other of the innumerable and profound subjects on which we heard him talk almost every day, I should have to compose another work and put aside the one which I have undertaken."[83]

In the next generation Honorius Augustodunensis (d. after 1140) was to take up again Anselm's definition of "free choice" in his dialogue *Predestination and Free Choice* (PL 172:1200). His *Elucidarium* borrows definitions from the *Cur Deus Homo*.[84] Still later, Richard of St. Victor's *On the Trinity* was modeled on the *Monologion*.[85] And in the fourteenth century Ockham appropriated Anselm's discussion of *nihil*.

Anselm's intellectual influence during his immediate lifetime was never as great as that of Augustine and of Thomas during theirs; still, from a historical standpoint, his ideas are as viable, his reasoning as rigorous, and his formulations as illuminating. If he did not found a school of his own, it was not because he lacked the gift of teaching. Eadmer is convincing on this point. As archbishop, Anselm's destiny lay in the unhappy controversy over investiture. Yet even in the midst of incessant and wearying disputes with William Rufus and Henry I, he never lost sight of the intellectual needs of the Canterbury community and never abdicated his role as a scholar.

humility, obedience, etc. *Memorials of St. Anselm*, ed. R. W. Southern and F. S. Schmitt (Oxford, 1969) contains the critical text.

82. Review of R. W. Southern's *Saint Anselm and His Biographer*, in *Theologische Literaturzeitung* (1965), p. 200.

83. *The Life of St Anselm, Archbishop of Canterbury*, ed. and trans. R. W. Southern (London, 1962), p. 78.

84. The general tenor of discussion is different from Anselm's since Honorius is under the influence of Erigena and neo-Platonism. See R. Crouse, "Honorius Augustodunensis: *De Neocosmo*" Ph.D. dissertation, Harvard Divinity School, 1970.

85. See S. Vanni Rovighi, "Notes sur l'influence de saint Anselme au XIIe siècle," *Cahiers de Civilisation Médiévale*, 7 (1964), 433.

Chapter II

Faith and Reason

From the very beginning of his systematic writings Anselm was self-consciously concerned with the relationship between faith and reason. The original title of the *Monologion* — "An Example of Meditating about the Rational Basis of Faith" (*de ratione fidei*) — implicitly generates the question of how to construe the *ratio fidei*. In this treatise Anselm adopts that method which was subsequently to characterize the *Proslogion* and the *Cur Deus Homo*: viz., suspending appeal to Scriptural authority and in its stead arguing by reason alone (*sola ratione*). By this means, he purports to demonstrate that certain truths of Scripture need not be accepted on authority alone, since they can be shown to coincide with conclusions yielded on an independent rational basis. This rational ground enables faith to understand itself and thus to become meaningful and living. Anselm builds upon the cornerstone of Augustinianism when he professes in *Proslogion* 1: "I do not seek to understand in order to believe; but I believe in order to understand."[1] This statement more than any other embodies Anselm's programmatic ver-

1. Cf. Augustine's sermon on Isa. 7:9 (PL 38:257). See also his exposition of Ps. 118 (PL 37:1552): "For although no one can believe in God unless he understands something, nonetheless the faith by which he believes, heals him, so that he may understand more fully. For there are some things which we believe only if we understand and other things which we understand only if we believe." One of the best places to detect Augustine's view of the relation between faith and reason is DT Bk. 1, Chs. 1–2.

sion of faith's relationship to reason. He is never to abandon it, but never does he fully explicate it.

Anselm works with the commonsense meanings of "believing" and "understanding." He offers no formal definition of "faith"; he neither utilizes nor acknowledges Augustine's rendering of *credere* as "to think with assent." [2] He presupposes whatever Scripture says about faith: that it is of things unseen, that it comes by hearing, that it is the gift of God, that without it one cannot "merit" salvation, and so on. But we never find him overtly explicating or distinguishing various notions of faith — e.g., distinguishing faith from mere believing, or differentiating faith as trust from faith as assent to the truth of a dogma. Yet we may be sure that he was familiar with and subscribed to Augustine's distinction between believing that Jesus is the Christ (*credere Christum esse*) and believing in Christ (*credere in Christum*).[3] And we may assume his concurrence with Augustine's judgment that *tempore auctoritas, re autem ratio prior est*: "in the order of time authority comes first, but in the order of reality reason is prior." [4] Though Anselm nowhere explicitly mentions this principle, it may be inferred from other statements he makes. The right order, he tells us, is first to believe the "deeper things" of the Christian faith as taught by Scripture and the Church, and then to go on to understand them, if possible (CDH I, 1).[5]

Anselm is here distinguishing between partial and full understanding. One must have a conception of God before he can believe that God exists. "We should understand the statement 'Faith comes by hearing' to mean that faith comes from what the mind apprehends or conceives through hearing, not in the sense that the mind's conception alone produces faith in man, but in the sense that there can be no faith without some conception." [6] When one exercises saving faith, he has a partial understanding of the divine plan of salvation as revealed in Scripture, but he does not — indeed cannot — understand all the truths of Scripture. He

2. PL 44:963 (*Predestination of the Saints* 2.5): "ipsum credere, nihil aliud est, quam cum assensione cogitare."

3. Sermon 144.2 (PL 38:788).

4. *On Order* 2.9.26 (PL 32:1007).

5. This is also Augustine's view of the right order in *Catholic and Manichean Ways of Life* 1.2.3 (PL 32:1312).

6. DC III, 6 (S II, 271:5–8). Anselm was undoubtedly familiar with the distinction between a necessary condition and a sufficient condition — if from no other place than Augustine's *Reproof and Grace* 12.34.

accepts the teachings of Scripture in the expectancy of progressively understanding them, as far as this is, for him, a human possibility. Anselm's rational justification of the incarnation is directed above all to *believers* who seek the reasons underlying their faith. Accordingly, he chooses as his interlocutor in the *Cur Deus Homo* the Christian monk Boso, who does not seek reasons confirmatory of faith but, instead, the joy which comes from understanding that his faith accords with reason.[7]

Rational justification serves the believer by exhibiting the intelligibility of the Supreme Being and His decrees. The apprehension of this intelligibility is understanding; and in the human being understanding is intrinsically associated with joy. Anselm never loses sight of the fact that the pursuit of understanding constitutes an act of obedience, since the Christian is commanded to know the bases of his faith (I Pet. 3:15). And obedience in itself fosters the experience of joy by being a necessary condition for its presence. In general, Anselm sees himself as discussing not whether the Christian faith is true but only *why* it is true.[8] Even in the *Proslogion* — directed against the Fool, who says there is no God — Anselm is attempting to show his own students that their faith is not groundless. For this reason he can describe the *Proslogion* as "faith seeking understanding." Yet the very arguments which enlighten believers in their faith likewise help to remove obstacles which keep unbelievers from faith. Even though unbelievers "seek a reason because they do not believe but we because we do believe, nevertheless we seek one and the same reason as they."[9] Anselm is an apologist, and as such recognizes that any set of arguments which defend the rationality of the Christian faith do so for both the Christian's sake and the non-Christian's sake. Not that the Christian faith ought to be defended to Christians. "Our faith," notes Anselm, "ought to be defended by reason against the impious, but not against those who admit that they delight in the honor of being called Christian. For while to the former it should be shown rationally that they irrationally despise us, from the latter it is right to require that they hold firmly to the pledge taken at their baptism. A Christian should advance through faith to understanding, not come to faith through understanding, or withdraw from faith if he cannot understand. Rather, when he is able to attain to understanding, he is delighted; but when he

7. CDH II, 15 (S II, 116:11–12).
8. DIV 1 (S II, 6:8–7:2).
9. CDH I, 3 (S II, 50:18–20).

cannot, he reveres what he is not able to grasp."[10] In other words, the purpose of finding reasons is different for the believer and the unbeliever. The believer should seek reasons not in order to defend his faith to himself, as if he were about to lose faith, but in order to comprehend it and advance it.[11] On the other hand, the unbeliever is given these reasons so that he may come to faith, even though he does not yet comprehend the full truth of faith.

Accordingly, Anselm appeals to the believer on a basis different from that on which he appeals to the unbeliever. He concludes his reply to Gaunilo with the statement: "Thus the Fool, who rejects sacred authority [i.e., Scripture], can easily be refuted if he says that by reference to other things he cannot conceive of that than which a greater cannot be thought. But if an orthodox Christian (*catholicus*) should say this, let him remember that 'since the creation of the world the invisible things of God (including His eternal power and deity) are clearly seen and are understood by reference to created things'" (Rom. 1:20).[12] Anselm quotes Scripture to the Christian, offers arguments to the unbeliever. Yet it would be going too far to contend that, for Anselm, arguments play no role with regard to Christian doctrine. We have already seen how they purport to show, negatively, that the truth revealed in Scripture and through the Church cannot be confounded by the dialecticians. In a positive sense, they supplement Scripture by deriving truths consistent with its teachings, but not actually found there.

The imperative *crede ut intelligas*[13] does not involve the high-handed and erroneous principle that any time someone believes a proposition he is better able to understand it than someone else who does not believe it. Rather, it embodies the modest but viable conviction that since the participant does not always share the same perspective as the onlooker,

10. *Letter to Fulco* (Ep. 136). S III, 280:34–281:41. Anselm is following Augustine's program of defending faith against the godless (*impii*) and commending it as a help to the godly. DT 14.1.3.

11. Attention is drawn to the distinction between *act* of faith and *content* of faith — a distinction which remains implicit throughout the present chapter. Note that although Boso does not seek to be confirmed, or strengthened, in the act of believing, nonetheless the reasons which Anselm adduces are (if good reasons) confirmatory of the content of faith. Hence, Boso is entitled to rejoice whenever he perceives a sound argument.

12. *Reply to Gaunilo* 8 (S I, 137:28–138:3).

13. The imperative formulation is Augustine's (Sermon 212.1), but Anselm should be thought of as accepting it.

there are some things which he, but not the onlooker, will understand. For insofar as understanding is a product of perspective and not simply of accumulated information, and insofar as the standpoint of the religiously committed individual differs from that of the nonreligiously committed individual — so far may understandings diverge.[14]

Anselm's notion of *credo* at this point surpasses the notion of mere intellectual assent and implies devotedness to God and to the pursuit of understanding His nature. It is belief *in* God as well as belief about God. "He who does not believe will not understand. For he who does not believe will not experience, and he who has not had experience will not know. For the knowledge of one who experiences is superior to the knowledge of one who hears to the same degree that experience of a thing is superior to hearing about it" (DIV 1. S II, 9:5–8). The sense in which the unbeliever will not experience cannot be the ordinary sense of "experiencing." Anselm's affirmation must be construed contextually: he who does not believe in God will not experience God, and thus will not know God. This is the sense of "know" in which the heathen are said to have lost the knowledge of God (Rom. 1:21). The experience of God is not for Anselm a mystical experience involving loss of the awareness of self-identity. It is, instead, that experience intimated by the Psalmist's exhortation to "taste and see that the Lord is good" (Ps. 34:8). Anselm is thinking of the religious life, which "sees" the Hand of grace operative in the midst of daily struggles. When a man comes to interpret his destiny in light of the Divine Being, he may glimpse with new insight the fuller meaning of mercy and grace. This kind of insight is associated with being able to appreciate. Accordingly, experience may lead to ap-

14. Cf. N. Malcolm's comment with regard to the ontological argument: "At a deeper level, I suspect that the argument can be thoroughly understood only by one who has a view of that human 'form of life' that gives rise to the idea of an infinitely great being, who views it from the *inside* not just from the outside and who has, therefore, at least some inclination to *partake* in that religious form of life." In *The Ontological Argument*, ed. A. Plantinga, p. 159. Anselm's "believing-understanding" formula implies (in general) something like the point Malcolm is making. However, Anselm thinks of the ontological argument, in particular, as so clearly sound that even the skeptic, who stands outside theism and looks on, can fully comprehend its logic apart from special experiences. In the *Proslogion* the "believing-understanding" formula functions for Christians as a kind of promissory note. Anselm is saying, as it were: "The ontological argument shows that our belief in God's existence is rationally (as well as Scripturally) justified. Other doctrines which the Christian faith teaches in accordance with Scripture, are also compatible with reason. Let the search for these reasons continue, in the expectation that God will Himself continue to illumine our minds."

preciation and appreciation to understanding. Such understanding is not merely understanding *that* a given set of propositions is true. It is understanding what-it-is-to-be-X. We commonly say that because the adolescent lacks certain experiences, he cannot himself understand what it is to be a parent with adolescent children. The man who has never experienced in himself human weakness may not be able to appreciate what it is for another to be failing, and thus may not be able to understand satisfactorily the other and his feelings. So too, on Anselm's theory, one who does not participate in the life of religious commitment may not view his life under the categories of sinfulness and holiness, and thus may not be able to understand the Psalmist's feeling of redemption or to see with the Christian something precious in the idea of the incarnation.[15]

The command *crede ut intelligas* is addressed fundamentally to the Christian: "continue to believe, in order that you may understand." The skeptic, on the other hand, is challenged first to understand — that God exists (*Proslogion*), that He is supreme Goodness and Justice (*Monologion*), that He has made provision for man's salvation in the only way possible (*Cur Deus Homo*) — and on the basis of this understanding to believe. Anselm does not and cannot (consistently) urge the skeptic to believe by a sheer act of will, with the promise of subsequently understanding. Rather, the *credo* for Anselm in *Proslogion* 1 is personal and confessional: I believe; for unless I believe, I will not understand. And if Boso in the *Cur Deus Homo* repeatedly acknowledges that his questioning indicates no personal doubts, he does so in contrast to the unbeliever, who questions because he doubts. *Crede ut intelligas* is thus seen to be a spiritual imperative and not a hermeneutical rule. Rather than abandoning faith when he does not comprehend, the Christian should reaffirm his faith and continue to strive toward intellectual clarity.[16] Herein lies the real meaning of faith in its contrast to knowledge. And here arises also the requirement of faithfulness. The believer discerns the reason for some of the doctrines he adheres to. And these reasons constitute the solid foundation which warrants his supposing that those "deeper things" which he has not fathomed — perhaps, cannot fathom — have their own

15. Note Anselm's use of the phrase *corde intelligere*, "to understand with the heart." DC III, 2 (S II, 265:5–6). Cf. Matt. 13:15.

16. Anselm is thus agreeing with Augustine's construal of this formula. DT 7.6.12: "But if it cannot be grasped by the understanding, let it be held by faith until God enlightens your hearts." Also note *On the Gospel of John* 39.3; 48.1; 48.6; 99.3.

43

hidden reasons. On this basis, he is justified in remaining faithful to his initial commitment.

Although "unless you believe, you will not understand" has an empirical basis, it is an essentially theological utterance. For it represents the theological conviction that *intellectus gratia est*: understanding is a grace.[17] In the first instance, the understanding which accompanies the conversion of the unbeliever is a grace; in the second, the progressive understanding subsequent to conversion is equally a grace. The Anselmian-Augustinian formula thus enunciates the conviction of the Church with regard to this second grace, viz., the conviction that understanding is a special gift of God which some, but not all, believers receive. This type of understanding has faith and obedience as its necessary, but not its sufficient, condition. "Not only is the mind prevented from rising to the understanding of higher things when it lacks faith and obedience to the commandments of God, but by neglect of good conscience even the understanding which has already been given to a man is sometimes removed and faith itself overturned" (DIV 1). In this sense, understanding is conceived as the reward of faith.[18]

REVELATION AND REASON

Anselm presupposes that the right use of reason can never contradict Scripture. If Scripture clearly teaches a doctrine, then any rational argument to the contrary will be an unsound argument. Anselm does not beg the question here by defining the argument as unsound simply because its conclusion contradicts Scripture. He thinks that an argument can be seen to be sound or unsound independently of its relationship to Scripture. But if prima facie its conclusion contradicts a teaching of Scripture, then this becomes a signal cautioning one to take a second look at the alleged soundness of the proof or at the allegedly clear interpreta-

17. DC III, 6 (S II, 271): "Faith comes into being when, by grace, uprightness of willing is added to the conception, because then a man believes what he hears. 'And hearing comes by the word of Christ,' that is, by the word of those who preach Christ. Now, there are no preachers unless they are sent. But the fact that they are sent is due to grace. Therefore, preaching is a grace, since what derives from grace is also a grace; and hearing is a grace, and the understanding which comes from hearing is a grace, and uprightness of willing is a grace."

18. Cf. Augustine, Sermon 139 (PL 38:770); "Fides enim debet praecedere intellectum, ut sit intellectus fidei praemium." Also, *On the Gospel of John* 48.1.

Faith and Reason

tion of Scripture. If Anselm intimates that reason can never be in conflict with Scripture, this is not because he could not, or would have refused to, recognize such a conflict were it brought to his attention. Instead, his conviction arises from three factors: his own feeling of having been able satisfactorily to harmonize prima facie conflicts which he himself encountered; his recognition that the adjudication of such a conflict is itself a rational enterprise; and, his view that human reason cannot in principle comprehend the full mystery of the Godhead as revealed in Scripture. Anselm operates on the further presupposition that a rational God cannot reveal to man anything essentially irrational. And if Scripture is the primary vehicle of divine revelation, then Scripture can never contradict reason.

A presupposition is not something which cannot be challenged, but something which can be challenged only in a special way. A presupposition is that with which we evaluate data, not something which is itself validated or invalidated by direct appeal to the data. Thus, the presupposition that reason and revelation never conflict becomes a structural principle for Anselm: he uses it to interpret the phenomena of theology. When the consistent interpretation of these phenomena becomes too costly — e.g., in terms of additional hypotheses needed or overall modifications required — the presupposition itself may be surrendered. But the cost is seldom so great as to *dictate* such surrender.

In accordance with his presupposition Anselm is ready to interpret Scripture so as to bring about its accord with reason, but without "forcing" this accord. For example, Scripture tells us that God creates evil (Isa. 45:7). But neither reason nor other parts of Scripture support this view.[19] This apparent conflict signals the believer to inquire further and to look beneath the surface reading. Anselm, like Augustine, interprets the biblical passage by invoking a distinction between evil as injustice and evil as disadvantage (*incommodum*). The evil which is disadvantage "is in some cases nothing, as with blindness; but sometimes it is something, as in the case of pain. When this evil is something, we do not deny that God causes it. . . . For He creates hardships and uses them to try and to purify the just, and to punish the unjust."[20] Hence

19. Note Anselm's presuppositions: (1) God is rational; (2) right reason cannot contradict Scripture; (3) Scripture cannot contradict itself.
20. DC I, 7 (S II, 258:23–27). Cf. Augustine, *Catholic and Manichean Ways of Life* 2.7.9.

45

God creates evil not in the sense of creating morally unjust natures but in the sense of causing sickness, floods, and the like. And this rendering, Anselm contends, is compatible with God's own nature as justice.

To take another example, Scripture speaks of God as having "established man's end, which cannot be escaped" (Job 14:5). This seems to imply a kind of fatalism which is inconsistent with free choice. Since Anselm thinks that philosophical reason proves that man has freedom of will (the argument of *De Libertate*), he must either reexamine his proof or interpret the passage in Job in such a way as to avoid the doctrine of fatalism. And here again he brings to bear a philosophical distinction to elucidate the meaning of Scripture. God "is said to have established immutably within Himself something which can be altered with respect to man before it actually comes to pass. . . . For it is not contradictory to say both that within eternity something does occur (never that it has occurred or will occur) and that within time this same event has occurred or will occur. Likewise, it is not inconsistent to maintain that an event which is unchangeable in eternity may, before it actually occurs in time, be changeable as a result of free will." [21]

However, Anselm will not always modify the interpretation of Scripture and thus comply with a purported proof of reason. "Even though our reason may seem unassailable to us, we should not believe that it is supported by any truth if Scripture is obviously opposed to our understanding." [22] In other words, some teachings of Scripture are so clear that their real meaning is their surface meaning. If in this case a rational argument is at odds with the Scriptural doctrine, one is obliged to reevaluate the argument — and to keep doing so until the mistake in reasoning becomes evident. Of course, if the reasoning continued to seem unassailable and if the biblical passage admitted of no other plausible interpretation, one might decide to give up the presupposition about the relationship between Scripture and reason. But the point is that he would not be rationally forced to do so because the type of argument at stake here is not the schematic proof of formal logic, which, if valid, can be mechanically known to be valid. Rather, it is the more characteristically

21. DC I, 5 (S II, 253:22–24; 254:2–6).

22. DC III, 6 (S II, 272:3–6). Cf. also: "I am certain that anything . . . obviously contradictory to sacred Scripture is false." CDH I, 18 (S II, 82:8–10).

Cf. Augustine, *Christian Doctrine* 2.7.9: "We must think and believe that what is written in Scripture is better and truer — even if the truth be hidden — than that which we can know by ourselves."

philosophical argument, whose soundness turns upon the informalisms of language as well as upon the logical rules of inference. And precisely these informalisms make it difficult to speak of clearly having a philosophical proof. The history of Anselm's own ontological "proof" bears out this point most vividly.

Scripture is, then, for Anselm a norm of truth.

For, if at times we cannot clearly show that a view we affirm by reason is also in Scripture, or if we cannot prove it from what Scripture says, then in one way we can still learn through Scripture whether such a view should be accepted or rejected. For Scripture opposes no truth and favors no falsity. So, if a view is derived on the basis of a clear reason and if this view is not contradicted in any part of Scripture, then it may be said to be supported by the authority of Scripture because of the fact that Scripture does not deny it. . . . In this way, then, when Holy Scripture either clearly affirms or else does not at all deny a truth derived rationally, it contains the authority of every rationally derived truth (DC III, 6. S II, 271:28–272:7).

This statement in *De Concordia* is a further specification of the statement in the *Cur Deus Homo*: "If I say something which a greater authority [viz., Scripture] does not confirm, then even if I seem to prove this point rationally, it should be accepted as only tentatively certain — awaiting the time when God somehow reveals something better to me." [23] Although Anselm does not forsake this view in the passage from *De Concordia*, he does note a sense in which Scripture can be said to support a given judgment of reason whenever Scripture does not explicitly, or by implication, *exclude* this view. He thus strengthens the case for reason by this acknowledgment of indirect Scriptural support. Accordingly, the conclusions of reason are no longer considered as being quite so tentative as suggested in the *Cur Deus Homo*.

One way reason can supplement the teachings of Scripture is to deduce the truths implied by the explicit statements of Scripture. For if Scripture teaches only true propositions, then any further proposition which follows validly from the set of Scriptural propositions will itself be true. Anselm views the Church's formulation of the creeds as a concrete attempt to summarize such rational deductions.

23. CDH I, 2 (S II, 50:7–10). Note also CDH I, 18 (S II, 82:5–16). Cf. Southern: "The demonstrations of reason are in varying degrees provisional. In Anselm's theology they are provisional in the same way that explanations in natural science are provisional." *Saint Anselm and His Biographer*, p. 56.

Where in the Prophets, in the Gospels, or in the Apostles do we read in just so many words that the one God exists in three persons, or that the one God is a trinity, or that God is from God? Nor do we encounter the words "person" and "trinity" in the [Nicene] Creed, in which the procession of the Holy Spirit from the Son is also not set forth. Nevertheless, since these things clearly follow from those things which we do read, we steadfastly believe them in our hearts and confess them with our mouths. Therefore, we ought to receive with certainty not only whatever we read in the Holy Scriptures, but also whatever follows from Scripture by rational necessity — as long as there is no reason against it (DP 11. S II, 209:9–16).

The creeds, for Anselm, are never an authority in their own right, as is Scripture. Yet they are *authoritative* precisely because, in addition to reciting Scripture, they form a collection of necessary inferences from Scripture. Since the creeds are confessional, they do not contain within themselves the patterns of inference which lend them support. But as a theologian, Anselm sets forth in various treatises what he takes to be these undergirding reasons.

LIMITS OF REASON

Necessity and suitability. In the preface to the *Cur Deus Homo* Anselm states his enterprise as showing "by necessary reasons — omitting reference to Christ, as if we had heard nothing of Him — that it is impossible for any man to be saved apart from Him." What he means by "necessary reasons" (*rationes necessariae*) and how he distinguishes such reasons from considerations of appropriateness (*convenientia*) constitute significant questions in regard to the methodology of the *Cur Deus Homo* as well as in regard to his treatment of faith and reason generally. It is clear that appeal to what is merely appropriate points up the limited scope of reason in its role of demonstrating the necessity of the incarnation. When deductions from the moral and metaphysical nature of God do not suffice to complete a total argument, Anselm has recourse to these *convenientiae*. The best example of this is in Book 2, Chapter 8, where he likens himself to an artist, painting a conceptual picture:

Then paint . . . that just as the sin of man and the cause of our condemnation had its origin from a woman, so it is very fitting that the remedy for sin and the cause of our salvation should be born from a woman. And lest women despair of obtaining blessedness since such great evil came

48

from a woman, it is appropriate that such great good should come from a woman in order to restore their hope. And paint this also: if a virgin was the cause of all evil for the human race, it is all the more suitable that a virgin should be the cause of all good for the human race. And paint too that if the woman whom God made from a man alone without a woman, was made from a virgin [viz., Adam], it is especially fitting that the man who was made from a woman alone without a man, should be made from a virgin.

Anselm thinks that for the Son of God to be born from a woman alone or from a man alone is morally more worthy and more pure than for Him to be born of their union.[24] Thus, he never completely breaks with the Augustinian notion that the conjugal act is tainted with concupiscence, and therefore with sin. But neither moral nor metaphysical considerations can establish that Jesus should be miraculously taken from a woman rather than from a man, as was Eve. And here Anselm resorts to an intuitive sense of decorum: it befits Jesus to be taken from Mary alone since this type of birth completes a pattern. In his role as conceptual artist Anselm realizes that his pictures have minimal apologetical content. He is here suggesting and surmising instead of polemicizing. For at this juncture there can be no rigor: the marshaling of strict arguments has reached a boundary point, and didactical analogies intervene. These analogies are not directed exclusively toward the believer, though.[25] When Boso calls Anselm's picture beautiful and reasonable, he is doing so with an eye to those opponents who, unfamiliar with this picture, see only repugnance in the story of the virgin birth.

Rationes necessariae are professedly reasons so cogent as to be capable of moving the intellect of unbelievers — if not to faith, then at least to the awareness that Christianity provides an intellectually viable world view. In Book I, Chapter 25, Anselm makes his most cryptic statement about such reasons: "What is proved true on the basis of a necessary reason ought not to be brought into doubt, even if the reason why it is true remains undiscerned."[26] This passage exhibits an unclarity in Anselm's use

24. CDH II, 8 (S II, 103:28–30).

25. Contrast McIntyre: " 'Necessity' is the quality of such relations as are self-evident to, or accepted after proof as true by, believers and unbelievers. 'Fittingness', on the contrary, can be applied only to such relations or situations as are seen by believers to be the case." *St. Anselm and His Critics*, p. 59.

26. "Quod enim necessaria ratione veraciter esse colligitur, id in nullam deduci debet dubitationem, etiam si ratio quomodo sit non percipitur." S II, 96:2–3.

of *ratio*. Here he seems to be implicitly distinguishing the reason *that* a proposition is true from the reason *why* it is true. But this distinction is hazy. Assume, for instance, that A, B, and C are exhaustively alternative. Then if we can eliminate A and B as false, we know that C is true. But we also know why C is true, viz., because A and B are false and because A, B, and C are logically exhaustive. Still — and this may be Anselm's point — we may not yet feel that we "really" understand why C is true. That is, we are not satisfied with the purely formal explanation, and we seek instead a different level explanation — one which proceeds other than eliminatively. If something like this is what Anselm intends, then his statement makes some sense as a comment on the notion of explanation. However, comparison with *Monologion* 64 suggests that he may be alluding to the fact that in some cases these other explanations *cannot* be forthcoming.[27] In such cases our desire for further illumination can never be fulfilled, since the subject matter lies essentially beyond human comprehension.

Anselm's unsystematic use of *ratio* embodies perplexities regarding his distinction between necessary reasons and fitting reasons. For although it seems unquestionable that he wanted to make some such distinction, there remains debate about the precise nature of the distinction. *Cur Deus Homo* II, 16, confirms that Anselm really was trying to indicate a difference between the two kinds of reasons. There Boso remarks concerning the topic at hand: "We can conclude that this [belief] is not only fitting (*conveniens*) but also necessary (*necessarium*)." [28] Earlier, Boso had suggested that necessary reasons serve as a solid foundation which supports pictures that are merely fitting, and that, therefore, the citing of necessary reasons must come first.[29] But Anselm responded by insisting that in the case under discussion it was a necessary enough rea-

27. Cf. M 64 (S I, 75:3–6): "Yet, even if because of their naturally deep incomprehensibility we cannot explain these doctrines which are supported by necessary proofs and opposed by no contradictory reason, we ought nonetheless to regard them with faith's certainty."

28. "Quod non solum conveniens sed etiam necessarium esse possumus concludere." S II, 119:13–14.

Anselm's words for "It is fitting" are *convenit* and *decet*; his phrase for "It is necessary" is *necesse est*. *Oportet* appears to be used sometimes as a substitute for *necesse est* and sometimes as a substitute for *convenit* and *decet*. Cf. CDH II, 8 (S II, 103:20) — *hoc inevitabiliter oportet esse* — with CDH I, 3 (S II, 51:3–7) — *quam convenienter. . . . Oportet namque . . .*

29. CDH I, 4 (S II, 52:3–6): "prius . . . necessitas . . . deinde istae convenientiae quasi picturae."

son (*satis necessaria ratio*) that something was not appropriate (*nec decebat*) in relation to God's plan for the human race. And in Book 2, Chapter 8, after having shown that two things are unfitting (*inconvenientia*) with respect to God, Anselm concludes: "Therefore it is necessary that . . ." (*ergo necesse est*).[30] It seems, then, that whenever something is inappropriate to God, or unbefitting of Him, it is necessary to think of Him as not doing that thing. Yet where an action is thought to befit God, it is not thereby, and for this reason, necessary that God be conceived as performing the action. In this way a fitting reason is not as strong as a necessary reason, even though whatever is unfitting is necessarily not the case with God.

Mystery and ineffability. In the *Monologion, Proslogion,* and *Cur Deus Homo* Anselm affirms the inability of reason to plumb the depths (*altiores rationes*) of the Divine Being and His activity. In *Monologion* 43 he speaks of the mystery (*secretum*) and ineffability of God. Indeed, the *Monologion* concludes with the words: "Truly, then, this Spirit is not only God but the only God — ineffably three and one." And *Proslogion* 11 concedes: "If we can somehow grasp why You can will to save the wicked, surely we cannot at all understand why from among those who are equally wicked You save some and not others because of Your supreme goodness, and condemn some and not others because of Your supreme justice." Consequently, Anselm never supposes that human reason can penetrate the mystery of the Divine Being. Yet this inability of reason does not cause any embarassment to his faith. From his viewpoint, only the undiscerning can take offense at the thought of there being in principle some truth which transcends the domain of human reason.

Yet even in the suprarational dimension, Anselm himself never totally abandons the pursuit of rational indicators. Assurance of this fact occurs in *Cur Deus Homo* II, 16, where he admits to not understanding how in Christ two natures come together in one person. Still, he has Boso remark: "I agree that in this life no man can open such a mystery; and I do not ask you to do what no man can do, but only to do as much as you can. For you will more easily persuade me that deeper reasons lie hidden in this matter if you show that you see some rationale in it than if by saying nothing you show that you do not understand it at all" (S II, 117:

30. S II, 103:17–18.

18–22). Here resides the limitation in scope of the Anselmic enterprise: to show that those doctrines which cannot be rationally comprehended are at least not altogether alien to reason. In other words, he aspires to demonstrate in some minimal sense of "reasonable" that it is not *unreasonable* to subscribe to these teachings in the absence of stricter argumentation. Precisely at this juncture he appeals to similarities, illustrations, and a sense of what is fitting. The distinction, therefore, between *rationes necessariae* and *rationes congruentes* must be viewed in relation to his acknowledgment of divine hiddenness. "Necessary reasons" comprise those arguments which purport to be objective in their independent witness to, and warrant of, the revealed tenets of Scripture — arguments so efficacious that even the unbeliever may perceive their soundness. "Fitting reasons," by contrast, include those more subjective considerations which indicate — still to unbelievers as well as to believers — that the Church's witness to deeper truths is not an arbitrary witness. In making this distinction Anselm conveys a position earlier adhered to by Augustine and later systematically articulated by Thomas, viz., the rationality of believing that certain theological truths cannot be proven.[31]

Anselm recognizes, but never emphasizes, the noetic consequences of the Fall. The Apostle Paul teaches that unbelievers have their "understanding darkened, being alienated from the life of God through the ignorance that is in them, because of the blindness of their hearts" (Eph. 4:18). Anselm holds with the Apostle that the Fall has corrupted human nature, so that the natural man, unaided by grace and revelation, cannot understand the requirements of justice or righteousness.[32] Yet the corrupting influence of sin is not such that it can prevent the natural man's reason from assenting to the "necessities" of the Christian faith once these are presented to him. Anselm's "rationalism" is such that he aspires to prove that God exists, that He is triune, that the soul is immortal, that salvation can be accomplished only by a God-man, and so on. On the other hand, though, he is aware that the mind needs grace as a precon-

---

31. Note Augustine, Ep. 120 (PL 33:453): "Thus, if it is reasonable that faith precede reason with respect to certain profound issues which cannot yet be comprehended, then without any doubt the very reason which persuades us of this, itself precedes faith."

32. "In those who are not baptized, not only the inability to have justice but even the inability to understand it is counted as sin, for this inability has also resulted from sin." DC III, 7 (S II, 273:20–23). See also DIV 1 (S II, 9:9–11): The mind which lacks faith cannot understand the higher things of God. Cf. Augustine, *Catholic and Manichean Ways of Life* 1.2.3.

dition for theological understanding and that the human intellect is inherently limited with respect to penetrating the mystery of the Divine Being. This recognition — rather than any conflation of *necessitas* and *convenientia* — modifies his rationalism.[33] That Anselm comments relatively little on the relationship between sin and the intellect manifests the absence of that fear of reason's deceptiveness which haunted Augustine after his experience with Manicheism.

Antidialecticians. The intention to "prove by necessary reasons" contains no guarantee of success. Some of the arguments deemed by Anselm to yield rationally necessary conclusions seem more properly described as considerations of fittingness. That is, the demarcating line between the two types of reasoning is not clearly drawn. But the fact that this distinction is not clearly made in every case constitutes no basis for denying that Anselm was intent on making it. In general, his insistence upon preserving *two* categories of reasons embodies his allegiance to the principle that there is no caprice at all in God. Accordingly — to return to a previous example — the Son of God's having assumed human nature from a woman instead of from a man could not have been arbitrary. Anselm wants to bring such doctrines under the aegis of reason: he can do this only by affirming that they belong to a different category of intelligibility. In this way, he self-consciously and staunchly confronts those of his day who viewed as presumptive any attempt to understand the activity of the Divine Being *sola ratione*.

Thus, Peter Damian (1007–72), though not in the strictest sense an antidialectician, asserted in his treatise *Divine Omnipotence* that God, as omnipotent, can restore virginity to someone who has lost it, and can bring it about that those things which now exist should not have existed.[34] And when we say that God can do all things, this does not contradict Scripture, which declares that God cannot lie. Indeed, Damian grants that God cannot lie because lying is an instance of doing evil; and since evil is nothing (rather than something), it is not encompassed by

33. We may disagree with D. Knowles's observation that "the adjective *necessarius* means [for Anselm] 'formally admissible', 'probable', rather than 'compelling.'" *The Evolution of Medieval Thought*, p. 101.

34. "Sicut ergo potuit Deus, antequam quaeque facta essent, ut non fierent; ita nihilominus potest et nunc ut quae facta sunt non fuissent." PL 145:619. (See also 145:600.) In *Against Faustus the Manichean* 26.5 (PL 42:481) Augustine had earlier tried to meet this very objection. Augustine, too, is the source for the view that sin is nothing. *On the Gospel of John* 1.13 (PL 35:1385).

the *omnia* which we say God can do (PL 145:610). In addition, Damian regards the miracles of God as confounding the rational schemes of the philosophers and the dialecticians. By contrast, Anselm does not cite the occurrence of miracles as a means to ward off the intellectual thrusts of philosophers. Although keenly aware of the limitations of reason in relation to revelation, and although regarding Scripture as the norm of reason, he unflaggingly pursues the rationale of revelation — in the hope of offering this rationale to unbelieving philosophers and dialecticians.[35]

The antirationalists proclaimed that mere appeal to the will of God suffices as an explanation for why various events occur in the history of the world. Anselm seems to embrace this position when he observes: "Recourse to the will of God ought to constitute a sufficient reason for God's doing something — even in those cases where we do not see why He wills what He does. For the will of God is never irrational."[36] Yet Boso renders this principle inoperative as an explanation. He rightly notes that if something seems unreasonable, there is no need to think that it coincides with the directive will of God. Mere appeal to the will of God offers no explanation for why an event occurred, because there is no independent way of knowing that God efficaciously wills this to occur rather than willing to permit it to occur. Moreover, the occurrence of the event itself may be in question — as with the incarnation. Against one who urges that the reason for the incarnation is the will of God, the reply might be given: "The doctrine of incarnation is unintelligible; therefore since God cannot will what is unintelligible, He could not have willed to become incarnate; therefore there was no incarnation."

35. Anselm does, however, partly agree with Damian: "It is wrong to say that it is impossible for God to make what is past not be past." CDH II, 17 (S II, 123:4–6). Simply because God wills something from eternity does not mean that His will is subject to any necessity; and if it is not subject to the necessity of doing a thing, it is also not subject to the impossibility of not doing that thing.

Anselm is not saying that God can do the logically impossible: he is making a comment on the application of the phrase "It is impossible for God . . ." Admittedly, God wills to create the world and with it time. It is now true and ever after will be true that there is a past. That is, it is now impossible that there should be no past. But to say "It is impossible for God to make what is past not be past," thinks Anselm, wrongly connotes the inconceivability of God's *not* having created the world and time. Since God does eternally will the creation of time, it is impossible that once there is a past, there should not always be a past. Hence, the impossibility of God's making the past not be past is the impossibility of God's willing what He does not will. Anselm rightly refuses to think of this as constituting a limitation on God's omnipotence. And this is precisely Damian's attitude as well.

36. CDH I, 8 (S II, 59:10–11). Note Augustine, Ep. 120.1.5 (PL 32:454) and *City of God* 21.5.2.

Because of the possibility of this reply, the voluntarist's unqualified introduction of the will-of-God principle has no theological value. It prescribes the limits of reason in the wrong way and at the wrong place. Anselm, for his part, always seeks the rational ground determining God's will, and never thinks of that will's activity as affording a reason in itself.

"The will of God is never irrational" makes no empirical claim, verifiable or unverifiable. It is, rather, definitional of the nature of God. If God seems to will the irrational, then Anselm is committed to say that either we have misapprehended or else the being is not God. Anselm is not prepared to surrender this principle in the light of experience, but only to use it in making sense of experience. The principle follows deductively from the higher order definition of God as supremely perfect. Our conception of perfection is such, explains Anselm, that a supremely perfect being cannot be thought to will what is irrational. In general, we attribute to God *quidquid melius est esse quam non esse*: whatever it is better to be than not to be (P 11). The notion of perfection is the normative a priori notion from which Anselm's entire apologetic takes its start.

We have seen Anselm's deep commitment to both revelation and reason. He employs reason to defend faith and to justify its existence. But at the same time he acknowledges the limitation of reason and avoids making it the standard determining all truth. He respects the mystery of the Godhead and concedes the noetic consequences of the Fall. Yet he does not falsely restrict the prerogatives of reason as do the extreme antidialecticians. Though he never adequately explores the various uses of *ratio* and *fides*, and though he never programmatically treats their interrelationship, it is clear that he is neither a relentless rationalist nor an unreflective fideist. In last analysis, faith and reason are ever coadjutors: in interpreting Scripture reason aids faith; in guiding reason, Scripture regulates understanding.

UNITY OF APPROACH

We have been speaking as if Anselm's view of faith and reason were unified. However, is this assumption justifiable? That is, does Anselm's account of faith and reason, after all, change during the course of the *Monologion, Proslogion,* and *Cur Deus Homo*? J. McIntyre observes, for instance, that the *Christo remoto* approach of the *Cur Deus Homo* conflicts prima facie with the *credo ut intelligam* perspective of the *Pros-*

logion.[37] And others have contended that the method of the *Proslogion* differs substantively from that of the *Monologion*: "In the *Proslogion* . . . we look in vain for the *Monologion's* confidence of the ability-to-know and for the recurrence of such words as *'necessitas rationis,'* *'absurdus.'* These words do appear — but only rarely." [38]

Monologion and Proslogion. It is generally conceded that Anselm's tack in the *Monologion* is stated clearly in the preface: viz., to prove doctrines by independent arguments and without appeal to authority. The exclusion of Scripture and the reliance upon philosophical argumentation goes so far that the Spirit of the Father and of the Son is never referred to as the *Holy* Spirit. And the designation "God" is introduced only at the last moment, after the Supreme Being has purportedly been shown to possess those attributes which are commonly associated with the Divine Nature. Although the *Proslogion* arguments do not themselves appeal to Scriptural authority, they are thought by some interpreters to be far less apologetically intended than the arguments of the *Monologion.* During the interval of time between the writing of the *Monologion* and the *Proslogion*, Anselm, it is said, came to believe that rational argumentation could never prove theological truths to the unbeliever. Hence, in the *Proslogion* he does not proceed *sola ratione* but *fide quaerente intellectum.* In other words, proponents of this theory assert that whereas the *Monologion* is intended for believers and unbelievers alike, the *Proslogion* is written essentially for those who are already Christians. Interestingly, the underlying continuity of Anselm's works is so strong that what begins as an attempt to drive a wedge between the *Monologion* and the *Proslogion* culminates in reappraising the *Monologion* itself as an intra-fideistic work. Thus Karl Barth concludes: "Not a single one of Anselm's writings can be regarded as directly addressing those who are outside of faith — i.e., as being apologetic in the modern sense. The readers whom he envisioned and in whom he was interested were the Christian theologians — more specifically, the Benedictine theologians of his day." [39] And again: "In the *Monologion* itself we are con-

37. *St. Anselm and His Critics*, pp. 1–7.
38. A. Antweiler, "Anselmus von Canterbury, Monologion und Proslogion," *Scholastik*, 8 (1933), 558.
39. *Fides quaerens intellectum* (Darmstadt, 1966), p. 60 (English ed., pp. 62–63).

fronted by decisive rejection of all speculation which does not respect the incomprehensible reality of the object of faith. . . ." [40]

According to Barth, the *Proslogion* does represent Anselm's intention to prove the existence of God. But Barth sees in Anselm no champion of natural reason. The proofs of *Proslogion* 2 and 3 are not meant for the man outside of faith. They do not seek to bring him to God; for Anselm realizes, Barth tells us, that no conclusions of natural reason can do that. Nor, on the other hand, do they confirm the believer in his faith, since the believer's faith is supposed to remain firm irrespective of proofs. To Anselm, continues Barth, "the purpose of theology cannot be to lead men to faith, nor to strengthen them in faith, nor even to free their faith of doubt. One who asks theological questions does not do so for the sake of his faith's existence; nor can the working out of theological answers, whether perfected to greater or lesser extent, have any meaning for the existence of his faith." [41] According to this interpretation, the arguments of the *Monologion* and the *Proslogion*, therefore, have no relation to faith. They neither induce the one man to come to faith nor the other to remain in faith. As the product of faith, they do not strengthen faith, but bring joy to faith by increasing understanding.

Furthermore, observes Barth, when Anselm addresses the Fool, he does so on the believer's ground; never does he himself subscribe to the unbeliever's universal reason, which is undirected by Scripture.[42] In *Proslogion* 4, Anselm notes that the unbeliever does not really understand what God is — otherwise he could not conceivably think God not to exist. That the Fool persists in thinking God not to exist — in the face of a "proof" to the contrary — exhibits his lack of understanding. Moreover, in replying to Gaunilo, Anselm appeals to Gaunilo's faith as evidencing that he, Gaunilo, cannot disavow understanding the phrase "that than which no greater can be thought." [43] Barth purports to detect in these passages Anselm's awareness of the apologetical ineffectiveness

---

40. *Ibid.*, p. 54 (English ed., p. 57). "Behind *Monologion* 1–6 stands the dogma of creation out of nothing. Behind the doctrine of the attributes of God (in spite of all the 'neo-Platonic' technique employed) stands the Christian confession of the oneness and the omnipotence of God. Behind the doctrine of the Divine Word stands, of course, the Christology of the Catholic Church. . . ." *Ibid.*, pp. 55–56 (English ed., p. 58).

41. *Ibid.*, p. 16 (English ed., p. 17).

42. *Ibid.*, p. 64 (English ed., p. 67).

43. *Reply to Gaunilo* 1 (S I, 130:15–16).

of rational argumentation vis-à-vis the skeptic. Natural theology offers no genuine common ground (*Anknüpfungspunkt*) for Christian and non-Christian. In fact, suggests Barth, "Anselm might not have known how to talk about the Christian *Credo* other than by addressing sinners as if they were non-sinners, non-Christians as if Christians, and unbelievers as if believers. . . ." [44]

Barth envisions Anselm, even in the *Proslogion*, as primarily reflecting upon the meaning of the *Credo*.[45] Hence, Scripture and the *Credo* at no point cease being the general basis for Anselm's philosophizing. That is, Barth chooses to emphasize the biblical presuppositions which encompass Anselm's argumentation — presuppositions of which he thinks Anselm could never have lost sight.[46] For Anselm does not proceed to deduce the tenets of reason within the context of nonbiblical presuppositions alone. Rather, he makes use variously of nonbiblical presuppositions as a means to the more limited task of exhibiting a rationale for the Christian faith. But since this rationale is not purely objective — i.e., since it is not developed totally outside the biblical framework — it cannot, concludes Barth, be of intellectual weight to the man who stands outside of faith.

In three articles, A. Stolz insists on the sharp line between the rationalistic methodology of the *Monologion* and the less conclusivistic approach of the *Proslogion*.[47] Stolz goes further than Barth by contending that in the *Proslogion* Anselm never considered himself to be proving the existence of God. Stolz agrees with Barth, though, that Anselm is concerned with examining the names of God and that one of the names of God is "He who truly is." [48] In this light he construes the title of *Pros-*

44. *Fides quaerens intellectum*, p. 68 (English ed., p. 71).

45. "Basically '*intelligere*' means for Anselm *legere*: reflecting on what has already been said in the *Credo*." *Ibid.*, p. 39 (English ed., p. 40).

46. Of the CDH Barth writes: "The decisive presuppositions which underlie the proof of the rationality, or necessity, of the incarnation and of the atoning death of Christ are: the existence of a divine plan for the human race, the essential duty of man to obey God, the regarding of sin as an infinite debt which man owes to God, the inviolability of God's negation of sin, the inability of man to redeem himself, and (last but not least) the aseity and honor of God. . . ." *Ibid.*, p. 53 (English ed., p. 55).

47. "Zur Theologie Anselms im Proslogion," *Catholica*, 2 (1933), 1–24. " 'Vere esse' im Proslogion des hl. Anselm." "Das *Proslogion* des hl. Anselm." Contrast the view of G. Söhngen, who speaks of the *Proslogion* as an example of *conclusio theologica*. *Die Einheit in der Theologie* (Munich, 1952), p. 25.

48. Exodus 3:14: "I am who I am." See Ch. 1, p. 18.

logion 2 ("That God truly exists") as indicating a discussion of a name attributed to God rather than indicating a speculative demonstration of God's existence. In *Proslogion* 2 and 3, argues Stolz, the existence of God is never in question. Anselm is assuming God's existence and is merely trying to understand its special features more clearly. What differentiates this existence from all other existents is that God "exists so truly (really) that He cannot be thought not to exist" (P 3). This notion of degrees of reality is derived from Augustine, who conceives of everything mutable as not fully real (*non vere est*), in contrast to the immutable, which is most real. "It is evident," concludes Stolz, "that [in the *Proslogion*] Anselm never thought of proving God's existence. He only wanted to deduce God's special mode of being and thus to take the first step toward that goal at which the entire *Monologion* aims, viz., the immediate experience of God and the knowledge of God as found in the dogmas." [49] Stolz views the *Proslogion* as an exercise in mystical theology, directed to the Fool not in order to bind his intellect but to unbind his heart by confronting him with a portrayal of the majesty of God.

The approaches of both Barth and Stolz seek to recast the perspective of Anselm studies by minimizing the apologetical nature of the *Proslogion*. Yet neither interpretation can be substantiated by a judicious reading of the texts. Barth has been rightly criticized for projecting into Anselm his own insistence upon the supremacy of biblical over natural theology. In particular, his claim that Anselm sees in philosophical argumentation no bearing upon faith needs to be qualified. As long as Barth allows that Anselm is trying to prove the existence of God, there is no basis in Anselm for contrasting the believer's ability to recognize the soundness of a proof with the unbeliever's inability to recognize this. If the arguments of the *Proslogion* do not *prove* to the unbeliever, it is because they also do not prove to the believer — i.e., because they do not prove at all.

In the absence of explicit statements to the contrary, we are justified in attributing to Anselm — even at the time of writing the *Proslogion* — the formula articulated in the *Cur Deus Homo*: Christian and skeptic seek the same set of reasons (CDH I, 3). When Anselm appeals to Gau-

49. "Zur Theologie Anselms im Proslogion," p. 23. Furthermore: "If someone wants to speak of an Anselmian proof of God, then he must show (in view of Anselm's strictly Augustinian terminology) that '*vere esse*' in the title of Chapter 2 does not have the sense of 'immutable and absolutely real being' but refers merely to God's existence. . . ." P. 409.

nilo's faith and conscience, he does not stop there but goes on to appeal to his intellect as well. Moreover, he seeks to increase the Fool's understanding in the hope that he will be led *by* grace *to* faith *through* understanding. But should the Fool remain in his state of unbelief, Anselm does not consider his own rational arguments objectively unsound but only, in this case, subjectively ineffective.[50] He recognizes that the Fool's being led to understanding is not tantamount to his being led to faith. This fact is borne out by the end of *Proslogion* 4: "I thank You, good Lord, I thank You that what at first I believed through Your giving, now by Your enlightening I so understand that even if I were unwilling to acknowledge that You exist, I could not fail to understand that You exist."

At stake here is the distinction between understanding, and therefore believing that God exists, on the one hand, and, on the other, believing in God, who does exist. Believing that God exists is only a necessary precondition for believing in God. And perhaps this distinction epitomizes the heart of Barth's point: Anselm recognizes that even if a rational argument brings the Fool to understanding, it can never by itself bring him to saving faith — *fides qua fiducia*. Nevertheless (and Barth does not sufficiently emphasize this) the intelligent Fool will never come to faith in the absence of preparatory understanding. And for this reason Anselm appeals directly to the intellect — setting forth, as best he can, what seem to him simple and straightforward demonstrations. If these demonstrations succeed in leading the Fool to understanding, then they may be instrumental in leading him also to belief *in* God. But the commitment of faith involves a deliberate choice of will; and in fallen man there is a pervasive discrepancy between what intellect apprehends and will chooses. In this light, then, Anselm discerns man's need for

50. In a noteworthy passage in the CDH Anselm again takes up the question of the Fool's understanding: "How are we to answer someone who maintains of something necessarily the case that it is impossible — and who maintains this simply because he does not see how it could be the case? *Boso*: Call him a fool. *Anselm*: So then, we ought to despise his opinion. *Boso*: Yes. But he should be shown the reason for that necessity which he wrongly considers an impossibility." I 25 (S II, 95: 18–23). Wherever possible, then, Anselm is concerned to give the Fool reasons. And he thinks of these reasons as objectively good ones in spite of the Fool's incomprehension. N.B. Augustine, Ep. 120.1.4 (PL 42:1080): The unbeliever is to be given reasons even when he is not able to understand them apart from faith in order that he may recognize his lack of understanding and come to faith. Cf. DT 15.17.27: "Let whoever does not see this point seek understanding from the Lord, not an explanation from us; for we cannot say it any more clearly."

grace in understanding and for grace in order to will what one comes to understand.

Barth's unassailable service to the history of theology has been to emphasize afresh Anselm's awareness of this need. Where Barth errs, however, is in maintaining that for Anselm philosophical and theological answers are irrelevant to faith and that Anselm finds no common ground between believer and unbeliever. Were these answers conceived of as irrelevant to faith, Anselm could not possibly have expressed such intense joy at having discovered them. Indeed, Barth's own comment on Anselm is itself partly irrelevant. "To my knowledge, no one has ever claimed that the 'arguments' set forth in the treatises on the incarnation of the Word (or rather, on the relation of nature to persons in God), on the procession of the Holy Spirit from the Father and the Son, on the virgin birth and original sin, and on the fall of Lucifer, are rational grounds in the sense of inferences from general truths." [51] Barth neglects to mention that in all these cases Anselm thinks of himself as partly adducing rational grounds. Sometimes these grounds are a priori principles, sometimes appeals to fittingness, sometimes appeals to moral reason. That at times Anselm turns to Scripture to furnish a needed premise shows only that he acknowledges the limits of reason, and that he thinks of reason as not *totally* availing in regard to these topics. From the fact that Anselm does not try to provide deductive inferences from general metaphysical truths, it does not follow — as Barth implies it does — that he seeks some special grounds intelligible only within the framework of faith. Rather, it follows that he construes the notion of "having rational grounds" in a looser sense than Barth is willing to construe it. Moreover, even in this reduced sense, Anselm supposes that reasons should still be offered to the unbeliever since they confirm the content of the Christian faith. In last analysis, Barth's non sequitur is based upon a prior refusal to regard the *Proslogion* proof as Anselm's attempt to find in natural reason a point of contact with the skeptic. [52]

If Anselm's program in the *Proslogion* is to understand, it is not to understand instead of to prove. Stolz's contention to the contrary cannot

---

51. *Fides quaerens intellectum*, p. 52 (English ed., pp. 54-55).

52. Barth is right in stating that the *Proslogion* is written primarily for the believer, but this does not mean Anselm envisions no common ground between believer and skeptic. For other criticisms of Barth, see the discussions by J. McIntyre, *St. Anselm and His Critics*, pp. 24ff; M. Charlesworth, *St. Anselm's Proslogion*, pp. 40–46.

be vindicated. A look at Anselm's summary of his enterprise suggests Stolz's misapprehension: "I have now shown, I believe, that in my earlier treatise [the *Proslogion*] I proved — not by inconclusive reasoning but by reasoning which is logically cogent enough — that something than which a greater cannot be thought exists in reality. And I have shown that this reasoning was not weakened by any strong counter-reasoning." [53] We may grant with Stolz that for Anselm "God truly (really) exists" refers to the manner of God's existence without denying, as Stolz does, that it also refers to the fact of God's existence. Here, after all, lies the subtlety of the ontological argument: reflecting upon the description of God, one is supposedly led to discern that God exists (= the fact of existing) and that He exists so really that He cannot even be thought not to exist (= the manner of existing). We must remember, too, that Anselm is addressing himself to the Fool, who says there is no God (Ps. 14:1). Anselm therefore is intent upon proving to the Fool that God does exist. Moreover, when Gaunilo interprets Anselm's reasoning as purporting to have established conclusively the fact of God's existence, Anselm in his reply does not disabuse Gaunilo of this interpretation. Finally, the *Proslogion*'s frequent references to illumination, as well as the recurrence there of the light-dark motif, do not indicate affiliation with the mystical tradition.[54] They testify instead that Anselm is modeling the style of the *Proslogion* on Augustine's *Confessions*. Consequently, the *Proslogion* as a whole takes the form of a prayerful meditation with invocations to God to reveal Himself from out of the inaccessible light in which He dwells, and with praise to God, whose mercy is manifested unto the wicked and whose joy fills those who truly seek Him. But at no time should this exalted style be construed as jeopardizing the intent to prove.

In last regard, we must affirm that the characterization of faith and reason does not change from the *Monologion* to the *Proslogion*. It is true that the *Proslogion* does not explicitly mention proceeding *sola ratione* and that the *Monologion* nowhere advocates *crede ut intelligas*. Yet what could be clearer than that the former exemplifies the suspending

---

53. *Reply to Gaunilo* 10 (S I, 138:28–30).

54. Note Gilson regarding the *Proslogion*: "Is it a mystical contemplation? Once again, I do not know. For P. Stolz every contemplation is *ipso facto* mystical, just as for K. Barth every meditation is rightfully theology." "Sens et nature de l'argument de saint Anselme," *Archives d'histoire doctrinale et littéraire du moyen âge*, 9 (1934), 42.

of authority just as the latter is at every point guided by the *Credo*? As a result, Anselm experiences no hesitancy in grouping them together: "I have written two small works, the *Monologion* and the *Proslogion*, which are intended particularly to show that it is possible to prove by necessary reasons, apart from Scriptural authority, those things which we hold by faith concerning the divine nature and its persons, apart from the incarnation." [55] And in the *Cur Deus Homo* Anselm extends the method of necessary reasons to cover the incarnation itself.

The Cur Deus Homo. The fact that this work proceeds by necessary reasons indicates a prima facie continuity between the *Monologion*, the *Proslogion*, and itself. We must remember too that the *Cur Deus Homo* builds upon the conclusions established in the *Monologion* and the *Proslogion*. In turning his attention to the incarnation Anselm wanted to show the metaphysical necessity of a given historical event. He attempted to prove that the nature of God is such as to will the very means of incarnation proclaimed in Scripture — and he tried to do this *Christo remoto*, i.e., without recourse to anything said about Jesus in Scripture. On occasion he self-consciously veers from this course, as in Book II, Chapter 10, where he speaks "for a moment not, as it were, about Him who never existed . . . but about Him whose life and deeds we know." But a few speeches later he returns: "Now let us go back to conducting our investigation as if Jesus did not yet exist."

There are those, as McIntyre suggests, who claim to have found a discrepancy between this *Christo remoto* method and the believing-understanding method of the *Proslogion*. Such discoverers are quick to point out that whereas the *Cur Deus Homo* suspends the Christian belief in incarnation in order to establish it anew rationally, the *Proslogion* exhorts one first to reaffirm the Christian faith and then to understand it. That is, the *Cur Deus Homo*, unlike the *Proslogion*, almost involves the principle *intelligo ut credam*.[56] However, this discontinuity between the two works cannot be maintained without insisting upon a discontinuity within the *Cur Deus Homo* itself. For in the very first chapter of Book I Boso remarks: "Just as right order demands that we believe the deep truths of the Christian faith before we proceed to discuss them ration-

55. DIV 6 (S II, 20:16–19).

56. McIntyre, *St. Anselm and His Critics*, p. 5. This is not, however, McIntyre's position.

ally, so too we seem remiss if, having been established in faith, we do not strive to understand that which we believe." [57] Here Anselm expressly intimates that the believing-understanding formula has not been abrogated. It seems hasty, then, to consider Anselm's interpretation of this formula as inconsistent with his argument *Christo remoto*.

We have observed earlier that the *credo ut intelligam* principle is fundamentally a principle for believers and that in a sense Anselm's charge to unbelievers is indeed something like *intelligite ut credatis*: understand in order to believe. One must view the *Christo remoto* principle not as an intrinsic violation of the believing-understanding relationship but as the embodiment of Anselm's commitment *against* introducing credal premises into the domain of argument. That is, if a set of arguments is to confirm the content of the Christian faith by defending it against the skeptic, then Anselm must present to the skeptic's natural reason a rationale for Christianity. This he attempts to do in the *Monologion*, the *Proslogion*, and the *Cur Deus Homo* alike. He does not require Boso to suspend his belief, but to suspend the appeal to his belief in developing arguments on the basis of rational necessity.[58] More specifically, Boso's belief may quite legitimately direct him to arguments, but it dare not become a constitutive element within these arguments.[59]

There is a further point of continuity between the method of the *Cur Deus Homo* and that of the two earlier works — viz., that already in the *Monologion* Anselm tacitly adopted the distinction between the fitting and the necessary. We see this plainly in *Monologion* 39, where he writes: "In no way can the Word more fittingly (*convenientius*) be

57. S II, 48:16–18. Note also that DIV explicitly articulates the principles of *credo ut intelligam* (Ch. 1) and *sola ratione* (Ch. 2).

58. Thus, when in the CDH Anselm brackets the Christian faith, he is doing no more or no less than what he had done in the *Monologion* and the *Proslogion*, viz., reasoning apart from the appeal to Scriptural authority. The semblance of difference results from the fact that in the CDH he is treating a historical topic. He suspends this historical dimension for the sake of metaphysical certainty.

59. In holding that in some ways believing conduces to understanding and in other ways understanding conduces to believing, Anselm does not waver from the Augustinian tradition. However, the relationship between believing and understanding should not be misconceived. Anselm is not asserting that from "If I believe, I am better able to understand" there follows "If I do not believe, I am less able to understand" — a logical fallacy. He is affirming both together, and not deriving one from the other. Moreover, he is not affirming them for all cases, but only for the "deeper truths of God." As for the less hidden truths, he implicitly holds with Augustine that understanding precedes, though not necessarily chronologically, the act of belief.

thought to exist from the Supreme Spirit than by being begotten." Although the distinction becomes fully operative in the *Cur Deus Homo*, it is nonetheless foreshadowed in the *Monologion*.

That Anselm sets forth a list of presuppositions in the *Cur Deus Homo* and that he frequently cites Scripture does not mean he is abandoning rational apologetics. In fact, these presuppositions are listed in the same chapter where he reiterates his rationalism. Book I, Chapter 10, explicitly assumes: (1) man was created for blessedness; (2) blessedness cannot be attained in the present life; (3) no man can be blessed unless his sins are forgiven; (4) no man is without sin. And it implicitly assumes: (5) God exists as trinity; (6) God wills to save mankind. In this same chapter Anselm gives Boso the role of speaking for those who believe nothing except what can be rationally demonstrated. His rule of procedure is twofold: to ascribe nothing unfitting to God, and to refuse credence to no reason unless there be a weightier reason against it. "For just as the least unfittingness is impossible in God, so even the smallest reason constitutes a necessity of argument as long as there is no stronger reason to contradict it." [60]

Anselm does not suppose himself in the *Cur Deus Homo* to be theologizing exclusively on the basis of a priori truths grasped by the light of natural reason and therefore acceptable to all men (and here Barth is right). His self-imposed task is more limited: to examine only the doctrine of incarnation while presupposing other aspects of Christian revelation. Some of these other aspects are presupposed because they have been previously argued, others in spite of their not having been argued, and still others because they cannot be argued. Hence, when Anselm sets aside *fides Christiana*, the Christian faith, he does not do so in the sense of reasoning apart from every Christian presupposition, but only apart from those doctrines defended exclusively by appeal to authority. Accordingly, Boso can deem it justifiable to summarize the overall result by saying: "You prove that of necessity God became man. And this proof is so cogent that even if the few teachings introduced from Scripture were eliminated (the teachings about Adam and about the three persons in God), you would still satisfy not only the Jews but also the pagans by reason alone." [61]

60. S II, 67:4–6. M 80 (S I, 87:2) also makes use of the notion of *inconveniens*.

61. II, 22. There is some controversy about whom the word "pagans" designates. Roques *Anselme de Cantorbéry: Pourquoi Dieu s'est fait homme* (Paris, 1963), main-

The much bantered question of whether or not Anselm is a rationalist is partly, though not entirely, a verbal question. He is of course an epistemological rationalist (as opposed to empiricist) because he thinks it possible to know some matters of fact a priori. And he is a theological rationalist (as opposed to fideist) because he thinks it both possible and desirable to defend the major doctrines of Christianity by reason. But if theologically he is a rationalist, he is not an extreme rationalist; for he acknowledges the authority of Scripture to judge the conclusions of reason, and he does not presume to accept as true only those biblical doctrines which can be established by independent intellect. Moreover, he interprets the Fall as having affected man's intellect as well as the relationship between intellect and will. Yet he remains enough of a rationalist to be an apologist [62] and to discover in the apology of St. Paul on Mars Hill an implicit imperative for all Christian philosophers — the imperative to formulate and defend the rationale of the Gospel. If Anselm's view of faith and reason does not change from one work to another, it is because from the very beginning he felt himself grasped by this divine imperative. Under its urging he endeavors believingly to understand and understandingly to believe.

tains that Anselm means the Muslims and others who may share some if not all of the Christian presuppositions. Charlesworth, *St. Anselm's Proslogion,* rejects this notion. Note the similar controversy over the reference of *infideles.* G. Van der Plaas, "Des hl. Anselm 'Cur Deus Homo,'" supposes that solely the Jews are meant, whereas Geyer, "Zur Deutung von Anselms Cur deus homo," thinks that they are the imaginary opponents addressed by Augustine in DT 13.10.13 (PL 42:1024).

62. See F. S. Schmitt, "Die wissenschaftliche Methode in 'Cur Deus homo,'" *Spicilegium Beccense,* 1 (Paris, 1959), 349–370.

Chapter III

Ontological Argument

Anselm's conception of the *ratio fidei* (rational basis of faith) led him to wonder how he might give intellectual support to his belief in God. The dispute over whether or not in *Proslogion* 2 and 3 Anselm is intent on proving God's existence also arises over the extended argument of *Monologion* 1–4. Karl Barth contends — and F. S. Schmitt has repeated the contention — that in the *Monologion*, unlike in the *Proslogion*, Anselm is trying to prove something only about God's nature, not about His existence.[1] Specifically, in *Proslogion* 2 Anselm unequivocally states his task as understanding both *quia es sicut credimus, et hoc es quod credimus*: "that You exist, as we believe, and that You are what we believe You to be." But in the *Monologion*, runs the interpretation, Anselm never mentions any attempt to prove "that You exist" but shows interest only in proving "that You are what we believe You to be." In fact, he explicitly says in the preface that he is giving an example of meditating on the divine Essence, or Nature (*de meditanda divinitatis essentia*).[2] Yet, with due respect to Barth and Schmitt, total separation of the question of God's existence from the question of His attributes is misleading in regard to the *Monologion*. For what Anselm is trying to prove is not simply that God — presupposed to exist as the cause of every other thing

1. *Fides quaerens intellectum*, p. 85 (English ed., p. 90). "Anselm und der (Neu-) Platonismus," AA I, 45–46.
2. S I, 7:3.

— is the Supreme Good, the Supreme Nature, the Supreme Being. Rather, he is attempting to show that the existence of good things requires the existence of one highest good, which is God; that the existence of superior and inferior natures requires the existence of one Supreme Nature, which is God; that the existence of beings *per aliud* requires the existence of one Being *per se*, which likewise is God.

Thus, in *Monologion* 3 Anselm does not baldly assume that all presently existing things have a cause, but in his own way he argues for it. (Might they exist *per nihil*, i.e., through nothing? No. So they must exist through something.) Neither does he assume that this something is singular; for whatever *is* might exist through a plurality of causes. His argument in Chapter 3 concludes, *Est igitur unum aliquid, quod solum maxime et summe omnium est*: "Therefore, there is one thing (being) which alone exists most greatly and most highly of all."

We may abbreviate the argument in Chapter 3 as follows:

(1) All the things which are presently existing exist either through something or through nothing.
    (a) But no thing can exist through nothing.
    (b) Therefore, whatever is, exists through something.
(2) This something through which everything exists is either one or many.
    (a) If many, then these many exist (i) from some one thing, or (ii) independently, each through itself (*per se*), or (iii) mutually through themselves (*per se*).
       (i) If the many exist through one thing, then whatever is exists also through the one thing through which the many exist.
       (ii) If the many exist independently, then there is some one power (*vis*) or nature (*natura*) to which they owe their existing *per se*. Hence, this one rather than the many is what, strictly speaking, exists *per se*.
       (iii) The many cannot exist mutually through one another, since what confers existence on another cannot itself exist through that other upon which it confers existence.
    (b) Therefore, whatever is, exists through some one being, which itself exists *per se*.
(3) Whatever exists through another is less than that other.
(4) There is, therefore, one Being which, in existing *per se*, exists in the supreme degree.

Only a special doctrine of universals allows Anselm to suppose that several things could not have independent powers of existing *per se*. He assumes that two or more beings existing *per se* would "share" a power of existing *per se*. Thus, that power would be what exists absolutely *per se*, so that these other beings, which could not exist without this power, would only in some respect exist *per se* (while in some respect existing *per aliud*). As the Supreme Being, God alone exists absolutely *per se*, for He shares His nature with no other.

What seems apparent is that Anselm, like Augustine, is operating with an attenuated requirement regarding what counts as a cogent argument. For surely there are so many metaphysical presuppositions needed in the *Monologion* (and so many biblical presuppositions needed in the *Cur Deus Homo*) that nowadays, when these presuppositions are not being made, one is not prepared to say that these arguments really prove anything. Still, Anselm thought they did. Yet, he recognized the problem about presuppositions — to such an extent, in fact, that in the *Cur Deus Homo* he tried to limit (never eliminate) them by proceeding *Christo remoto*, while in the *Monologion* he tried to presuppose no more than his method required and no more than he thought the educated man of his day would be likely to grant. In general, he wanted to find arguments that depended upon as few controversial assumptions and as few authorities as possible. And this desire led to his hitting upon the *Proslogion* argument for God's existence. For in the preface to the *Proslogion* he alludes to a difference between that work and the earlier *Monologion*. This difference is not that the *Proslogion* proves the existence of God, whereas the *Monologion* does not. Nor is it that the *Monologion* alone deals with God as Supreme Good and as Supreme Being, without which no other being could exist; for the preface to the *Proslogion* indicates that these very themes are to be taken up. Rather, the difference is that Anselm is seeking a single argument (*unum argumentum*) which, because of its simplicity, can be presented to every man: "Considering this work [the *Monologion*] to be a chain of many interlinking arguments, I began to ask myself whether perhaps one argument could be found which constituted an independent proof and sufficed by itself to demonstrate that (1) God really exists, that (2) He is the Supreme Good, needing no one else yet needed by all else in order to exist and to exist well, and that (3) He is whatever else we believe about the Divine Substance" (S I, 93:4–10).

In the *Proslogion*, then, Anselm presents what he takes to be a single argument from which may be inferred the fact of God's existence together with various features about His nature. However, since the time of Barth's powerful book on Anselm, in which he treats separately the arguments of *Proslogion* 2 and 3, it has become common to distinguish two (sometimes three, rarely four) different versions of the proof in Anselm (even though Anselm did not consciously make this differentiation).[3] The first version is that of Chapter 2; the second takes off from Chapter 3 but includes comments made in reply to Gaunilo. One interesting reconstruction of this second line of argument is presented by Norman Malcolm, who in 1960 published an article defending this version's soundness. We shall inquire in turn into both of these ontological proofs.[4]

Any full discussion — perhaps any adequate discussion — of the ontological proofs has to take account of the following issues: (1) What is the relationship between the "two" proofs? (Does the one depend on the other? Is one a continuation of the other? Is each independent of the other?) (2) Is existence a perfection (predicate)? (What does this question itself mean? Is Kant's criticism of this thesis correct?) (3) What is the difference between conceiving something and conceiving that thing to exist? (4) Does Anselm confuse logical necessity with ontological necessity? (5) Does Anselm confuse predicating a modality *de dicto* with predicating a modality *de re*? (6) Does Anselm mean to be distinguishing understanding (*intelligere*) from thinking (*cogitare*), and, if so, how? (7) Does the argument presuppose that there are degrees of perfection, and, if so, what does this mean? (8) Is "necessary existence" an inconsistent notion? (9) In what sense is it impossible to think of God as not existing? (10) Is Anselm's notion of *conceivability* interchangeable with the notion of *possibility*? (11) What does Anselm mean by "greater"? (12) Does Anselm have a fully intelligible conception of perfection? (13) What does Anselm mean in *Proslogion* 15 by God's exceeding our ability to conceive of Him? (I.e., how is it that the greatest conceivable

3. Note especially Barth, *Fides quaerens intellectum*, pp. 126–129 (English ed., pp. 132–135); N. Malcolm, "Anselm's Ontological Arguments," *Philosophical Review*, 69 (January 1960), 41–62; D. P. Henry, *The Logic of Saint Anselm*, pp. 142–150; G. Nakhnikian, "St. Anselm's Four Ontological Arguments," in *Art, Mind, and Religion*, ed. W. H. Capitan and D. D. Merrill (Pittsburgh, 1965), pp. 29–36; Charles Hartshorne, *Anselm's Discovery* (LaSalle, Ill., 1965), pp. 99–106.

4. The label "ontological argument" derives from Kant's *Critique of Pure Reason*. In mounting his attack on this argument Kant seems to have had Christian Wolff and G. W. von Leibniz in mind rather than Anselm.

being cannot be conceived?) (14) Does Anselm's description of God imply a contradiction? (15) Does "the most perfect conceivable being" mean the same as "the being which embodies all perfections"? In this chapter it will be possible to touch upon only a few of these questions.

"FIRST" ONTOLOGICAL ARGUMENT

The argument of *Proslogion* 2 proceeds toward a *reductio ad impossible*:

(1) We properly conceive of God as something than which no greater can be thought.

(2) We understand what the words "something than which no greater can be thought" describe.

(3) What is thus described exists either in the understanding alone or both in the understanding and in reality.

(4) Assume that this thing than which no greater can be thought exists in the understanding alone.
(a) Existing both in the understanding and in reality is greater than existing solely in the understanding.
(b) This thing, existing in the understanding alone, can also be thought to exist in reality — and hence can be thought to be greater than it is.
(c) It is not therefore something than which no greater can be thought (which is impossible *ex hypothesi*).

(5) Therefore, something than which no greater can be thought exists in reality as well as existing in the understanding.

With this brief demonstration Anselm considers that he has shown the atheist's denial of God's existence to be inconsistent. For the atheist must conceive of God in order to deny His existence. But having understood God to be something than which no greater can be thought, the atheist is logically constrained, on the basis of the argument above, to conclude that God exists in reality, while at the same time he is disavowing that God does so exist.

Anselm's criterion for something's existing in the understanding (*in intellectu*) is simply that it be understood (*quidquid intelligitur in intellectu est*).[5] The Latin idiom whereby something may be said to exist *in* the understanding need not in itself give rise to confusion — any

5. In PF Anselm qualifies this criterion by stating that it does not apply to infinite nouns such as "not-man" or to the word "nothing." See the section on *aliquid*, which must have been written after the *Proslogion*.

more than need the English idiom "to have something in mind." Having established, then, to his own satisfaction that God exists both in the understanding and in reality, Anselm now turns in Chapter 3 to a point about conceivability: God's existence is so real that He cannot even be thought of as not existing. Thus, even though *Proslogion* 3 will later be treated as if it were opening up an altogether new line of argument, Anselm presents it as a rounding-off of his main argument in Chapter 2. To say, as he does, that God cannot be conceived of as not existing (in reality) is to say that it belongs to the definition of "God" that He cannot not-exist. On this basis, there is a perfectly legitimate sense in which we "cannot think of God as not existing," inasmuch as to do so would be in effect not to be thinking of God but to be thinking of some being which is less than God. But in one sense the Fool[6] *is not* conceiving of God as not existing, for he recognizes that a greatest conceivable being must be conceived of as existing in reality. However, he contends that conceiving of something as existing in reality is not inconsistent with denying that it does exist in reality. In another sense, then, the Fool *is* conceiving that there is no God — i.e., he is "envisioning" an exhaustive state of affairs which does not include a God, and he is affirming that this envisioned state of affairs corresponds to what is the case. Thus, on his view, God exists in the understanding alone even though He must be conceived of as not existing in the understanding alone. The Fool, therefore, thinks that God does not exist, without thinking of God as not-existing.

It seems, then, that the unbeliever might well insist that Step 5 of the proof is misformulated and that when it is correctly reformulated, a sixth step is necessary to complete the argument. According to him Step 5 should read: Therefore, something than which no greater can be thought cannot consistently be assumed (thought) to exist in the understanding alone. Step 6 now completes the demonstration: Therefore, in properly conceiving of God we must conceive of Him as existing in reality as well as in the understanding. And with this final inference the Fool agrees. For he does think of God (according to the description) as existing in reality even though (according to fact) he does not think (i.e., he denies) that God exists in reality. Moreover, no inconsistency attends his both thinking and not thinking that God does not exist in reality, since

6. Psalms 14:1: "The fool has said in his heart: There is no God." Note Augustine's reference to this verse in *Free Choice* 2.2.5. Augustine also mentions that Evodius is filled with joy at having a proof for God's existence (2.15.39). Cf. Anselm's acknowledgment of his joy over his own discovery. *Proslogion* preface.

the conception and the denial take place in different respects, on different levels.

Alternatively, the unbeliever's intuitions may be such as to lead him to disqualify the claim in Step 4 that existing in the understanding and in reality is greater than existing solely in the understanding — i.e., he can plausibly deny that existence is a perfection. For surely (he may urge) there is something strange about comparing, say, a real house with a merely imaginary house of exactly the same description and judging that the real house is better than the imagined one. One real house may be better than another; but real houses are neither better nor worse than imagined ones. Even though the Fool may not be able to argue for his intuition (since it is but an intuition), still he does not have to; for the burden of proof is on Anselm, the soundness of whose demonstration dare not turn upon mere counter-intuitions.

In *Proslogion* 4 Anselm shows himself alert to the Fool's predicament of both thinking and not thinking of God as existing. For in this chapter he distinguishes two senses of "thinking."

In one sense an object is thought (*cogitatur*) when the word signifying it is thought (*cogitatur*), and in another when what the object is [i.e., its essence] is understood (*intelligitur*). In the first sense but not at all in the second, God can be thought not to exist. Indeed, no one who understands what God is can think that God does not exist, even though such a person says in his heart "God does not exist" — saying it either meaninglessly or else bizzarely. For God is that than which a greater cannot be thought. Whoever comprehends (understands) this, surely discerns (understands) that God so exists that He cannot even be thought not to exist.[7]

Anselm grudgingly grants that in a certain sense the Fool may legitimately say in his heart "There is no God." This is the subjective or psychological sense in which the Fool can repeat the words to himself and give them some special or private meaning. But once the Fool thinks of God in accordance with the Anselmian description — i.e., once he *understands* the description — he cannot rationally fail to see, argues Anselm,

7. "Aliter enim cogitatur res cum vox eam significans cogitatur, aliter cum id ipsum quod res est intelligitur. Illo itaque modo potest cogitari deus non esse, isto vero minime. Nullus quippe intelligens id quod deus est, potest cogitare quia deus non est, licet haec verba dicat in corde, aut sine ulla aut cum aliqua extranea significatione. Deus enim est id quo maius cogitari non potest. Quod qui bene intelligit, utique intelligit id ipsum sic esse, ut nec cogitatione queat non esse. Qui ergo intelligit sic esse deum, nequit eum non esse cogitare." S I, 103:18–104:4.

that the existence of such a being is logically entailed by the description. Anselm's distinction in *Proslogion* 4 between *cogitatur* and *intelligitur* is simply this: *intelligere* represents a correct form of *cogitare*. Many things may be conceived; but when they are correctly conceived, then they are understood. When Anselm notes that the Fool thinks the *words* "God does not exist" without understanding the *essence* signified by the word "God," he is saying in effect that the Fool does not really understand (i.e., correctly think) the meaning of the *word* "God." For if he understood the meaning of the word "God," he would understand what kind of being God is; and if he understood what kind of being God is, he would recognize that God (as that than which no greater can be thought) cannot be thought (i.e., correctly thought, or understood) not to exist. Yet, in the end, it is not the Fool who fails to comprehend what "God" means but Anselm who fails to comprehend what the Fool means. The Fool may admit that God must be conceived of as existing; but he need not understand God to exist, i.e., he need not take it to be a fact that God, conceived of as having to exist, does exist.

The distinction between *cogitatur* and *intelligitur* as witnessed in *Proslogion* 4 should not be construed as reflecting a distinction of terminology which Anselm in the *Proslogion* itself is generally insistent on. In fact, he has no rigid rule governing the use of these terms in the *Proslogion*. With one exception (P 9. S I, 108:12–13) he does regularly use *cogitari* in the phrase *id quo maius cogitari nequit*.[8] But this one exception proves that Anselm does sanction interchanging *cogitari* and *intelligi* in some contexts. To be sure, the difference between the use of *intelligere* in stating the argument of *Proslogion* 2 and the exclusive use of *cogitare* in formulating the additional reasoning of *Proslogion* 3 appears striking. Yet, Anselm's switch is partly explainable in light of his attempt in Chapter 3 to exhibit the Fool's position as self-contradictory. The Fool conceives of *id quo maius cogitari nequit*. Hence, Anselm tells him that this being whom he is conceiving as existing is such that *non cogitari potest non esse*. To say *intelligi* here would minimize the appearance of contradiction which Anselm is intent on exhibiting. But at the end of *Proslogion* 4 he resumes the use of *intelligere*:

8. And in the variants: "aliquid quo nihil maius cogitari potest"; "aliquid quo maius cogitari non valet."
That Anselm is not assigning a rigid meaning to *intelligere* may also be discerned from his interchanging it with *scire* in *Meditatio Redemptionis Humanae* (cf. S III, 88:110 with 88:114).

74

Ontological Argument

"I could not fail to understand that You exist." [9] In this same chapter Anselm is focusing attention on the close relationship that exists between words and things. His aim is not to distinguish between *cogitare* and *intelligere* as such.[10] He might just as well have said: "In one respect a thing is thought (*cogitatur*) when the word signifying it is thought (*cogitatur*); in another respect, when what the object is is [correctly] thought (*cogitatur*)." His *not* having said this, results from his desire to emphasize the two different respects of *cogitare*.

What is happening in the *Proslogion* with regard to *intelligere* and *cogitare* seems to be something like what is happening in *De Veritate* with *oratio*, *enuntiatio*, and *propositio*. Following Aristotle and Boethius, Anselm in *De Veritate* takes *oratio* to indicate any sentence, i.e., any utterance containing a subject and a verb. But he implicitly restricts the use of *oratio* to cover only a subclass of all sentences — viz., the class of those sentences which are said to be either true or false, i.e., the class of propositions (*enuntiatio*, *propositio*). This restriction allows him to interchange these terms to avoid monotony. He is not in *De Veritate* insisting on the distinction between *oratio* and *enuntiatio*, although he recognizes that there is such a distinction. Similarly, in the *Proslogion* proper, he sometimes uses "thinking" and "understanding" interchangeably, even though he recognizes that there are various ways to distinguish them.

Gaunilo's reply, however, forces Anselm to take up explicitly this distinction between *intelligere* and *cogitare*. For in Section 2 Gaunilo suggests the semantic equivalence of "to understand that X exists" and "to apprehend with certainty that X exists." [11] And in the second half of Section 7, where he speaks for himself and not for the Fool, he maintains that falsities and unrealities cannot, strictly speaking, be understood but can only be thought. Accordingly, he interprets the argument of *Pros-*

9. ". . . ut si te esse nolim credere, non possim non intelligere."

10. N.B. *Reply to Gaunilo* 1 (S I, 130:12–18), where Anselm is *not* making any special distinction between *intelligitur* and *cogitatur*; "But I contend that if that than which a greater cannot be thought is not understood or thought and is not in the understanding or in thought, then surely either God is not that than which a greater cannot be thought or else He is not understood or thought and is not in the understanding or in thought. But I point to your faith and conscience as the strongest indicator of how false these inferences are. Therefore, that than which a greater cannot be thought is indeed understood and thought and is in your understanding and in your thought."

11. S I, 125:21–126:1.

logion 2 as implying that God can *only* be understood to exist, and can never be merely thought to exist [as even unreal things can be (mistakenly) thought to exist]. Moreover, he applies the same distinction to the reasoning of *Proslogion* 3, "improving on" Anselm's statement that God cannot be thought not to exist. According to Gaunilo, Anselm, who thinks that God is the most real being, should maintain exclusively that He cannot be *understood* not to exist.[12] That is, the Fool considers God an unreal being, just as he thinks of unicorns as unreal beings. But Anselm has allegedly proven in *Proslogion* 2 that God is and must be a real being. Therefore, Anselm should say that since God is known for certain to exist as a real being, He is understood to exist. And just as God cannot be known not to exist, so He cannot be understood not to exist. But of course, continues Gaunilo, God can be mistakenly *thought* not to exist by the Fool, who (Anselm allows) may misapprehend the proof of Chapter 2.

In reply Anselm leaves no doubt that he does accept a distinction between thinking and understanding (S I, 131:15–17). But he does not linger over this distinction. In last analysis, he concedes that there may be a sense of "understand" in which existing things cannot be understood not to exist — and hence in which God cannot be understood not to exist (as Anselm has already argued). But there is the further sense in which God cannot even be thought not to exist — whereas all other objects, even while they do exist, can be so thought. And this fact about God indicates His unique nature. Nevertheless, Anselm does not take up anew the sense in which the atheist may consistently deny God's existence. He is content to refer Gaunilo once again to the previous statements of the *Proslogion*.[13] This omission on Anselm's part constitutes a major deficiency. For precisely at this turn his original argument was extremely frail. Indeed, his unclarity on this point initially prompted Gaunilo's objections. And one cannot remove the force of these objections by so convenient a referral. Yet it is perhaps too demanding to expect from Anselm an additional statement. The essential plausibility of his argument arises from his confusion over this particular distinction. To expect him to be clear in this regard is tantamount to expecting him to recognize the unsoundness of his entire proof.

12. *Ibid.*, Section 7 (S I, 129:10–12).
13. *Reply to Gaunilo* 4 (S I, 134:18–19).

Although Gaunilo's expressed dissatisfaction with the proof's soundness is partly well grounded, it gives rise to a misapprehension. For in his summary of *Proslogion* 2 Gaunilo begins by using the phrase *natura qua nihil maius cogitari potest* ("a nature than which nothing greater can be thought") but he soon switches to the phrase *maius omnibus* ("that which is greater than all other beings"). Anselm criticizes him for this transformation since it destroys the *reductio ad impossibile* structure of his argument and thus its validity. Yet Gaunilo probably intended *maius omnibus* as an abbreviation for *illud maius omnibus quae cogitari potest*: "that which is greater than all other beings that can be thought." [14] But Anselm interprets it as an abbreviation for *maius omnibus quae sunt*: "that which is greater than all other existing beings" (S I, 135:8–10); and so he accuses Gaunilo of distorting his argument. To be sure, Gaunilo does use the description *maius omnium quae sunt* (Section 7. S I, 129: 8). But here he is not supposing that it is equivalent to Anselm's formula. Rather, he is urging Anselm to formulate a totally new argument which would utilize this new description and would not beg the question of God's existence. Whether or not Gaunilo is guilty of a distortion, he surely does fail to do justice to the *reductio* structure of the proof. Accordingly, he does not even regard the proof as plausible. Indeed, this low estimate is what leads to his demand for a revised approach: "First of all, then, a compelling argument must be adduced to prove the existence of a higher (i.e., a greater and better) Nature than all other existing natures, so that on the basis of this proof we can go on to deduce all the characteristics which such a Nature must have." [15] In other words, Gaunilo is attempting to reintroduce the approach of the *Monologion*.[16] He finds this approach superior to that of the *Proslogion* because it seeks to establish the existence of a supreme being without recourse to positing a dubious relationship between existence and conceivability. Yet it is precisely this "dubious" relationship that accounts for the unique subtlety of the *Proslogion* argument.

14. Cf. *On Behalf of the Fool* 1 (S I, 125:3–4 and 125:11) with Section 4 of the same work (S I, 126:30 and 127:23). Note also S I, 126:26–27.

15. *Ibid.*, Section 7 (S I, 129:7–10).

16. "Although some natures are indisputably better than others, nonetheless reason persuades us that one of them is so preeminent that no other nature is superior to it. For if such an order of gradation were limitless, so that for each degree a higher degree could be found, then it would follow that the number of these natures would be infinite. But everyone deems this consequence absurd . . ." M 4 (S I, 17:3–8).

"SECOND" ONTOLOGICAL ARGUMENT

Proslogion 2, we have seen, constitutes the essential argument by which Anselm purports to refute the atheist. It is this argument which Eadmer had in mind when he recorded Anselm's excitement at having developed a single decisive proof of God's existence. It is in fact the only proof fully developed in the *Proslogion*. Chapter 3 is a further statement about how real God is: not only can God not not-exist, He cannot even conceivably not-exist. Chapter 4 attempts to explain how the Fool can nonetheless meaningfully say in his heart "There is no God." However, once we go beyond the *Proslogion* itself to the reply to Gaunilo, we see that Anselm reasons in such a way as to imply a second proof: "I contend that if this being can be even thought to exist, it is necessary that it exist. For that than which a greater cannot be thought can only be thought to exist without a beginning. Now, whatever can be thought to exist but does not exist can be thought to begin to exist. Thus, that than which a greater cannot be thought cannot be thought to exist and yet not exist. Therefore, if it can be thought to exist, it is necessary that it exist." [17] Though Anselm nowhere indicates awareness of opening a second line of proof, his statement here can be joined with *Proslogion* 3 to yield a new line of argumentation.[18] Before examining this version, however, we should note certain facts about Anselm's use of the term "necessity."

In the *Proslogion* Anselm does not at all use the word "necessity" in formulating his argument. In fact *necessarium* occurs only twice — both times in the last paragraph of Chapter 23, where Anselm quotes from Luke 10:42: "But one thing is necessary." [19] He goes on to say, "This

17. *Reply to Gaunilo* 1 (S I, 131:1–5). Note D. P. Henry, "Proslogion Chapter III," AA I, 101–105.

18. N. Malcolm, "Anselm's Ontological Arguments," *Philosophical Review*, 69 (January 1960), 41–62. Reprinted in *The Ontological Argument*, ed. A. Plantinga (New York, 1965), pp. 136–159. All page references are to the Plantinga anthology.

19. "But one thing is necessary. And Mary has chosen the best part, which shall not be taken away from her." Anselm is not attempting to interpret the Scriptural passage or to regard its context. He simply uses the first part of the verse as a trimming for something he wants independently to say.
  Augustine used the verse in the same way in Sermon 103.3.4 (PL 38:614–615), where he makes it unmistakably clear that the one necessary thing is God: "Quia unum est necessarium, unum illud supernum, unum ubi Pater et Filius et Spiritus sanctus sunt unum. Videte nobis commendari unitatem. Certe Trinitas est Deus noster. . . . Ista tria non tres dii, non tres omnipotentes, sed unus Deus omnipotens,

is that one necessary being in which there is every good—or better, who is every good, one good, complete good, and the only good." This reference to God is the *Proslogion's* sole explicit mention of necessary being. And it indicates that Anselm thinks of God alone as a necessary being—unlike Thomas after him and Boethius before him. Boethius had earlier introduced a distinction between two types of necessity: natural and propositional.[20] First, there is the necessity by which certain things occur. The movement of the sun, for example, takes place by necessity—inasmuch as the sun is perpetually in motion and will never stop moving. Following Aristotle, Boethius defines "necessary" as "what is not possible not to be." And he thinks of what perpetually occurs as not possible not to occur. In another passage he refers to unchangeable things as necessary beings; and here again his example is the sun. Although changeable with respect to position, the sun is constant (*immobilis*) with respect to its substance as light. And since the sun will never not-exist and will always exist as light, its existence is necessary.[21] Secondly, Boethius observes that there is a kind of necessity which can be ascribed to propositions rather than to events. While Socrates is sitting, necessarily he is sitting; and when he is no longer sitting, necessarily he is not sitting. That is, it is necessary that "If X is occurring, X is occurring."

Anselm's distinction between preceding and subsequent necessity likewise uses the example of the heavens:

There is a preceding necessity, which is the cause of something's occurrence; and there is a subsequent necessity, which the thing itself causes. When we say it is necessary that the heavens be turned around, we are speaking about a preceding and efficient necessity, for by necessity the heavens are turned. However, subsequent necessity produces nothing, but is itself produced. Thus when I say that of necessity you are speaking, because you are actually speaking, I mean that it is impossible for you not to speak so long as you are actually speaking; I

ipsa Trinitas unus Deus: quia unum necessarium est." See also Sermon 255.6.6 (PL 38:1189).

20. "Duplex modus necessitatis ostenditur, unus qui cum alicujus accidentis necessitate proponitur, alter qui simplici praedicatione profertur, ut cum dicimus solem moveri necesse est, non enim solem quia nunc movetur, sed quia nunquam non movebitur, idcirco in solis motu necessitas venit. Aliter vero qui cum conditione dicitur talis est, ut cum dicimus, Socratem sedere necesse est, cum sedet, et non sedere necesse est, cum non sedet." PL 64:514.

21. PL 64:381.

do not mean that something is compelling you to speak. For a natural chain of circumstances compels the heavens to be turned. But no necessity constrains you to speak (CDH II, 17. S II, 125:8–14).

Anselm, then, allows that the motion of the heavens is a necessary motion because the heavens naturally revolve.[22] Yet he declines to ascribe the title "necessary being" to these physical objects which move necessarily. Only God is a necessary being. All things less than God receive their existence from Him. And even though some of these things may never actually go out of existence, still their nonexistence is conceivable. That is, there is a sense in which it is possible for them not to be, as well as a sense in which it is not possible for them not to be. Should God at any moment will their nonexistence, they would no longer be. However, since God does not in fact will for them not to be, they shall exist perpetually in the future. Thus their nonexistence, while actually impossible, is nonetheless conceivable. In this respect they are unlike God, whose nonexistence cannot be conceived without self-contradiction. Accordingly, on Anselm's view, God is uniquely characterized as a necessary being — a being whose nonexistence is neither actually possible nor even conceivable. Thus, various contingent beings may have respective necessities of nature without being themselves necessary beings. As God is superior to all other beings in eternity and limitlessness, so He is also superior to them in necessity.

You alone are eternal because You alone of all beings neither begin to exist nor cease to exist. But how are You alone unlimited? Is a created spirit limited as compared with You, though unlimited as compared with something corporeal. Now what exists somewhere as a whole without being able at the same time to exist elsewhere is certainly limited in every respect — as is the case with corporeal objects only. And what exists at once everywhere as a whole is unlimited — as is the case with You alone. But what exists somewhere as a whole while being able at the same time to exist as a whole elsewhere, but not everywhere, is both limited and unlimited — as is the case with created spirits. For if the soul were not wholly in each of the different parts of the body, the soul as a whole would not experience feeling in each of these parts. Therefore, O Lord, You are uniquely unlimited and eternal; and yet other spirits are also unlimited and eternal (P 13. S I, 110:17–111:5).

22. In this context Anselm is contrasting *necessity* with freedom rather than with *possibility* or *impossibility*. But he seems to hold that the heavens will always continue to exist, just as the corporeal structure (*moles corporea*) of the present world shall be renewed. CDH I, 18 (S II, 79:28).

Ontological Argument

Although Anselm explicitly calls beings other than God eternal and unlimited in derivative and restricted senses, he is never prepared to call these beings necessary. For he identifies necessary being with *esse per se* and contingent being with *esse per aliud* (note *Proslogion* 12). At this point he is not yet the equal of Thomas in the thirteenth century, who was willing to designate some beings existing *per aliud* as necessary beings. Thus, Thomas's Third Way, after purportedly having established the existence of at least one necessary being, asserts that if this being has its necessity *per aliud*, then there must exist another being who has necessity *per se* (and this other being is God). That is, the series of *per aliud* necessary beings cannot regress infinitely. For Thomas, then, the necessary/contingent distinction is not coincident with the distinction between God and all other beings.[23] Rather, what sets God apart from all other beings is that He alone exists *per se*. By contrast, Anselm follows the Augustinian position in terms of which God's uniqueness is understood as constituted by His necessity, since necessary existence is viewed as characterizing only *esse per se*.

In *Proslogion* 3 Anselm uses the modal phrase *"non possit cogitari non esse."* That he does not explicitly use the word "necessary" may be attributable to his desire to formulate a proof so lucid and unproblematical that even the ordinary man could understand it. Norman Malcolm distinguishes Anselm's *Proslogion* 2 proof, which does not employ the notion of necessary being, from a further proof beginning roughly with *Proslogion* 3, where the idea of necessary being and impossible being is implicit in the notion of inconceivability. For another way of saying that God is a being whose nonexistence is inconceivable is to say that His nonexistence is logically impossible. And if a thing's nonexistence is logically impossible, then its existence is logically necessary. On this basis, runs the argument, a being whose existence is logically necessary is greater than a being whose existence is not logically necessary. That is, whereas the first ontological argument contends that a being which

23. Aristotle regards a temporal being as necessary if and only if it exists at all times; as possible if and only if it exists at some time; as impossible if and only if it exists at no time. Thomas agrees that if a temporal being exists at all times, it is a necessary being. But he allows as well that human souls — created subsequently to the beginning of time, but continuing to exist forever thereafter — are also necessary beings. Moreover, he maintains that beings necessary *per aliud* are possible not to be in the sense that God can annihilate them if He wills to. But in the Third Way Thomas does not employ this sense of "possibility" since it would presuppose the existence of God, whom he aims at demonstrating to exist.

exists in reality is greater than a being which exists merely in the understanding, the second contends that a being whose nonexistence is logically impossible is superior to a being whose nonexistence is logically possible. Thus, discerns Malcolm, the second demonstration avoids treating existence as a perfection and does not compare things really existing with things only conceptually existing. Rather, its reasoning turns upon dividing all being into three logically exhaustive categories: contingent, impossible, and necessary. Anselm's description of God precludes His being contingent. Thus either it is impossible for God to exist or else it is necessary that He exist. But it can only be impossible for God to exist if the concept of God is self-contradictory. Since it cannot be shown that the description of God as that-than-which-no-greater-can-be-thought is logically inconsistent, God must exist. According to Malcolm, "We are not to think that 'God necessarily exists' means that it follows necessarily from something that God exists *contingently*. The a priori proposition 'God necessarily exists' entails the proposition 'God exists,' if and only if the latter also is understood as an a priori proposition: in which case the two propositions are equivalent. In this sense Anselm's proof is a proof of God's existence" (p. 147).

From the interpretation presented above Anselm is seen to be arguing that either God must always exist or else He can never exist. By blocking the latter alternative, Malcolm is able to maintain the former. But it is still not clear what is being asserted by this first alternative. Malcolm assumes a symmetry between logically impossible and logically necessary, such that if what is logically impossible (e.g., a round square) does not and cannot actually exist, then what is logically necessary (e.g., God) does and must actually exist. However, this symmetry does not hold. That the concept of a round square is self-contradictory guarantees that there are no round squares in existence. But from the fact that the concept of God necessarily includes the concept of existence, it does not follow that God actually exists.

Malcolm comes to Anselm's rescue by reducing his assailants' position to "If God exists (and it is possible that He does not) then He necessarily exists." Next, Malcolm finds fault with the opponents who allegedly advance this claim.

Their position is self-contradictory in the following way. On the one hand, they agree that the proposition "God necessarily exists" is an a priori truth. . . . On the other hand, they think that it is correct to analyze this proposition in such a way that it will entail the proposition "It is possible that God does not exist." But so far from its being the case that the proposition "God necessarily exists" entails the proposition "It is possible that God does not exist," it is rather the case that they are *incompatible* with one another! Can anything be clearer than that the conjunction "God necessarily exists but it is possible that He does not exist" is self-contradictory? (pp. 155–56).

Malcolm is thus thoroughly Anselmian in declaring that the Fool is ensnared by his own inconsistent position. Yet in sharing Anselm's conviction, Malcolm also shares his mistake. In the first place, the Fool is not maintaining that "God necessarily exists" logically entails "It is possible that God does not exist." In fact, it is foolish to accuse him of this logical howler. If anything, the Fool is committed to the view which Malcolm himself (we have seen) subscribes to: viz., "The a priori proposition 'God necessarily exists' entails the proposition 'God exists,' if and only if the latter also is understood as an a priori proposition . . ." (p. 147). Now, regardless of what Malcolm means by this comment, he is only justified in meaning the following: (1) "God necessarily exists" is analytic of the definition of "God." (Otherwise Malcolm has begged the question of God's existence.) (2) "God necessarily exists" analytically entails "God exists," since what exists necessarily, exists. (3) "God exists" is known a priori because it follows analytically from "God necessarily exists," which is known a priori. (4) Just as "God necessarily exists" says something only about the concept of God, so "God exists" says something only about the concept of God. But it does not follow from this analytic meaning-relationship that in fact God does exist. So in last analysis, the Fool is maintaining that the proposition "God necessarily exists" logically entails the proposition "God exists" and not the proposition "It is possible that God does not exist." And he has nothing to fear from this admission. For he can consistently maintain that there is no God (factual construal) but that the concept of God is such that if He were to exist, it would be necessary for Him to be without beginning and end (linguistic construal).[24]

24. Note the implicit difference in saying (a) necessarily God exists, (b) God necessarily exists, and (c) God exists necessarily. Saying *a* is like saying, "It simply must be the case that God exists — in fact I can prove it." This rendering tends to be more epistemological in that it suggests something about our preparedness to defend the claim that God exists. The use of *c*, however, tends to be more metaphysical, in that it purports to tell us something about God's nature: He is the kind

In the second place, Malcolm miscontrues the Fool's notion of "possibility." The latter is not saying "If God exists (and it is possible that He does not) then He necessarily exists." Instead, he is saying "If God were to exist (but He does not) then He would necessarily exist." The difference is the difference between an indicative conditional and a contrary-to-fact conditional. A contrary-to-fact conditional statement cannot be satisfactorily analyzed into a simply corresponding indicative conditional statement. But Malcolm is suggesting exactly such an analysis when he puts forth the Fool's argument in indicative terms and then declares it self-contradictory. Because the Fool does not believe that God exists, he is committed to the view that God's existence is impossible; for if God does not exist, He can never come to be. However, the Fool is not committed to the view that God's existence is *logically* impossible in the sense that the definition of "God" is inconsistent. In other words, he is committed not to the logical inconsistency of the proposition "God exists," but to the logical inconsistency of the proposition "A being by definition necessary and in fact not presently existing does at some time exist." God's existence is impossible, thinks the Fool, because God does not presently exist *and* because of the kind of being He is defined as. Since the definition of "God" is *not* self-contradictory, there is a sense in which (contrary to fact) God might have existed. And this is the sense in which the Fool can urge the possibility of that existence: possible because not self-contradictory; impossible because not actually existing. In still other words, if God does not exist (as the Fool is contending), then, to be sure, His nonexistence is possible; for what does not exist is possible not to exist. Yet the possibility by which God does not exist (supposing He does not) is the possibility logically entailed by an impossibility to exist — whereas in the case of nonexistent contingent beings, no such logical entailment holds. Thus the Fool is really saying: "If (contrary to fact) God exists [and it is (trivially) possible that He does not exist because it is (nontrivially) impossible that He exist (for reasons already given)], then (contrary to fact) He necessarily exists." And there is absolutely no contradiction here of the necessary/possible variety alleged by Malcolm.

In the third place, allow that the Fool is a skeptic instead of an atheist; i.e., allow that he only suspends judgment about whether or not God

of being who can never fail to exist. We say *b* ambiguously, since it may be substituted for either *a* or *c*.

exists. Then, perhaps, he might have said what Malcolm attributes to him, viz. (once again), "If God exists (and it is possible that He does not) then He necessarily exists." But in this context the notion of "possibility" would be not so much logical possibility as epistemic possibility. That is, the Fool would be claiming that *as far as is known*, it is possible that God either does or does not exist; relative to the available evidence, it might be a fact (it is possibly a fact) that no such necessary being actually exists. Now since the notion of "possibility" here is primarily epistemic, there is no self-contradiction in the Fool's utterance. He is certainly not asserting the logical self-contradiction that a necessary being, while *not* possible not to be, is likewise possible not to be. And anyone who thinks this is being claimed radically misunderstands the Fool's position — as radically as the Fool is alleged to have misunderstood Anselm's position.

That Malcolm nowhere attempts to analyze the various uses of the word "possible" points up a major deficiency in his defense of Anselm. If Anselm's initial version of the proof fails, at least it fails openly — whereas Malcolm's reconstruction, which introduces the modal terms, tends to camouflage the proof's flaw without rendering its unsound statement sound. Interestingly, the complex problem of the possible and the necessary is the very problem over which Aquinas was to stumble as he constructed his Third Way. In the *Summa Theologica* he reasons:

We find among existing things certain ones which are possible to be and not to be — since some things are seen to be generated and to be corrupted and consequently to be possible to be and not to be. (S_1): *Impossibile est autem omnia quae sunt talia, semper esse: quia quod possible est non esse, quandoque non est.* (S_2): *Si igitur omnia sunt possibilia non esse, aliquando nihil fuit in rebus.* But if this were the case, nothing would now exist, because that which does not exist only begins to exist through something else which is already existing. Therefore, if in the past nothing existed, then it would have been impossible for something to begin to exist, and hence nothing would now exist — which is clearly false. Therefore, not all beings are contingent beings (*possibilia*), but rather some necessary being must exist. However, every necessary being either has or does not have the cause of its own necessity from other than itself (*aliunde*). But it is not possible that there should be an infinite series of beings which have the cause of their necessity from another — just as we have shown this to be impossible in the case of efficient causes. Therefore, we must posit a being which is necessary *per se* and does not have the cause of its necessity from elsewhere. And all people call this being God.[25]

The crucial statements here are S_1 and S_2. The former is subject to important alternative construals.[26] For some manuscripts omit the word *semper*, and some interpreters of Thomas are inclined to place the comma after *sunt* instead of after *talia*. Depending upon which of these combinations is adopted, we have the following viable translations: [27] (1) It is impossible that all things which are such [viz., possible to be and not to be] should always exist — because what is possible not to exist, at some time does not exist. (2) It is impossible that all things which exist should be such [viz., possible to be and not to be] — because what is possible not to exist, at some time does not exist. (3) It is impossible that all things which exist should always be such [viz., things which exist] — because what is possible not to exist, at some time does not exist.

However, it is important to note that regardless of which reading one chooses, Thomas's argument will still remain unsound. For the universal assertion that "whatever is possible not to exist, at some time does not exist" cannot be successfully defended. And neither can its successor S_2: "Therefore, if all things were possible not to be, then at some time nothing would have existed." In the first case Thomas is working with a vacuous notion of possibility. In the second, he makes a mistake in logical inference.

Thomas's notion of possibility is borrowed from Aristotle — specifically from *De Caelo* I, 12: "In another way, clearly, it is impossible for the corruptible not to be corrupted at some time. For otherwise it will be at once both corruptible and actually incorruptible. Hence, it will at once be possible always to be and possible not always to be. Therefore, the corruptible is corrupted at some time. And if some existing thing is generable it has been generated, since it is possible for it to have been generated and possible for it at some time not to have existed." [28] Aristotle is maintaining, accordingly, that what always exists *cannot without contradiction* be said to be capable of not existing. Neither Aristotle nor

25. Translated from the Leonine text.

26. I am indebted to Professor Herbert W. Richardson for calling this point to my attention.

27. Some combinations do not make sense within the argument, and hence are not viable.

28. 283^a25–29.

Thomas introduces here the distinction between logically "possible not to exist" and "at some time caused not to exist." [29] Grant that some temporally existing thing has always existed and will continue always to exist. It is still possible to conceive of this thing as at some point (past, present, or future) not existing. That is, it is logically possible that this thing which always exists in time should either never have existed or else should at some particular time not exist. And this is the case even though, by hypothesis, this thing is never caused not to be. Anselm sees this point in *Reply to Gaunilo* 1 when he distinguishes God's existence from the existence of all spatial and temporal beings: "Therefore, whatever at any place or at any time does not exist as a whole can be thought not to be — even if it does actually exist. But if that being than which no greater can be thought, exists, then it cannot be thought not to be. Otherwise, if it exists, it is not that than which no greater can be thought — an inconsistency. Therefore, this being than which no greater can be thought always and everywhere exists as a whole, and never and no place fails to exist as a whole." [30]

By using the phrase "not possible to be thought not to be" instead of merely "not possible not to be," Anselm successfully avoids the Aristotelian-Thomistic problem. In other words, unlike Thomas, Anselm is not committed to the principle (P_1) that "at some time or other every possibility (potency) is realized." Thomas thinks that if something never occurs then its occurrence is not a genuine possibility (potency), but rather an impossibility. And this point of view leads him to say that those beings which are not possible not to be — inasmuch as God wills (causes) them always to exist from the beginning of time and for all time — are *necessary*, even though they hold this necessity *per aliud*. So then, Thomas is defining "what is possible" as "what is realized at some time." [31] And substituting this definition within P_1 betrays the fact that the principle with which Thomas works is but a tautology: "whatever is realized at some time, is realized at some time." On this rendering, the Thomistic principle is (trivially) true — but at the price of telling us nothing about matters of fact. In effect, what Thomas is saying is that if an event is pos-

29. The latter sense of "possibility" corresponds to the metaphysical potentialities which Aristotle and Thomas attribute to material substances.

30. S I, 131:31–132:1. Note Augustine, DT 5.1.2.

31. Elsewhere Thomas calls *possible* (for God) anything which does not involve a self-contradiction (ST 1st, 25, 3). But this notion of possibility is not operative in the present argument. Cf. n. 23 above.

sible, then necessarily there is a time at which the event occurs. However, we now see that this necessity is not even causal necessity, but only the necessity whereby the analytic proposition "What is going to take place is going to take place" is always true.

The continuation of the proof involves a fallacy of inference. Thomas has asserted S_1: For every X (where X is a thing which is possible not to be) there is some time at which X does not exist. But from this proposition he illicitly infers (*igitur*) the more restricted proposition S_2: If everything be X, then there is some time at which *no* X exists. But in fact, he is entitled to infer only S_3: If everything be X, then for any given thing there is some time at which it does not exist.[32] In other words, "Every thing is such that at some time it does not exist" does not entail "At some time nothing exists." On the assumption that all things are contingent, it might still be the case that each particular thing has its own time for not existing, and that many particular things cease to exist only in connection with causing another thing to begin existing. Within his proof Thomas has no way of justifying S_2. And this fact alone is enough to render the proof unsound.

Thomas's identification of the eternal with the necessary allows him to hold a view foreign to Anselm's. But in spite of entertaining differing notions of the necessary and the possible, both Anselm and Aquinas become entangled in the linguistic web of their respective versions of these modal terms. Anselm recognizes the sense in which the concept of God logically implies that God's nonexistence is impossible. But he wrongly goes on to infer therefrom *quod Deus est in re*. Aquinas, by attributing necessity to that which is eternal, fosters the impression that the question "Does X hold its necessity from itself or from another?" must be and can be meaningfully raised. By contrast, the unadorned question "Does X hold its eternity from itself or from another?" does not appear quite so intriguing. For one might reply that because X is by nature eternal, X "holds eternity from itself"; but we can dispense with the circumlocution.

Accordingly, nothing seems to coax us toward saying that the universe, for instance, or matter-as-such cannot in themselves be eternal. But something does seem to invite us to say that the universe or matter

32. The fallacy may be seen more readily in an analogous argument: S'_1: For every boy there is a girl whom he likes. Therefore, S'_2: There is some (one) girl whom every boy likes.

cannot be necessary in itself (*necesse per se*). For neither of these has its *reason for being* in itself. What this means, according to interpreters of Thomas, is that the universe or matter can be conceived as at some time not existing. But — we may want to ask — if something exists which can conceivably not exist, need it follow that something else exists which cannot conceivably not exist? The answer must be — not any more so than it follows from the inconceivability of something's not actually existing that that thing itself *does* actually exist. Aquinas and Anselm here move on intersecting paths. The latter's "necessity" is the former's "necessity *per se*"; and the former's "necessity *per aliud*" is the latter's "contingency." The Third Way does not collapse into the ontological argument as Kant would have us believe. But in its last stage it does implicitly appropriate the notion of "inconceivability of not existing," which lies at the heart of the ontological argument. And after its own fashion, it proceeds as illicitly as does the ontological argument.

The history of Anselm's *Proslogion* argument testifies amply to its subtle richness. Except for Zeno's Achilles' paradox, perhaps no philosophical argument has been so fertile in engendering sustained and vigorous controversy. Rejected by Aquinas, it was revived in one form or another by Descartes, Spinoza, and Leibniz. Kant dealt it a crippling blow; but in recent times Kant's own criticism has come under attack. Advocates of the argument's essential soundness have not always been few and far between. They have not always propounded the same type of defense; yet for one reason or another they have always made the same mistake — the mistake of inferring from a unique and self-consistent description something affirmative about matters of fact.

Chapter IV

Doctrine

of the Trinity

Anselm supposes that not only can God's existence be proven but also God's nature as trinity. The *Monologion* represents the extended attempt to formulate this proof. *De Incarnatione Verbi* and *De Processione*, by contrast, are not intended to *prove* philosophically that God is triune but rather to show that the notion of triunity as applied to God is at least rationally consistent. In one respect Anselm's two later works build upon the foundation of the *Monologion*, whose arguments he never repudiates; in another, they are more oriented toward explicating and defending the creeds. In arguing against Roscelin and the Greeks, Anselm is able to assume a larger field of theological common ground than he could effectively have done in the *Monologion*, where his argument aims in part at the total unbeliever.[1] As a foundational work, the *Monologion* sets out to justify first theism and then Christian theism.

MONOLOGION

The *Monologion* contains no sound demonstration of the triunity professed by Christian theism. What it does contain, though, are various analogies and similarities from the domain of human experience which

1. Note DIV 6 (S II, 21:1–3): In the *Monologion* and the *Proslogion* I have attempted "to answer, on behalf of our faith, those who, while unwilling themselves to believe what they do not understand, deride others who do believe."

tend to suggest a relationship of three-in-one. Anselm hopes that under the guidance of these patterns, the human mind may come to glimpse, as through a glass darkly, the rationale inherent in the Godhead. By invoking these patterns of similarity, Anselm's program is thoroughly Augustinian, as are the linguistic forms through which God's trinity is referred to.

Terminology. In *On the Trinity* Augustine refers to God as *una substantia, tres personae*: three persons in one substance.[2] Already by Augustine's day this linguistic form had become standard within the Latin Church. The Greeks, however, spoke of μία οὐσία τρεις ὑποστάσεις. And this phrase presented the following problem for the Western Church: whereas οὐσία was customarily translated as *essentia*, ὑπόστασις was *not* customarily translated by *persona* but by *substantia*. Thus the Greeks seemed to be saying that God is *una essentia, tres substantiae*: three substances in one essence. And although the notion of God's being one essence was acceptable to the Latins, the further notion of three "substances" in the Godhead was ostensibly contradictory to the Latin profession that God is but one substance. Boethius takes up the intricacies of this problem in *The Person and the Two Natures* 3, and concludes that *substantia* is, after all, the most appropriate translation of ὑπόστασις. Thus, he notes, were it not contrary to tradition, it might be better to speak of God as three substances.[3] However, Boethius's conclusion must be qualified by his own earlier observation: what the Greeks call ὑποστάσεις, they also call πρόσωπα (*personae*). That is, the Greeks do not use ὑποστάσεις for animals and for things which have no *persona*.[4] And this fact furnishes credibility to the claim that the Latin terminology is conceptually equivalent to the Greek.

Anselm does not veer from the traditional recitation stemming through Augustine and the Quicumque. He sees that Greeks and Latins are in conceptual agreement and is willing to allow either terminology as long as it does not hide the conceptual truth. Perhaps because he was not engaged in translation projects and did not know Greek, he was

2. DT 5.8.10–5.9.10 (PL 42:917–918).

3. PL 64:1345. Boethius proposes the following equivalents: οὐσία — *essentia*; οὐσίωσις — *subsistentia*; ὑπόστασις — *substantia*; πρόσωπον — *persona*. PL 64:1344.

4. Ch. 3 (PL 64:1344). In DT 5.8.10 Augustine also expresses some hesitation about what the term ὑπόστασις means.

(unlike Boethius) scarcely occupied with the problem of finding linguistic equivalents. At any rate, his terminology is more flexible, if indeed less consistent than Boethius's. In the preface to the *Monologion* he ascribes to the Greeks the wording whereby God exists as three substances in one *person* — a wording exactly opposite to that of the Western Church (S I, 8:14–18). In the *Monologion* itself he no longer views the Greek wording as indicating that God exists as one person, but rather as one essence, or nature. In fact, he identifies essence with nature in *Monologion* 4; and throughout this work he speaks of God as one in essence, nature, or substance — interchangeably. In the last chapters he goes so far as to use *substantiae* as an alternate for *personae* (S I, 86:4ff).

If Anselm vacillates in his use of these terms, it is because he is uneasy about the impressions they convey. "Substance," for instance, implies the correlative idea of accidents; for substance is that which underlies accidents and accounts for the unity and continuity of an object as it undergoes change. But in God there is no change and no accidental feature of being. Hence, as applied to God, the word "substance" can only mean "essence," or "nature"; and this is Anselm's justification for using all three interchangeably.[5] The word "person" is likewise inadequate to convey the notion of plurality in the Trinity.[6] For "person" ordinarily suggests individuals existing separately — whereas, in the Trinity, the persons are distinct but do not exist as independent individuals. Anselm's understanding of "person" is the same as Boethius's[7] and involves three factors: "person" is predicated only of natures; "person" is predicated of particulars rather than of universals; "person" is predicated only of that which is rational. Thus, "person" always refers to an individual rational nature — whether in God, in the angels, or in men. Since natures exist in substances, Boethius defines "person" as the individual *substance* of a rational nature. Although Anselm nowhere uses this exact formula, his understanding of person does not differ from Boethius's. And this understanding accounts for his willingness in the *Monologion* to describe God as either three persons or three substances. But his final posi-

5. Augustine had authorized the interchangeability of these terms with regard to God. See *Catholic and Manichean Ways of Life* 2.2.2; DT 2.18.35; 5.2.3. Anselm's hesitancy in M 79 to call God a substance is paralleled by Augustine's earlier hesitancy in DT 7.5.10.

6. M 79 (S I, 85:23–86:5).

7. See p. 30.

tion is presented in *De Incarnatione Verbi*, where he says simply, "The Latins call these three persons, the Greeks [three] substances. For just as we say that in God there is one substance and three persons, so they say one person and three substances. But they mean by 'substance' what we mean by 'person,' so that in faith they do not differ from us in any respect" (Ch. 16). Here he reverts to the language of the *Monologion* preface, according to which the Greeks call God one person. But he himself holds fast to the Latin confession of *una substantia, tres personae*, and no longer accommodates a more flexible terminology.

Vestigia Trinitatis. Augustine argues that since man is made in the image of God, this image must be reflected in man's very nature. Moreover, the very triunity of God must be reflected, since Scripture uses the plural form when it represents God as saying "Let us make man in our image" (Gen. 1:26). This image is primarily detectable in the human soul. For one way to view the soul is as a triad of memory, understanding, and will. Augustine sees clearly that these are distinct functions of a single soul, or mind:

> Memory, understanding, and will are not three lives or three minds but one life and one mind. Hence, they are not three substances but only one. Insofar as memory is called life and mind and substance, it is being spoken of with respect to itself. Insofar as it is called simply memory, it is spoken of in relation to something else. The same thing holds for understanding and will — both of which may be spoken of relatively. But with respect to itself, each is life, mind, and essence. Thus, these three are one insofar as each is one life, one mind, one essence. . . . But they are three insofar as they are spoken of in relation to one another. If they were not equal — each to the other and each to all — they would not comprehend one another. For not only is each one comprehended by each one but all are comprehended by each. I remember that I have memory, understanding, and will; I understand that I understand and will and remember; I will that I will and remember and understand; and at one and the same time I remember my entire memory, understanding, and will.[8]

Here then is the striking analogy which Augustine detects between the human soul and the Divine Being. This analogy is not argumentative but illustrative. That is, Augustine does not envision himself as proving a truth about the Trinity on the basis of an analysis of human being. He aspires only to elucidate, if possible, the nature of God's triunity by ap-

8. DT 10.11.18 (PL 42:983). Note also Augustine, Ep. 169.

pealing to this similarity. At the same time he is interpreting the text of Genesis 1:26.

Anselm, by contrast, purports to show by necessary reasons that God exists as three persons in one essence. But even though the movement of his argument is more systematic than Augustine's, he does not accomplish more than does Augustine. Whereas Augustine moves from the analysis of the human mind to the statement about the nature of the Trinity, Anselm tries to deduce the doctrine of the Trinity from purely a priori principles. Thus his deduction of the existence of the second member of the Trinity in Chapter 29 makes no substantive use of analogical comparison:

Nothing at all could ever have existed or can ever exist except the Creating Spirit and its creatures. But it is impossible that the Expression of this Spirit should be in the class of created things; for every existing creature was created through this Expression — which could not have created itself. Indeed, nothing can be created through itself, because whatever is made exists later than that through which it is made, and because nothing exists later than itself. Thus, the other alternative holds, viz., that the Expression of the Supreme Spirit — since it cannot be a creature — is identical with the Supreme Spirit. Finally, this Expression can be understood to be nothing other than the understanding (*intelligentia*) of the Supreme Spirit by which the Supreme Spirit understands all things (S I, 47: 12–21).

The analogical comparison enters when Anselm identifies the Expression of the Supreme Spirit with the Word (or Image) of that Spirit, just as man's mental expression (i.e., thought) of something may be called a word representing that thing.[9]

Anselm views the third member of the Trinity as the love that proceeds from the first two members; for God must be thought to love Himself, just as He must be thought to understand Himself. Anselm is here guided by an analogy with human love, but appeal to the nature of human love does not become an intrinsic part of his argument. Rather, he appeals to a principle he regards as a priori true: viz., that "the remembrance and understanding of anything is in vain and altogether useless except that this thing be loved or hated to the extent required by reason." Therefore, he concludes, the Supreme Spirit loves itself even as it remembers

9. Augustine also compares the Word of God with concepts in the human mind. Just as these concepts (which Augustine also calls words) become embodied in spoken sounds and written signs, so the Word of God became manifest in human flesh. DT 15.11.20.

Doctrine of the Trinity

and understands itself (M 49). So then, in the end, he describes Father, Son and Holy Spirit as memory, understanding, and love — a variant which Augustine himself uses.[10]

Unity and plurality in God. What is important about the *Monologion* is not its alleged proof of the Trinity or its correlation of the three persons with three similar functions of the soul, but rather its clear distinction between the relational and the substantial aspects of the Godhead, as witnessed in Chapter 43: "The Father and the Son are so opposite in relation that the one never sustains the property of the other; and they are so concordant in nature that the one always has the essence of the other. For with respect to the fact that the one is the Father and the other is the Son they are so different that the Father is never called the Son nor the Son called the Father; and with respect to their substance they are so identical that the essence of the Son is always in the Father and the essence of the Father is always in the Son" (S I, 60:5–10). This statement provides the basis upon which Anselm will build in *De Incarnatione Verbi* and *De Processione*. It becomes his way of reconciling trinity and unity in God. Father, Son, and Holy Spirit do not differ as God but in the way each is God in relation to the others. Relations, Anselm sees, are not accidental features of the Godhead; for God is eternally related to Himself as Father, Son, and Holy Spirit — so that these relationships do not constitute contingency.[11]

Anselm is indebted to Augustine's *On the Trinity* for this approach toward reconciling God's plurality and singularity. According to Augustine, a statement about an object may be either *secundum substantiam*, *secundum accidens*, or *secundum relationem*.[12] A statement about the *nature* of an object is a statement "according to substance"; and an assertion about those features of an object which are subject to change, and

10. DT 15.6.10.

11. Note Southern regarding DIV: "Anselm was reported to have said — and he did not deny the report — that the Persons of the Trinity were to God what the qualities *albus, justus, grammaticus*, and so on, were to an individual man. In other words, the relationship was like that of Substance and Accidents. In the first draft of his reply to Roscelin Anselm attempted to justify this parallel by explaining the sense in which it was true. But it opened the way to so many misunderstandings that he suppressed this passage in his final version." *Saint Anselm and His Biographer*, p. 80.

12. 5.3.4–5.5.6 (PL 42:912–914). See also DT 5.8.9; 15.5.8; *On the Gospel of John* 22.14; 39.3–4; Sermon 244.3.

which when changed do not determine a change in that object's nature, is an assertion "according to accident." With respect to created and mutable beings, notes Augustine, every description of objects must fall into one or the other of these categories. The case is different, however, with respect to God. Since there are no accidents in God and since not everything is said about God according to substance, we discern that some things are said of Him "according to relation." So then, we may speak of God insofar as He is God (*ad se ipsum*) — i.e., with respect to His substance — or we may speak of Him insofar as He is Father, Son, and Holy Spirit (*ad aliquid*) — i.e., with respect to His relationships. For God cannot be Father except as He is Father of a son; and God cannot be Son except as He is Son of a father. Since "father" and "son" are correlative terms, they can only be understood with respect to each other. And what is understood *secundum relationem* cannot in the same way be understood *secundum substantiam*. In the following passage Augustine makes this clear.

If the Father were called father only with respect to Himself and not with respect to the Son, and if the Son were called son only with respect to Himself and not with respect to the Father, then in speaking of the Father or of the Son we would be speaking according to substance. But because the Father is so called only with respect to the fact that He has a son, and since the Son is so called only with respect to the fact that He has a father, we do not apply these designations according to substance. For each of the two persons is spoken of in relation to the other and not exclusively in relation to Himself. Moreover, we do not predicate paternity and filiation according to accident, inasmuch as [in God] fatherhood and sonship are eternal and unchangeable. Therefore, although being the Father is different from being the Son, the Father and the Son are not two different substances. For in speaking of them we are speaking relationally rather than substantively. Yet this relation is not itself an accident, since it is unchangeable.[13]

Augustine's distinction between *secundum relativum* and *secundum accidens* must not be misconstrued. He is not suggesting that the former is altogether inapplicable to created things, but simply that the latter is altogether inapplicable to God. That is, for created and mutable things, relationships are always sustained accidentally, so that the one category is subordinated to the other. But in speaking of God we do not subordinate a category: we exclude a category. In *Monologion* 25 Anselm

13. DT 5.5.6 (PL 42:914).

subscribes to Augustine's position. He also sees that some relationships which finite beings enter into do not constitute a change in those beings, and hence are not necessarily to be considered accidents of those beings. Thus, for instance, it is certain that "I am neither taller nor shorter than, equal nor similar to a man who will be born after the present year. But after he will have been born, I will surely be able to entertain all of these relations to him — according as he will grow or change in various of his qualities — without any change in myself." [14] Since Anselm does not view these relations as modifying one's existence, he does not want to call them accidents in the strict sense — even though they happen to one and come and go (and thus are accidents in a broader sense). This type of relationship which does not determine change in the relatum is considered by Anselm to reflect obliquely the unchanging and nonaccidental relationships within the Trinity. In addition, it helps to explain how God can be related to a changing world without His nature being affected by these changing relations. Therefore, since what is said of God relationally in no way touches upon His substance, He may consistently be conceived as one substance existing in multiple relations with Himself. In this way, plurality is never predicated of the essence nor singularity of the persons. [15]

Eternally and ineffably Three-in-One. Although the persons in the Trinity are distinct, they are not separate, for each is essentially God. As one, God's nature is not even conceptually divisible, observes Anselm. It can neither be thought not to be nor thought to be more than one. For if God were more than one essence, there would then be two or more gods. But the argument of *Monologion* 3 purports to show that only one Supreme Being can and does exist. Because this Supreme Being exists *per se*, He is eternal; and He is immutable because of His indivisible nature. If God is unchangeable in relation to Himself, He is also unchangeable in relation to the world. Yet how can that which is *eternal* be immutably related to that which is constantly changing through *time*? In answer

14. S I, 43:14-18. In DT 5.6.17 Augustine uses a different example but makes the same point about relationships.

15. Note Boethius: "Terms which are not predicable in accordance with something's nature cannot indicate alteration or any kind of change in that thing's essence. For this reason, if the terms 'father' and 'son' are correlative, differing only relationally, and if a relation tells us nothing about the nature of a thing, then it [and likewise these terms] will indicate no essential change . . . but only a difference of persons." *Unity of the Trinity* 5 (PL 64:1254). Note also PL 64:217.

Anselm maintains that God is related to the world as if it were present to Him in its entirety.[16] Accordingly, the eternal encompasses the temporal without itself becoming temporalized. God's omnipresence must be construed as being other than spatiotemporal. "Properly speaking, then, the Supreme Essence is not *in* any space or time, because the Supreme Essence is not contained by anything else. Nevertheless, in a sense it can be said to be in every place and time inasmuch as all things which are other than it are sustained by its presence lest they should fall away into nothing."[17]

Predicates of place and time may be applied to God so long as these predicates do not, then, beguile us into supposing that God's decrees are temporally ordered or that His persons are individually separate. "We commonly and acceptably use spatial language of things which are neither spatially located nor themselves places. For example, we say that the intellect is there in the soul where rationality is. Although 'there' and 'where' are spatial terms, the soul does not contain anything spatially, nor is the intellect or rationality so contained."[18] In this sense Scripture itself describes God in spatiotemporal categories. Anselm is well aware of Augustine's reference to Aristotle's ten categories in *On the Trinity* 5.7.8. Augustine sees that when we ascribe position, state, place, and time to God, we do so *per similitudines*, through likenesses. Thus, God is said in the Psalms to sit above the Cherubim (position), to cover the deep as does a garment (state), to be unfailing in years (time), and to be in Heaven, where one may ascend (place).[19] Like Augustine, Anselm has no objection to such figurative use of language. He recognizes that after this fashion the human mind does intelligibly express a truth about God's presence. In *De Concordia* he argues this point effectively:

When the Apostle declares that God foreknew, predestined, called, justified, and glorified His saints, we must understand that none of these occurs earlier or later than the others for God, but that all of them are together at once within an eternal present. For eternity has its own "si-

16. Cf. DCD 21. For Augustine's statement of this viewpoint see DT 15.7.13; *On the Gospel of John* 38.10.

17. Ch. 22 (S I, 41:4–7). Note Augustine, DT 5.1.2.

18. Ch. 23 (S I, 41:26–42:2).

19. DT 5.8.9 (PL 42:917). For the use of Aristotle's ten categories note also *Confessions* 4.16; DT 5.1.2; 5.7.8.

multaneity" and encompasses all the things that occur at the same time and place and that occur at different times and places.

In order to show that he was not using these words in their temporal signification, the same Apostle used verbs in the past tense to refer even to future events. For, temporally speaking, God has not already called, justified, and glorified those who He foreknows are still to be born. From this we can see that for want of a verb that would adequately signify the eternal present, the Apostle used verbs of past tense; for things which are temporally past are altogether immutable, and in this way resemble the eternal present. In this respect the temporal past is more like the eternal present than is the temporal present (DC I, 5. S II, 254: 10ff).

God's eternity, then, can be apprehended by human intellect and can be given expression in ordinary language. This fact makes it possible for Anselm to argue in behalf of the eternal begottenness [20] of the Son and the eternal procession of the Holy Spirit — a discussion he takes up in *De Incarnatione* 15. As a point within a point is still one point, so eternity within eternity is one eternity. Thus, the eternity of the Father and of the Son and of the Holy Spirit within the eternity of God forms a single eternity. Likewise, the eternal begottenness by which the Son comes from the eternal Father does not constitute intervals within the one eternity.

Anselm never forgets that the patterns of similarity by which he apprehends the Trinity cannot suffice to fathom the depths of God's mystery. In this light, the last sentence of the *Monologion* is doubly significant. For it shows not only what Anselm thinks he has accomplished but also what he knows he can never accomplish. "Truly, then, this Spirit is not only God but the only God, ineffably three and one." As Anselm supposes God's triunity to be demonstrable by reason alone, so he recognizes that reason alone can never comprehend the triunity it apprehends. Thus, even in the *Monologion*, reason does not replace faith: it seeks to bring faith into focus, to illuminate the object of faith. And this program of illumination with respect to the Trinity continues in *De Incarnatione* and *De Processione*, where Anselm consistently interprets Scripture and Scripturally orients reason. If there is a prominent difference between the *Monologion* and the two later treatises, it is not that the two, more than the one, proceed by "believing in order to under-

20. For Augustine's teaching of eternal begottenness see DT 5.5.6; 6.2.3; 15.26.47; *Christian Combat* 16.18.

stand" — the watchword of *De Incarnatione* 1. It is rather that the *Monologion* envisions a universal audience, whereas the audiences of *De Incarnatione* and *De Processione* are envisioned as restricted. Furthermore, the *Monologion* undertakes a general task, while *De Incarnatione* and *De Processione* contend with particular points of controversy within the dogmatic life of the Church. Hence, the one treatise is more apologetical, the other two more theological. But who can fail to see that even *De Incarnatione* and *De Processione* are extensive apologies on behalf of the credal formulations of the Western Church? Moreover, although the primary purpose of these two works is intended as intra-fideistic, Anselm never loses sight of their secondary role — viz., to exhibit at large the rational consistency of the Christian faith. And this secondary function is identical with the main goal of the *Monologion*.

DE INCARNATIONE VERBI

Anselm's quarrel with Roscelin developed over how to construe "three persons in God." In particular, Roscelin is reputed to have contended, "If the three persons in God are only one thing (*res*), and not three things, each separate in itself, like three angels or three souls — being one in such a way, however, that the three are wholly the same in will and power — then the Father and the Holy Spirit were incarnate with the Son" (DIV 1). While still at Bec, Anselm began a work against Roscelin but discontinued it when Roscelin recanted at the Council of Soissons in 1092. Subsequently, however, Roscelin resumed his position; so Anselm felt obliged to deal with it once and for all. He thus began a second version of his interrupted manuscript, addressing it to Pope Urban II under the title *Epistola de Incarnatione Verbi*.[21] Anselm seems to have had no firsthand knowledge of Roscelin's work. In Chapter 11 he admits, "I have had access to nothing from the writings of the opponent to whom I am responding in this letter except the statement I quoted above. . . ." And earlier, in Chapter 4, he even casts doubt on whether the quotation attributed to Roscelin is entirely accurate: "It may be that he himself does not actually use the words, 'like three angels or three souls.' Perhaps the one who passed the question on to me introduced this example him-

---

21. Although Anselm nowhere in this treatise mentions Roscelin by name, it is clear from the letter to Bishop Fulco of Beauvais (#136) that the view under discussion is indeed Roscelin's.

self, while the man whose views we are discussing affirms only that the three persons are three things without the addition of any illustration." This uncertainty about the exactitude of the statement attributed to Roscelin is paralleled by uncertainty about how Roscelin intended the statement to be interpreted. Thus, before Anselm can contend with the position of his opponent, he must seek to determine just what that position is. And this he can only do — given the secondhand nature of his investigation — by scrutinizing the quotation before him.

Interpretation of Roscelin's position. "If the three persons are only one thing, and not three things . . . then the Father and the Holy Spirit were incarnate with the Son." But how, asks Anselm, does Roscelin understand "three things"? Does he use this phrase substantially or only relatively when referring to the persons of God? That is — as the *Monologion* has already pointed out — we may speak about the persons with respect to what is common to all or with respect to what is proper to each. So then,

The person of the Father is both God (which is common to Him with the Son) and Father (which is proper to Him). Similarly the person of the Son is God (which is common to Him with the Father) and Son (which is said of this person alone). In these two persons, therefore, one thing is common, viz., God, and two things are proper, viz., Father and Son. Now, whatever properties are common to them — such as omnipotence and eternity — are to be understood solely in this common aspect; while such properties as are peculiar to each — such as Begetter or Begetting (for the Father), Word or Begotten (for the Son) — are signified by the two names "Father" and "Son." [22]

If Roscelin means that the three persons are three things so that the re-

---

22. Ch. 2 (S II, 11:17-25). Cf. DT 5.11.12 (PL 42:918-919). "What is predicated properly of each member of the Trinity is in no way predicated with regard to what they are in themselves but with regard either to the other members of the Trinity or else to creatures. And so it is evident that these things are said relatively and not substantively. For the Trinity is called one God, great, good, eternal, omnipotent, and can also be called its own deity, its own greatness, its own goodness, its own eternity, its own omnipotence. But the Trinity may not be called father — unless perhaps metaphorically, in relation to creatures because of the adoption of sons."

Note also that in DT 5.6.7 (PL 42:915) Augustine distinguishes between the terms "unbegotten" and "begetter" as applied to the Father. The latter is a straightforward relational term; the former is the negation of the relational term "begotten," and hence is itself also a relational term. Augustine thinks that if "unbegotten" were regarded as a nonrelational term, it would then designate the Father with respect only to Himself (*ad se ipsum*) — thus implying that His essence is different from that of the Son.

lation of the Father is not the relation of the Son and not the relation of the Holy Spirit, then he stands in fundamental agreement with the Christian faith.[23] For the Christian faith allows that in God, the Father differs from the Son precisely because He is related to the Son as father; and the Son differs from the Father precisely because He is the Father's son. The Father cannot be His own father, and the Son cannot be His own son. But these differences of properties are not thought to interfere with the simplicity and indivisibility of the divine essence, or substance.

However, Roscelin seems to intend "three things" substantially. For he specifies that (1) "each is separate in itself" (2) "like three angels or three souls," and yet (3) each is "wholly the same in will and power." If the persons of God exist separately as do three souls, notes Anselm, then they exist as substantially plural, since "soul" denotes a substance. In this case Roscelin cannot call himself a Christian, inasmuch as he is subscribing to tritheism (Ch. 3. S II, 14). But he may protest that he is not a tritheist; for these three things (he may say) are not three gods, but rather are *together* one God (Ch. 4. S II, 17:8–9). Against such a possible reply Anselm raises two objections. First, if the three things, so construed, are together one God, then God exists as a composite — so that no one of the persons would Himself be God, but God would be only the three in combination. However, the Christian faith declares that the Father is God; the Son, God; and the Holy Spirit, God; and that the one God is Father, Son, and Holy Spirit.[24] Secondly, if the nature of God is composite, then something can be conceived to be greater than God. For a being whose nature is simple is superior to a being whose nature is composite. But since no being can be thought to be greater than God, the nature of God cannot be composite. Thus, the ontological argument itself defeats Roscelin's possible response.

If the persons of the Trinity are not three substances, then according to Roscelin the Father and the Holy Spirit would have to have been incarnate with the Son. Anselm conjectures Roscelin's reasoning as follows:

23. Anselm tacitly distinguishes the Christian faith (*fides christiana*) from the Catholic faith (*fides catholica*). By the latter he means (in the present context) primarily the dogmas formulated in the Athanasian Creed, whereas the former encompasses the broader range of ecclesiastically defined theological truth. Yet, Anselm sometimes uses the expressions as if without distinction.

24. In DT 7.4.8 Augustine meets the objection that "if there are three persons there are three gods" by appealing to Scripture.

Doctrine of the Trinity

If God is numerically one and the same thing, and this very same thing is both Father and Son, then when the Son became incarnate, how is it that the Father also was not incarnate? For where two different things are involved, there is no reason why something should not be affirmed of one thing while at the same time it is denied of the other. But if we are speaking of one and the same thing, the affirmation of something and the denial of it cannot both be true at the same time. For example, it is not true that the same Peter both is and is not an apostle. And even if under one name he is affirmed to be an apostle, while under another name this is denied — as, for example, "Peter is an apostle," and "Simon is not an apostle" — these propositions are not both true. One of them is false. But "Peter is an apostle" and "Stephen is not an apostle" can both be true, because Peter and Stephen are different people. If therefore the Father is numerically one and the same thing as the Son, we cannot truly affirm something of the Son and deny it of the Father, or affirm it of the Father and deny it of the Son. Therefore, whatever the Father is, the Son is also; and what is said of the Son ought not to be denied of the Father. But the Son was incarnate. Therefore, the Father also was incarnate (Ch. 3. S II, 14:23–15:12).

In accordance with this interpretation Anselm accuses Roscelin of Sabellianism; i.e., he views Roscelin as suggesting that God is but one person who assumes three different modes of existing.[25] For if all the predicates which apply to the Father, apply equally to the Son, and vice versa, then Father and Son can no longer be distinct by virtue of their relationship to each other. And in this case they cannot be two persons, but only one. (The same reasoning holds with respect to the Holy Spirit.) Therefore, if "the Father is whatever the Son is" means that if the Son is begotten, the Father must also be begotten, or that if the Son is incarnate, the Father must also be incarnate — then Father and Son are the same person, for they have the same substance *and* the same characteristics of relation. Such a view constitutes a denial of the Christian faith, which maintains the plurality of persons and the incarnation of the Son alone.

Anselm claims, then, that Roscelin's position terminates in either tri-

25. The simultaneous incarnation mentioned by Roscelin is one version of what came to be called Sabellianism. Sabellius claimed that God as Old Testament Lawgiver is Father, as Incarnate One is Son, and as Sanctifier in the hearts of men is Holy Spirit. These modalities were not understood to exist at the same time, however. They were said to be successive appearances in terms of which God manifests Himself in history. Sabellianism in its different versions is also known as patripassianism and modalism. See Augustine's attack on this theory in *On the Gospel of John* 36.8 (PL 35:1667). For his rejection of both Sabellianism and Arianism see *On the Gospel of John* 36.9; 37.6. Also note Ep. 11, which raises the question of why the Father and the Holy Spirit were not incarnated with the Son.

theism or Sabellianism, and, accordingly, violates Christian dogma. In particular, it violates the doctrinal articulation of the Athanasian Creed, or Quicumque. And this Creed constitutes the background against which Anselm and Roscelin take up their controversy. For although the Quicumque is nowhere mentioned in *De Incarnatione* or in *De Processione*, it *is* referred to in Anselm's letter to Bishop Fulco (Ep. 136) — the same letter in which Anselm delivers an explicit judgment against Roscelin.[26] Because Anselm holds to the Creed, he sees Roscelin's argument as objectively entailing the rejection of Christianity. (But Roscelin, as Anselm hints, may well have thought of himself as subjectively holding to the faith.) Anselm is not content to challenge Roscelin's position by pointing out that it is inconsistent with the Creed; for the question might once more arise, Is the Creed right? Nor does he repudiate Roscelin by appeal to Scripture — even though Scripture nowhere favors either tritheism or simultaneous incarnation. Rather, since Roscelin might perversely interpret Scripture, Anselm confronts him head-on and attempts to defeat his argument by proving rationally that the incarnation of the Son entails neither that the three members of the Trinity are separate things nor that the other two members must have been incarnate with the Son.[27]

Anselm's three tasks. In meeting Roscelin on the common ground of reason, Anselm sets himself three tasks: to show that even if there were three gods, this would not prevent the Father and the Holy Spirit from also having been incarnate; to demonstrate that nevertheless there is not a plurality of gods; to prove that the incarnation of any one person of the Trinity does not necessitate the incarnation of the other two, but rather makes it impossible (Ch. 6. S II, 21:20–25).

If there are three gods, implies Anselm, then each of these must be essentially (but not numerically) what the other two are; otherwise one would be greater than the others, so that he and not the others would be God. Moreover, they must be essentially omnipotent and omnipresent since any being lacking these perfections is less than God. If each, then, exists *everywhere* with respect to his being and power, each must be

26. In Ep. 136 Anselm refers to the Quicumque as a creed. See J. Hopkins and H. Richardson, "On the Athanasian Creed," *Harvard Theological Review*, 60 (July 1967), 483–484.

27. Ch. 2 (S II, 11:5); Ch. 6 (S II, 20:11–13).

where as well as *what* the other two are. Thus, if the Son is incarnate, the Father and the Holy Spirit must also be incarnate. "Hence, when our self-styled defender of the faith says that there are three gods, he cannot show how they are separated from one another in such a way that the Father and the Holy Spirit are freed from the incarnation. In other words, positing a multiplicity of gods cannot help him to keep the Father and the Spirit from being incarnate, because he cannot discover in this multiplicity of gods that distinction (*disiunctio*) which he himself argues is absolutely necessary if this freedom from incarnation is to be achieved" (Ch. 7. S II, 22:14–20).

Secondly, God must be identical with the Supreme Good, since God embodies every conceivable perfection and since He cannot be less than anything else. But the Supreme Good can never be plural. "For if there are several supreme goods, they are all equal. But the Supreme Good is that which so excels other goods that it has neither an equal nor a superior. Therefore, there is only one Supreme Good" (Ch. 8. S II, 22:27–23:2).

Thirdly, even though Father, Son, and Holy Spirit are numerically one God, the incarnation of any one of them does not necessitate the incarnation of all of them. For God is numerically one with respect only to His nature; with respect to His persons He is numerically three (Ch. 9. S II, 23:21ff). Now, in the incarnation God assumed manhood either into a unity of nature with Himself or into a unity of person. Since it is blasphemous to suppose that God and man are one and the same nature, it follows that God assumed manhood into a unity of person. But different persons can never be one and the same person. Therefore, when God assumed manhood into a single person with the Son, the other persons of God were necessarily excluded from this incarnation.

Anselm's first two arguments constitute the weakest points in *De Incarnatione*, for they turn on verbal distinctions which beg the question. The third is plausible, granted the distinctions Anselm has been at pains to make within the preceding sections of the treatise. If these three considerations, taken collectively, were the only objections he could muster against Roscelin, Anselm would have done better to contend with his opponent's view on the basis of Scripture alone. Even though Roscelin might perversely have interpreted Scripture (as Anselm feared), it is better that Roscelin should wrongfully have interpreted than that Anselm should tenuously have reasoned. However, the three arguments advanced above are neither the heart of *De Incarnatione* nor the only considerations at Anselm's disposal. They are important in manifesting, not in executing, his intent. In *De Incarnatione* Anselm is concerned to make clear the substance/relation distinction which he first articulated in the *Monologion* and which he brings to conclusion in *De Processione*. If he can successfully elucidate this distinction with respect to God, then he will have gone a long way toward clarifying the faith of the Church as expressed in the Quicumque. And it will not so much matter whether or not he has beaten back Roscelin at every turn along that way.

Unambiguity of the relations. In an effort to encompass the entire range of issues connected with Roscelin's statement, Anselm takes up the question of why the Son rather than the Father or the Holy Spirit was incarnate, if only one member of the Trinity could take on human form (Ch. 10). His answer centers on what is fitting to believe.[28] If the Holy Spirit alone had been incarnated, then the Holy Spirit would be called the Son of the Virgin. In that case there would have been two sons in the Trinity: the Son of God (i.e., the second member of the Trinity) and the Son of the Virgin (i.e., the Holy Spirit). And this situation would have led to confusion when one spoke of "God the Son," since the reference would no longer be unambiguous. Moreover, this state of affairs would seem to imply an inequality in the Trinity. For of the two sons, the one who is begotten from God would seem to have a loftier birth than the other, who is begotten of Mary. But there should not even be a seeming inequality between the persons of God. Likewise, had the Father become incarnate, there would have arisen the same ambiguity with respect to "God the Son" — as well as the additional problem of there having been two members of the Trinity called grandson. (The Father would be the grandson of Mary's parents, and the Father's son would be the grandson of Mary — even though nothing belonging to Him would have originated from Mary.) However, none of these confusions arise if the Son is incarnated. Moreover, since the Incarnate One is supposed to offer prayers to the Father on behalf of man, it is most appropriate, as in human relationships, that the Son should implore the Father. "Therefore, since even a small incongruity (*inconveniens*) is impossible in God, no person of God ought to be incarnate except the Son. For nothing incongruous

28. Note Ch. 2, pp. 48-51. Cf. CDH II, 9, where the argument discussed above is repeated.

follows if He is incarnate. Even when it is said that the Son is inferior to the Father and the Holy Spirit from the point of view of His humanity, this still does not mean that these two persons are superior to the Son. For that very majesty by which they are greater than the humanity of the Son belongs to the Son as well; and together with His Father and the Holy Spirit, the Son Himself is superior to His own humanity" (Ch. 10. S II, 26:3–9).

Example of the Nile. In *De Incarnatione*, as well as in the *Monologion*, Anselm is in search of analogies and patterns of similarity which will elucidate the mystery of triunity as far as is humanly possible. If amidst common discourse about created natures he can find a parallel to the Church's discourse about the Divine Nature, then he will have made it easier for Roscelin and others like him to believe what they do not fully understand — as Anselm himself believes what in this case he also does not fully understand. Just such an example occurs to Anselm with regard to the Nile. The Nile is a *spring* flowing through a *river* and accumulating into a *lake*. The spring is not the river or the lake, the river is not the lake or the spring, and the lake is not the spring or the river. Yet the spring is the Nile, river is the Nile, and the lake is the Nile. Moreover, the three collectively are called the Nile; and the combination of any two of them is also called the Nile. There are not three Niles, but only one. The Nile is one nature, one water. Although the whole Nile is the spring, the whole Nile the river, the whole Nile the lake, yet the spring, the river, and the lake are all distinct from one another. The river is not the spring; but the river is what the spring is, viz., the Nile. In this respect all three have the same nature. Likewise, the whole river exists from the whole spring, and the whole lake from the whole river and the whole spring.[29]

Anselm sees in this example an illuminating approximation to the Church's language about God's three-in-oneness. The Son exists from the whole essence of the Father; the Holy Spirit proceeds from the whole of the Father and the Son. The Son is not the Father or the Holy

29. Note Augustine's similar example: "It is not strange to say these things about the ineffable Nature, since an analogue to these statements can be found in what is said about objects perceived with bodily eyes and distinguished by the sensible faculty. For although we cannot say of a spring that it is the river, nor of the river that it is the spring, nor of a draught taken from either of these that it is either the river or the spring — nevertheless we call all three water, both individually and collectively." *Faith and the Creed* 9.17 (PL 40:189).

Spirit; yet the Son is what the Father and the Holy Spirit are, viz., God. There are not three gods or three sets of consciousness, but only three distinct spheres of relationship within one indivisible consciousness. Anselm's effort to clarify the Christian concept of God relies upon analogies because these alone, in the absence of additional proofs, seem to him to suggest with some vividness that the formulations of the Christian Church are not meaningless. In the *Proslogion* Anselm succeeded in constructing what he assumed to be a more effective proof for God's existence than the proofs expounded in the *Monologion*. But in *De Incarnatione* and *De Processione* he could not improve upon the *Monologion*'s demonstration of God's triune nature. So he presupposes the *Monologion* proof of triunity and goes on to analyze the concept of the divine nature in relation to the concept of the divine persons. He seeks, therefore, to prove that tritheism and simultaneous incarnation are false by setting forth a clear *explication* of orthodox teachings and by showing that neither of the two heresies is implied by orthodoxy — as Roscelin wrongly thought. Because Anselm does not have a further *metaphysical* proof of God as triunity, along the lines of the *Monologion* proof, he elaborates upon *Monologion* 43 in the attempt to exhibit to Roscelin and those "heretics of dialectic" the internal consistency of the orthodox profession of *una substantia, tres personae*.

DE PROCESSIONE SPIRITUS SANCTI

In *De Processione* Anselm continues to refine the distinction between the indivisible unity and the incompatible diversity in the Trinity. Turning to contend with the Greeks, he tries to establish that the Holy Spirit proceeds from the Son as well as from the Father. After the amended phrase *qui ex Patre Filioque procedit* became part of the Latin version of the Nicene-Constantinople Creed, the renowned *filioque* controversy had never ceased to be a divisive theological issue between East and West. Anselm thinks that from the trinitarian views which Greeks and Latins hold in common, he can deduce the doctrine of procession from the Son, and thereby explain why the Latins added its statement to the Creed. *De Processione*, therefore, begins with a summary of these common views. Here Anselm does not have to ward off tritheism or "Sabellianism," or to worry about the distinction between begottenness and procession. For the Greeks confess fundamentally the same thing as the Latins. Throughout the treatise Anselm distinguishes two basic expressions: (1) "God from whom God exists" and (2) "God from God." These expressions are used to distinguish the persons of God from one another. The Father is uniquely characterized because He is *1* but not *2*, the Son because He is *1* and *2*, the Holy Spirit because He is not *1* but *2*. That is, God the Father is "God from whom God exists" because the Son is begotten from Him and because the Holy Spirit proceeds from Him; He is not "God from God," since He neither proceeds nor is begotten. God the Son is "God from God" since He is begotten; and He is "God from whom God exists" since the Holy Spirit proceeds also from Him. God the Holy Spirit is "God from God" since He proceeds from the Father and the Son; but He is not "God from whom God exists," since neither the Son nor the Father proceeds from Him or is begotten from Him.[30] On this basis, the persons of God must be plural since their differing properties prevent their being identical. The Father cannot be the Son or the Son the Father since the one from whom another exists cannot be that other who exists from Him[31] — the principle appropriated from *Monologion* 43. Unlike Roscelin, the Greeks see that this plurality does not jeopardize God's essential indivisibility. Anselm may therefore turn immediately to the question occasioning the treatise.

Does the Holy Spirit exist from the Son? It is clear to the Greeks that both the Son and the Holy Spirit exist from the Father in differing ways. The Holy Spirit exists from God who is Father, whereas the Son exists from God who is *His* Father.[32] This difference embodies the distinction between procession and begottenness (Ch. 1. S II, 179:1–3). Now if the Holy Spirit exists also from the Son, then it must be by procession, since, according to *De Incarnatione*, it is unfitting to suppose that the Holy Spirit would be begotten from the Son and thus be the Son's son as the Son is the Father's son.[33] But does the Holy Spirit proceed at all from the Son? In affirming that He does, Anselm adopts a twofold course: first, to maintain that "either the Holy Spirit exists from the Son or else the

30. Ch. 1 (S II, 182:17ff). Cf. Ch. 15 (S II, 216:2ff).

31. This is also Augustine's principle in DT 1.4.7.

32. Augustine: The Father is not father of the Holy Spirit but only of the Son. DT 7.4.7.

33. Note Augustine, *On the Gospel of John* 99.9; DT 5.14.15: the Holy Spirit is not begotten, because then He would be a son; rather He is sent; i.e., He proceeds.

Son exists from the Holy Spirit"; and secondly, to block the latter alternative by showing that the Son cannot exist from the Holy Spirit.

If the Holy Spirit exists from the essence of the Father, then, since Father and Son are one in essence, the Holy Spirit exists also from the Son (unless some relationship in the persons opposes this). Likewise, if the Son exists from the essence of the Father, then, since the Father and the Holy Spirit are the same essence, the Son exists also from the Holy Spirit (unless some relationship in the persons opposes this). But, as the Greeks concede, both the Holy Spirit and the Son exist from the essence of the Father. This fact would seem to necessitate the conclusion that "both the Son exists from the Holy Spirit and the Holy Spirit exists from the Son." But this conclusion is impossible (because A's origin from B precludes B's origin from A). Therefore, because of this opposition of relations, either the Holy Spirit must exist from the Son or the Son from the Holy Spirit (Ch. 1. S II, 183:15–29).

The Greeks, still wanting to repudiate the disjunction above, may possibly claim that Anselm's argument raises an internal difficulty for the Christian faith.

Suppose that since the Father and the Holy Spirit are one God, and since the Son exists from the Father, it follows that the Son also exists from the Holy Spirit; or suppose that since the Father and the Son are one and the same God, and since the Holy Spirit exists from the Father, it follows that the Holy Spirit also exists from the Son. If the Father begets the Son, the Father must also beget the Holy Spirit — since the Son and the Holy Spirit are one and the same God. And if the Holy Spirit proceeds from the Father, then because the Son and the Holy Spirit have the same unity of deity, the Son also proceeds from the Father in the same way as the Holy Spirit. But if the unity of God in the Son and Holy Spirit does not lead us to conclude that each is begotten by or proceeds from the Father in the same way, then it seems that from the fact of the Father and the Holy Spirit's being one God it does not follow that the Son exists from the Holy Spirit, or that from the fact of the Father and the Son's being one God it does not follow that the Holy Spirit exists from the Son . . . (Ch. 1. S II, 184:16–185:1).

The Greeks, accordingly, seek to disqualify Anselm's argument by maintaining that either it implies abrogating the distinction between begottenness and procession or else it does not imply that the Holy Spirit proceeds also from the Son. Anselm counters by denying that his argument could possibly entail fusing the distinction between begottenness and procession. The unity of essence in God is never able to interfere with the plurality of persons. Hence, this unity, as posited by Anselm's argument, cannot entail conflating begottenness and procession, since such conflation would confuse the persons of the Son and the Holy Spirit. Consequently, this further implication which the Greeks extract from Anselm's initial argument must itself be illicit. The Son and the Holy Spirit are distinct from each other because the former is begotten, whereas the latter proceeds. If both proceeded from the Father or if both were begotten by the Father (without the Holy Spirit existing from the Son or the Son from the Holy Spirit), then there would be no basis for their difference in person.

Having established to his satisfaction that "either the Holy Spirit exists from the Son or else the Son exists from the Holy Spirit," Anselm now contends that the Son does not exist from the Holy Spirit — neither as begotten by nor as proceeding from the Holy Spirit — and that consequently the Holy Spirit must exist from the Son. In particular, the Son is not begotten from the Holy Spirit because if He were, the Holy Spirit would be His father; but the Holy Spirit is not the Father. The Son does not proceed from the Holy Spirit because then He would be the spirit of the Holy Spirit; but the Holy Spirit is rather believed to be the spirit of the Son.[34] This second step completes Anselm's central argument in *De Processione*. He is satisfied that it effectively deduces the *filioque* doctrine from theological premises which are held in common by the Western and the Eastern churches. In the remainder of the treatise he defends this basic argument against other objections which (he hypothesizes) the Greeks might raise against it.

Six possible objections by the Greeks.

1. "The Holy Spirit does not exist from the essence of the Father." The Greeks may deny outright that the Holy Spirit is God from God, since the Nicene-Constantinople Creed nowhere uses this phrase for the Holy Spirit, but only for the Son. If they take this posture, then they will have no basis for distinguishing the Father and the Holy Spirit. The reason the Holy Spirit differs from the Father is that He exists from the Father (since the one who exists from another cannot be that other from whom he exists). In other words, that the Father has a son existing from Him while the Holy Spirit does not only

---

34. Ch. 1 (S II, 185:24-25). Here Anselm's argument is sustained by appeal to Scripture and the creeds rather than by *rationes necessariae*. Cf. Ch. 2, pp. 38, 49.

shows that the Father and the Holy Spirit are two persons; it is not the reason for their being two persons, says Anselm (Ch. 2. S II, 186:9–18). Because they are two persons nothing prohibits the one from having a son and the other from not having a son; yet having or not having a son does not make them two persons. By the same token, the Holy Spirit is not a different person from the Father simply because He proceeds from another, whereas the Father does not — or simply because He does not have a spirit existing from Him, whereas the Father does. Even if the Father did proceed from someone else, and even if the Holy Spirit did have a son and a spirit existing from Him, the Father and the Holy Spirit would still be different persons.

Moreover, if the Holy Spirit is not God from God, then the fact that He is the *spirit of the Father* would not *make* Him distinct from the Father. Rather, His being *of the Father* would *presuppose* that He is distinct from the Father. "For example, when one man is said to be the lord of another man or the vassal (*homo*) of another man, his being the other's lord or vassal presupposes that the two men are distinct. Likewise, then, even if the Holy Spirit did not exist from the Father, His being distinct from the Father would be logically prior to His being *of the Father*. Therefore, the fact that He is the spirit of the Father could not be the *reason* for His being distinct from the Father . . ." (Ch. 2. S II, 187:9–14).

Finally, the Greeks may allege that the Holy Spirit can proceed from the Father without existing from the Father, and that this procession suffices to differentiate Him from the Father (Ch. 2 S II, 188:8ff). In that case, they are thinking of procession as the Holy Spirit's being sent or being given by the Father (John 14:26). But the Son also gives and sends the Holy Spirit (John 15:26), so that, even on this account, the Holy Spirit must proceed also from the Son. Furthermore, the Holy Spirit is sent only to the creature; but He was different from the Father even before there was an existent creature. Hence, His procession cannot consist merely in His being sent, but must involve His existence from the Father.

2. *"The Holy Spirit exists from God because He exists from the Father."* If the Greeks are willing to acknowledge that the Holy Spirit is God from God, something which the Creed does not state, then they should not hesitate to confess that the Holy Spirit proceeds from the Son — provided their sole basis for this hesitation is the absence of this statement

from the Creed (Ch. 2. S II, 189:17–22). But they seem to think, observes Anselm, that the Holy Spirit's being God from God is deducible from the Creed whereas the Holy Spirit's procession from the Son is not. On their view, the Creed's statement that the Holy Spirit proceeds from the Father implies the further statement that the Holy Spirit exists from the Father as God from God; but it does not imply the consequence that the Holy Spirit exists also from the Son. By contrast, Anselm affirms that both doctrines are equally derivable. For the Holy Spirit's proceeding from the Father must be understood in either of two ways: The Holy Spirit is from the Father because He is from God, or the Holy Spirit is from God because He is from the Father. If in the second way, "then when it is said that He exists from the Father, we must not understand that He exists from that in virtue of which the Father is God, i.e., from the divine essence. Rather, we must understand that He exists from that in virtue of which God is the Father, i.e., from that in virtue of which He is referred to the Son. And then the divine essence in the Holy Spirit will not be from the deity of the Father but only from the relation of the Father. But this is very foolish" (Ch. 2. S II, 190:3–7).

For this reason, concludes Anselm, the Holy Spirit must be from the Father because He is from God, as the first alternative states; and therefore because the Holy Spirit exists from the Father insofar as the Father is God, He must also exist from the Son — as has already been established. But even if the second alternative were to hold, it would still follow that the Holy Spirit exists from Father and Son alike. For the relationship of father cannot be separated from the relationship of son; so if the Holy Spirit exists from God-as-Father, He must also exist from God-as-Son (Ch. 2. S II, 190:8–19). Thus, since the Creed's statement that the Holy Spirit proceeds from the Father implies that He exists from the Father insofar as the Father is God, it likewise implies that He exists from the Son.

3. *"Scripture does not confirm the Latin view."* Since Scripture nowhere teaches the *filioque* doctrine, the Greeks could claim that there is no justification for having changed the Creed. But Anselm reminds them that Scripture's silence is not tantamount to Scripture's denial of this doctrine. Although Scripture does not say explicitly that the one God exists in three persons [35] or use the phrase "God from God," no one (among the Greeks) would suppose that Scripture precludes these credal utter-

35. Augustine makes this point in DT 7.4.8.

ances (Ch. 11. S II, 209:9–16). Scripture teaches things from which the *filioque* doctrine follows directly. For instance, in the fourth Gospel Jesus speaks of His sending the Holy Spirit from the Father (John 15:26), and the Father is said to send the Holy Spirit in Jesus' name (John 14:26). Now, if the Holy Spirit is sent from the Father, He is therefore sent by the Father; and if He is sent from the Father by the Son, then the sending of the Holy Spirit by the Father is identical with His being sent by the Son. And this accords with what we should expect, indicates Anselm, since the Father and the Son are one God (Ch. 4. S II, 191:15–192:27). Furthermore, in giving His own spirit to the Son,[36] the Father did not give what the Son at any time was lacking. The Son does not receive the Holy Spirit from the Father: He receives the essence from which the Holy Spirit proceeds. Thus, as the Son owes His existence to the Father, so He owes to the Father His having a spirit proceeding from Himself.[37]

Another example of how Anselm deduces the *filioque* doctrine from Scripture may be seen in Matthew 11:27: "No one knows the Son except the Father, nor does anyone know the Father except the Son and anyone to whom the Son chooses to reveal Him." Now, the Holy Spirit must have knowledge of the Father and the Son, since otherwise He would be less than they and therefore not God. So then, He has this knowledge either because the Son reveals it to Him, or else because He is one essence with them and, accordingly, shares their knowledge.

So if the Greeks choose the first alternative, which asserts that the Holy Spirit knows the Father and the Son through the revelation of the Son, then the Holy Spirit has this knowledge from the Son, and this is the same as for Him to have existence from the Son. Therefore, the Holy Spirit exists and proceeds from the Son, since He proceeds from the one from whom He exists. And if they choose the second alternative, they assert that when the Father and the Son are said to know themselves, the essence through which they know themselves is the same for the Holy Spirit, so that the Holy Spirit shares the same knowledge. Hence when they read that the Holy Spirit proceeds from the Father, about whom the Son says "I and the Father are one" (John 10:30), then let them confess with us that because of the essential identity of Father and Son, the

36. Cf. John 5:26: "Just as the Father has life in Himself, so He gives to the Son to have life in Himself."

37. DP 14 (S II, 213:27–29). Note Augustine, DT 15.26.47; *On the Gospel of John* 99.8.

Holy Spirit also doubtlessly proceeds from the Son (Ch. 7. S II, 199:15–23).

These two examples from Scripture — John 15:26 and Matthew 11:27 — support Anselm's claim that instead of opposing the *filioque* doctrine, Scripture implicitly confirms it, since it teaches those things from which the doctrine of procession from the Son logically follows. Therefore, as the position of the Eastern Church has no basis in reason, so it also has no basis in revelation. Anselm therefore calls upon the Greeks to join with the Latins in a common confession.

4. *"The Greek view is supported by an analogy."* The Greeks might attempt to uphold their view by invoking the analogy of heat and brightness existing simultaneously from the sun. The heat does not exist from the brightness, or the brightness from the heat. In the same way, it is fitting to speak of the Son and the Holy Spirit as existing equally from the Father, so that neither the Son nor the Holy Spirit exists from the other. If the Greeks were to adopt this comparison, it would be in order to offset the impression that the *filioque* doctrine posits intervals in eternity (Ch. 8. S II, 199:25–31). For if the Holy Spirit proceeds from the Son, think they, He can only do so after the Son has been begotten from the Father. Yet the idea of there being intervals in eternity is unacceptable — as is then the Latin view.

In *De Incarnatione* Anselm has already commented on the notion of eternity.[38] In *De Processione* he refers to this earlier discussion without taking up the topic again at length (Ch. 16. S II, 218:8–21). He is content merely to deny that the Latin view involves the consequence ascribed to it by the Greeks and, additionally, to fault the comparison they set forth. "When we say that the Son and the Holy Spirit both exist from the Father, we confess that God the Son and God the Holy Spirit both exist from God the Father; and we confess that these three persons are one God, and that this very God exists from Himself. But in the case of the sun, we do not say that the sun exists from the sun when brightness and heat exist from the sun; nor do we say that the brightness and heat which exist from the sun are also the sun; nor that the three are one sun" (Ch. 8. S II, 200:16–21). Moreover, if the Son and the Holy Spirit existed equally from the Father as brightness and heat exist equally from the sun, then there would be no basis for calling the Holy Spirit the spirit

38. DIV 15. In DT 15.26.45 Augustine also rejects the notion that there are intervals of time in the Trinity.

of the Son instead of calling the Son the son of the Holy Spirit. For there is no more reason to term brightness "the heat's brightness" than to term heat "the brightness' heat." Thus, Anselm purports to expose the deficiency of the analogy which the Greeks are conjectured to put forth as a stepping-stone toward understanding the relation of persons in the Trinity. He sees too, but does not mention, that if the Holy Spirit's procession from the Father and the Son posits intervals in eternity, then the Son's begottenness from the Father would itself already have posited such an interval. But as the Son's begottenness is eternal and ungraded, so the Holy Spirit's procession is also eternal and ungraded, irrespective of whether it is procession from the Father alone or from the Father together with the Son.

In disagreeing with the Greeks' possible appeal to the heat-brightness analogy, Anselm is at the same time rejecting Augustine's actual recourse to this example: "In fire we behold a certain threeness: the fire, the brightness, the heat. And although these are three, they are one light. They arise together and continue together. The fire does not precede the brightness, nor the brightness the heat. They are neither confusedly one nor separately three. Yet they are both one and three." [39] That Anselm knew this analogy to be Augustine's is confirmed by a letter from John the Monk (#128), where the reference to Augustine is explicit.[40] While rejecting this particular analogy, Anselm opts for another of Augustine's comparisons — the one with water.[41]

    5. "The Holy Spirit proceeds per filium." If the Greeks contend that the Holy Spirit proceeds *per filium* (through the Son) instead of *a filio* (from the Son), it is not clear exactly what they are claiming. They may be thinking of Romans 11:36, which states about God that "all things are from Him, through Him, and in Him." [42] If they construe "all

39. *Sermon on the Creed (for the Catechumens)* 9.9 (PL 40:659). Cf. *Free Choice* 2.11.32.

40. John writes: "But St. Augustine's comparison of trinity and unity with the sun (which although one thing is nevertheless also heat and brightness inseparably) thoroughly opposes [Roscelin's] comparison of trinity and identity with three angels and three souls." S III, 271:13–16.

41. See n. 29, p. 107. In DP 14 Anselm allows, as does Augustine, a sense in which the Holy Spirit proceeds *principally* from the Father. But neither he nor Augustine construe this sense as denying that the Holy Spirit proceeds from the essence of the Father and Son. Note DT 15.17.29; Sermon 71.16.26 (PL 38:459).

42. Anselm neglects to mention here I Cor. 8:6: "But to us there is but one God, of

things" to refer to all created things, then Anselm agrees that all things are from the Father, through the Son, and in the Holy Spirit. However, if they include the Holy Spirit Himself in the designation "all things," then Anselm rejects their exegesis as entailing a confusion of the three persons. For if the Holy Spirit is included in the designation "all things," then so too are the Father and the Son.

At this point Anselm must be viewed as being concerned with the terminology used to express the Holy Spirit's procession. In this way he reflects the earlier efforts of the patristic Church to crystallize its theological doctrines into dogmas. Never regarding the terminological question as important for its own sake, he refuses to quibble about verbal distinctions where they involve no conceptual distinction. In the present instance, he sees no conceptual difference between saying *a filio* and *per filium*. Since the Father and the Son have the same essence, then if the Holy Spirit proceeds *from* the deity of the Father and *through* the deity of the Son, how can He not proceed *from* the deity of the Son? Anselm views the two expressions as not importantly differing from each other. Even if Romans 11:36 meant that the Holy Spirit existed from the Father through the Son, there would be no basis in Scripture for a real distinction between *a filio* and *per filium*. For Scripture also teaches that "Whatever the Father does, this the Son does likewise" (John 5:19). So then, what was created by the Father through the Son may also be said to have been created by the Son. And likewise, the Holy Spirit, who proceeds from the Father through the Son, may also be said to proceed from the Son (Ch. 9. S II, 203:1–6). Anselm is thus willing to say *per filium* as long as he may also say *a filio*. Far from being contentious, he compliantly allows a range of expressions, none of which he feels to be completely adequate to describe the nature and persons of God. Yet he still thinks that the most satisfactory of these only partly adequate expressions are those decided upon by the earlier Church councils after vigorous disputation. For these very disputations forced the Church to refine the terminology with which it defined orthodoxy. Because such terminology has an established usage within orthodoxy, Anselm is hesitant to change it simply to please the Greeks — for fear, too, that the very change might confirm the Greeks in their misunderstanding. Anselm's flexibility extends to the point of allowing him to admit a sense in which the Son,

whom (*ex quo*) are all things, and we in Him; and one Lord Jesus Christ, through whom (*per quem*) are all things, and we through Him."

as well as the Holy Spirit, may be said to proceed from the Father (Ch. 9. S II, 204:17). But he continues to maintain the conceptual point that the Son proceeds in one way, the Holy Spirit in another.

Because the Greeks can find no basis in reason or in Scripture for an exclusivistic use of *per filium*, Anselm in no way concedes that *per filium* is incompatible with *filioque*. Rather, he reintroduces from *De Incarnatione* the example of the Nile to concretize the Western Church's terminology and doctrine of procession. Let the Greeks say that the Holy Spirit proceeds from the Father *through* the Son as a lake proceeds from a spring through a river. But then let them also say that the Holy Spirit is from the Son as well as through the Son; for a lake is from a river, even though it is from a spring through a river (Ch. 9. S II, 203:11–13). Anselm utilizes this analogy to supplant the heat-and-brightness analogy of the Greeks. In analogical terms he is able to repeat specifically the basic argument throughout *De Processione*: "Just as the lake does not exist from that in virtue of which the spring and the river are different from each other, but rather from the water which they have in common, so the Holy Spirit does not exist from that in virtue of which the Father and the Son are different from each other, but rather from the divine essence in which they are one" (Ch. 9. S II, 205:11–14).

6. *"The Holy Spirit cannot proceed from two sources."* If the Holy Spirit exists from both the Father and the Son, then He exists from two causes or sources (*principii*), the Greeks may assert. Anselm replies in accordance with his standard formula: the Holy Spirit does not exist from the Father and the Son insofar as they are different persons but insofar as they are one God. Therefore, the Holy Spirit, who is God from God, has only one source – if God may be said to have a source (Ch. 10. S II, 205:18–31). Accordingly, there is no discrepancy involved in affirming the doctrine of joint procession.

Concluding practical and metaphysical questions. Having stated and sustained his major argument on behalf of joint procession, Anselm now deals with the practical issue of why this doctrine should have been added to the Nicene-Constantinople Creed. Why should the Creed, confessed commonly with the Greeks, have been altered without consulting the Greeks? Are the Greeks not rightly offended? The Creed was supplemented, explains Anselm, because various individuals within the Church did not understand that this doctrine is implied by Scripture and is necessitated by reason. So that these individuals should not fail to confess that which is unfailingly true, the Latin Church incorporated the *filioque* doctrine into the Creed. That the Greek Church has become confused over this doctrine testifies to the need for public articulation. Moreover, at the time, it was extremely difficult to convene the Latin and the Greek bishops from such vast distances. And since the doctrine was undisputed in the Latin Church, there seemed to be no reason against its addition. Finally, the Latin Church exercises the prerogative of determining what is to be read and sung in its domain, so long as these words accord with right faith (Ch. 13. S II, 212:4–6). Anselm thus bears witness to the liturgical nature of the creeds. The Greeks have no grounds for taking offence at the liturgy of the Latin Church or with the dogmas contained in the liturgical forms. In particular, the doctrine of joint procession is above reproach since it follows from premises taught by Scripture and since Scripture nowhere teaches anything which either directly or by implication contradicts this doctrine.

Having dispensed with the practical question, Anselm now raises a final metaphysical issue: How can the Holy Spirit exist from the Father and the Son without being inferior to them? For in general it seems that if one thing exists from another, it must be dependent on, or subordinate to, or in some way less than, that other. Anselm's answer is the only answer possible for orthodoxy:

Just as the essence of God is quite different from created essence, so when we say that God exists from God by generation or procession, this generation or procession is to be understood quite differently from our speaking of things being born or proceeding from created things. For in God there is neither naturally nor temporally nor in any other sense anything either before or after, or greater or lesser; nor is there anything that God in any respect needs. But everything that God is, is not so much equal or similar to God and coeternal with God as it is identical with God Himself. For God is completely sufficient unto Himself, and there is nothing begotten and nothing proceeding from Him in the sense of something passing from not-being into being. . . . In God neither that which is born nor that which proceeds is different from that from which it is born or proceeds, namely, the one and only God. Therefore, just as the same God is not greater or lesser than Himself, so with respect to the three persons . . . no person is more or less what He is than the other two; and this conclusion still holds true even though God exists from God by generation and by procession (Ch. 14. S II, 214:12–215:4).

Anselm professes with the Church the dogma of eternal generation and eternal procession. Thereby he is able to maintain the economic subordination of the Son and the Holy Spirit without jeopardizing their equality to, and full deity with, the Father.

Anselm's doctrine of the Trinity is at every point orthodox. He propounds a theory which is opposed to monarchianism, subordinationism, and tritheism. Through Augustine he becomes aware of the distinction between *dictum secundum substantiam* and *dictum secundum relativum* as applied to God.[43] In terms of this distinction he sets forth more pointedly and coherently than Augustine an array of reasons buttressing the dogmas of the Western Church. Stated tersely in the *Monologion*, this fundamental distinction is developed further in *De Incarnatione* and is carried to its full conclusion in *De Processione*. In the *Monologion* Anselm confronts the skeptic; in *De Incarnatione*, Roscelin and tritheism; in *De Processione*, the Greeks and the *per filium* doctrine. This doctrine seems first to have been openly formulated by Gregory of Nyssa; it then became the standard affirmation of the East. The disputes that occasioned the councils of Soissons and Bari forced Anselm to cover much the same ground as did Augustine between 400 and 416 when he was preparing *On the Trinity*. Anselm unfolds Augustine's arguments, remodulates their emphases, and gears them to the problematics of his own intellectual and ecclesiastical situation. In this situation he seeks to do justice to the rational credibility, the historical continuity, and the Scriptural basis of Western orthodoxy. Although he does not succeed in proving the trinity of God to the skeptic, he does perfect the Church's self-understanding of its own witness through the creeds. Thus, while defending the emendation of the Nicene-Constantinople Creed, he is at the same time supporting the Athanasian Creed.

Given the philosophical, historical, and revelational presuppositions of Western orthodoxy, Anselm's discussion of the nature and the persons of God is as fine a statement as can be found. If his presentation fails to be thoroughly satisfying, the difficulty may lie in the presuppositions that generate and focus the questions which Anselm takes up. Or it may lie in the scope of the topic itself — a scope which, as Thomas was to assert more emphatically, transcends the very limits of human reason.

43. The trinitarian application of this distinction goes back at least as far as Gregory of Nyssa (334–394).

Doctrine of the Trinity

Yet what Boso asks of Anselm with regard to the incarnation is undoubtedly what Anselm is demanding of himself with regard to the Trinity: "I do not ask you to do what no man can do, but only to do as much as you can. For you will more easily persuade me that deeper reasons lie hidden in this matter if you show that you see some rationale in it than if by saying nothing you show that you do not understand it at all."[44]

44. CDH II, 16. Note Anselm's reference in DIV 16 to Augustine's having studied the doctrine of the Trinity carefully, but "through a glass darkly" (I Cor. 13:12). Cf. Augustine, DT 15.23.44.

Chapter *V*

Doctrine of Man, Freedom, and Evil

"Human nature was created in order that the whole man, i.e., body and soul, should one day enjoy a blessed immortality."[1] With these words Anselm expresses one aspect of the purpose underlying the creation of man, while at the same time disclaiming the view that the real man is the bodiless soul. God created man body and soul together; and He created him happy and just together. Because happiness and justice coincided, Adam's sense of well-being derived doubly from his relation to the world of nature and his relation to the Divine Nature. Adam was created to enjoy (*frui*) God,[2] in that he was to find delight in God's presence. His natural delight in God was itself to God's honor; and the receiving of this honor was itself a further end of creation. Nevertheless, God's purpose in creation was not selfish, since He did not receive honor at the expense of His creature's well-being and perfection but rather through this well-being and perfection. Anselm therefore examines human nature with an eye to its reflecting the image of God and with the intent of vindicating God against those who would make Him responsible for man's fall.

1. CDH preface (S II, 42:15–16).

2. CDH II, 1: "It ought not to be doubted that rational nature was created by God to be just, so that by enjoying Him it should be happy." S II, 97:4–5. Cf. Augustine, *Christian Doctrine* 1.22.20: "Among all these things, then, only those which we have cited as eternal and unchanging are to be enjoyed; other things are to be used . . ." PL 34:26.

Man, Freedom, and Evil

HUMAN NATURE AND TRUTH

Man as body and soul. Anselm's account of the body-soul relationship in man is not in general Platonistic. As early as the *Monologion* we read: "When a man is called a body and rational and man, these three things are not said in the same way, in the same respect. In one respect he is a body, in another rational; and neither of these constitutes the whole man." [3] The whole man, or "the whole of human nature," includes man's corporeal as well as his spiritual and rational nature. [4] For this reason, Anselm views Adam as created not only with an immortal body but also with an immortal soul. Bodily death came as a result of the Fall — and together with death came the corrupting influence which the body exerts on the soul. Although in various places Anselm defines man as "a rational, mortal animal," he makes it clear in the *Cur Deus Homo* that this definition applies only to fallen man. [5] There Anselm speaks of *veritas humanae naturae* (true human nature) as having been distorted by the Fall in such a way that Adam lost his conditional bodily immortality. [6] But a new immortality will be bestowed on Adam and all redeemed men in the next life; for "this corruptible must put on incorruption, and this mortal must put on immortality" (I Cor. 15:53). Augustine had already taken up this position against the Pelagians, who maintained that Adam's fall did not affect human nature as such but only Adam's person. Therefore, according to them, death was the natural condition of Adam before the Fall and was not a penalty of sin. In rejecting this view, Augustine distinguished Adam's original immortality from that future immortality which the redeemed shall possess. Adam was able not to die; the

3. Ch. 17 (S I, 31:27–30). Cf. *De Grammatico* (S I, 156:18–19): "*Man* signifies a substance with all the differentia which are in man — e.g., sensibility and mortality."

4. DCV 2 (S II, 141:15–16). Note also CDH I, 18 (S II, 81:23–27).

5. Cf. M 10 with CDH II, 11 (S II, 109:8–11): "I do not think that mortality belongs to the uncorrupted, but only to the corrupted, nature of man. Indeed, if man had never sinned and if his immortality had been established unchangeably, he would have been no less a true man. And when mortals rise again to incorruptibility, they will be nonetheless true men." See also CDH I, 9 (S II, 61:25–28); I, 22 (S II, 90:20–23); II, 2 (S II, 98: 10–11); II, 3. Note Boethius, *On Aristotle's Categories* (PL 64: 163); *On Cicero's Topics* (PL 64:1096). Cf. Augustine, DT 7.4.7; 15.7.11; *On Order* 2.11.31.

6. Cf. Rom. 5:12. Note R. Heinzmann, "Veritas humanae naturae. Ein Beitrag zur Anthropologie Anselms von Canterbury," in *Wahrheit und Verkündigung* (Munich, 1967), pp. 779–998.

redeemed shall not be able to die.[7] Accordingly, redeemed men shall be elevated to a state loftier than the original state of Adam — a state which he lost for himself and his descendants.

Augustine should not be thought of as consistently identifying the real man with the soul, and therefore as differing from Anselm.[8] Although Augustine in his early writings was surely influenced by neo-Platonism, he does not in his later works fail to identify human being with the *embodied* soul, thereby drawing a parallel with Christ: "As every man is a body and a rational soul in one person, so Christ is both Word and man in one person."[9] And this view, expressed in the *Enchiridion*, is the same view which Anselm puts forth in the *Cur Deus Homo*: "Therefore, since it is necessary that a God-man be found in whom both natures remain integral, it is no less necessary that these two integral natures be present in one person (just as a body and a rational soul are present in one man). Otherwise the same person could not be perfect God and perfect man."[10] Any attempt to drive a wedge between Augustine and Anselm on the question of the body's relationship to the soul cannot be defended. Augustine is perfectly clear in stating his view that the whole man (*totus homo*) is body and soul. The oft-cited passage in *Catholic and Manichean Ways of Life* does not suffice to show that Augustine, unlike Anselm, calls the soul alone the real man: "Body and soul are numerically two, and neither one alone could be called man (for the body would not be man if there were no soul; nor would the soul be man if it did not animate a body). Nevertheless, it might be the case that one of these alone can be considered and called man. . . . Yet it is difficult to settle this issue. . . . For whether both together or whether the soul by itself should receive the title *man*, the

7. Anselm repeats this statement in CDH I, 18 (S II, 80:14–16). Note also Augustine, *Incomplete Work against Julian* 1.96; 6.12 (PL 45:1112, 1522); *City of God* 22.30.3; DT 13.16.20; *Enchiridion* 28.105–106.

8. But note E. Gilson, *The Spirit of Mediaeval Philosophy* (London, 1936), pp. 168–188; R. Schwarz, "Die leib-seelische Existenz bei Aurelius Augustinus," *Philosophisches Jahrbuch*, 63 (1955), 323–360; R. O'Connell, *St. Augustine's Early Theory of Man* (Cambridge, Mass., 1968).

9. *Enchiridion*, Ch. 36 (PL 40:250). Cf. *Expositions of the Psalms* 37:11: "Wherever there is a whole man (*totus homo*) there is flesh and a soul." PL 36:402. The doctrine that a human nature comprises both a body and a soul is found everywhere in Augustine. E.g., *City of God* 14.5; DT 6.2.3; 7.4.7; 13.9.12; 13.20.25; *Confessions* 10.6; *On the Gospel of John* 19.15; 26.13; Ep. 137.3.11 (PL 33:520).

10. CDH II, 7 (S II, 102:17–21). Cf. the Quicumque: "For just as a man is a rational soul and a body, so Christ is God and a man."

highest good for man does not coincide with what is the highest good for the body. Rather, it coincides either with the highest good for the soul by itself or else with that of both body and soul together." [11]

Here Augustine is not *in vacuo* identifying the human being with the soul. He is suggesting that the soul is superior to the body with regard to its degree of perfection and that consequently the human being ought to be identified with his nobler component.[12] Moreover, Augustine is not disparaging the body (or the bodily state) as such, but only the corrupted body (or bodily state) which has resulted from the Fall. Adam in his fallen condition became victimized by his animal nature, so that he was beset by carnal desire. Anselm adopts this same theory in *De Conceptu* 2: "After sin, the body was like the bodies of brute animals – subject to corruption and carnal appetites; and the soul was infected with carnal feelings both because of the corruption of the body and its appetites, and because of the lack of the goods that the soul lost."

Neither Augustine nor Anselm embraces the doctrine that the soul's embodiment represents a punishment for a sin committed by the soul in a preexistent state, i.e., the doctrine that the Fall was a fall into corporeal incarceration.[13] To be sure, Augustine does refer to the mortal body as a prison – but he is quick to add that God did not create it a prison, and that for unfallen man it was no burden.[14] That the soul in this life uses (*utens*) an earthly body [15] and that in the next life it shall *rule over* an

---

11. 1.4.6 (PL 32:1313).

12. When Augustine uses *anima* to signify *homo*, he does so in the context of the (Latin) Old Testament, where this substitution is frequent. PL 34:517, 588. The use of these terms interchangeably does not in itself indicate Platonism. In another context Anselm testifies to this kind of substitution: "It seems to me that we should first ask why the sin by which the human race is condemned is more often and more particularly imputed to Adam than to Eve, although she sinned before Adam did, and he sinned because of her. . . . I think Scripture speaks this way because a union of two things often takes its name from the chief member of the union, just as a whole often takes its name from one of its parts." DCV 9.

13. Note Augustine, *The Soul and Its Origin* 1.12.15 (PL 44:482): "Nor do I support the third view, viz., that souls sinned before their embodiment, with the result that they deserved to be condemned to incarnation. Indeed, the Apostle very clearly taught that those who are not yet born have done nothing good and nothing evil" (Rom. 9:11).

14. *Expositions of the Psalms* 141.18. N.B. Both Anselm and Augustine are mindful of Wisdom 9:15: "For the corruptible body is a load upon the soul. . . ." Cf. Augustine, Ep. 131; DT 8.2.3; *Merits and the Remission of Sins* 2.10.12.

15. *Catholic and Manichean Ways of Life* 1.27.52.

incorruptible body indicate the superior nature of the soul.[16] Of course, if emphasis upon this superiority were to count as Platonism, then Augustine — and with him Anselm — would be Platonistic. But one dare not forget the other respect in which Augustine affirms clearly and repeatedly that the body itself belongs to the description of human nature.[17] Augustine takes the likeness of the body to a garment cloaking the soul more from Saint Paul than from Plato.[18] This notion of *vestimentum animae* should not be construed as invalidating the idea of a fundamental unity between body and soul. It is rather Augustine's way of pointing out that the body in its earthly form shall pass away, as shall the present form of the earth (cf. Heb. 1:11–12). But in the renewal at the end of history, the soul shall be clothed anew with an unchangeable garment, since the bodily state is essential to human being.

Augustine's mature philosophy of man should be called Platonistic, if at all, primarily because it tends to disparage bodily pleasure and the bodily appetites, and because it emphasizes the deleterious effects of the body on the soul. Yet Anselm's subsequent praise of the monastic virtues is simply the obverse side of Augustine's derogation of the sensual. In whatever way, then, that Augustine's final account of the body is really Platonistic, in that same way Anselm's view of man is Augustinian; for there is no important respect in which Anselm differs from Augustine on this topic.

Anselm and Augustine do argue for the immortality of the soul and do think of the interim state following physical death and preceding resurrection as a bodiless state. But this interim state is not the state of *totus homo*. Whereas the Fall damaged the human soul, it did not remove immortality from the soul as it did from the body. Anselm contends that it is unreasonable to consider the punishment for sin as entailing the death of the soul: "Before the soul existed it was not able to have guilt or to be aware of punishment. Therefore, if after despising the end for which it was made the soul were so to die that it did not experience anything or

16. Note Anselm, M 27: "The spirit is of more worth than the body." S I, 45:16–17. Cf. Augustine, *Free Choice* 2.18.48; 3.5.16; *Catholic and Manichean Ways of Life* 1.5.7.

17. *City of God* 1.13 (PL 41:27): "These bodies are not a mere external adornment or aid, but belong to human nature itself." Also DT 13.9.12 (PL 42:1023): "Faith promises . . . that the whole man — who certainly consists of a soul and a body — is going to be immortal."

18. II Cor. 5:1–4. Cf. Augustine, *Expositions of the Psalms* 101.14.

so that it were absolutely nothing, its condition would be the same in the case of greatest guilt as in the case of no guilt. Moreover, supremely wise Justice would not be discriminating between (1) what can do no good and wills no evil, and (2) what can do the greatest good but wills the greatest evil" (M 71). Anselm's line of thought is strange because it compares two states of not-being as if these were themselves conditions of the soul rather than the absence of all conditions. The other side of this argument is equally problematical and in a sense even begs the question. God is supposed to have created the soul intending for it to love Him forever. But the soul cannot do this unless it lives forever. Therefore, the soul was created immortal; and for the reason already given, this immortality could not (like the body's) have been conditional (M 69). The soul lives on, then, beyond the death of the body. In its intermediate bodiless existence it is neither the person (*persona*) nor the human being (*homo*; *humana natura*). If the soul is nevertheless the principle of the individual man, it is in the sense of constituting psychical identity between the person of the earthly man and that of the resurrected man.

Anselm nowhere utilizes Augustine's "proofs" of immortality. But the reason for this may be that he deals only minimally with the question of immortality and that he died before having written his projected treatise on the soul.[19] Anselm's notion of the body and soul as constituting *true* human nature is itself already in a sense Augustine's notion. For it was Augustine who interpreted for Anselm John 8:44, according to which Satan is said not to have remained in the truth when he fell. And it was Augustine who applied this same reasoning to Adam, so that the first man is viewed as having been created in the truth and in the likeness of Truth (God).[20] When we remember that it was from Augustine that Anselm learned to construe bodily death as a consequence of the fall from truth, it no longer seems strikingly unique that Anselm should characterize the relationship existing between body and soul before Adam's fall as *veritas humanae naturae*.

Status of universals. We have seen from Chapter I that Anselm's major argument for the eternity of truth is exactly Augustine's argument.[21]

19. Eadmer, *The Life of St. Anselm*, ed. R. W. Southern (London, 1962), p. 142.

20. *Expositions of the Psalms* 143.11 (PL 37:1863): "Nam quando [homo] est primum conditus, veritati similis factus est; sed quia peccavit, quia recepit digna, *vanitati similis factus est.*" Cf. *City of God* 14.4.1.

21. See p. 17.

Truth, for Augustine, whenever it is thought of as universal and eternal, is to be identified with God. And man's having been created *veritati similis* (in the likeness of truth) is identifiable with his having been created *in imagine Dei* (in the image of God). Augustine's procedure is to regard all universals as being within the mind of God. He thus follows Plotinus's interpretation of Plato — while remaining true to that principle expressed in the *Parmenides* whereby everything eternal is equated with everything most valuable; for what exists in the mind of God prior to creation is more valuable than creation itself. In *Eighty-Three Different Questions* 46.2 Augustine writes: "Certain archetypal ideas, forms, or reasons exist unchangeably in the Divine Mind" (PL 40:30). And this is effectively Anselm's position in *Monologion* 9. Since all things are created in accordance with their pattern in the Divine Mind, they accord with whatever they are in the Supreme Truth (i.e., in God). To this extent and in this respect they may be said to exist truly.[22]

In *De Incarnatione* 1 Anselm makes his most explicit statement on the theory of universals; yet this very statement is in many ways unhelpful in determining his actual position.

Certainly those dialecticians of our time (or rather, the "heretics of dialectic") who think that universal substances are mere words (*flatum vocis*), and who are not able to understand color as something different from a material object, or human wisdom as something different from the soul, ought to be blown right out of the discussion of spiritual questions. Indeed, in the souls of these men, reason — which ought to be the ruler and judge of all that is in man — is so covered over by corporeal images that it cannot extricate itself from them, and cannot distinguish from among them those things which ought to be considered purely and in isolation. For how can someone who does not yet understand how several men are one man in species comprehend how in that highest and most mysterious Nature several persons — each one of whom is perfect God — are one God? And how can someone whose mind is so dark that it cannot distinguish between his own horse and its color distinguish between the one God and His several relations? (S II, 9:21–10:9).

Nowhere in this extended passage does Anselm intimate that universal substances exist as eternal entities independently of the mind of God —

22. DV 7. Cf. M 5 (S I, 18:15): "Through the Supreme Nature all existing things are what they are. . . ." In M 31 Anselm notes that created things are the imperfect copy (*vix aliqua imitatio*) of the Word of God. Note Augustine's reference to eternal reasons in DT 9.6.9; 12.14.23.

the doctrine of Platonic realism.[23] Rather, the passage seems best interpreted in the light of Augustine's *On the Trinity*, Book 7. For there Augustine comments on the difference between a color and a material substance, such as a horse, in which the color, an accident, is present. There too appears a discussion about the soul in relation to wisdom, as well as a reference to several men being one man in species — topics presented as propaedeutic to understanding the doctrine of the three persons and the one nature in God.[24] So it seems that Anselm likewise is drawing attention to the difference between an individual substance (a man, a horse) and a universal substance (a species); and he is differentiating between a material quality (a color) and an immaterial quality (wisdom).

Now, it might seem prima facie that an important difference arises between Anselm and Augustine. For the latter expressly speaks of the soul as *participating* in wisdom, which is identified with the *substance* of God (DT 7.1.2). Were wisdom a *quality* in God, then God would have wisdom rather than be Wisdom. Moreover, continues Augustine, God would not be simple in nature since He would be a subject possessing attributes in such a way that the attributes would be really other than the subject (substance). Hence, in God wisdom is identical with the divine essence; accordingly, as the Son is the Wisdom of the Father, so He is the same essence (substance) as the Father. (And thus the Arians are wrong in teaching that the Son merely participates in the Father.) Augustine leaves no doubt that goodness, greatness, justice, eternity, omnipotence, omniscience, and truth are also identical with God's essence, and hence are not qualities of the Divine Nature.

By contrast, in the first chapter of the *Monologion* Anselm speaks of justice as a quality; and *Monologion* 16 extends this notion by suggesting that created things are just through *participation* in the *quality* of justice. Accordingly, on the interpretation in question, we may infer that for Anselm, unlike for Augustine, the soul is not regarded as partici-

23. M 27 (S I, 45:6-12): "Every substance is classified either as a universal, which is essentially common to many substances (as manhood is common to individual men), or else as a particular (*individua*), which has a universal essence in common with other particulars (as individual men have in common the fact that they are men). Accordingly, how could anyone understand the Supreme Nature to be contained in the same classification as other substances? For neither is it common to many substances nor does it share with any of them a [universal] essence."

24. DT 7.1.2; 7.4.7.

pating in God. In fact, it may be urged, Anselm's idea of participation is less Platonistic than Augustine's. For example, in *Monologion* 9 and 10, where Anselm acknowledges that there is an eternal exemplar in the mind of God, he does not refer at all to created objects' participation in God. Moreover, in *De Veritate* 2, where the Student maintains that "nothing is true except by its participation in truth," the Teacher does not himself adopt the language of participation. Instead, since Truth is identified with God, the Teacher prefers to conclude the entire dialogue by observing: "When some thing is in accordance with Supreme Truth (*secundum illam*), then we speak of the truth, or rightness, of that thing." The expression "in accordance with truth," continues the interpretation, replaces "participating in truth." Why Anselm prefers this replacement is presumably to avoid the appearance of pantheism. Perhaps talk about the soul's participation in God or in God's goodness, a la Augustine's *On the Gospel of John* 39.8 and Letter 120.4.19, conjured up in Anselm's vision something philosophically or theologically suspect. For there is no passage in Anselm which corresponds to *On the Trinity* 14.8.11, where Augustine declares that as a result of the Fall the unregenerate human mind (*mens*) has lost its participation in God while retaining a remnant of the image of God (PL 42:1044).

However, according to a second interpretation, the line of reasoning above draws too sharp a division between Anselm and Augustine vis-à-vis the doctrine of participation.[25] It is true that Anselm is not fond of the word *participatio*; nonetheless the *Monologion* abounds with the concept. For *Monologion* 16 makes clear that if something has a quality by participation, then it has that quality *per aliud* (through something else) rather than *per se* (through itself). And the passage seems to warrant the converse: if something has a quality *per aliud*, then it has it by participation.[26] According to the second interpretation, *Monologion* 16 shows that Anselm uses the phrase *per aliud* as a substitute for *participatio* — as a substitute for, not as an exclusion of. Consequently, when Anselm refers to justice as a quality, he is thinking of Augustine's catalogue of Aristotelian categories in *On the Trinity* 5.7.8, where the example of predication according to quality is the statement "He is white." In 7.1.2

25. Attention is drawn again to the controversy between F. S. Schmitt and K. Flasch in articles appearing respectively in ΛΛ I and II. The reader is cautioned that the two interpretations offered above correspond only roughly, and not exactly, to the positions of Schmitt and Flasch.

26. S. I, 30:9–11.

Augustine argues that wisdom (also supposed to come under the category of quality) is not like whiteness. For whiteness exists only in material objects which are colored white. If the objects change color, then whiteness will cease to exist. By contrast, wisdom does not cease to exist when the souls that once had it no longer retain it. Wisdom, insofar as it characterizes God rather than the soul, is not a quality but a substance — one and the same substance as God. Similarly, greatness (a quantitative notion) is not predicated of God other than substantially. God is not great, notes Augustine, by a greatness which He has from elsewhere (i.e., in which He participates). Rather, He is great by a greatness which He Himself is.[27] Thus, Augustine can summarize his view: "Let us understand God (if we are able, and as best we are able) to be good without quality, great without quantity, creator without need, ruling from no position, containing all things without Himself being shaped, wholly everywhere without place, everlasting without time, making mutable things without Himself changing, and Himself suffering nothing."[28]

According to this second interpretation, then, Anselm's view coincides exactly with Augustine's. For Anselm too identifies goodness and greatness with God's essence (M 17). Hence, God does not participate in goodness (or justice) as if it were a quality which He possessed. God *is* justice (M 16). Consequently, as the just man has justice but is not justice, so God is justice but does not have justice (M 16). "When someone asks what the Supreme Nature is, the answer 'He is justice' is as appropriate as the answer 'He is just.' The intellect is bound to perceive rationally that what we see to have been established in the case of justice also holds true for all the characteristics predicated similarly of the Supreme Nature." Anselm also points out that to think of justice or goodness (or greatness) as a quality (or a quantity) of God's nature would constitute a denial of the divine simplicity: "We accept nothing, then, as predicated truly of His essence with respect to quality or quantity but with respect [only] to what He is. For whatever is spoken of with respect to quality or quantity is still something else with respect to what it is. Hence, it is not simple but composite" (M 17. S I, 32:1-4).

If we need a passage which shows that Augustine no less than Anselm

27. "God is not great by a greatness which is not that which He Himself is so that (as it were) God, when great, is so by participation in this other greatness. For then this other greatness would be greater than God; but there is not anything which is greater than God. . . ." DT 5.10.11 (PL 42:918).

28. DT 5.1.2.

could envision participation as participation in qualities, then we need only look at *On the Trinity* 7.1.2 (PL 42:935): "If the Father, who begot Wisdom, were made wise from [participation in] that very Wisdom and if for Him to be were not the same as for Him to be wise, then the Son would be His *quality*, not His offspring, and so God would no longer be Supreme Simplicity." So then, in the opinion of both Augustine and Anselm, because God exists *per se* He does not participate in another, whereas other things have justice or goodness or truth as qualities, and so are thought to possess these *per deum* and thus in a reduced (and nonpantheistic) sense to participate in God, from whom they have their existence. Neither Augustine nor Anselm develops this theory further. For instance, neither discusses whether or not white things participate in a whiteness which exists as a form in the mind of God. Nevertheless, at precisely this point, Anselm introduces a second notion of participation. In *De Grammatico* he follows Boethius in treating a thing as participating in a quality which it has *and* as participating in the name which derives from the name of the quality.[29] A white thing has the quality whiteness, and therefore is said to participate in whiteness; moreover it participates in the name "white," which derives from the name "whiteness." But the fact that Anselm employs *participatio* in this Boethian sense does not take anything away from that use which corresponds to the Augustinian sense and to the doctrine of exemplarism. Also noteworthy is that in a letter to Lanfranc, newly consecrated as archbishop of Canterbury, Anselm introduces a third and nontechnical sense of *participatio*. There he refers to his prayer that Lanfranc's candle of wisdom and faith should be transferred to eternal participation in the divine light in company with the angels, after it has permanently given light to the English.[30] Interestingly, this prayer with this use of "participation" represents the very kind of statement that Augustine himself might be expected to have uttered.

In last analysis, Anselm does not appear in the *Monologion* to be di-

29. Note Boethius, *On Aristotle's Categories* (PL 64:167–168): "Hence, whenever some thing participates in another, this participation is given in the name as well as in the things, as when a certain man's participation in justice results in his being called 'just', the name thus reflecting the state of affairs. Hence those names are called 'paronyms' which differ from their root-name only by case-termination, i.e., by alteration only." Quoted from D. P. Henry, *The Logic of Saint Anselm*, pp. 62–63.

30. Ep. 1 (S III, 97:6–9). Note Augustine's use of "partaker of God" in *City of God* 22.30.3.

vesting himself of the Augustinian notion of participation; rather he seems to be supplementing it in *De Grammatico* by recourse to the Boethian linguistic construal. Had Anselm been averse to the Augustinian theory of participation, he would either not have introduced the Student's comment about participation (in *De Veritate* 2) or else, having introduced it, he would explicitly have taken exception to it. We must also keep in mind that in *Free Choice* 2.12.34 Augustine's argument claims that true judgments are made *according to truth* (*secundum illam*) and that here he does not lean upon the word "participation."

As for Anselm's leaving unmentioned in *Monologion* 1 Augustine's allusions to the good as impressed on the mind and the seeing of Goodness itself (DT 8.3.4), it is not obvious that he is passing over them because he disagrees with them. In *On the Trinity* 9.10.15 (PL 42:969) Augustine says that "everything which is known is called a word impressed on the mind (*verbum animo impressum*)" — a doctrine with which Anselm could have no quarrel. When Augustine thinks of justice (DT 14.15.21) or goodness (DT 8.3.4) as impressed upon the mind, he is thinking of these as a priori rather than empirical concepts — and hence as impressed other than by means of experience. It would be strange for Anselm to reject this feature of Augustinianism. Perhaps in *Monologion* 1 he does not mention *impressa notio* because it is not germane to the focus of his discussion. When we remember how unfocused *On the Trinity* is, it is not surprising that Anselm is highly selective in his borrowings from Augustine. For instance, he nowhere discusses Augustine's teachings about the inner and the outer man, a distinction that looms large in *On the Trinity*. Nor in the *Monologion* does he extensively examine epistemological issues of the kind that Augustine explored with regard to sight (DT 11.2.2). Anselm's logical mind and concise style did not permit him Augustine's ramifications.

Regarding Anselm's "failure" in *Monologion* 1 to mention seeing Goodness itself, we must remember that when Augustine uses the expression "seeing the Good itself," he means seeing with the "mind's eye" — that is, conceiving of Goodness itself (God). Now, with this construal Anselm *agrees*. In *Monologion* 1 he speaks of turning the *mind's eye* to investigating the source from which all goods are derived; and in *Monologion* 3 he argues that this source is the cause of every other good and is not itself good through another. When we compare *Monologion* 1 and 3 with *Reply to Gaunilo* 8, we recognize that Anselm teaches that the

human mind can conceive of (see) Goodness itself (i.e., supreme Goodness, Goodness *per se*, supreme Perfection) and that this Goodness must
exist, for the existence of things which *have* goodness (i.e., whose goodness is *per aliud*) requires the existence of that which *is* Goodness (i.e.,
whose goodness is *per se*). The difference between Anselm and Augustine is simply that Augustine does not furnish an argument for why one
thing's *having* goodness requires that another *be* Goodness. By contrast,
Anselm wants to spell out the necessity of this requirement. He therefore goes beyond Augustine. But in surpassing Augustine at this point,
Anselm is not repudiating the Platonistic requirement: he is simply arguing for it in a way in which Augustine did not. Thus, in *Monologion*
3 and 4, respectively, Anselm introduces two different proofs for the existence of a supremely excellent Nature. The first proof purports to establish the existence of one Being who in existing *per se* and in the highest degree is the cause of all other beings, and to infer that since these
other beings are good, they must derive their goodness as well as their
existence from this Supreme Being, who is also supreme Goodness.

The second proof assumes that a series of beings, each better than the
preceding, cannot continue infinitely, for the notion of an infinite series
of graded beings is (Anselm thinks) irrational. The reason, then, for
Anselm's not moving *directly* from contemplating good things to contemplating Goodness itself is *not* that he finds Augustine's approach too
Platonistic but rather that he wants to strengthen the approach by em-
ploying two ancillary arguments. And the appearance of these two arguments shows that unlike Augustine in *On the Trinity* 8.3.4–5, where
the *existence* of the Supreme Good is taken for granted, Anselm is trying to *prove* the existence of this unique Being. He therefore needs intermediate steps. Indeed, in *Proslogion* 24, where the discussion takes for
granted God's existence (because it was already "proved" in *Proslogion*
2), Anselm does move *directly* from reflecting upon the various goods
(*singula bona*) to reflecting upon "that Good which contains the joyful-
ness of all goods." And, again, in *Proslogion* 25 he proceeds equally directly: "O insignificant man, why do you then go from one good to
another in quest of what is good for your soul and good for your body?
Love the one Good in which are all goods, and it shall suffice you. Desire
the simple Good which itself is every good, and it shall be enough for
you." Only where the existence of God (e.g., M 3 and 4) or the conception of God (e.g., *Reply to Gaunilo* 8) is at issue does Anselm feel the

Man, Freedom, and Evil

need to be more explicit about *how* the mind, by reference to created goods, can arrive at a knowledge of the Supreme Good. (To possess this knowledge is to see God and to be illumined by divine light (P 14)). Indeed, Augustine himself — even though traveling a different route in *Free Choice* 2.15.39, where he takes up the question of proving God's existence — becomes equally explicit about the issue of *how* the knowledge of God is possible.

The truth of propositions. In *De Veritate* 1 (and *Monologion* 18) Anselm argues that a proposition [31] cannot be true unless truth exists. Moreover, since some propositions are never false, truth must always have existed and always be going to exist. In chapters 2 and 13 he explores an argument for the unity and independent existence of Truth (identified with God).

In general, Anselm regards truth as rightness: everything which is as it ought to be is right; and everything which is right is true. This formula enables him to speak of actions, for example, as true and false. Moral actions ought to be done, and thus are right and true; immoral actions ought not to be done, and thus are wrong and false. Yet, in another sense even immoral actions, he maintains, are right and true inasmuch as they ought to be done because they are *permitted* by God. Thus, an action can be right, or true, in two different senses. In the first sense, it is right if it is morally proper; in the second sense, it is right simply by virtue of being performed. Now, this theory seems strange to us because we are not ordinarily prepared to call *actions* true or false and because even were we to call them such, we would be inclined to do so in the first sense only. However, Anselm's notion of truth is so much broader than ours that he predicates "true" and "false" of whatever is as it ought to be.

According to him, then, a proposition is true when it is right. And being right has two senses which parallel the two senses for actions. On the one hand, a proposition is right when it signifies what is the case. (Signifying correctly parallels acting correctly.) On the other hand, a proposition is right when it signifies anything at all — that is, when it is meaningful. (Signifying anything at all parallels doing anything at all.) Thus, even when a proposition signifies what is *not* the case, it retains a

31. On Anselm's use of *oratio, enuntiatio,* and *propositio,* see Ch. III, p. 75. Note Augustine, *Christian Doctrine* 2.35.53 (PL 34:60): "'Falsity' is defined by saying that the signification of a thing is false when the thing is not as it is signified to be. . . ."

residual truth by virtue of being meaningful. Anselm admits that all of this may sound a bit strange. "It is rather unusual to call a proposition true when it signifies that something exists which does not exist; nevertheless, such a sentence has a certain truth and correctness, for it signifies as it should *in one respect*. But when a sentence signifies that something exists which does, in fact, exist, it functions as it should *in two respects*: for it signifies (1) in accordance with its power of signifying and (2) in accordance with the purpose for which it has its power of signifying" (DV 2).

In part, Anselm is following Aristotle, who taught that contingent propositions may change their truth values. "Socrates is sitting" is true as long as Socrates is sitting. It becomes false when Socrates rises. Adopting this theory, Anselm also accepts the view that a proposition is true by virtue of according with the way things are. (*Enuntiat quemadmodum res est.*) However, he goes beyond Aristotle by defining a sense of "truth" which a proposition does not lose when the corresponding state of affairs changes. For were it to lose this truth, it would no longer be a proposition, since it would have lost its nature. So, then, even when a proposition no longer corresponds to what is the case, it retains a natural, or residual, rightness.

Anselm now argues that the natural rightness in propositions is one and the same as the natural rightness in actions, in wills, in thoughts, in perceptions, and in the essences of all things.

Teacher. I mean that if the rightness which is in signification [i.e., correctness] were different from the rightness which is in the will [i.e., uprightness] simply because the former rightness is in the signification and the latter in the will, then the former rightness would owe its existence to signification and would be changed in accordance with it.

Student. But isn't this the case? For when a sign signifies the existence of what does exist or the non-existence of what does not exist, then its signification is correct, and it is evident that the correctness exists without which the signification could not be correct. But if a sign signifies the existence of what does not exist, or the non-existence of what does exist, or if it signifies nothing at all, then there will be no correctness of signification, since that correctness could only be in the signification itself. Hence, this correctness has its existence through the signification and changes with it — just as color has its existence or non-existence through a material object. For as long as a material object exists it is necessary that its color exist, but when a material object perishes, it is impossible for its color to remain (DV 13. S I, 197: 16–27).

But the teacher rejects the comparison between correctness and color on the ground that correctness is not dependent on a proposition.[32] Although one type of correctness perishes when a proposition is false, correctness itself, which is common to its many types, does not perish; for if it did, the proposition could not retain its natural truth. Now, however strange this argument may appear, it is Anselm's way of dealing with truth in relation to propositions. By defining truth as "rightness perceptible only to the mind," he is able to maintain that truth, as immaterial, is one and is common to all those things which are as they ought to be. Indeed, truth exists independently of the things which are true.[33] And since some propositions are always true, this independent truth, which is a cause of the truth of these true propositions, is also eternal.[34]

Perception and language. We have seen in Chapter I that Anselm thinks of the senses as reliably conveying information to the soul in accordance with their natural abilities.[35] Perceptual error results from the soul's misjudgment of the sensations it receives through the body. Anselm attempts to explain simple perceptual errors such as our looking at an object through a sheet of glass and mistakenly believing that the object rather than the glass has a given color. His theory is straightforward enough:

When sight passes through a body which has the color of air, it is no more prevented from receiving the likeness of the color it sees beyond the glass than when it passes through the air. And this is always the case except insofar as the body it passes through is denser or darker than air. . . . When sight passes through some other color (for example, through tinted glass), it receives the color which it first encounters. Thus, having received and been modified by the color of the medium, either it receives

32. This comparison is reminiscent of Augustine's comparison between a color and wisdom in DT 7.1.2.

33. "Now time, when considered in itself, is not called the time of any particular thing; but when we consider things which are in time, we say 'the time of this thing' or 'the time of that thing.' So too, Supreme Truth, subsisting in and of itself, is not the truth of any particular thing; but when some thing is in accordance with Supreme Truth, then we speak of the truth, or rightness, of that thing." DV 13 (S I, 199:25–29).

34. DV 10: "The truth of the proposition could not always be unless its cause always were. . . . Therefore, if it could never have been false that something was going to exist and if it could never be false that something has existed in the past, then it is impossible that the Supreme Truth could have had a beginning or could ever have had an end." S I, 190:21, 30–32.

35. See p. 21.

imperfectly whatever additional color it encounters, or else it doesn't receive it at all. Therefore, sight reports the color it apprehends first, and reports it to the inner sense either by itself or in combination with the color it apprehends subsequently. So if sight is modified by the first color up to its full capacity for receiving color, then it cannot at the same time sense an additional color (DV 6. S I, 184: 3–15).

In this way Anselm plausibly explains perceptual error without impugning the general reliability of the sense-faculty itself. The senses were bestowed by the Creator as instruments through which man could have veridical perceptual access to his environment.

From *Monologion* 33 and 62 we gather that, for Anselm, the soul perceives objects by way of images or likenesses conducted into the mind through the senses. These images are then stored in memory and may be recalled in the absence of the object itself. Anselm says no more about perception. He considers perceptual experience as providing the foundation for language; and he regards language as primarily an intricate system of *names* linked together according to rules which may be taught. In *Monologion* 32 he states that every word is a word representing something.[36] Yet he never loses sight of the flexibility of ordinary usage, which sanctions expressions that from the grammatical rigorist's point of view "ought not to be said."

The key to Anselm's view of language may be discerned from his statement in *De Casu Diaboli* 1: "We should not so much cling to inappropriate words which conceal the truth, as we should seek to discover the genuine truth hidden under the many types of expression." Anselm's interest lies on the side of semantic communication even though he actually gives more weight to the formal features embodied in grammatical rules. In *De Grammatico* these formal considerations lead him into semantical nonsense; but he does not for that reason renounce them.[37] From Anselm's perspective on grammar, an expression may be either proper or improper. To take one of his standard examples: "Just as someone is said to cause something, though not himself directly causing it but rather causing another to do it . . . so a man is said to be under obligation, though not himself owing anything, but being (in a certain manner) the cause of someone else's having an obligation. After this

36. "Nempe omne verbum alicuius rei verbum est." S I, 50:20. But cf. his discussion of *nihil* in DCD.

37. See D. P. Henry's superbly clear translation and analysis of *De Grammatico* (Notre Dame, Ind., 1964).

same fashion we say that the poor ought to receive from the rich, although the poor have no obligation, but rather the rich. That the poor are in need is the reason (cause) for the rich being obliged to expend money." [38] In this example, Anselm terms it proper to say "The rich ought to give" and improper to say "The poor ought to receive." But since we use the latter expression as an alternate for the former, no confusion arises. Wherever an improper statement can be translated equivalently into its proper counterpart, Anselm sanctions its use. He insists only on the possibility of such translation and does not demand that ordinary discourse be changed to accommodate the grammatical difference.

In other places Anselm points out special characteristics of theological language. For instance, Scripture sometimes speaks as if actions occurring through free choice were necessary (DC I, 5), and sometimes speaks as if a thing were already accomplished when in fact it is yet to be accomplished (DCV 7). Moreover, God is said to be impassible and, at the same time, to have compassion (P 8). In dealing with these and other theological considerations, Anselm exhibits an understanding of language which does not fail to take account of the multiple roles to which a given expression may be put. He shared the interest of his day in fostering the studies within the *trivium*. *De Grammatico* is fully intelligible only in the light of the eleventh century's desire to revive the exploration of *grammatica latina*. Concern with language dominates Anselm's doctrine of truth, inasmuch as he approaches the latter through the former. In turn, concern with truth dominates his philosophy of man, since the human mind is viewed as imitating the Divine Mind (M 32). Man is related to truth not only through his rational faculty but also through his volitional faculty. Insofar as the will wills rightly, truth may be said to be in it (cf. DV 4). Since Adam was created possessing an upright will, he was created "in the truth." Anselm's discussion of human nature now leads him to examine the freedom of will through which Adam could have chosen to remain steadfast in the truth.

FREEDOM OF CHOICE

Although the Old Testament declares that man was created in the image of God, it does not specify what this image consists in. Early church

38. PF 35.22 – 36.2. Cf. CDH II, 18, where the example also appears.

theologians considered the *imago Dei* to be reflected in man's rational and moral nature, since these natural features distinguish man from brute animals and at the same time liken him unto God. As rational, man has the capacity for both self-knowledge and knowledge of the Creator. As moral, he is capable of recognizing the obligations enjoined upon him by authority as well as by his own nature. Thus, a sense of obligation together with an ability to distinguish right from wrong belonged to Adam before he partook of the "tree of the knowledge of good and evil" — for otherwise, he would not have understood the meaning of the prohibition. A theologian like Augustine, therefore, construes the Genesis story not as depicting a fall from nonmorality into morality but as recording a falling away from morality into immorality. Adam's violation of the prohibition rendered his imagination susceptible to the solicitations of evil by destroying the original harmony between reason, the will, and the appetites. Out of harmony with himself and his Creator, Adam fell prey to the domination of his passions, so that his imagination voluntarily yielded up, and involuntarily yielded to, the delights of the flesh and the vaunting of pride. Having lost his original justice[39] and become a servant to sin (Rom. 6:17), Adam's very freedom seemed to Augustine to be threatened: "By evilly using his free choice, man destroyed himself and his free choice. For whoever kills himself does so through living; but through killing, he loses his life and cannot bring himself back to life once dead. Likewise, when man sinned through free choice, he lost free choice, and sin was his victor."[40]

But if freedom is a constituent part of the *imago Dei*, then even as the capacities for rational and moral discrimination were not completely lost to Adam, so free choice would also not have been totally lost to him. Therefore, in Adam, was freedom like rationality or was it like justice? If like rationality, then it belonged to Adam by nature and was characteristic of him after the Fall, even though in imperfect form. If like justice, then it belonged to him as a supernatural gift and was forfeited at the time of his fall. Moreover, if it was forfeited, then like original justice it is also lacking in all those who are descended from Adam, so that every member of the human race sins unfreely as a result of Adam's hav-

39. *Iustitia* is the Vulgate translation of δικαιοσύνη. Thus, in the context of the medieval Latin church, justice is always understood as righteousness. Anselm, in fact, defines "justice" as "uprightness of will kept for its own sake."

40. *Enchiridion* 30.9 (PL 40:246-247). Note Augustine's fuller position, pp. 156-157, below.

ing freely relinquished original righteousness. How would it then be just for God to punish human beings other than Adam for that which they do through no free choice of their own? Furthermore, irrespective of whether freedom is a natural possession or a supernatural gift, how could Adam himself have chosen freely, inasmuch as God foreknew how he would choose, and inasmuch as whatever is foreknown by God will necessarily occur as it is foreknown? Finally, in the case of the second Adam, viz., Jesus, how could He have freely chosen death, since His death is said to have been necessary, and how could He have freely avoided lying, since He is said to have been unable to lie? These puzzles were a major concern to the Church since they posed questions relevant to the doctrine of salvation. For without freedom a man can never be truly just; and without justice there is no hope of redemption. Anselm states that fallen man, like unfallen Adam, is always free; yet he rejects the Pelagian view that fallen man can actually perform works of justice which will merit him salvation. He interweaves these two themes on the basis of a special definition of "freedom." And this definition constitutes a unique contribution to the history of thought.

Definition of "freedom." Anselm tends to speak of *voluntas libera* (free will) and *arbitrium liberum* (free choice) interchangeably.[41] But he makes it clear that the right order is *libertas arbitrii rationalis voluntatis*: freedom of choice of a rational will.[42] By including the word "rational," he means to distinguish deliberative choice from mere appetitive inclinations. The appetites are in themselves neither good nor bad but become so when they are given expression at the wrong time, in the wrong place, for the wrong reason, and so on (cf. DCV 4). Thus, they ought always to be subordinate to the will, as the will should be subordinate to reason. In relation to reason the will is the faculty of *consent* whereby a person chooses to act upon certain of his desires. But the will itself is also an instrument of desire (*concupiscentia et desiderium*).[43] This fact makes it possible — even essential — to render Anselm's one Latin word *velle* by the English infinitives "to will," "to want," "to wish for," "to be willing." "To will" and "to be willing" convey more the notion of rational consent — whether actual consent or the disposition to

41. E.g., DC I, 6 (S II, 257:27).
42. DL 13 (S I, 225:24ff).
43. DCD 7 (S I, 245:1).

consent. "To want" and "to wish for," on the other hand, convey more the notion of desire. When Anselm speaks of free will, he is thinking of the will as that function of the soul which is responsible for choosing. But because "choosing to" and "wanting to" are complexly interrelated expressions, they tend to be conflated in the exclusive use of *velle*. Thus, as we shall see, Anselm has no use for the statement "I choose to, but I do not wish to."

In *De Concordia*, however, Anselm does take a step toward explicating the distinction between the actual and the dispositional notions of willing. For there he distinguishes three wills — or as we say, three different meanings of the word "will" (DC, III, 11). The *instrument* of willing is not the same as the *affection* and the *use* of this instrument (*voluntas instrumentum, voluntas affectio, voluntas usus*). The will as an instrument is a faculty of the soul, just as reason is a faculty of soul. In this sense of "will" a man is always said to have a will, whether or not he is actually *using* this will. Anselm introduces a comparison to help make this distinction. A person who is not blind is said to have the instrument, or the power, of sight, i.e., to be able to see. And even when he is standing in the dark, he is still said to have this power, though at the moment he cannot actually see anything, i.e., he cannot use his power of sight at all. We ascribe sight to him because we know that if light were present, he would be able to see all the various objects around him. By the same token, a man has the instrument of will even when he is not actually willing anything at all. For example, while he is sleeping, he still has the instrument of will, even though it is not being used. We attribute to him, asleep, not only an instrument of will but also a disposition to will. Thus, by *voluntas affectio* Anselm intends to indicate various dispositions, inclinations, or affections, in accordance with our saying that a person is willing to do X even when he is not thinking about doing X.

This usage occurs when we say that man always possesses the will for his own well-being. For here what we call will is the affection of that instrument by which a man wills well-being. In this way we say that a saint continually has the will to live justly, even when he is sleeping and not thinking about it. When we say that one person has more of the will to live justly than another person, the only will we are referring to is the affection of that instrument by which he wills to live justly. For the instrument is not greater in one person and less in another (DC III, 11. S II, 280:10–17).

The instrument of will has two primary affections — one by which it is disposed to will what is beneficial (*commoditas*) and another by which it is disposed to will uprightness (*rectitudo*).[44] The latter is lost to fallen man and can only be regained through the gift of God. The former is intrinsic to the human soul and therefore can never be lost. In terms of this inalienable affection, a man wills those things which he deems to be goods, whether earthly or heavenly. This is the sense in which Anselm in *Monologion* 1 argues that all men desire only what they suppose to be good (*bonum*). When a man chooses evil, he aims not at the evil itself but at the ephemeral good which he detects amidst the evil. Augustine himself had earlier stated that no man does wrong except with the desire to procure a good or to avoid a harm.[45]

These three *voluntates* correspond to what can be called the faculty of will, the volitions of this faculty, and the dispositions of this faculty. Having distinguished the three, Anselm is in a position to raise the question of the will's freedom. Now, a disposition or a set of inclinations is not ordinarily thought to be either free or unfree. Yet Anselm calls *voluntas affectio* free insofar as it is considered a will.[46] But he realizes that the general question of man's freedom is to be posed with respect to the instrument of will and its particular uses, or volitions. As if to reinforce this awareness, he prefers the expression "free choice" to "free will" and entitles his major work on this topic *De Libertate Arbitrii*.

Freedom of choice is, then, "the ability to keep uprightness of will for its own sake." On the basis of this definition Anselm constructs an entire theory. Freedom must be thought of as an ability because a man is free to choose X only if he is able to choose X; and his being-able analytically entails the attribution of an ability. In quest of a definition of the freedom which is common to God and man, Anselm refuses to view free choice as "the ability either to choose the good or not to choose the good"; for God cannot choose evil, and yet He must be conceived as free. Freedom is not, therefore, a mere neutral power, but rather the

44. By *commoditas* Anselm means those things which we ordinarily consider goods: e.g., life, health, pleasure. These goods are regarded as useful, or advantageous, in the sense of conducing to happiness. Anselm seems nowhere openly to appropriate Augustine's distinction between *fruor* and *utor*. Cf. Augustine, DT 10.10.13 (PL 42:981): "We enjoy things that we know; and the will rests in them, delighting in them for their own sakes. But we use things which are a means to something else which is to be enjoyed."

45. *City of God* 14.4.1 (PL 41:407).

46. DC III, 13 (S II, 287:8–12).

power of choosing rightly.[47] One might object that if freedom does not include the ability to choose evil, then Satan and Adam were not free when they chose to disobey God; for (according to Anselm) they could only have chosen evil through an ability to choose evil and not through an ability to choose the good. If they chose unfreely, they thereby chose necessarily. And if necessarily, then their act of choosing could not itself be blameworthy, even though their choice was in fact evil. Anselm responds by indicating that Satan and Adam "sinned through their own choice, which was free, and not through that by which it was free, namely, the ability not to sin and not to serve sin. Rather, they sinned by the ability they had for sinning, which neither helped them towards the freedom of not sinning nor compelled them into the service of sin" (DL 2. S I, 210:6–10).

Because Satan and Adam had the ability not to sin, they had free choice. Therefore, *any* choice they made, Anselm suggests, would have been made freely — even should it not have been made *through* this defining ability. Indeed, Anselm makes it logically impossible that the choice of evil should ever occur by means of the ability to choose the good. Satan and Adam chose freely not because they chose the good but because they could have done so — they were able to do so. And by definition anyone who has this ability is free, even on those occasions when he does not exercise his ability. According to Anselm, having the ability to sin is an accidental feature of free choice and as such implies having the ability not to sin; for to possess the accident of a nature is to possess the nature itself. But having the ability not to sin does not in itself imply having the ability to sin; for one may possess a nature without possessing every accident of which that nature admits. Therefore, Anselm can consistently maintain that God, who cannot sin, and Satan, who can, are both free with respect to their choices.

Yet in one way the distinction between these abilities appears prima facie strange. There seems to be something suspect about supposing that the ability to sin and the ability not to sin are two different abilities. A man who is able to kill another may do so in self-defense or in murder. In the one case he acts admissibly, in the other inadmissibly. But he exercises the same ability in both cases. That is, the description of the act changes, but the ability to act remains unchanged. However, there may

47. Augustine makes the same point with respect to God and to men who will have been confirmed in goodness in the next life. *City of God* 22.30.3.

144

be cases in which an ability changes when a description changes. Though a psychological anomaly, it is possible that an individual who perceives a situation as one of self-defense is able to kill, whereas the same individual in a situation perceived as murder is psychologically unable to kill. At any rate, Anselm does not resort to paradigmatic cases; he is making the conceptual and, as it were, definitional point that one does not choose evil through an ability to choose the good.

Extent of freedom. Anselm holds that a man *always* has the ability to keep uprightness of will. And he has this ability even on those occasions when he does not choose the good or even if he should never choose the good. Therefore, a man's choice is always free. If he does not choose the good, the reason is not that he is unable but rather that he is unwilling, i.e., he does not *use* his ability-for-choosing-the-good, but rather he *uses* his ability-for-choosing-evil. To illustrate this difference between ability and use Anselm invokes an example of physical capacity: "Suppose you know a man so strong that when he is holding a wild bull, the bull cannot get away. What if you should see the same man holding a ram, and see the ram shake himself loose from the man's hands: would you think the man less strong when he is holding a ram than when he is holding a bull?" And the Student responds: "I should think that his strength was the same in both cases, but that he didn't use his strength equally — for to hold a bull is harder than to hold a ram. The man is strong because he has strength, but his action is said to be strong because it is done in a strong way" (DL 7).

By comparison, a man may have the strength of will to vanquish temptation but may not use his strength of will against temptation. In such cases he yields to the allurement; but his yielding does not show that his will was unequal to the allurement but only that he did not exercise his will strongly enough. Thus, we find some men resisting a great temptation who later give in to a lesser one. And the explanation for this state of affairs must be grounded in the distinction between ability and use, thinks Anselm.

Someone may suppose that Anselm's distinction is unintelligible on the basis of the following argument:

Granted that the ability to resist temptation is the same as the ability to choose the good, why does a man ever fail to use his ability-to-resist-temptation? Is it because he is *unwilling to* or because he is *unable to*? If he is unable, then, you Anselm, are caught in a self-contradiction: a man has an ability which he is unable to use. If he is unwilling, then you are caught in a misleading circumlocution: a man is unwilling to use his ability to choose the good. This is a circumlocution because it does not differ from saying, simply, that the man is able to choose the good but does not want the good. It is misleading because it suggests that the man is "unwilling to use his ability," whereas in fact he is "unwilling to choose the good." [48]

Anselm might face this argument by adopting the second alternative: a man fails to use his ability simply because he does not will the good.[49] That is, Anselm may cut through the ensnaring circumlocution just as the argument against him does. He need not talk at all about being willing or unwilling to use an ability. A person is always able to will the good; and when he fails to, it is simply because he does not will to. And this "not willing to" is what Anselm means when he says that such a person does not exercise his ability.

But if "not using an ability with respect to X" means "able but not actually willing with respect to X," then Anselm must do two things: he must explain why, if each person is always able to will the good, any particular individual should ever fail to will the good (i.e., fail to use his ability with respect to the good); and he must abandon his example about the bull and the ram.

Anselm must give up his example because the man's "not using his ability" to hold down the ram is not identical with his "being able but not actually willing" to hold down the ram. On the contrary, the man is willing to but is not able to. At this point it becomes apparent that Anselm has not adequately analyzed the notion of "having an ability" and that his distinction between the possession and the use of an ability is not so clear after all. Anselm wants to say that the man has the ability but does not use it when confronting the ram. That the man does have the ability is known from his having been able to subdue the bull, which is stronger than the ram. But then why was he unsuccessful with the ram?

48. The argument is suggested by the following phrases: (a) ". . . quamdiu hac libertate voluerit uti" (DC I, 6. S II, 256:21–22); (b) ". . . sic tantummodo quando rectitudo illa nobis deest, tunc habemus illam impotentiam, quam facit nobis eius absentia" (DL 12. S I, 224:18–20). (c) ". . . est in servando vitam potestas volendi servare et potestas servandi" (CDH II, 16. S II, 120:21–22).
   N.B. Augustine's reference to free will using itself. *Free Choice* 2.19.51.

49. This move will ultimately force him back to the first alternative.

Clearly, because in some non-self-contradictory sense he was unable to use his strength, or ability, to hold down this weaker animal.

"Ability" sometimes indicates a skill, an aptitude, a residual strength, or a developed or native capacity. In this sense a sturdy man who without defeat repeatedly tests his physical power against that of a bull can justifiably be accredited with strength enough for a less difficult feat. Should he fail in the less difficult case, it does not follow that he lacks the capacity to succeed. (Indeed, if he were to attempt the same feat a second time, he might even triumph.) Some reason must be found for his failure. This reason, or set of reasons, will explain why *in this particular instance* he was unequal to the task even though *in general* he is superior to the task. And now such reasons as the following type become relevant: he slipped on a stone, his hands were moist, he didn't sleep well last night, his leg suddenly cramped up, he felt dizzy, or he was nervous. These reasons are sought in order to explain his present *inability*; for his willingness is not in question. Therefore, to say that he is able to do X is to say something both positive and negative. Positively, he has exhibited himself capable of repeatedly performing various tasks of specified difficulty, and this performance justifies our claim to know that he can perform tasks of lesser difficulty, provided no new skills are involved. (This claim holds independently of whether he ever does actually perform these lesser deeds.) Negatively, we must assume that the conditions under which he is seeking to perform X do not in some unusual way prevent him from exercising his ability, or even temporarily remove this ability from him (as in the case of sickness). Should some "extra" condition, c_i, interfere, then it will make sense to say of the man "He could have done X if c_i had not occurred." In other words, he was both able and unable to do X. In general, he was able; in particular he was unable. And this inability may be attributed to either environmental, physical, or mental factors.

By comparison, a morally disposed man may in general be able to resist a specified level of temptation. Yet it is conceivable that on a given occasion the very same level of temptation may prove stronger than the man's will. He struggles with himself and against the enticement. But in the end, because of his own momentary weakness, he is vanquished by the greater force of the temptation. This weakness constitutes a momentary inability of his will. Thus, to say that he has the ability to resist but does not *use* this ability is misleading; for at the very moment of choice, we want to say, his strength to resist is crippled. And this state of psychological incapacitation underlies our calling him unable. We may account for this passing inability by such reasons as the following: at the time, the man was slightly depressed; or he was overwrought and therefore more readily vulnerable; or he was experiencing extreme anxiety. (The belief that in every such case there are these reasons does not result from empirical findings. Rather, it embodies a methodological commitment toward viewing the world as intelligible.) Thus, the assertion that a man is "unable to use his ability" is neither a self-contradiction nor a redundancy. It is simply a way of speaking about a person's unexpected subperformance, or even nonperformance, in the light of certain types of intervening conditions. So then, Anselm must withdraw his example about the bull and the ram. He must do so since he is suggesting that in all cases where a person is overcome by temptation, he is overcome because he does not will more strongly, even though he is able to will more strongly. But the application of the example suggests a condition in which a person *cannot* will more strongly, regardless of how hard he should try.

The second thing Anselm must do is to explain why someone who can always will the good should ever will otherwise. He handles this problem by commenting on the relation between motivation and free choice, and by restricting the legitimacy of the question. He draws a sharp distinction between "ability to will X" and "motivation to will X." Only the former is intrinsic to freedom, since it alone enters into the definition of "free choice." In De Libertate 5 he considers the example of a man who is confronted with a forced option between telling a lie or being killed.[50] Now, this man is not free with respect to the situation thrust upon him, since he is unable to escape having to make a choice. That is, the choice-necessary situation arises against his will and represents a constraint imposed upon him. But within this broader constraint his choice either to tell a lie or to be killed is free; for he is able to do the one or the other in accordance with his preference. It is necessary that he "either lie or be killed." But it is not necessary for him to lie, since he can let himself be killed; and it is not necessary for him to let himself be killed, since he can tell a lie. He chooses whichever of the two he wants more. Anselm does not doubt that inducements guide a person's choice. He only refuses to concede that they overpower that choice and

50. Cf. DC I, 6 (S II, 257:5-27).

therefore render it unfree. Thus, if immediately before choosing, a person were to have a vision of the divine rewards and punishments contingent upon his choice, he would not fail, claims Anselm, to choose the rewarded alternative. For the prospect of the glorious reward would motivate him to choose in its favor.[51] God withholds this vision from men in order that they should choose not only the right object but also for the right reason. And a choice simply for the sake of a future reward is not, morally speaking, a sufficiently praiseworthy choice — since moral choice aims at willing the right end for its own sake. Indeed, a person's wants and preferences are not properly said to be free or unfree. In a loose sense they simply flow from his nature. Thus, maintains Anselm, it is natural for a man to be motivated generally by a desire for his own happiness and unnatural for him, even as fallen, to be motivated by a desire knowingly to kill God (i.e., the God-man).[52] The human will is naturally governed by these conditions. Yet the will of a man is free inasmuch as it has a given ability to choose the good, even when in fact the man does not resist temptation but, by yielding, chooses the wrong means for satisfying his natural desire for happiness.

Thus, Anselm's first way of answering the question why a man fails to choose the good (*bonum*) is to say: the man chooses a lesser good (*commodum*) which he thinks will bring him happiness; and this good, in being less than righteousness demands, is an evil.[53] This evil is chosen in accordance with the man's particular preferences and individual patterns of motivation. Yet, these preferences do not interfere with his ability to choose the greater good and therefore do not contravene his inherent freedom of will.

51. DL 9. Note also DC III, 9 (S II, 276:23–26): "In the Celestial City there will be no human procreation as there would have been in Paradise. So if converts to Christ immediately passed over into that state of incorruptibility, there would be no men left from among whom the perfect number could be gathered; for no one would be able to resist rushing for the happiness he would then see." Cf. *City of God* 13.4 (PL 41:379). Cf. DCD 23 (S I, 270:20–23): "Satan ought not to have had the knowledge that he would be punished if he sinned. For if he had known this, then even while willing and possessing happiness, he wouldn't have been able freely to will that thing which would make him wretched. And in such a case, he wouldn't have been just when he didn't will what he shouldn't, because he couldn't have willed it." This passage shows that Anselm is not always true to his sharp distinction between ability and motivation. For here he speaks as if a person's positive motivation in one direction "incapacitated" him to choose in a different direction. This is the same confuson which underlies his sharp distinction between ability and use.

52. DCD 4; CDH II, 15.

53. DCD 4; DC III, 13. Cf. Augustine, *Free Choice* 2.19.53; 3.1.1.

But if a person chooses a lesser good because he prefers it to a greater one, why does he have this preference? Here Anselm recognizes that no further answer is possible. In *De Casu Diaboli* 27 the student asks the teacher to explain why Satan willed what he was not supposed to will.

Teacher. When I say that he deserted uprightness by willing what he was not suposed to will, I am showing clearly why and how he deserted it. For he deserted it because he willed what he was not supposed to will: and he deserted it in this way, viz., by willing what he shouldn't have willed.

Student. But why did he will what he was not supposed to will?

T. No cause preceded this willing except his mere ability to will.

S. Then he willed to desert justice because he was able to will?

T. No, because the good angel was also able to will, but he didn't will to desert justice. For no one wills what he is able to will simply *because* he is able to will; there must be still *another* cause — although, of course, he would never will anything at all if he were *not able to will*.

S. Why, then, did he will?

T. Only *because he willed*. For there was no other cause by which his will was in any way driven or drawn; but his will was both its own efficient cause and its own effect — if such a thing can be said!

Thus, Anselm's second response to the question "Why does someone not will the good?" indicates his awareness that the question does not in every case admit of a satisfactory answer. I may prefer X to Y, because I judge that X has features which make it objectively better than Y — or at least because I judge it more subjectively suited to my purposes than Y. But take a case where Y is apprehended as both objectively better, and subjectively more suited to my purposes, than X. If in the light of this judgment, I still prefer and go on to choose X in favor of Y, then no rational (noncausal) explanation is possible. And since Anselm views Satan's choice of a lesser good as a choice made against his better judgment, he finds no other explanation for the decision than to say: Satan chose as he did simply because he wanted the lesser good; and he wanted the lesser good simply because he wanted it. Nothing compelled him psychologically toward this end (DCD 27). Moreover, in the case of human beings Anselm tends to think of a man as choosing irrationally, more often than ignorantly, when he chooses other than what is morally upright. For in so choosing, he goes against what is ultimately best for him, and caters to a preference which his better judgment should not condone.

Central argument for freedom. Up to this point Anselm has done a number of things: (1) he has defined "free choice" as "the ability to keep uprightness of will for its own sake"; (2) he has identified this ability to keep uprightness with an ability always to resist temptation; (3) he has asserted that because every man always has the ability to resist temptation, he always has free choice; and (4) he has supported this ascription of freedom by distinguishing between having an ability and using it. Anselm is now ready to consolidate his position by showing that no power, not even the power of God, can overcome a man's will so as to constrain it to choose unfreely. This argument must be thought of as Anselm's central defense of free choice, since it allows him to claim that no temptation is ever irresistible, because no power whatsoever can ever deprive the human will of freedom.

We sometimes say that a person is constrained to act or to choose against his will. In the case of the man who must either lie or be killed, there seems to be a sense in which he is unwilling to do either; and therefore whichever he opts for, he does so *against his will.* But Anselm, we have seen, calls this sense of "against his will" misleading: against his will the man is confronted by an unfortunate option, but he does not actually opt *against his will.* "A man can be bound against his will because he can be bound unwillingly; a man can be tortured against his will because he can be tortured unwillingly; a man can be killed against his will because he can be killed unwillingly. But a man cannot will against his will, because he cannot will unwillingly. For everyone who wills, wills willingly." [54] If the man chooses to lie, he does not will the lie for its own sake but rather for the sake of his life. Therefore, he may be unwilling to have to lie, even though he does not actually lie against his will. Anselm regards it as self-contradictory to say that someone chooses, or wills, against his will. That is, he regards it as logically (semantically) impossible for an *act* of will to be itself described as unwilling. If a man were unwilling, he would not will; if he wills, he is not unwilling, though he may be reluctant.

54. DL 5 (S I, 214:19–23). Note Augustine, *Free Choice* 3.3.6 (PL 32:1274): "We can correctly say that we grow old unwillingly and by necessity, or that we die unwillingly and by necessity. . . . But who is so mad as to say that we will unwillingly?" Also *City of God* 5.10.1.

Thus, if "choosing against one's will" refers to choosing amidst a special type of circumstance, viz., a forced-option circumstance, then it has a legitimate use, thinks Anselm. But if it refers to the act of choosing, then it can have no conceivable use. But since by "free choice" Anselm has been discussing the act of choosing rather than the range of options, he can consistently maintain his thesis about the will. No temptation can possibly overpower the will because to do so, it would have to wrest a man's consent from him; i.e., it would have to move the will against its will. If temptation merely incapacitated the will, no choice would ensue; therefore, a man could not choose the enticing object. Temptation must take possession of the will and thereby force the will to choose unwillingly — if the will is to choose unfreely. But on Anselm's view it is logically impossible that temptation should ever succeed in doing this. Therefore, temptation can never overpower a man's will unless the man himself consents to yield. And by consenting to yield, he freely sins — even though he does not sin through that ability in terms of which "freedom" is defined. And the fact of his freely sinning disallows our saying that temptation has, after all, *overpowered* him — though it has indeed beset him and *induced* him.

   With this central argument, Anselm has consolidated his position on the human will's freedom of choice. But he has done so at the expense of introducing an analysis which makes it either meaningless or self-contradictory to say that a man ever chooses unfreely. He completes this analysis by contending that even as Satan, the Tempter, could not have removed uprightness from Adam's will against his will, so also, for a different reason, God could not have removed it either.[55] A will which keeps uprightness for its own sake is a just will. And a just will is one which wills what God wills for it to will. If God were to remove uprightness from a man's will, He would have to do so either willingly or unwillingly. But God cannot unwillingly choose to act, since, as we have just seen, no one can will unwillingly. Hence, if God were to remove uprightness from a man's will, He would have to do so willingly. But if He willingly removed uprightness, He would be willing that that man not (continue to) will what He wills for him to will. And this is impossible. Therefore, God could not have violated Adam's will by wresting uprightness from it. When Adam abandoned uprightness, he did so of his own accord.

55. DL 8. Cf. DC I, 6 (S 11, 256:24-30).

Man, Freedom, and Evil

Paradox of freedom. Having assured us that every man is always free because, like Adam, every man has the ability to keep uprightness, Anselm now confronts us with a paradox. Although fallen men retain the ability to keep uprightness, they no longer have the uprightness to keep; for when Adam deserted uprightness, he lost it not only for himself but also for all his descendants. Moreover, fallen men do not have the ability to regain uprightness by themselves, although they could keep it if it were given to them again. So then, if a man does not have uprightness of will, he cannot will uprightly; and if he cannot will uprightly, he cannot always avoid resisting temptation in the way we have been led to believe. Anselm's theory seems, accordingly, to pose the following paradox: because a man has the ability to keep uprightness of will, he is free; because a man has no uprightness which his will may actually keep, he is in fact unable to choose what is absolutely good. This paradox arises from Anselm's attempt to reconcile the philosophical demand that the human will be free (in order for man to be meaningfully blameworthy for his wrong choices) with the theological teaching that unredeemed fallen man can do no work sufficiently good to repay the debt of sin and thereby to merit him salvation. For even where such a man objectively performs the right action, he does not act from an absolutely good will. However relatively good his deeds may be, they do not succeed in elevating him from his state of sin and restoring original righteousness to his will. And salvation is contingent upon exactly this restoration.[56]

Anselm senses this paradox and allows it to be pressed against him. If we are free, asks the student, then why does Scripture speak of us as "servants of sin" (John 8:34)? How can a man be both servant and free? Anselm's reply draws upon his definition of "freedom": "In one respect, because he is unable to escape from sin, he is a servant; in another respect, because he is unable to be forcibly drawn away from uprightness, he is free. But he can be turned away from sin and from servitude to sin only by another; and he can be turned away from uprightness only by himself; but he cannot be deprived of his freedom at all — either by himself or by another. For a man is always naturally free to keep uprightness,

56. Note DC III, 4 (S II, 268:15–17): "I do not believe that eternal life has been promised to all who are just but only to those who are just without being at all unjust. For it is the latter who are properly and absolutely said to be just and upright in heart."
Augustine: Without grace a man can do nothing good. *Grace of Christ* 1.19.20 (PL 44:370).

ST. ANSELM

whether he has it in his possession or whether he does not" (DL 11). Anselm reinforces this reply with his earlier example about sight. A man is said to have sight if he can see the sun or an object in the sun's light. And even if the sun has set — so that, at the moment, it is no longer to be seen — the man's sight remains unaffected. For he could see the sun if the sun were present.[57] By the same token, a man is free if he can keep uprightness when it is present. Should it happen not to be present, the man's ability-to-keep (and therefore his freedom) remains undiminished.

Even though a man without uprightness of will is both servant and free, Anselm prefers to call him free rather than to call him servant. He bases this preference upon the continued analogy with sight: we say "A man has the ability to see the sun even when the sun is absent, because he would be able to see it if it were present"; and we prefer this statement to the statement "A man lacks the power to see the sun when the sun is present, because, if it were absent, he could not make it present" (DL 12). By substituting in these statements "ability to keep uprightness" for "ability to see the sun," Anselm defends his having spoken of man as free rather than as servant. Now, however strange this analogy between freedom and sight may seem, it is precisely Anselm's way of dealing with the paradox resulting from the philosophical and the theological demands. If nothing else, his recognition and clear articulation of these demands hallmark his contribution to the history of medieval debate.

In drawing the comparison with an object of sight, Anselm tends to reify uprightness and to speak of it as a gift which can be cherished or discarded. This is his reason for using the word "keeping" (servare) and for distinguishing so sharply between the will's ability-to-keep, the will's inability-to-regain, and the object which the will can keep but cannot regain. In the absence of the object, the ability and the inability remain. Thus, the will is naturally free without being actually free — in the case of unredeemed fallen man. For lacking uprightness, the will cannot actually will uprightness.

There is certainly no doubt that the will wills rightly only because it itself is upright. No man's sight is acute because he sees clearly; rather, a man sees clearly because his sight is acute. So too, the will is not upright because it wills rightly, but rather it wills rightly because it is itself upright. There is no doubt that when a man wills this uprightness he wills

57. Cf. Augustine's example which distinguishes (1) a color, (2) seeing the color, (3) the ability to see the color were it present. Free Choice 2.3.9.

154

rightly. Therefore, he wills uprightness only because his will is upright. But it is the same for the will to be upright and for it to have uprightness. Thus, it is clear that a man wills uprightness only because he has uprightness. I do not deny that an upright will wills an uprightness which it does not yet have when it wills more uprightness than it already has. But I maintain that the will can will no uprightness if it has no uprightness at all by which to will it (DC III, 3. S II, 265:26–266:7).

Now, although human nature in Adam retained some justice even after the Fall, this justice did not pass on to Adam's descendants.[58] Without justice, they cannot will uprightly and therefore cannot of their own accord free themselves from bondage to sin. Uprightness is thus conceived as both the object and the rule of the will. A person is said to will the object when he wills in accordance with the right rule. But this is precisely what, on Anselm's view, fallen man cannot perfectly do. Therefore, Anselm is forced to conclude: "Without justice the will can never [actually] be free, because without justice the natural freedom of choice is useless (*otiosa*). It is even made a servant to its own affection for what is beneficial; for once justice is taken away, a man can will only what this affection wills" (DC III, 13. S II, 287:5–8). This observation indicates that although man may be able to perform relatively good deeds, he is not actually free to keep uprightness by abstaining from all evil intent and desire. But if the natural freedom of choice is useless, or futile, then it seems more sensible (against Anselm) to call man *servant* than to call him free, and more sensible to stress that man cannot always resist temptation than to stress that he always can.

Anselm's tendency to hypostatize uprightness leads him to speak as if a man had an ability which he lacked the opportunity to exercise. Anselm is influenced by such examples as someone's being able to read but having no reading material, and therefore in another sense not being able to read — for lack of the opportunity. By comparison, someone may have an ability to choose X without ever having X available to his choice, and therefore in another sense not be able to choose. But the comparison masks an important difference: in the first case the ability to read remains unaffected by the absence of books to be read; but in the case where "X" stands for "uprightness," the unavailability to choice is at the same time, and thereby, a severe impairment of the ability to choose. When a man lacks a book, he lacks something external to himself; but when he lacks

58. Note DCV 24 (S II, 166:19–22). Anselm defines "justice" as "uprightness of will kept for its own sake" (DV 12).

uprightness, he lacks an internal state of soul. And this internal deficiency makes it almost pointless for Anselm to claim that the man retains an ability to keep uprightness were it only present. The presence of uprightness in the will is nothing more or nothing less than the will's continually willing uprightly — i.e., continually willing the right end for the right reason. By Anselm's own admission, this willing is something which the human will (unaided by grace) simply cannot do.[59] The statement that the will *could* keep uprightness were it available amounts to saying that the will could will uprightly if it could will uprightly (though it cannot). At this point the viability of Anselm's position seems to have collapsed.

Anselm and Augustine. Anselm's treatment of free choice appears, at first, radically different from Augustine's; but as his discussion proceeds, his thought becomes increasingly similar to Augustine's. Augustine maintained that fallen man is free to sin but not free totally to avoid sinning. He calls fallen man free because he thinks of freedom as the opposite of prohibition and constraint.[60] Since a man who sins chooses in accordance with his wants and not under constraint, he chooses freely.[61] But this freedom is not true freedom, states Augustine.[62] True freedom is the ability to will, and to delight in, upright deeds. Adam originally possessed this freedom but lost it in the Fall. That is, Adam did not utterly lose his freedom; he lost the predisposition toward the good as well

59. Note especially DC III, 6 (S II, 271:13–15): "But sending, preaching, hearing, and understanding come to naught unless the will wills what the mind understands. But the will cannot do this unless it has received uprightness."

60. In CDH II, 17 (S II, 123:23), Anselm evidences that he too thinks of necessity as either compulsion or prevention — and therefore of freedom as the absence of both.

61. "If by 'necessity' we mean that which is not in our power but which, even though we be unwilling, causes what it can (e.g., the necessity of dying), then it is obvious that our wills, by which we live rightly or wrongly, are not under such necessity. For we do many things which we certainly would not do if we were unwilling." *City of God* 5.10.1 (PL 41:152).

62. "He serves freely who performs the will of his master with pleasure. By this token, a man who is a servant to sin is free to sin. Hence, he will be free to do what is upright (*juste*) only if, after having been freed from sin, he becomes a servant to justice. In the case of someone's being a servant to justice there is both true freedom, because of delight in upright deeds, and holy servitude, because of obedience to God's commands." *Enchiridion* 30.9 (PL 40: 247).
  In *Reproof and Grace* 13.42 (PL 44:942) Augustine says that unredeemed fallen man's choice is free (*liberum*) but not freed (*liberatum*). It is free of justice but a servant to sin.

as the power of choosing the good.[63] But he retained the power to choose evil. In the case of God, Augustine thinks that "freedom" should not be defined so as to include the ability to sin.[64] But in the case of men in this life, the ability to sin constitutes part of the notion of freedom. At times Augustine tends to think of free choice as a neutral power (*media vis*) for performing good or for performing evil — even though he acknowledges that in the next life the redeemed shall not have the power to choose evil.[65]

Anselm, by contrast, consistently includes references to the object of choice, viz., uprightness, within the definition of "free choice"; and he invokes the same definition of "freedom" in the case of God and of man, although he recognizes that the "use" of this freedom is different for God and for man. In a sense, Anselm's entire contrast with Augustine arises out of his unique definition, which, together with the peculiar distinction between ability and use, generates Anselm's theory. But it is important to remember that aside from these two features, Anselm's position coincides roughly with his predecessor's. Augustine is Anselm's source for the central argument that no one can will against his will and hence that no one can be *forced* to will what temptation suggests.[66] And it was through Augustine's interpretation of Scripture that Anselm learned to appreciate the futility and the servitude of fallen man's natural freedom. In *De Libertate* 12 Anselm utilizes Augustine's very terminology in describing fallen man: *non potest non peccare.*[67] Both Anselm and Augustine are anti-Pelagian. But Anselm, by invoking his special definition and by simultaneously proclaiming that every man has free choice, fosters the illusion of being less anti-Pelagian than Augustine. Only his statements on the relation of grace to free choice make his theological kinship to Augustine perfectly clear. For here, like Augustine, he

63. "Who among us would say that because of the first man's sin the human race lost free choice? To be sure, the freedom which the first man had in Paradise was lost — the freedom to have immortality and complete justice. . . ." *Against Two Letters of the Pelagians* 1.2.5 (PL 44:552).

64. *City of God* 22.30.3.

65. "First, then, let us see whether we can deal with this problem by saying that the natural free choice given to the rational soul by the Creator is a neutral power (*media vis*) which can either be directed toward faith or be inclined toward unbelief. . . ." *The Spirit and the Letter* 33.58 (PL 44:238).

66. *City of God* 5.10.1 (PL 41:152): "non enim vellemus, si nollemus" ("For we would not will if we were unwilling").

67. S I, 224:1. Cf. *City of God* 22.30.3 (PL 41:802); *Reproof and Grace* 12.33.

emphasizes the *inability* of human nature to perfect itself without divine assistance. "Just as no one receives uprightness unless grace precedes it and enables him, so no one keeps uprightness unless the same grace follows it and helps him. Even though the keeping of uprightness, when it is kept, is done through free choice, this keeping must not be attributed to free choice so much as to grace; for free choice possesses uprightness only through prevenient grace and keeps it only through subsequent grace" (DC III, 4. S II, 267:15–19).

Baptized infants, who have not yet reached the state of rational choice, are saved by grace alone.[68] Those who have reached the age of understanding either receive uprightness by grace or else they do not receive it at all. Those to whom God gives His grace should recognize that the gift is not based on antecedent merits; i.e., it is truly a gift, and not a reward.[69] Those who are offered divine grace and accept it are to be numbered among the redeemed. Grace further assists them by reducing the power of temptation against the will and by increasing the will's affection for uprightness.[70] Although the initial acceptance of grace is done through free choice, this acceptance is not a meritorious work. For the acceptance is identical with an act of faith. And this act of faith is itself encompassed by grace.[71] Thus Anselm can speak of faith as coming through grace; and like Augustine, he can silently leave it a mystery why this grace, which cooperates with the act of faith by being its necessary precondition, should be given to some men and not to others.[72]

Freedom and foreknowledge. If an event is foreknown, then it is necessary for that event to occur; otherwise it would be incorrectly said to be foreknown. Now, if the "event" which is foreknown is a choice and if it is necessary for this choice to occur, then the choice appears to be un-

68. DC III, 2 (S II, 264:20–22). DC III, 3 (S II, 266:19–20).

69. "Although God does not give His grace to everyone, since 'He has mercy on whom He will have mercy, and whom He will He hardens' (Rom. 9:18), nevertheless He does not give grace to anyone as a reward for some antecedent merit, for 'Who has first given to God and shall be recompensed by Him?' (Rom. 11:35). If, however, the will through free choice keeps what it has received and in this way merits either an increment of received justice, or even power for a good will, or some reward, then all these are the fruit of the first grace and are 'grace for grace' (John 1:16)." DC III, 3 (S II, 266:24–267:1).

70. DC III, 4 (S II, 268:7–10).

71. DC III, 6 (S II, 271:8–9).

72. E.g., Augustine, *The Spirit and the Letter* 34.60; *Predestination of the Saints* 14.26.

free. Anselm raises this argument against himself in order, by rebutting it, to show once and for all that freedom and foreknowledge are not opposed to each other. Neither the formulation of the puzzle nor its solution is new with Anselm. He is relying here (as always) upon Augustine. But he is also mindful of Aristotle's comments about the truth and falsity of propositions expressing future contingencies (relayed through Boethius's analysis of *On Interpretation*) and of Boethius's limited remarks on foreknowledge in *Consolation of Philosophy*, Book 5.

Anselm handles the ostensible threat of foreknowledge to free choice in three ways: by distinguishing two senses of "It is necessary for . . ."; by deriving God's foreknowledge from His eternity; and by introducing a special *argumentum ex concesso*.

According to the first argument, then, "It is necessary for X to happen" does not always mean the same thing as "X happens by necessity." For it is not redundant to say "It is necessary for X to happen by necessity" or self-contradictory to say "It is necessary for X to happen freely." That is, whereas "X's happening by necessity" is opposed to "X's happening freely," "being necessary for X to happen" is compatible with "X's happening freely." "Its being necessary for . . ." has a noetic as well as a causal use. In accordance with the noetic use, a thing which is certain to occur may be said necessarily to occur — i.e., may be said to be necessary to occur. Thus, what is foreknown to be going to occur is certain to be going to occur; and if it is certainly going to occur, then it is necessary that it not fail to occur; and if it is necessary that it not fail to occur, it is necessary for it to occur. Assume that a free choice is foreknown to occur. (Anselm has previously established to his own satisfaction that there are free choices.) Then Anselm's argument runs: if it is foreknown, then it is certain; if it is certain, then (in a sense) it is necessary; and if it is necessary, then it cannot fail to occur as it is foreknown, viz., freely. Hence, far from interfering with freedom, foreknowledge guarantees it.[73] The necessity by which a will is free cannot at the same time be a necessity which deprives the will of freedom.

Anselm sees that this kind of necessity — subsequent necessity — does not *affect* anything. It is simply a *modus loquendi* by means of which we indicate that what happens cannot both happen and not happen. (This way of speaking goes back to Aristotle.) To say *merely* "It is necessary

73. DC I, 1 (S II, 246:14–23). Augustine makes this same argument in *Free Choice* 3.3.8 and *City of God* 5.10.2.

for X to happen" leans in the direction of saying "X happens by necessity." But to say "It is necessary for X to happen as foreknown" has a very different sense. For what is signified by "foreknowledge" is knowledge of what will occur. Therefore, it is logically necessary that if something is foreknown, it will happen. In *De Concordia* I, 3, Anselm recognizes this fact,[74] and it becomes his basis for speaking of subsequent necessity. Nowadays instead of saying "It is necessary for X to happen as foreknown," we would say "The proposition 'If X is foreknown to happen in way Y, then X happens in way Y' is necessarily true." Anselm is saying essentially the same thing, but not saying it as explicitly. When he posits a future choice as free, states that God foreknows this choice, and then concludes by declaring "It is necessary that this choice be freely made," he invites the confusion of supposing that this choice *must* occur rather than will occur, and hence that its occurrence cannot really be free. "It is necessary for . . ." tends needlessly to blur the distinction between being certain to happen and happening by necessity. In last analysis, however, Anselm is always clear that there is such a distinction.

Anselm's second argument maintains that all free choices of the human will are contingent in the sense that before they occur, it is possible for them not to occur. But if it is really possible for them not to occur, then how can they be foreknown (since what is foreknown is necessary to occur)? And if they are foreknown, how can they possibly not occur? Here again the phrase "It is necessary for" generates puzzles which Anselm must try to resolve. Having explained the sense in which what is foreknown is necessary to occur, he must now explain the sense in which what can possibly not occur is foreknown. He does this by recalling the difference between eternity and time: "We have no basis for denying that something can be mutable in time while being immutable in eternity. Indeed, something's being mutable in time and immutable in eternity is no more contradictory than something's not existing at a certain time but always existing in eternity, or its having been or its going to be in the order of time while being neither past nor future in the order of eternity" (DC I, 5. S II, 255: 10–14). Thus, whatever is going to happen, as well as what has already happened, is present to the mind of God without temporal distinction. Accordingly, God views all things as if they were pres-

---

74. "In 'praescire' intelligitur futurum. Nam non est aliud praescire quam scire futurum, et ideo si praescit deus aliquid, necesse est illud esse futurum." S II, 250:28–30.

ent, so that rather than having *foreknowledge* of the future which we await, He has knowledge of an eternal present (DCD 21). In viewing all human choices from within this eternal present, His knowledge no more interferes with the freedom of these choices than does one human being's awareness of another's (temporally) present choice interfere with that other's freedom.

Anselm's first argument did not introduce the reference to God in an intrinsic way. That is, the distinction between "X's happening by necessity" and "Its being necessary for X to happen" is applicable to the problem of free choice and foreknowledge irrespective of whether God or man might have this foreknowledge. However, the second argument restricts the possession of "foreknowledge" to God, for only God knows the future.[75] This foreknowledge is a constitutive part of God's omniscience and as such is unique to Him. The fact of God's omniscience does not intrude upon the fact of there being real metaphysical contingencies relative to the human will—any more than the fact of God's eternity intrudes upon the fact of there being real temporal distinctions relative to the human mind.

Anselm's third argument begins from his description of God as the greatest conceivable being. This description entails both that God's will is free and that God knows everything that He wills. For were His will not free or were He not to know His own will, then a being greater than God could be conceived—which by definition is impossible. If, then, God knows His own will, His knowledge either does or does not impose necessity on His will. But His knowledge cannot impose necessity, because then God would not will freely—something just shown to be impossible. Therefore, since we must concede that God's knowledge does not impose necessity on His own will, there is no basis for believing that His knowledge in any way imposes necessity on the human will.[76]

With these three arguments Anselm eliminates the danger which divine foreknowledge seemed to pose for human freedom. But now he must deal with a new and special threat, viz., that particular threat whereby Jesus was unable to turn away from death (CDH II, 16). For if Jesus had avoided the cross, Mary could not have been justified by

75. Note Anselm's argument in DCD 21 (Appendix II below) to the effect that Satan could not have foreknown his own fall. Augustine has the same argument in *Reproof and Grace* 10.27, and Ep. 73.3.7.

76. DC I, 4 (S II, 252:7–22). This is essentially Augustine's argument in *Free Choice* 3.3.6.

faith in His future death. And had Mary not been made righteous through faith, the Son of God (it seems) could not have been sinlessly born of her — or better, He could not have assumed human nature from *any* of Adam's descendants. Therefore, the very fact of Jesus' birth seems to have necessitated His dying. According to this line of reasoning, Jesus had the power to lay down His life and to take it up again (John 10:15–18), but He did not have the power not to lay it down. Because of His divine nature Jesus foreknew His death. Anselm has shown that this foreknowledge did not prevent Jesus from freely choosing to die. But now for another reason His death seems to have been predetermined and unavoidable — and hence, from this point of view, impossible not to be willed.

Freedom in the God-man. Anselm observes that Jesus' death was impossible not to be willed, simply because Jesus steadfastly willed it — i.e., He steadfastly willed to let Himself be put to death for the sake of justice. This impossibility-of-not-willing is identical with a subsequent necessity of willing;[77] no antecedent necessity or compulsion determined Jesus' will. And thus His will to undergo death was at every point free. Even though that will affixed the necessity of His dying, it freely affixed this necessity. The Father Himself did not compel the Son to undergo death; nor did He love the Son's suffering. He willed the Son's death only in the negative sense that He did not will for human beings to be saved apart from some meritorious work, and He knew that the Son was the only one who could perform this work on man's behalf.[78] Moreover, He approved of the Son's will, since the will of the Father and of the Son is the same divine will.[79] With this analysis Anselm is grappling with Boso's syllogistic objection:

> Whatever God wills, must happen.
> God wills that Christ die.
> ———————————————————
> Therefore, Christ must die.

By pointing out that the will of Christ is identical with the will of God, Anselm makes it clear that Christ willingly underwent death and was not constrained by an independent will of the Father. Because this com-

77. Regarding subsequent necessity see p. 79.
78. CDH I, 9 (S II, 64:6-10).
79. CDH II, 16 (S II, 121:28-30).

mon will of Father, Son, and Holy Spirit determines what is necessary and impossible, and in some sense is not itself subject to necessity and impossibility, it is rightly spoken of as free.[80] Thus, the "must" in terms of which Jesus' death occurs is that whereby what He wills must follow in accordance with His will—not that whereby something precedes and constrains Him to will.

Boso is not satisfied. For Anselm is contending that Jesus could not have avoided death because He did not will to avoid it. But Boso points out that, once born, Jesus could not have escaped death *even had He willed to*; for He could not have been taken from Mary unless she were pure. And she was pure, teaches Anselm, by faith in her Son's future death. Therefore, once born from her purity, Jesus had to die. Hence, the necessity of His death seems to be not simply a necessity which *follows* from His will, but seems rather to be a necessity which lies outside His will and directs His earthly life toward death irrespective of His will.[81] Anselm confronts this objection by recalling that the will of Christ was identical with the will of the Son of God *before* the incarnation.[82] *Ab aeterno* the Son of God, foreseeing the fall of some angels and of all men, willed to undergo death. Because from eternity He willed to submit to death, He could not as incarnate will to avoid death; for He could not be both actually willing and not actually willing the same thing. Accordingly, Boso's phrase "even if He had willed to" is inoperative; hence the statement containing it can no longer conjure up the false imagery of Jesus struggling against an external necessity. Within the system of Anselm's theology, the statement of Jesus' birth from Mary's purity, when taken together with other propositions, logically entails the statement of Jesus' death. But among these other propositions is the statement of the volitional freedom through which the Son of God planned for man's salvation.

In *De Conceptu* Anselm qualifies the *Cur Deus Homo* assertion that "Jesus could not have been taken from Mary unless she were pure": her purity befit His sinless birth rather than His sinless birth having required her purity. With this clarification of the intent of the passage from the

80. CDH II, 17 (S II, 122:26–27).

81. CDH II, 16 (S II, 122:1–7).

82. Anselm is affirming the presence of the divine will in Christ. By itself this passage should not be construed as monothelitism, which CDH I, 9 (S II, 63:27ff) shows Anselm as rejecting.

Cur Deus Homo, Boso's objection loses plausibility. Had Mary's purity been *necessary* to Jesus' sinless birth, and had her purity resulted from faith in His future death, then the picture of His *having to die* would be plausibly generated. For the statement of His death would then indeed follow with logical necessity from the other statements. And this logical entailment might conduce to the confusion of thinking that a causal or metaphysical necessity was operative. But once Mary's purity is not a necessary precondition of Jesus' sinless birth, but only a fitting precondition, the phrase "He *could not have* been taken from her unless she were pure" loses its rigor. Accordingly, it is no longer sufficient to generate even a prima facie philosophical puzzle.

Anselm's treatment of *ability* with respect to the God-man allows him to claim with Scripture that Jesus had the power to preserve His earthly life (Matt. 26:53), while at the same time maintaining that Jesus *could not* actually will to preserve His life because He *did not* actually will to preserve it. And He did not actually will to preserve it because He steadfastly willed man's salvation, which could only be accomplished by incarnation and death. However, in some cases, Jesus' not actually having willed something was not the result of His having willed some other incompatible end. Rather, in these cases He is said not to have willed that thing because His divine *nature* did not allow Him to will it. For example, His nature as Justice prevented Him from willing a lie. Yet this "language of prevention" must not mislead us into supposing that the divine nature in God and in the God-man somehow prohibits or restrains the will. We may say simply that God's nature is such that He never wills to lie — without introducing the word "prevent" at all. In a sense, the language of prevention embodies a logical rather than a metaphysical way of specifying a moral end of God's will, so that it is definitionally impossible for Him to will immorally. If God willed a lie, He would not be God. Therefore, by definition He cannot will a lie. But neither this definition (from the logical point of view) nor God's nature (from the metaphysical point of view) can be properly thought of as curtailing divine freedom.

The inability to lie is properly thought of as an ability to abide by the truth. The notion of God's having an *inability* suggests the idea that God's nature is deficient. By translating the statement about inability into an equivalent statement about ability, Anselm hopes to make it clear that God's "inability" to lie is really a perfection. And a perfection does not limit a nature but completes it. Consequently, as God's nature is not limited by His inability to lie, so His will is not prevented by His nature as Justice. To say that God must always act in accordance with His nature is simply to express a necessary truth; it is not to ascribe an antecedent necessity to God's will.[83]

Although God cannot lie, Boso has an argument which purports to prove that Jesus could have. And he asks Anselm to resolve this discrepancy. Scripture records Jesus as replying to His accusers, "If I shall say I do not know Him [the Father], then, like you, I shall be a liar" (John 8:55). Having uttered this sentence, Jesus uttered all its parts. He therefore said the words "I do not know Him." Now, had He said these words alone, He would have uttered a lie and thus have sinned. But the very fact that He did say the words proves that He could also have said them alone. Therefore, Jesus could have sinned, contends Boso (CDH II, 10). Anselm's reply once again manifests the entanglement implicit in the word *posse*. He distinguishes between the ability to tell a lie and the ability to will a lie — i.e., between an ability of action and an ability of choice. Jesus was able to perform the act of telling a lie, concedes Anselm, but He was able to do so *only if* He willed to tell a lie. Yet because of His divine nature He was unable to will to tell a lie. Therefore, He was both able and not able to sin.

Anselm's reply is peculiar. He is really saying something like this: "Although the God-man was conditionally able to tell a lie, He could never actually tell a lie, because fulfillment of the condition under which He could do so is logically impossible. (By definition the God-man cannot will a lie.)" But because of this impossible condition, Anselm should say outright that Jesus could not have sinned by telling a lie — instead of maintaining that He was able to tell a lie but not able to will a lie. For if someone cannot will a lie, then he can *in no sense* tell a lie. (This principle holds true irrespective of the reason why such a person cannot will a lie.) Anselm, through Boso, seems to be thinking of a lie as simply the utterance of a false statement, so that had Jesus ever uttered the words

83. Anselm wants to avoid speaking of the *necessity* of God's doing something (such as preserving His honor) or of the *impossibility* of His doing something (such as making the past not be past), because these expressions, he feels, wrongly connote inability, imperfection, and lack of freedom. Cf. CDH II, 5 (S II, 100:20-26); CDH II, 17 (S II, 123:4-6). See Ch. 2, n. 35. Note also P 7 (S I, 105).

Augustine calls God omnipotent because He can do everything that He wills. The fact that God cannot will everything (e.g., a lie) does not affect His omnipotence. *City of God* 5.10.1; DT 15.15.24.

"I do not know the Father" and only these words, He would have been lying. Yet the contrary is evident: Jesus could have spoken these words without lying, for He could have said them hypothetically. If His accusers had asked, "What would You have to say in order to be a liar like us?" He might didactically have answered, "I do not know the Father." But with these words He would not have been telling a lie even though He would have been giving an example of a lie by saying something false. If Anselm denies that Jesus could ever have said anything false, then the problem repeats itself. Clearly He might have said something false without having said it falsely, i.e., without having been committed to it. For instance, He might have found and read aloud an old parchment on which was inscribed "Xerxes II died in his fifth year." He would then have been uttering a false sentence without having committed a falsehood. In this way, Jesus both could and could not have said something false. But there are not two corresponding senses in which He could and could not have lied, or sinned.[84] For telling a lie presupposes willing a lie, i.e., presupposes intending the falsehood one utters. Hence, being incapable of willing a lie logically entails being incapable of telling a lie. Accordingly, there is *no* meaningful sense in which Jesus could have lied, granted Anselm's orthodox Christology.

Earlier, Anselm himself recognized this point when he noted, simply, that Jesus could not have sinned because He could not have willed to sin.[85] And to Boso's response that Jesus could not therefore have held to justice freely, Anselm recalls that the definition of God's freedom does not include reference to an ability to sin. Why then did God not endow men with an inability to sin, since the possession of the "inability" is compatible with their having been free?[86] Anselm contends that it was reserved for the God-man to be made incapable of sinning. Adam was created free from sin and was able to merit a persevering will for uprightness. But Jesus, from the moment He possessed a rational will, possessed a will persevering in uprightness.

In his desire to reconcile the philosophical thesis that all men have free choice with the theological doctrine that no unredeemed fallen man can

84. Augustine calls every sin a lie. *City of God* 14.4.1.

85. CDH II, 10 (S II, 106:21–107:9).

86. The *inability* to sin is the *ability* to will only uprightness. Augustine, too, grants to God the power to have made man unable to sin. *On Continence* 6.16 (PL 40:359).

actually choose the good, Anselm begins with a special definition of "free choice." In so doing he moves on two different levels. On the one level he is urging that every man has the power to resist temptation by deciding between alternative options. On the other level he talks not about the choice of particular ends but about choices insofar as they are describable as either upright or not upright — i.e., insofar as through the choice of particular ends one either does or does not "keep uprightness." Anselm confuses these levels when he begins to think of uprightness not merely as a description of choice but as an object available to the will. What results is the paradox of fallen man's freedom and servitude. In view of this paradox Anselm's further distinction between ability and use, which at first seems to place him so far from Augustine, becomes modified so as to bring him into accord with Augustine's anti-Pelagianism. Anselm views the grace required for salvation as something bestowed by God apart from individual merits. Those who by faith and through grace commit themselves to God receive anew the gift of uprightness, although they shall not possess this gift in its fullness until the next life. That God foresees their acts of faith does not injure the freedom of the faith-act; for God's foreknowledge serves as a guarantor not as a usurper of human freedom. Moreover, the necessity with which the God-man underwent death for the salvation of the human race is not a necessity of will but a necessity of instrumentality relative to God's purpose for mankind. Adam, fallen men, and the God-man are all free in the sense of Anselm's definition. Yet why did Adam spurn the gift of uprightness and choose what was evil? Why did he cast away justice for himself and his descendants and impair the use of his freedom, thus making it necessary for the God-man freely to atone for the human race? Anselm must deal with the question of what evil is and of what it is we dread when we hear the word "evil." He must explain how Adam's good will could have been turned toward evil and how God could justly allow human nature to have become corrupted. For only then will man's destitution and need for salvation not obscure the fact of his having been created in the image and glory of God.

EVIL AND THE FALL

Anselm's treatment of free will makes it possible for him to assess the fall of Satan and of Adam in terms which relieve God of direct responsibility. God gave freedom to Satan and Adam because it was a good appropriate to their natures. But Satan and Adam of their own accord misused freedom by setting their own wills over against the will of God. In discussing the fall of man and angels, Anselm attempts to relate the concept of freedom to the condition of sin in such a way as to preserve the honor of God. For if God's honor was manifested in the glory and perfection of His creature and if the creature's glory and perfection became corrupted and distorted by his defection from uprightness, could not this defection have resulted from a *defect* in the created nature? And if God is omnipotent, could He not have created rational beings without the defect which resulted in sin? Beset by such objections, Anselm intends to show that the creature's free choice of something other than uprightness did not stem from an imperfection in his nature, and that, accordingly, God is not blamable for the origin of moral evil. Moreover, since the evil which we call injustice is metaphysically privation and nothingness, God cannot be its source, since from God come only being and goodness.

Giving and receiving perseverance. Anselm discusses the fall of Satan for two reasons: it represents a theological problem in its own right; and the puzzles which arise with respect to the will and fall of Satan arise *mutatis mutandis* with respect to the will and fall of Adam. If Anselm can show that God is not responsible for Satan's plight, then ipso facto he has gone a long way toward alleviating God of responsibility for Adam's depravity. Allow, then, that Satan and the other angels were created in equal possession of uprightness. Why did the one group of angels desert uprightness while the other persevered? In particular, if all angels were created having nothing from themselves (I Cor. 4:7), then their wills, together with their perseverance of will, must have come from God. But if some angels did not persevere, was it not because God failed to give them the gift of perseverance? In *De Casu Diaboli* the Student formulates this objection tersely: "If giving is the cause of the good angel's receiving, then not-giving is the cause of the evil angel's not-receiving; and if not-giving is postulated, I see not-receiving as a necessary consequence. We all know that when we do not receive what we want, it is not the case that it is not given because we do not receive it, but it is rather the case that we do not receive it because it is not given. As far as I remember, everyone I've read or heard dealing with this question has put it in the form of the following argument: if the good angel received perseverance because God gave it, then the evil angel did not receive it because God did not give it" (DCD 2).

Anselm's reply is equally laconic and distinguishes two different senses of "cause." There is the actual cause of something and there is the cause, or reason, for *inferring something* (DCD 3). To borrow Boethius's example, hostility is an actual cause of war; however, it does not *follow* from the existence of mutual hostility that two countries are in a state of war, but rather from a state of war that two countries are hostile.[87] On the basis of this distinction Anselm can argue that A's giving might be an actual cause of B's receiving, while A's not-giving might be only a cause for inferring C's not-receiving; C's not-receiving might actually cause A's not-giving. Correspondingly, from the statement of the good angel's having received perseverance because God gave it, it does not follow that the evil angel did not receive it *because* God did not give it, but only that if God did not give it, the evil angel could not have received it.

Satan refused to accept the perseverance which God offered; this is the sense in which his not-receiving actually caused God's not-giving. God could not give this gift against Satan's will, for the very attempt to do so would have transformed the gift into an imposition. Anselm is thus thinking of a gift as something which must be accepted by a person before it can ever be a gift *to him*. To have perseverance is simply to be able to will only uprightness. God was going to confirm Satan's and Adam's wills in uprightness had each during a probational period persisted in willing uprightness.

At this point it is important to remember that Augustine had distinguished between Adam's situation and that of redeemed fallen men: "Adam was given an aid to perseverance — not an aid by which he would be made to persevere but an aid without which he could not persevere through free choice. But now no such aid is given to the saints, who are predestined into the kingdom of God through the grace of God. Rather, perseverance itself is given to them as an aid — not only so that they cannot persevere without this gift but also so that through this gift they cannot fail to persevere."[88] So then, in Adam's case perseverance was to have been partly merited, even though grace was a necessary condition

87. *On Cicero's Topics*, Bk. 2 (PL 64:1066).
88. *Reproof and Grace* 12.34 (PL 44:937).

for the possibility of this meriting.[89] In the case of redeemed fallen men, however, perseverance is not at all merited.[90] Unlike Adam's will their wills "are aroused by the Holy Spirit so that they are able to persevere because they will to; and they will to because God brings about (*operatur*) their willing to." [91] Adam was able not to forsake the good in order that he might come to deserve and receive the gift of being unable to forsake the good. Among those of his descendants who through faith have had uprightness restored to their wills, not all have received perseverance. Accordingly, some who are now upright believers will fall away.

In *De Casu Diaboli* Anselm does not concern himself with all the topics raised by Augustine in *Reproof and Grace*. The reason for this is twofold. First, Anselm focuses on the fall of Satan and of Adam and on the possibility of their not having fallen. Therefore, he brackets the question of the perseverance of the saints. Secondly, in *De Casu Diaboli* unlike in *De Concordia*, Anselm does not intend to detail the role of grace but only to vindicate the righteousness of God. On his view, as on Augustine's, both Satan and Adam sinned by willing to be like God. Yet, Anselm asks himself, "if God cannot be conceived except as a unique being, so that nothing else can be conceived to be like Him, how was Satan able to will what he could not conceive?" (DCD 4). In taking up the question Anselm distinguishes between the object and the rule of the will. Satan could not will to be like God as the object of his will. But in willing something which was contrary to the will of God, he presumed to set his own will above God's.[92] For it belongs to God alone to act from an absolutely independent will. Thus, in the attempt to absolutize his will, Satan sought to elevate himself to the position of God. He therefore willed to be like God through the rule governing his will. In the case of Adam, the same situation reoccurred. In willing to partake of the forbidden tree, Adam sought to act on the basis of an independent will. He thereby presumed to the likeness of God, even though the object of his will was *something less than God*. As for Satan, however, it is not clear what the object of will was when he willed something other than

89. *Ibid.* 11.32.

90. *Ibid.* 8.17.

91. *Ibid.* 12.38 (PL 44:939).

92. "The will of an angel or a man is independent when it wills contrary to the will of God." DIV 10 (S II, 27:4–5).

what accorded with God's will for him. Yet on the basis of the distinction above between object and rule, and on the basis of the ontological
argument itself, Anselm can say the following: although the object must
have been some good less than God, nevertheless, because it did not agree
with God's will, Satan willed in principle to be like God (cf. DIV 10).

Anselm here is recasting Augustine's interpretation of Fall. Augustine
maintains that Satan's evil willing had no *efficient* cause but only a *deficient* cause. That is, Satan's evil willing did not arise from his nature,
for his nature was good and could not effect an evil choice. Therefore,
Satan willed wrongly because his will-for-the-good failed him. Influenced by neo-Platonism, Augustine wants to give some sense to saying,
metaphysically, that Satan's evil will arose from nothing. Augustine
views created things as made from nothing and therefore as subject to de-
cay and falling away.[93] Exactly why Satan's defective movement of will
occurred, Augustine does not claim to know. But he insists that it could
not have occurred through any fault of God's.

Precisely the fear that someone might accuse God for having en-
dowed Satan and Adam with imperfect wills leads Anselm to speak of
Satan's evil will not as having a deficient cause but as being the efficient
cause of itself (DCD 27). Anselm recognizes the difficulties in this expression, but he uses it to ward off every appearance of blameworthiness
on the part of God. "Deficient cause" suggests deficiency; deficiency
in turn suggests that God is at fault in having created defective rational
beings. Thus, Anselm takes pains to introduce a further distinction —
one which seems casuistic and overly subtle, yet one which he feels is
theologically necessary. In *De Casu Diaboli* 3 he asserts that "willing to
desert X" is sometimes prior to "being unwilling to keep X." Anselm
thinks that if he can make this point, then he will have shown how Satan's will to desert uprightness *preceded* his being unwilling to keep
uprightness. On this basis, the unwillingness (which seems to indicate a
deficiency) would not have originated his fall: rather a deliberate and

93. *City of God* 12.7–8. Note especially: "I know that the nature of God can never,
nowhere, and in no respect fail. Yet those things made from nothing can fail. Those
which insofar as they are do good (thereby doing something) have efficient causes.
Insofar as they fail and thereby do evil (for what do they do except nothing?) have
deficient causes." PL 41:355.
Free Choice 2.20.54: "That movement of turning away [from good] which we
call sin is a defective movement. And every defect is from nothing. Therefore, seeing to what this movement pertains, do not doubt that it does not pertain to God."
PL 32:1270.

efficient willing of something other than uprightness would have originated the unwillingness and at the same time the fall. Anselm offers an
example to illustrate his distinction. A miser may have to part with some
of his money in order to purchase food and to stay alive. His will to
"desert" his money precedes his unwillingness to keep it. He does not
desert his money because he is unwilling to keep it, i.e., because he shuns
money as such; he is unwilling to keep his money only because he prefers to obtain food and cannot do so without spending money. Correspondingly, because Satan preferred, and efficiently willed, something
which was incompatible with uprightness, he was unwilling to keep uprightness. "Therefore, I say it is not the case that Satan did not will what
and when he should have willed because his will had a deficiency which
came from God; but when he willed what he should not have willed, he
expelled his good will by means of a supervening evil will. For this reason, it is not the case that Satan didn't have, or didn't receive, a good
persevering will because God did not give it; rather, God didn't give
him a good persevering will because he deserted it by willing what he
ought not; and by deserting it he didn't keep it" (DCD 3). Anselm
agrees with Augustine that the will to desert uprightness did not arise
from Satan's nature and that its origin is not properly explainable. Still,
he finds that an inexplicable efficient cause is theologically more service-
able than an inexplicable deficient cause.

Evil as privation and nothing. Because Satan and Adam sinned, their
natures became corrupted. But corruption is not *something*: it is the
absence of something — namely, the absence of a perfection which properly belongs to a nature.[94] From this point of view, injustice is the absence of uprightness in the will. Therefore, Satan's and Adam's natures

94. Augustine's purpose in calling evil a form of not-being had been to assert, against
the Manicheans, that evil is not a *nature*. He did not mean that evil is devoid of all
reality. Rather, he thought of it as having the kind of reality that corruption (i.e.,
the *loss* of a perfection) has. Anselm's position, stated by the Student at the beginning of DCD 10, corresponds to Augustine's *Nature of the Good* 17 and 20. Anselm
uses the word *essentia* instead of *natura*, but Augustine had himself pointed to the
interchangeability of these terms (*Catholic and Manichean Ways of Life* 2.2.2).
Moreover, *essentia* also derives from *esse* and carries with it the notion of *being*
(DT 5.2.3). Accordingly, Anselm's use of *essentia* combines the notions of *esse* and
natura. It may, therefore, be translated in DCD as either "a being" or "a nature."
   N.B. PF 42:30; 42:32–33; 43:14–15, where Anselm interchanges "*non existit in re-
rum natura,*" "*est absque omni essentia,*" and "*habet nec ullam existentiam.*" Cf.
Gaunilo's use of *essentia* for "existence" in *On Behalf of the Fool* 6 (S I, 128:30).
Anselm also uses *essentia* for *what* a thing is (M 4. S I, 17:14–15).

became corrupted by the will's having lost a perfection, not by its having lost a native power. Allow that this state of injustice is metaphysically describable in terms of a lack (or a privation), and furthermore that injustice itself may be said to be nothing. Then, one might ask, is not God the cause of this state of not-being, even though he may not be blamable for it? In *De Casu Diaboli* 1, the Student observes: "Who but God causes the many things which we see passing from being to not-being to become other than what they were — even if they don't become absolutely nothing? Or who makes not to be whatever is not, except He who makes to be whatever is? If there is something only because God makes it, then it follows that whatever is not is not because He doesn't make it. Therefore, just as those things which exist have their 'being something' from Him, so those things which do not exist, or which pass from being to not-being, seem to have their 'being nothing' from Him."

Anselm denies that God may properly be called the cause of not-being, but he does allow a certain "improper" sense to the expression. A person who makes something become different from what it was is properly said either (1) to *cause* it *to be* or (2) to *cause* it *not to be*. Yet we sometimes use these same expressions of a person who can cause a thing to be, but does not, or who can cause it not to be, but does not. Strictly speaking, such a person is not causing anything at all. That is, he is not *doing* (*facere*) something, but he is not-doing something. Accordingly, he is (3) *not causing* a thing *to be* or (4) *not causing* it *not to be*. Anselm considers the use of these negative expressions to attribute causation to be grammatically improper. Nevertheless he grants that the expressions have a common role, and he favors their continued use as long as they do not mislead. In the *Philosophical Fragments* he notes the interchangeability of *1* and *4*, and of *2* and *3*. In each of these two cases an affirmation and a negation are substituted for each other. For example, God may be said to harden a man's heart when He does not soften it; or He may be said to lead a man into temptation when He does not deliver him from it.[95] But in fact, God is not doing anything at all, and so He is called a cause only in a negative sense. This negative sense, it is important to see, does not constitute an omission on God's part. He is not-doing something which He *can* do rather than not-doing something which

95. That is, (1) "to cause X's heart to be hard ≡ (4) "not to cause X's heart not to be hard"; and (1) "to cause X to be tempted" ≡ (4) "not to cause X not to be tempted." Cf. DC II, 2 (S II, 261); DCD 20 (S I, 265:7–10).

173

He *should* do. In this negative sense, continues Anselm, God is said to be the cause of not-being. For by not causing something not to be, or by not causing something to be, God is in a certain (improper) sense a cause of not-being. But this sense in no way contradicts the (proper) statement that He causes only being and goodness.

As ever, Anselm has an example with which to illustrate his point. If one man has no clothes and another man refuses to give him clothes, then, nonetheless, the first man's state of nakedness is from himself. The second man does not actually cause the first man's nakedness — though he does cause it in the sense of not causing the man to be dressed. Now, Anselm supposes that even if the second man had temporarily given a garment and later taken it back, still he would not properly be called the cause of the other's nakedness. For the other was naked before he received the garment; and when the garment is recalled, he returns into his original state — a state for which the man who temporarily loaned the clothing is not responsible. Likewise, Anselm considers God's bestowing existence upon something and preserving it in existence as similar to bestowing a garment: "A being only exists by His causing it to exist, and a being only remains what He has made it be by His preserving it. When He stops preserving what He has made, then that thing returns to not-being, not because He makes it not to be, but because He ceases to make it to be. For when, as though through anger, God destroys a thing and removes its existence, He is not the cause of its not-being; but by His reclaiming what He had bestowed, then that thing which He had made and was keeping in existence returns into not-being. It had this not-being before it was made, and hence had it from itself and not from Him" (DCD 1).

Anselm thus interprets God's causing a being not to exist as His ceasing to preserve it in existence. Like Augustine, he tends to view the universe and the objects within it as constantly in need of being sustained, lest they slip away into nothingness (*ne in nihilum cadat*).[96] Yet by thinking of receiving and losing existence as analogous to receiving and surrendering a garment, he fosters the misconception that existence is a property. In fact, however, what he means by claiming that a thing has not-being from itself is simply that it does not have existence from itself (but from another). The language of Anselm's example wrongly suggests that a thing *possesses* existence, rather than rightly indicating that it must exist in order to possess any attribute at all. It possesses attributes

96. M 22 (S I, 41:61).

as soon as, but no sooner than, it exists. But existence is not itself an at-tribute (not a possession).

In the *Monologion* Anselm has putatively shown that no being other than God has existence from itself. If a thing returns to not-being once it ceases to exist, then it is only because it was created from not-being. We have just seen that its "possessing" not-being from itself is Anselm's way of saying that it does not exist from itself but from the Divine Be-ing. Yet how are we to understand the nothing from which God cre-ated all things? Anselm avoids the danger of reifying nothingness; the world could not have been created from nothingness itself (*de nihilo ipso*) because nothingness has absolutely no ontological status.[97] "Noth-ingness" is not the name for a preexistent matter — halfway between be-ing and not-being — from which God fashioned the world. Plotinus's in-terpretation of Plato's doctrine of the Receptacle in the *Timaeus* does not find its way into Anselm's philosophy. Moreover, not even Augus-tine's adaptation of Platonism is borrowed by Anselm. Augustine had in-terpreted Genesis 1:2 as referring to a *materia informis* from which God formed the ordered universe. Although this formless matter was not it-self nothing, it was almost nothing (*prope nihil*).[98] But unlike Plato, who insisted on the eternity of the Receptacle, Augustine insisted that *materia informis* was created *ex nihilo*. It was not something which limited God by being eternally set over against Him; rather, whatever being it had, it owed to God. For it was created together with time and existed only logically, not temporally, before the material objects that were formed out of it.[99]

Although Anselm has no use for Augustine's exegesis, he does agree with him in two respects. First, he accepts Augustine's theory that the word "nothing" has no reference; i.e., it does not refer to something whose ontological status is in between not-being and being.[100] Secondly, he agrees with Augustine against those who assert that God is the mate-rial cause, so to speak, as well as the efficient cause, of the world. In *Nature of the Good* Augustine distinguishes between *de ipso* and *ex ipso*. The

97. Anselm's view therefore differs from that of Fredegisus. See Ch. I, p. 34.

98. *Confessions* 12.19.28 (PL 32:836).

99. *Confessions* 13.33.48. Although Augustine thought of *materia informis* as *prope nihil*, he still maintained that this *prope nihil* was created from *omnino nihil* — so that creation was not creation from an eternally preexistent matter.

100. *The Teacher* 2.3.

world may be said to be from God (*ex ipso*) because He created it; but it is not of God (*de ipso*) because it is not of His substance.[101] Augustine finds it necessary to invoke this distinction since he faces opponents who argue as follows: "To state that God created the world from nothing (i.e., not from an eternally pre-existent matter) is to render the doctrine of creation unintelligible unless 'creation from nothing' is simply a way of saying 'creation from nothing other than from out of God' — so that God is both the efficient cause of the world and the substance out of which the world emanated." Augustine rejects this reasoning because he regards its conclusion as heretical. What is of God can only be God. Thus, the Son is God begotten of God (*de deo*) and the Holy Spirit is God proceeding from God (*de deo*). If the universe were from the substance of God, then it would be equal to the Son and the Holy Spirit, i.e., it would itself be God.[102] This conclusion, however, is not only heretical, but also (thinks Augustine) impossible. For God must be conceived of as an immaterial being — unchangeable and unchangeably beyond the course of time.

In *Monologion* 7 Anselm feels obliged to ask whether or not the world could have derived its existence as if through the matter of God. He concludes, "Therefore, since it is thoroughly obvious both that the essences of all things besides the Supreme Essence have been created by the Supreme Essence and that the essences of all things exist from no matter, nothing could be more clear than that the Supreme Essence through itself alone produced from nothing (*ex nihilo*) so great a complex of things — so vastly numerous, so beautifully formed, so well-ordered in their variety, so harmonious in their diversity" (S I, 21:29–22:10).

Having dismissed both the view that the world derives from God as if from a material cause and the view that *nothing* has a kind of being, Anselm is now ready to complete his interpretation. When we say that God created the world *ex nihilo*, we mean that He did not create it from something. That is, "nothing" and "not something" are equivalent expressions.[103] According to this rendering, to say that nothing existed before the Supreme Being is to say that not anything existed (logically and ontologically) before Him. It is not to suggest that there was a *time* when

101. Ch. 27 (PL 42:560). Note Rom. 9:36, which Augustine is interpreting: "Quoniam ex ipso [i.e., Deo], et per ipsum, et in ipso sunt omnia."

102. *Confessions* 12.7.7 (PL 32:828).

103. Note Augustine, *Incomplete Work against Julian* 5.31 (PL 45:1470).

no being (including the Supreme Being) existed (M 19). Yet, after having equated "nothing" and "not something," Anselm introduces a parallel which seems to threaten this equation: "We can say consistently that those things which have been made by the Creative Substance were made from nothing in the way that a rich man is commonly said to have been made from a poor man, or that a sick man has returned from sickness to health. That is, he who previously was poor is now rich, and he who previously was sick is now healthy. Similarly, we can consistently say that the Creative Essence made all things from nothing or that through the Creative Essence all things have been made from nothing. That is, things that once were nothing are now something" (M 8. S I, 23:26–33).

A rich man's now being what earlier he was not is fundamentally different from a thing's now existing whereas earlier it did not. For we can sensibly compare a rich man with the poor man he once was, but we can scarcely compare him with what he was before he existed. Anselm's illustration only compounds the difficulty inherent in talking about a *thing* as not existing. Having made it clear that "It is the case that X does not exist" means "It is not the case that X does exist," he falls back upon an example which obscures rather than elucidates his point.

One reason Anselm keeps treating existence as a property is that he thinks of things as existing archetypally in the mind of God before they exist in time.[104] In other words, before they existed, they both were and were not something. With respect to themselves they were nothing and not something; with respect to God they were something and not nothing (M 9). The clearest discussion of this topic occurs in *De Casu Diaboli* 12:

Teacher: I think that the world was nothing before it was made.

Student: True enough.

T. Therefore, before it was, it had absolutely no ability [potency].

S. This follows.

T. Then before it was, it was not able to be.

S. I don't agree. If it were not able to be, it would have been impossible for it ever to be.

T. Before there was a world, it was both possible and impossible for it to be. It was impossible for the world, since the world had no ability to be; but it was possible for God, since it was in God's power to make the

104. See Ch. I, p. 20.

world be. Therefore, the world exists because God had the ability to make a world before there was a world, and not because the world itself possessed an ability to be, before it was.

In this passage Anselm uses the Latin word *potestas* to express both capability and possibility.[105] A world which does not exist has no capability, but it is possible-to-be if God has ordained that it be. In general, we often say "X is able" or "X can," not because X itself has an ability, but because some second thing has an ability with respect to X. Thus, remarks Anselm, we say "Hector is able to be overcome by Achilles." Yet while saying "Hector can," we really mean to indicate that "Achilles can with respect to Hector" (DV 8). This fact about the conventions of language, taken together with the theory of exemplarism, helps explain the unhesitating and recurrent way in which Anselm speaks of nonexistent things which are destined to be, as if they had an ability (or possibility) to be.

Although nonexistent things possess from God (*ab illo*) their possibility-to-be, existent things possess from themselves (*a se*) their possibility-not-to-be.[106] When God ceases to cause a thing to be, it returns into its original state of not-being. And this state, Anselm has told us, is caused by God only in a negative sense — a sense which is not "properly" a causing at all. Although Aquinas was later to retain this negative sense, he was to reject Anselm's notion that the world and everything in it holds its possibility-not-to-be intrinsically: "If anyone says that those things which exist *ex nihilo* tend towards nothing insofar as they exist from themselves (*de se*), so that there is a *potentia* towards not-being in all created things, then this is clearly false. For created things are said to tend towards nothing in the same way they exist *ex nihilo*, viz., only according to the power (*potentia*) of their efficient cause. Therefore, there is no *potentia* towards not-being in created things. Rather, their Creator has the *potentia* to give being to them or to cease giving being to them, since He causes the production of things not by any necessity of nature, but by His own willing. . . ."[107] Thus, Thomas extends Anselm's analysis of *potestas* so that the world's possibility-to-be and its possibility-not-

---

105. Anselm uses *potestas*, *possibilitas*, and *potentia* interchangeably. See CDH II, 17 (S II, 123:11–12) and M preface (S I, 7:7).

106. "Redit in non esse, quod non ab illo sed a se, antequam fieret, habebat." DCD I (S I, 234:25–26).

107. *Summa Contra Gentiles*, Bk. 2, Ch. 30.

to-be derive equally from God, even though the one derives affirmatively, the other negatively. Thomas finds no more reason to ascribe to created things an inherent tendency toward not-being than to ascribe to things before their creation a tendency toward being.

Status of assertions containing the word "nothing." Since God created the world from nothing at all, and not from some *quasi nihil* analogous to Plato's Receptacle, Anselm feels obliged to examine how statements using the word "nothing" can be meaningful. In *De Casu Diaboli* the Student observes that if the word "nothing" really signifies nothing, then it has no signification. But if it has no signification, then it is meaningless; and if meaningless, it cannot properly be regarded as a name. By reverse reasoning, if "nothing" were properly a name, then there would have to be *something* which it named; but what it properly names cannot be something but must rather be nothing. Therefore, either way of taking up the question seems to force the conclusion that sentences containing the word "nothing" are meaningless because "nothing" is not a name.

In response to the Student's argument, Anselm notes that we do as a matter of fact say such things as "Nothing caused it" and "Evil caused it," and that these expressions do seem to have a meaning which accords with their use. He explains this meaning by recalling the equating of "nothing" with "not something." He thereby transforms the Student's problem into a question about how we speak of something and about how we deny that something is the case. In the *Philosophical Fragments* he distinguishes four different roles of the word "something." (1) Most naturally, we say that things such as stones, trees, and animals are something because they have names, are concepts in the mind, and exist in reality. (2) However, mythical creatures such as unicorns and chimeras are also said to be something, even though they do not exist in reality. (3) Furthermore, we say that *injustice* and *nothing* are something when we say that whoever is punished on account of his own injustice is punished for something, or when we say of some circumstance "It is nothing." Nevertheless, injustice and nothing neither exist nor are concepts in the mind, although they have names. (4) Finally, we also designate as something that which has no name, is not a concept, and has no existence at all. "For we say that the sun's not being above the earth causes it not to be day. And if every cause and every effect are said to be something, we will not deny that its not being day and the sun's not being above the horizon are something, since the one is the cause and the other the effect. Moreover, we say that not-being *is*, when, upon hearing someone maintain that something is not the case, we say that the state of affairs is as he says it is. But we ought rather, properly speaking, to say that the state of affairs is not, as he says it is not" (PF 43:14ff).

In these four ways Anselm attempts to account for the meaningfulness of a variety of linguistic expressions which we ordinarily use. In the case of the phrase "not something," he draws a comparison with the phrase "not man," noting that everyone understands what "not man" means. It signifies by indicating a removal. But to indicate removal, it must indicate what is to be removed. Therefore, "not man" obliquely indicates *man* in the very process of signifying the class removal of man. By the same token, Anselm is contending that "not something" obliquely indicates something in the process of signifying the removal of whatever is something. In this light, the word "nothing" is seen in a special way. It does not get its meaning by naming, since what it putatively names never exists — either in reality or as a determinate concept in the mind. "Nothing" owes its meaning to its unique role within a practice of language expressions which everyone understands. Yet what is readily understood at the level of common discourse tends to become paradoxical at the philosophical level. Anselm studiously avoids these paradoxes by articulating a philosophical position which is flexible enough to accommodate what we say regularly and without misunderstanding.

On the basis of the approach stated above, Anselm feels that he has defended the meaningfulness of two statements: "God created the world from nothing"; and "Evil and injustice are nothing." These statements become construed as the denials: "God did not create the world from something"; and "Evil and injustice are not something." But now an important difference arises. The two denials embody philosophical theses in an essential way, whereas the ordinary language expressions "Nothing caused it" and "Evil caused it" do not. (That is, the ordinary language expressions are compatible with any number of philosophical theses.) Having made his general point regarding the meaningfulness of the ordinary language expressions, Anselm should not suppose that he has *thereby* defended the intelligibility of his particular philosophical position. The philosophical position must be argued on its own merits and not on the basis of a theory about how the word "nothing" gets its meaning. It is conceivable that the theory should be right and yet that the philosophical statements containing the word "nothing" should themselves be unintelligible. Anselm does not seem to recognize this difference when dealing with creation *ex nihilo*. If God did not create the world from something external to Himself and if He did not create it from His own substance, how then can He be understood to have created at all? The intelligibility of the act of creation appears no less threatened by our having been told that God did not create from something. Anselm would have done better to concede that the doctrine of creation *ex nihilo*, as he expounds it, can never be made intelligible, since it transcends the bounds of human reason. Instead, he confused giving a semantical interpretation with providing a rational defense of a metaphysical thesis.

However, in the case of the doctrine of evil, Anselm self-consciously attempts to defend the intelligibility of his metaphysical thesis while at the same time tying it in with the semantical interpretation: "Blindness is called something according to the form of speaking, although it is not something according to fact (*secundum rem*). For just as we say of someone that he has sight and that sight is in him, so we also say that he has blindness and that blindness is in him — although this blindness is not 'something,' but rather is 'not-something.' For to have blindness is not to have something but to lack what is something, since blindness is not anything other than not-seeing, or the absence of sight where sight should be" (DCD 11). By treating evil (in the sense of corruption) as analogous to blindness, Anselm sheds some light on the notion that evil is nothing. For insofar as blindness is a privation, it is the loss of a perfection which ought to be present.[108] And if moral evil is a privation, then it also is the loss of a required perfection. Whether or not one agrees with Anselm that all moral evil is to be regarded as privation, the fact remains that this is how Anselm regards it. We have seen that he defines evil in the will (i.e., injustice) as the absence of uprightness. This absence, insofar as it is an absence, is not anything at all. Therefore, the statement "Evil is nothing" makes some kind of "philosophical" sense. Yet Anselm's

108. "When we say that injustice causes robbery, or that blindness causes a man to fall into a pit, we should not think that injustice or blindness do something. But we are to think that if justice were in the will and sight in the eyes, then neither the robbery nor the fall into the pit would have taken place. It is as if we were to say, 'The absence of a rudder drives the ship onto the rocks,' or 'The absence of reins causes the horse to run wild.' In these statements we mean only that if a rudder or reins were present, then the winds would not drive the ship onto the rocks nor would the horse run wild." DCD 26.

critics would be justified in challenging the notion that moral evil is properly analogous to blindness and in maintaining that Anselm's definition of "injustice" is tendentious.

God's responsibility for Satan's and Adam's sins. Up to this point Anselm has sought to do four things: to explain why the lack of a persevering will in Satan and in Adam did not result either from a malcreation or from a malicious withholding on God's part; to expose the presence of evil as really an absence, and thus a kind of not-being; to deny that not-being comes from God, while affirming that God created *ex nihilo*; to explore how the words "nothing" and "evil" can mean nothing and not-something. Having argued for these theses, he must now deliver himself from an apparent inconsistency. If evil is always privation and not-being, then the evil turning of Satan's will was itself nothing and privation. But Anselm has contended that Satan sinned through an *efficient*, and not a *deficient*, willing. So how can an efficient willing be nothing? *De Casu Diaboli* 8 deals with this problem by distinguishing between relative and absolute evil:

I think that both the will and the turning of the will are something. For although they are not substances, nevertheless it cannot be denied that they are beings of some sort, since there are many beings besides those which are properly called substances. Now a good will is not something more than an evil will, and the one is not a good thing more than the other is an evil thing. The will which wills to give a thing mercifully is not anything more than the will which wills to take something rapaciously; and the latter is as much an evil as the former is a good. Therefore, if an evil will were the very evil by which someone were called evil, then a good will would be the very good which would make someone good. But an evil will would be nothing if it were the very evil which we believe to be nothing; and conversely, a good will, since it is not anything more than an evil will, would be nothing also. . . . So we must conclude that an evil will is no more the very evil that makes creatures evil, than a good will is the very good that makes creatures good.

Anselm makes it clear that an evil will is not absolutely nothing. Insofar as it is a will it is something. Only insofar as it is evil is it nothing. Total evil is injustice; and hence injustice is absolutely nothing. By placing evil itself and evil volitions into different categories, Anselm is able, within his own philosophy, to make sense of the doctrine of privation.

Because Satan's will came to be deprived of uprightness, it came to be evil. But it came to be evil by efficiently willing a good (*commodum*) which was incompatible with the good of justice and therefore noncoincident with the will of God. A will wills insofar as it is a will, not insofar as it is evil — even when it wills evilly. Hence, even in the case of unredeemed fallen man, whose will lacks uprightness, every act of will must be viewed as something positive.

By distinguishing the evil act of will from the description of the will insofar as it is unjust, Anselm points to three different kinds of evil: the *will* is evil because (a) it chooses evilly and (b) lacks absolute goodness (viz., uprightness); and (c) certain *deeds* chosen by the will are evil (e.g., murder, stealing, lying). Anselm thinks of *a* and *b* as related in the following way: for Satan (and Adam) before the Fall, *a* causes *b*; for all fallen angels (and unredeemed men) *b* causes *a*. That is, Satan's evil choice "caused" his lack of uprightness: but his having lost uprightness in a sense "causes" his inability to choose other than evilly. Evil deeds, *c*, have a status analogous to that of volitions: they are something insofar as they are actions but not something insofar as they are evil. To these three distinctions Anselm adds a fourth: evil as pain or disadvantage (*incommoditas*): "The evil which is injustice is always nothing; but the evil which is disadvantage sometimes is nothing, as in blindness, and sometimes is something, as in sadness or grief. We always regard with aversion the disadvantage which is something. Therefore, when we hear the word 'evil,' we do not fear an evil which is nothing, but an evil which is something, and which follows the absence of good. For the evil of many disadvantages which are something, follows upon the evil of injustice and blindness, which are nothing; these disadvantages are what we dread when we hear the name 'evil' " (DCD 26). Only in this sense can evil be said to come from God, who causes natural disasters such as storms and earth tremors. God does not properly cause any evil relating to the will.

Anselm cannot yet close his argument. For if an evil act of will is something, and if everything which is something comes from God (as Anselm, like Augustine, has argued), then it still seems that Satan's unjust act of will must *in some respect* have come from God. Anselm admits that there is a respect in which God is responsible for Satan's evil willing. This is the sense in which we sometimes say that the one who permits something to happen, *when he could have prevented it*, wills its happening. In this way God bears responsibility for having permitted Satan to exercise his will evilly (though God did not approve of this will).[109] For God could have prevented Satan's willing *had He chosen to*. But Anselm implicitly suggests that God could not have chosen to, because to have done so would have been to violate Satan's freedom. Since this freedom was a good, the removal of freedom would have been an injustice — and God can do no injustice. Therefore, in Anselm's peculiar sense, God both could and could not have directly prevented Satan's evil willing. But the way in which He could have warrants the legitimacy of saying that God permitted Satan the use of his will for evil. Therefore, Satan both did (by permission) and did not (by approval) sin with a willing which came from God.[110]

The notion of permissive willing relates to Anselm's notion of causation in the following way: if A wills to permit X, then A is an indirect cause of X's occurrence. If A stands by while B stabs C, and if A could easily disarm B but does not, then B directly causes C's wound, whereas A indirectly causes it. A *indirectly causes* C's wound by *not directly causing* B *not* to be armed.[111] God indirectly caused Satan's evil willing by *not directly causing* Satan *not* to will what he did. In the case of the stabbing, A's inactivity is possibly an evil (depending upon the further description of the action). In the case of Satan, however, God's inactivity is necessarily a good; for God was indirectly causing a will which was keeping uprightness not to be removed from Satan before he sinned.[112]

Anselm's argument now concludes. He has claimed to show that God both is and is not the cause of Satan's sinning. Because God is only an indirect cause in a sense restricted to mere permitting, He may be said to bear some responsibility for Satan's fall without Himself in any way having done evil or having been a source of evil. By asserting both God's responsibility and nonresponsibility for Satan's fall, Anselm is iterating his oft-repeated observation that opposite characteristics are at times ascribable to the same thing in different respects. The sun in its circular course approaches the point it is leaving. And while moving from east

109. DCD 20 and 28. See PF 37:29ff for a further distinction between *voluntas efficiens*, *voluntas approbans*, *voluntas concedens*, and *voluntas permittens*.

110. On the two senses of "could" see Ch. 6, p. 197 below.

111. Cf. PF 29.20ff.

112. Thomas altogether disallows the statement that God is an indirect cause of man's sin (ST, 1st of 2nd, 79, 1).

to west (diurnally), it moves from west to east (annually).[113] Jesus both ought and ought not to have been put to death (DV 8). From the point of view of the divine program of salvation, His death ought to have occurred; from the point of view of human action, His death ought not to have occurred.

So too, Satan's sin both ought and ought not to have occurred. With respect to God, who indirectly caused it, it ought to have occurred; with respect to Satan, who directly "caused" it, it ought not to have occurred. These respects are always different. Hence, Satan's evil will can never be ✓ related to God in the sense in which it ought not to be. Only if this sense could be applied to God, could God be adjudged the ultimate Author of evil. But Anselm has argued — consistently and deductively — that from God come only being and goodness. This last point Anselm could have argued on the basis of his description of God alone. For if God is the greatest conceivable being, then He cannot be the Source or the Cause of moral evil. Otherwise, a being which is greater than God could be conceived — and so on. Yet Anselm is not content with this utterly general approach. He seeks particular arguments with which to counter the particular inconsistencies that seem to arise from theologizing upon Scripture. He does assert formally that God necessarily acts justly, but at the same time he pursues the special reasons which the problem at hand seems to demand. Because of the general proposition, Anselm is entitled to believe that there must exist some set of reasons whereby God's justice and goodness in relation to the Fall can be defended. But the general proposition entails only that there is such a set — without determining this set exactly. In the assurance that such reasons do exist, Anselm has proceeded to specify a set which he thinks solves the theological problem posed by the origin of moral evil.

Although Anselm's discussion of evil and the Fall primarily concerns Satan, the chain of argumentation which he develops has a direct bearing upon the fall of Adam as well. Thus, *De Casu Diaboli* may be viewed as an attempt to defend the perfection of creation — while allowing that human nature, through a wayward will, injured itself and, as it were, robbed God of honor. Because of the Fall, Adam faced the prospect of physical death. But as the soul thus brought corruption to the body, so

113. DC I, 4.

the corrupted body lay an additional weight upon the soul.[114] In man's movement toward physical death Anselm sees a sign of the general tendency of all created things toward not-being. The soul itself holds intrinsically the possibility not to be, even though at every moment its existence is sustained by God. God is thus the Creator, who calls the world forth from nothing, and the Sustainer, who holds creation together lest it fall back completely into nothing. He is the Savior, who redeems man from the not-being of evil, and the Comforter, who fills the empty heart with joy. As the Highest Being, God is metaphysically the antithesis of nothing; as both merciful and just, He is morally the antithesis of evil. In the Fall, Satan and Adam lost uprightness — the one irredeemably, the other redeemably. To restore fallen men to the place of fallen angels, God became incarnate in human form. The doctrine of divine incarnation poses a series of theological problems with which Anselm must further cope.

114. DCV 8 (S II, 150:2).

Chapter *VI*

Christology
and Soteriology

Although having forsaken God, Adam remained unforsaken by God. In the eternal order of decrees God had provided for the human race a means of salvation, viz., the divine incarnation. No one but God could make satisfaction for man's sin, and no one but man ought to make satisfaction. Therefore, it was necessary that a God-man repay the debt of sin (CDH II, 6). In a sense, the entire *Cur Deus Homo* is directed toward proving this thesis. For Anselm thinks that if he can show the impossibility of human redemption's occurring other than through the agency of a God-man, he will have removed the stigma which seems to accompany the notion of incarnation. According to Anselm's unbelieving opponents, the Christian doctrine of salvation abases God by depicting Him as suffering in human form. Against these opponents Anselm contends that they do not really understand what the Christian faith teaches.

We affirm without doubt that the divine nature is impassible, that it cannot be abased, and that it cannot expend any effort with regard to what it wills to do. But we say that the Lord Jesus Christ is true God and true man, one person in two natures and two natures in one person. Hence, when we say that God experiences weakness or lowliness, we do not understand this in accordance with the sublimity of His impassible nature but in accordance with the weakness of the human substance which He bore. Thus, no reason is known to interfere with our faith. So we signify no abasement of the divine substance; rather we show that the person of God and of man was one. Therefore, we do not understand the incarnation of God to have involved any abasement; instead, we believe that the nature of man was therein exalted (CDH I, 8. S II, 59: 18–28).

Thus, in developing his particular interpretation of the incarnation, Anselm must at the same time commit himself to a Christology, for these work themselves out *pari passu*.

WHY A GOD-MAN WAS NECESSARY

Devil-ransom theory. To begin with, Anselm rejects the Augustinian theory which maintains that the death of Christ served to ransom mankind from the captivity of Satan. In *On the Trinity* 13 and *Free Choice* 3 Augustine viewed Adam's yielding to Satan's solicitation as bringing the human race into Satan's power.[1] Satan retained this dominion until he unjustly slew Jesus, who, because He had not sinned, was undeserving of death. By undergoing death, Jesus paid to Satan the debt which man owed, and thereby ransomed the human race. Yet Satan was allowed to keep possession of those men who chose to remain in his dominion. In this way God dealt with Satan through justice rather than through force. For had God seized mankind by force, He would unjustly have injured Satan, who was justly in possession of man.[2] But Satan, by unjustly afflicting a just man, forfeited his right of possession and his claim against God, making it morally admissible for God to free human beings from capitivity.

In *Cur Deus Homo* I, 7, Anselm, through Boso, asserts that there is no reason why God should not have dealt with Satan through force, for Satan had no right to punish man.[3] Even if it were just for man to be punished, it was unjust for Satan to administer this punishment. For Satan afflicted man out of malevolence, not out of zeal for righteousness. To be sure, fallen man is in bondage to sin; and since Satan is the father of all sin, the human race is in a sense captive to him. But this sense does not by itself necessitate the further notion that God must pay a ransom to

1. DT 13.12–15; 15.25.44. *Free Choice* 3.10.31. Also *Enchiridion* 49.14. Anselm took the statement of this theory from the school of Laon. But he was certainly directly familiar with Augustine's own statements. See J. Rivière, "D'un singulier emprunt à S. Anselme chez Raoul de Laon," *Revue des sciences religieuses*, 16 (1936), 344–346. Note R. W. Southern, *Saint Anselm and His Biographer*, p. 87.

2. DT 13.14.18.

3. For a restatement of Anselm's view see also *Meditatio Redemptionis Humanae* (S III, 85:46–86:58).

Satan. On Anselm's view, God must not be thought of as transacting with Satan, who is himself God's own creature. God did not pay Satan a debt which He did not owe, but Satan owed God a debt which he could not pay. Although the ransom theory arises from the Pauline teaching that fallen man is a servant of sin,[4] Anselm points out that God need not purchase this servant from Satan in order to set him free. He need not do so because Satan is at no time man's owner, even though he may in some reduced sense be his master.[5]

In *Cur Deus Homo* I, 22–23, Anselm argues that God intended man to overcome Satan through resisting his promptings. Thereby man would have honored God by manifesting that a creature weaker than Satan and solicited toward evil nonetheless remained steadfast in uprightness — whereas Satan, stronger than man and unprompted, abandoned uprightness for something he preferred more. Had man defeated Satan, the perfection with which God had created angelic nature would thus have been visibly vindicated. But man was defeated to the dishonor of God. So with the fall of the human race there remained the original obligation to conquer Satan. "Attend to strict justice and judge according to it whether man makes satisfaction equal to his sin unless by conquering Satan he restores to God that very thing which he took away from God by allowing himself to be conquered by Satan. Thus, just as through man's having been conquered, Satan stole what belonged to God and God lost it, so through man's conquering, Satan would lose something which God would regain" (CDH I, 23. S II, 91:10–16). Anselm admits a sense in which Satan stole man from God and in which man is in captivity to Satan and to sin. What Anselm objects to in the Augustinian theory is its insistence that the purpose of the incarnation was to effect the salvation of man *by dealing with Satan justly*.[6] If man's redemption

4. Rom. 6:16–17. Also Eph. 4:8: "Ascending up on high, He led captivity captive. . . ." Augustine is also influenced by Acts 26:16–18 and Col. 1:13.

5. Cf. Luke 16:13.

6. "For although on account of the unity of person God is said to have done what that man did, nevertheless God did not need to descend from Heaven in order to conquer the Devil, nor did He need to act against the Devil through justice in order to free man. But God required of man that he conquer the Devil, and He required that the one who through sinning had offended against Him should make satisfaction through justice. Indeed, God owed the Devil nothing except punishment, and man owed him nothing except requital, so that man should conquer the one by whom he was conquered. Yet [properly speaking] whatever was required of man was owed to God, not to the Devil" CDH II, 19 (S II, 131:17–24).

were only or essentially a question of dealing with Satan, Anselm teaches, then God could have accomplished this without Himself having taken on human form.

Thus the Augustinian theory, maintains Anselm, fails satisfactorily to explain the incarnation. And it alleges that Satan was justly in possession of man, whereas, in fact, his possession was a form of robbery. Both Anselm and Augustine concede God's power to save the human race by means other than incarnation were He so to will. But Augustine finds the way of incarnation more befitting (*convenientior*) to God since it is more suitable that God redeem man by treating Satan justly than merely by treating him forcibly.[7] By contrast, Anselm tries to show that the incarnation was the necessary [8] (but freely chosen) means for accomplishing man's salvation. For only a God-man would be able to make satisfaction for the dishonor done to God through man's sin, and satisfaction must be made before God can forgive man's sin. Finally, in the *Meditation on Human Redemption* Anselm indicates still another objection to the theory of ransom: viz., the theory implies that one of God's purposes in incarnation was to conceal His divine power, and thereby to deceive Satan into unjustly acting against this power in the person of Jesus. But since God is not a deceiver, any theory which implies that He is must be rejected.

Boso's four main questions. Relative to God's redemptive purpose, then, why was it at all necessary for God to become incarnate? By posing four main questions, Boso presses Anselm to articulate this rationale.

(1) Why did God not make another man like Adam? God made Adam from no other man, but miraculously from the clay of the ground. When Adam fell, why could God not have made another man by the same miraculous means, and through this second man have provided redemption for Adam and his descendants (CDH I, 5)? For like original man, the second man would have been created sinless. Therefore, his life and death could have been as efficacious as that of a God-man. And in this way God could have spared Himself even the ostensible ignominy of incarnation.

Boso develops this question no further: it remains the brusk expression of a possible stance taken by unbelievers. Anselm's fuller response has

7. DT 13.10.13 (PL 42:1024). Cf. DT 13.14.18; 13.18.23. *Christian Combat* 11.12.
8. CDH I, 25 (S II, 95:9–14).

two parts. First, had the death of a non-Adamic sinless man been instrumental in effecting salvation for Adam and his descendants, then Adam and his race would have been reckoned as indebted to this other for his meritorious work on their behalf. In such case, Adamic man would be servant to someone in addition to God — something improper to believe. After the fall of the angels and of man, God intended to replace the number of fallen angels by redeemed men in such a way that these men would be equal in position to the good angels.[9] Since the good angels are servants only to God, it is necessary that redeemed men be servants only to God. Moreover, as the Adamic human race would have remained upright without the help of any other creature, had Adam not sinned, so the Adamic human race must be restored through the aid of one of its own members once Adam did fall.

Secondly, a new man, not of Adam's race, would not be under obligation to make satisfaction for the sin of the race. "For just as it is right that man should make satisfaction for the fault of man, so it is necessary that satisfaction be made by the very man who commits the offence or else by someone of his race. Otherwise neither Adam nor his race will make satisfaction for themselves. Therefore, just as sin was propagated unto all men from Adam and Eve, so no one except themselves or someone begotten from them ought to make satisfaction for the sin of men. Accordingly, since they are unable to do this, the one who shall do it must be from them" (CDH II, 8. S II, 103:1–6).

At this point Anselm's reasoning appears to involve special pleading. For it seems to lay down the moral necessity that satisfaction for the sins of a race be made by some member of that race — without laying down the further moral necessity (but only the moral obligation) that each member of the race make satisfaction for his own *personal* sins. That is, it might be argued against Anselm that a member of the Adamic race could admissibly be thought to make payment for the sin of Adamic nature (i.e., original sin, or racial sin), which he himself owes, as one who possesses this nature. But how could he owe the debt of all other men's

---

9. See, Ch. I, p. 24. Cf. Luke 20:36. Note J. McIntyre: "The primary ground [for the necessity of salvation, according to Anselm] is to be found in God's purpose for rational creatures; in creating rational beings it is His will for them that they should serve Him and give Him honour by obeying His commandments, and so achieve their highest blessedness. . . . The 'secondary ground' for the necessity of salvation is that God has resolved to substitute men for the fallen angels." *St. Anselm and His Critics*, p. 81.

personal sins? And if he does not owe *this* debt, how can he (any more than a non-Adamic man) make payment for these sins? Indeed if, as Anselm thinks, such a man could admissibly make satisfaction for personal sins which are not his, then why should it be thought morally illicit for a non-Adamic man to make satisfaction for both racial and personal sins which likewise are not his? Moreover, if the one who shares Adam's nature does not himself possess original sin (as in the case of a God-man), then in what sense does his human nature bring him at all under the obligation to make satisfaction? Is not the possibility of his performing a meritorious deed due precisely to his being under no obligation? Anselm's complete response to these possible objections must be sought in his treatment of Boso's explicitly remaining questions.

(2) Why could God not simply forgive man? Boso's second question is urgently central. Would not an incarnation have been superfluous? For if God is omnipotent, surely He could have forgiven man's sin by a direct act of will rather than through the death of a God-man (CDH I, 6). That is, God's willingness to forgive could itself have been unconditional and noninstrumental. Forgiveness would thus follow immediately from His merciful nature. Anselm answers that for God to remit sin without repayment is unfitting. Were He to proceed in this way, then both the sinner and the non-sinner would have equal status before Him. If sin is not punished, then it is subject to no law. And if subject to no law, then there is a respect in which the sinner more than the non-sinner resembles God, who also is subject to no external law. But this belief is incongruous (CDH I, 12).

As God's creature, every human being owes obedience to God's will. We have already seen how Anselm views the fall of Satan and of Adam as involving acts of will contrary to the will of God. In other words, each sinned by not paying his debt of obedience; and the non-payment of this debt tended to dishonor God (CDH I, 11). Now, no one can honor or dishonor God as He is in Himself, because no one can either add to or detract from God's perfection (CDH I, 15). Nevertheless, by not submitting to the will of God, Satan and Adam destroyed the original order which had been bestowed upon rational nature, so that *as it were* God's honor was diminished. For when a work of art loses its beauty and its original form, its marred state tends to deflect praise from the artist. So by marring itself, rational nature did a disservice to the Creator. Having robbed God of honor, human nature incurred a debt in addition to the debt of obedience.[10] Moreover, human nature must repay more than it took away from God because it must not only return what was stolen, but it must also repair the injury which accompanied the loss. This, then, is Anselm's formula for the notion of rendering satisfaction: viz., repayment plus reparation (CDH I, 11).

But how, continues Boso, can punishment of the sinner honor God (CDH I, 14)? Anselm points out that punishment proves to the sinner that *nolens volens* he is the creature of God and accordingly cannot escape God's will. God preserves His honor by the continued exercise of His Lordship over creation. In sinning, man took away what was rightly God's. In punishing, God takes away what would have been man's. For God deprives man of the blessedness which he was to possess had he not rebelled against the divine commandment. To avoid this punishment, man must make satisfaction for sin. Were a sinful man forgiven by God apart from the making of satisfaction, he could not possibly be the equal of those angels who have never sinned. And this fact constitutes another reason why repayment must be made before man can be restored to the state of dignity for which he was created (CDH I, 19). What, then, does a man have with which to pay the debt of sin? Boso suggests repaying God by adhering to the monastic virtues: "Do I not honor God when out of love and fear of Him I cast aside temporal pleasure with contrition of heart, when through fastings and good works I spurn the delights and tranquility of this life, when by giving and forgiving I generously bestow my own belongings, and when in obedience I subject myself to God?" (CDH I, 20. S II, 86:28–87:2). But Anselm disqualifies this suggestion by indicating that each man would have owed all these things to God even had he not sinned. Therefore, by means of these he cannot make payment for his sin. Accordingly, Boso must now concede: "If even when I do not sin I owe myself and all my abilities to Him so that I might not sin, then I have nothing with which to make restitution for my sin" (CDH I, 20. S II, 87:27–28).

Yet even if the good works mentioned above were to count toward payment for sin, contends Anselm, they would not outweigh even the slightest of sins. Should someone turn his head to look in a direction which God has proscribed (as Lot's wife turned to look at Sodom),

---

10. We must not forget that Augustine's devil-ransom theory makes use of the language of debt and repayment. *Free Choice* 3.15; DT 13.16.21.

then even this violation of God's will is so grave that it cannot be atoned for by contrition and mere works of penance. And even if by such a single glance one could save the entire universe from perishing, one ought rather to choose to obey God (CDH I, 21). Now, whoever dishonors God should offer as reparation *something greater than that with respect to which he was obligated not to dishonor God*.[11] Since no man ought to dishonor God even at the expense of the whole world's perishing, the satisfaction for sin must surpass everything that is other than God. And no one who is merely a man (not even a sinless non-Adamic man) can render this satisfaction.

Anselm concludes his discussion of Boso's second question with the observation that man's present inability to pay for his sin does not excuse him from blame. A servant who casts himself into a pit against his master's command, and then cannot extricate himself, has no excuse for being unable to carry out the duties previously assigned him. So too, man, who freely and against God's command gave himself over to sin, is without excuse for his inability to fulfill his duties toward God. Were God to remit the penalty for sin simply because man is now unable to repay, this would be tantamount to His remitting what He cannot obtain. Were God not to take away man's blessedness, then He would in effect be rewarding sin (CDH I, 24). "I do not deny that God is merciful. . . . However, we are discussing that ultimate mercy by which he makes man blessed after this life. By means of the arguments given previously I think I have proved that this blessedness ought to be given only to one whose sins are completely forgiven and that forgiveness ought to come only if the debt of sin has been repaid . . ." (CDH I, 24. S II, 94: 10–16).

(3) How could Jesus' death honor God? God will not allow His work in creation to be frustrated but will provide some means of making satisfaction for man's sin. This means, we have seen, comes through the life and death of a God-man: only God can make satisfaction for sin and only man ought to make it; therefore, it must be made by a God-man if it is to be made at all (CDH II, 6). This man who is also God will be able to offer to God a gift which He does not personally owe — a gift which will honor God to such an extent as to count as payment for all men's sins. This gift can only be the voluntary submission to death for the sake of

11. CDH I, 21; II, 6. *Meditatio Redemptionis Humanae* (S III, 86:75–87:81).

justice. Since this man, Jesus,[12] is fully just, He is not obliged to die. Therefore, His death, unlike the deaths of all other men, can be meritorious. In Book I, Chapter 8 Boso asked how God could justly condemn an innocent man in order to free a guilty one. And Anselm pointed out that God did not condemn Jesus or require death from Him against His will. Rather, Jesus freely underwent death on man's behalf, so that His death honors rather than reproaches God. But now Anselm observes that because Jesus willed to submit to death, He was not wretched. "As an advantage possessed against one's will does not conduce to happiness, so a disadvantage freely and wisely embraced does not lead to wretchedness" (CDH II, 12). The justice of this man's death assures the restoration of honor to God and the availability of salvation to all men.

(4) How can Christ's sacrifice outweigh the sins of all men? It is not yet clear to Boso how the death of Christ could outbalance the sins of all men. Accordingly, Anselm notes that assault on the person of Christ is the greatest sin possible, inasmuch as this is an attack on the person of God (CDH II, 14). Therefore, since Christ willed to undergo this greatest of all injustices, the merit of His death is the greatest possible. Consequently, it suffices to outweigh all the sins of mankind. Justice requires that the Son of God be given a reward for honoring God by defeating Satan. But since, lacking nothing, the Son has everything which the Father has, no payment can constitute a reward to Him. Nonetheless, since a reward is due Him, it may be rightly transferred to whomever He wills to have it paid. Therefore, it is paid to man on the Son's behalf, thereby canceling the debt of sin.

With this move Anselm's main line of reasoning is systematically complete. Yet it retains the unresolved problem of how Christ ought, as man, to redress human nature's injury to God's honor. For as sinless, Christ gave to God perfect obedience, which even He owed and which did not make restitution on behalf of man. But as sinless He also offered to God that which is meritorious precisely because it was not owed, viz., His life. It becomes clear that when Anselm argues "Only man ought to; only God can; therefore, necessarily a God-man," [13] he is equivocating on the meaning of "ought." For the sense in which man *ought* is the uncondi-

12. Although Anselm is arguing "as if nothing were known of Christ," we may without confusion to his argument identify the God-man by His historical name "Jesus."

13. Augustine's reasoning proceeds differently: Unless the mediator were human He could not be killed; unless He were God men would not believe that He voluntarily underwent death; therefore, a God-man was required. DT 13.14.18.

tional sense in which he *owes*. (The Latin verb *debere*, used repeatedly by Anselm, contains the notion of owing.) But the sense in which the God-man *ought* is the conditional sense in which He ought since (if) He *wills to*. In *Cur Deus Homo* II, 18 Anselm acknowledges these two different senses (S II, 129:3–8). But he fails to realize that their appearance invalidates his argument.

So then, in the sense of owing, Anselm would not really say "Christ ought, as man, to redress the dishonor done to God." For not Christ, but every other man, owes. Perhaps, then, Anselm would prefer to say "Human nature ought, and through Christ *is able*, to redress the dishonor done to God." But even here a difficulty would remain. For although human nature *ought*, nonetheless in Christ not the human nature *is able* but only the divine nature. Yet, Anselm might state his position more precisely by saying: "As in Adam human nature sinned, thereby incurring a debt for itself and all other human natures (men) propagated naturally from it, so in Jesus a sinless human nature repaid the debt of sin on behalf of all other human natures (all other men) and did so by means of the assistance of the divine nature" (cf. n. 21 below). This formulation would allow Anselm to say that in Jesus the human nature, assisted by the divine nature, *is able* to make satisfaction. But though this formulation is more precise and more consistent than the previous ones, it still does not save the main argument of the *Cur Deus Homo* from equivocation. For the sense in which sinful human nature *ought* to make satisfaction is not the sense in which sinless human nature *ought* to make satisfaction. At times Anselm tends to regard human nature as if it were an unindividuated universal. For instance, in the *Meditation on Human Redemption* he writes: "In *that* man [Jesus] human nature freely gave to God something its own which was not owed, so that it might redeem itself in others in whom it did not have what it owed and what it was required to repay" (S III, 87:99–101). But this passage, we shall see later, does not consistently convey Anselm's position that the human nature in one man is numerically distinct from that in another.

When Anselm says "Only man ought to," he is also tacitly saying "Only man can"; and this sense of "can" is different from the sense of "can" in the statement "Only God can." Only God can — in the sense that only God has the power to make satisfaction; only man can — in the sense that only man can consistently be thought to make satisfaction. That is, only God *can effectively*; only man *can acceptably*. For it is theologically unacceptable (i.e., inconsistent with other theological tenets) for man to be forgiven immediately, apart from any satisfaction's having been made; and it is theologically unacceptable (inconsistent) for anyone who is not a man (of Adam's race) to make payment for Adam and his descendants' debts.

So, then, Anselm is operating with equivocal senses of "ought" and "can." Only Adam and his natural descendants ought$_1$ in that only they owe; but Jesus ought$_2$ in that He wills to. Only God can$_1$ in that He has the power to; but only man can$_2$ in that no other alternative is theologically admissible. Anselm's confusion occurs when he infers, invalidly, that because only man ought$_1$ and only God can$_1$, only a God-man ought$_2$ and can$_1$. And his confusion continues when he implies that only Adamic man can$_2$ because only Adamic man ought$_1$ — that is, that non-Adamic man can$_2$ not because he ought$_1$ not. But if Jesus both ought$_1$ not and can$_2$, why should the case be different for a non-Adamic man? Why, in other words, should we predicate "can$_2$ not" rather than simply "can$_1$ not" of a non-Adamic man? Clearly, a non-Adamic man who was not also God could$_1$ not render satisfaction, for he would not have the power to make a payment greater than everything which is other than God. But why could$_2$ not God have become incarnate by assuming a non-Adamic human nature in order for a non-Adamic God-man to render satisfaction?

It becomes increasingly clear that Anselm's thought is influenced by the following analogy: a servant who has dishonored his good master brings disgrace upon himself and his whole family. That disgrace can be removed only through the future merits either of the servant himself or of some member of his family. An outsider may, to some extent, redress the grievance on behalf of the family; but his actions, by themselves, can never remove the family disgrace. This analogy, or something like it, governs Anselm's statement that reparation for human nature's sin ought to be made only by someone who himself belongs to the family of Adamic man. For only such a person will restore honor to God by exhibiting the original glory of human creation through defeating Satan. Moreover, such a person's merits may justifiably be imputed to the other members of his family — restoring them, if they will, to favor with their Lord, and removing, if they repent, the stigma of sin.

Anselm's attempt to make the doctrines of incarnation and atonement plausible does not escape the marks of feudal imagery. His theory may, it is true, be restated independently of this imagery; but this reformulation could not then even preserve the semblance of escaping the non sequitur in the fundamental argument of the *Cur Deus Homo*. However, if we look beyond this argument's difficulty, we witness an otherwise vigorous effort to defend the mercy of God in relation to His justice. The *Proslogion* had already taken up the problem cursorily; now on a fuller scale Anselm joins issue with Boso, who speaks for the opponents of the Christian faith rather than for himself. The underlying correspondences with feudal honor and vassal service, as well as with commercial transaction, never eclipse the exemplary nature of Christ's death. Boso sees that Christ presented a matchless example of acting and willing for the sake of justice, and that men should be His imitators (CDH II, 19). God's mercy toward man is manifested in, rather than apart from, the process of atonement. There can be no mercy toward fallen angels because there can be no atonement for their sins. A God-angel could not atone for all angels, since angels do not constitute a race — thereby all descending from a common ancestor.[14] Redemption belongs only to man, in whom God wondrously restores human nature to a state higher than the state it originally enjoyed.[15]

ASSUMPTUS HOMO

In the incarnation the Son of God *assumpsit hominem*. This phrase, a standard expression in *De Incarnatione, Cur Deus Homo*, and *De Conceptu*, presents a problem of translation and interpretation. Did the Son of God assume *manhood* or did He assume *a man*? That is, did He assume a nature or did He assume a person into a unity with His own nature and person? The Latin wording alone will not help us decide Anselm's meaning, since the phrase is essentially ambiguous, and therefore, from the point of view of English, admits of either translation. Only a look at the systematic context in which Anselm uses the term will serve to clarify his real meaning. It is noteworthy that Augustine uses the same expression in *On the Trinity* 13.18.23 and in his treatise *Against a Sermon of the Arians* 8.6.[16]

14. See Appendix II, p. 250, n. 5.
15. CDH II, 16 (S II, 117:6–7).
16. PL 42:1032, 688. Augustine also uses *suscepit hominem*. And in *Eighty-Three*

Christology and Soteriology

Anselm's most detailed statement comes in *De Incarnatione* 11, where he argues that God assumed another nature, not another person. So then, if God did not assume another person, He could not have assumed *a man*, since every man is a person. *Assumere hominem* must therefore be understood as "to assume manhood" or "to assume a human nature."[17] In making this point, Anselm summarizes one view of his opponents in order to fault it: "Must we not say that there are two persons in Christ, just as we say that there are two natures? For before the assumption of manhood God was a person, and He did not cease being a person after He assumed manhood. Moreover the assumed man (*homo assumptus*) is a person, because every individual man is known to be a person. This means that the person of God who existed before the incarnation is one, and the person of the assumed man is another. Therefore, just as Christ is God and man, so there seem to be two persons in Him" (DIV 11. S II, 28:15–21).

In rejecting this reasoning, Anselm is rejecting Nestorianism. In contrast to Nestorius's affirmation of a merely moral unity of two persons, Anselm pleads for the doctrine of the hypostatic union of two natures. On this rendering, the Son of God assumed a human nature into a real unity of person with Himself. "As in God one nature is a plurality of persons, and a plurality of persons is one nature; so in Christ one person is a plurality of natures, and a plurality of natures is one person. For as the Father is God, the Son God, and the Holy Spirit God, and yet there are not three gods but only one God; so in Christ God is person and man is person, and yet there are not two persons but only one person. Although God and man are different natures, yet in Christ they are not different persons; for in Christ the person who is God is also man" (DIV 11. S II, 28:23–29:3). So the man Jesus, called by Anselm the assumed man (*assumptus homo*), was originated when the second member of the Trinity (called both Word of God and Son of God) assumed a human nature (*assumpsit hominem*) into His own person. Thus, Jesus had, unconfused, both a divine and a human nature — the one derived from

Different Questions 73.2 (PL 40:85) he uses both senses of *homo*: "id est, habendo hominem, inventus est ut homo."

See also Boethius, *The Person and the Two Natures* 5 (PL 64:1348) and 8 (PL 64:1353).

17. N.B. the discussion by R. Roques, ed., *Anselme de Cantorbéry. Pourquoi Dieu s'est fait homme*, pp. 140–161. Note also that in CDH II, 8 (S II, 102:26–27) Anselm substitutes *assumere humanam naturam* for *assumere hominem*.

the substance of the Father, the other derived from the substance of Mary.[18] And although the Son of God existed prior to the incarnation, the man Jesus did not.[19] Anselm's use of *homo* in the expression *assumptus homo* is, then, different from his use of *homo* in *assumere hominem*. The former designates an individual, whereas the latter indicates a nature. To say *assumptus homo* is simply the obverse of saying *incarnatus deus*, for in being the incarnate God Jesus was the assumed man.

At this point Anselm makes a statement of utmost importance:

Taken by itself "man" does not signify the same thing as "man assumed by the Word," which signifies Jesus. For by the word "man" is meant simply "human nature," as has been said. But by "the assumed man" or by "Jesus" we indicate, together with a human nature, a collection of properties which is the same for the assumed man and for the Word. Therefore, we do not say that *man*, in an unrestricted sense, is the same person as the Word — lest we should imply that any man whatsoever, no less than that man [Jesus], is the same person as the Word. Rather, we say that the Word and the assumed man, viz., Jesus, are the same person. Likewise, we do not believe that that man is the same person as God, in

18. As stated in the Quicumque and also by the Council of Chalcedon (451). Anselm follows the Quicumque both in his doctrine of the Trinity and in his Christology. By insisting that a human nature consists of both a body and an immortal soul he is repudiating (1) Arianism, which taught that the Word (Logos) took the place of the soul when it assumed a human nature, and (2) Apollinarianism, which allowed that Jesus possessed an animal soul but not a rational soul. N.B. Augustine, Sermon 5.7. *On the Gospel of John* 47.9; 78.3. *Gift of Perseverance* 24.67. *Christian Combat* 19.21. Anselm would agree with Augustine that while Jesus lay dead the Word was in Paradise, the soul in Hell, and the body in the tomb. *On the Gospel of John* 111.2.

Because Jesus could die He was in the *likeness* of sinful flesh (Rom. 8:3). Since he was without sin, he ought not to have died — death being a consequence of sin. Yet because he was of Adam's nature he was able to die, even though he was not under the necessity of dying. *Against Julian the Heretic* 5.15.54.

19. Augustine: Jesus is God without beginning, man with a beginning. *Enchiridion* 35.10.

N.B. Anselm's terminology in DIV 11 (S II, 29:5–15): "When we say 'man,' we signify only the nature which is common to all men. But when we say, demonstratively, 'This man' or 'That man,' or use the proper name 'Jesus,' we designate a person who consists of a nature together with a collection of properties which individuates the nature common to Him and others, and which distinguishes Him from others. Thus, these expressions do not designate just any man, but designate the man to whom the angel referred in the Annunciation, who was divine and human, Son of God and Son of the Virgin, and whatever can be said truly about Him either according to His divinity or according to His humanity. For in designating or naming the person who is the Son of God we cannot avoid designating and naming the person who is the Son of man, and vice versa. For the one who is the Son of God is also the Son of man; and the same collection of properties belongs to the Word and to the assumed man."

an unrestricted sense. Rather we believe that He is the same person as the Word and Son — lest we should seem to profess that He is the same person as the Father or the Holy Spirit. Yet, since the Word is divine and since the assumed man is human, it is true to say "The same person is God and man." But by "God" must be understood "the Word," and by "man" must be understood "the Son of the Virgin" (DIV 11. S II, 29:26–30:6).

Anselm's point stands out more vividly when it is viewed in contrast with the position that the second person of the Trinity did not assume a particular human nature but human nature as a whole. Thus, as original man (Adam) was universal man, so the God-man (second Adam) was also universal man. As the whole human race was present in Adam, so Adamic human nature as a whole was present in Jesus. As Adam's fault passes to all other men (except the God-man), so Jesus' merit passes to all other men (without having to be accepted by them). In refusing to contemplate this position Anselm teaches that the Son of God united Himself with *a* human nature rather than with human nature as such. Therefore, the incarnate Word was a man and not Man. Accordingly, the title *Cur Deus Homo* should be interpreted (not translated) as: Why God in the person of the Son assumed a human nature.

Having followed Anselm's discussion of *homo simpliciter* (unindividuated human nature, i.e., human nature as a species) and *ille assumptus homo* (the assumed man), we are better able to understand his attack on "nominalism" in *De Incarnatione* 1. The nominalists of his day supposed that a term such as *homo* designates individual men only. By contrast, Anselm contended that *homo* also designates human nature as it is commonly and really present in all men. Thus, individual men with individuated natures are classified under the same species because each has a human nature which is objectively similar to other human natures. Although a nature does not exist apart from an individual (excepting its archetypal existence in the mind of God), it is something real and not a mere word (*flatum vocis*). In this respect Anselm's view of what a nature is coincides with Augustine's.[20]

Because human nature is something real in individual men, the Son of God could assume a real humanity in Jesus. Nevertheless, in Jesus the human nature remained distinct from the divine nature. Neither nature was changed into the other; nor did the two mingle together to become a

20. See Augustine's discussion of species in DT 7.4.7.

single nature (CDH II, 7). Anselm thus explicitly dissociates himself from Eutychianism (strict Monophysitism), which affirmed that after the hypostatic union there were no longer two distinct natures in Jesus. By holding steadfastly to the Chalcedonian formula, Anselm is able to affirm that Jesus was fully human and fully divine — and therefore could *legitimately* and *effectively* repay the debt incurred by every Adamic human nature other than His own.[21] At this point Christology and the theory of atonement intersect in Anselm's theology. When Jesus suffered, He suffered as a man; but the will by which He allowed Himself to be exposed to these sufferings was the will of God. In one person, therefore, man and God meet. And this meeting of natures in the same person opens the way for the reconciliation of individual men with their divine Savior.

VIRGIN CONCEPTION AND ORIGINAL SIN

In the *Cur Deus Homo* Anselm argued that the Son of God is *most fittingly* born of a virgin. Moreover, this virgin is most suitably thought to have been pure of sin — as accomplished by faith in the future death of her Son.[22] In *De Conceptu* he argues that the Son of God *could only have* assumed a human nature by means of a virgin birth; only in this manner could He have remained free of original sin while at the same time belonging to the Adamic race. But He could have assumed a human nature from a *sinful* virgin without Himself having become infected with original sin. This difference of argument points up the difference between *necessary reasons* and *fitting reasons*.[23] The former purport to show that something can happen in one and only one way because anything else would be inconsistent with the system of basic truths about God's nature and will. The latter, by contrast, suggest that something which might or might not consistently have happened in an alternative way happened as it did because this way, more than any other, is congruent with the notion of honor or majesty or worthiness in God. This

21. "In Christ the diversity of natures and the unity of person was such that if the human nature could not do what was necessary for the restoration of men, then the divine nature did it; and if it did not befit the divine nature, then the human nature did it. Yet not two persons but one and the same person, existing perfectly in two natures, paid through His human nature what was owed, and was able through His divine nature to do what was of help." CDH II, 17 (S II, 124:19–24).

22. See Ch. V, pp. 163–164.   23. See Ch. II, pp. 49–51.

difference is best seen when in place of the word "reasons" the word "reasoning" is substituted. Necessary reasoning represents the attempt logically to deduce a theological conclusion from a system of premises deemed to be essential to the concept of God as the most perfect of all possible beings. Fitting reasoning, on the other hand, represents the attempt to elicit a conclusion which accords with God's worthiness, but which does not by itself rationally close all other alternatives within the theological system. In last analysis, then, the *Cur Deus Homo* without elaboration suggests that Jesus' birth from a pure virgin was fitting; and *De Conceptu* purports to furnish more cogent reasons which show that whereas His birth from a *pure* mother was only fitting, the absence of a human father was not only fitting but also necessary.

Underlying the discussion in *De Conceptu* is the issue of how original sin is transmitted from Adam to his descendants. Anselm is not entirely able to divorce himself from the Augustinian view that original sin is associated with the concupiscence of the sexual act and is contracted in offspring in conjunction with parental concupiscence.[24] According to Augustine, Jesus was born free of original sin because his birth was not accomplished through Mary's sexual communion with an earthly father, but through communion with the Holy Spirit, apart from all concupiscence. When Anselm comes to interpret Psalms 51:5, which looms so large in Augustinianism, he concludes with Augustine that being conceived in iniquity and in sin refers to being conceived from seed "inseminated with the sense of pleasure which would have been proper only to irrational animals, had man not sinned" (DCV 14). For Anselm as for Augustine, original sin has to do with the inheritance of a nature (a will being an operation of a nature) deprived of justice. Lacking justice, human nature is beset by carnal desire associated with sexuality. The *Cur Deus Homo*, accordingly, makes a point of referring to the conception of Jesus as free of concupiscence.[25] Augustine and Anselm distinguish between what original sin is, how it is transmitted, and what its effects are. (It is injustice; it is transmitted through the male seed; its effects are a corrupt and concupiscent human nature.) But Augustine emphasizes the topic of sensual transmission, Anselm the lack of justice (which he *defines* as original sin).

24. DT 13.18.23; *Enchiridion* 41.13; *Against Julian the Heretic* 5.15.54; *Incomplete Work Against Julian* 2.45.
25. CDH II, 16 (S II, 116:20–24).

Anselm's major argument in defense of the sinless birth of Christ is at the same time a defense of the sinless birth of anyone conceived from a virgin.

It is completely absurd that Adam's sin, or debt, or penalty should be transmitted to a man born of a virgin. And this would be the case even if such a man were not assumed into the person of God, but were only and entirely a man. For it is absurd that Adam's sin, debt, and penalty should be passed down through a seed which is produced solely by the will of God — a seed which is not produced or brought forth by any created nature, or by the will of any creature, or by a power given by God to anyone else; for in order to beget a man by means of a new power, God takes from a virgin this seed which is free from sin. In this case, a rational mind understands that for the same reason that God ought to create Adam fully just and unburdened by any debt or disadvantage, so a man who is begotten by God's own will and power ought to be created free from subjection to any evil. For it would be utterly repugnant to God's omnipotent and wise goodness for Him to make — by His own will alone and from matter (in which there is no sin) — a rational nature which was subjected to evil (DCV 13. S II, 155:16–28).

This extended argument constitutes Anselm's chief contribution to the controversy over how God could have assumed a human nature without assuming a sinful human nature. For unless Jesus is shown to have been begotten sinlessly, His death cannot be thought to have honored God by being a payment not already owed. The background against which this defense is presented must now be examined more closely.

Meaning of "original sin." Original sin gets its name from the fact that the descendants of Adam, at their origin, inherit a sin together with a nature (DCV 1). It is contrasted with that personal sin which they themselves commit but do not transmit. Sin of person and sin of nature are therefore different. Adam's personal sin caused human nature to become corrupt; for when Adam sinned, human nature (*homo*) sinned (DCV 23). The inheritance of this corrupted human nature causes his descendants to sin personally. But Adam's descendants do not inherit a corrupted nature without inheriting the sin of that nature. That is, they do not inherit the *penalty* of Adam's sin without also inheriting the *guilt*. Since human nature lacks justice, which it ought to have, it is guilty. And this guilt passes to every individual who possesses the unjust nature. Even though Adam's personal sin is the cause of his descendants' natural (original) sin, still, by being a cause, it is different from theirs, which is an effect (DCV 26). Therefore, in being condemned for original sin, an individual is not condemned for Adam's sin but for his own.[26]

In other words, characteristics of person and characteristics of nature are related so as to pass over into each other.[27] Adam's human nature was such that he could hunger and thirst, but his natural will did not cause him to eat of the forbidden tree. When by a personal willing he partook of the tree's fruit, he sinned. And this sin passed over into his nature, since the person of Adam did not sin apart from his nature (DCV 23). When infants inherit this nature, its sin passes over into their persons and contaminates them; for their nature does not exist apart from their persons. In this way, the persons of infants are sinful even should infants die before having sinned personally (DCV 23. Cf. DC III, 2 and 3). Though their inherited sin is incommensurate with Adam's personal sin, it is punished by exclusion from the kingdom of God, since no one with any sin at all can enter this kingdom.

When Anselm writes that "the whole of human nature was weakened and corrupted" by Adam's sin, he means that the whole extent of human nature, viz., body and soul, was affected by sin (DCV 2). Moreover, since human nature did not exist outside of Adam and Eve, their fall corrupted human nature as it was transmitted to all of their natural descendants. Anselm suggests that Adam retained some measure of justice, even though this could not be passed on to his offspring (DCV 24). But in saying that these offspring are totally without justice, Anselm is not implying that they can perform no relatively good works, from the human point of view. Rather, he means that they cannot perform that absolutely good work which will merit them salvation and restore justice to their wills; therefore whatever works they do perform will be of no avail before God. Hence, from a theological point of view they are totally without the required righteousness. To affirm this deprivation of justice is to affirm the presence of original sin. Anselm understands original sin, then, to be the inherited lack of justice in the will of every fallen man. This deprivation is transmitted through the human seed and is associated (but not identified) with the concupiscence, or carnal desire, of the sex-

26. DCV 26. Anselm follows the tradition of the Church in regarding baptism as removing the guilt of all prior sins, including original sin (DCV 28–29). Note Augustine: "In unbaptized infants Adam is seen; in baptized and, hence, reborn infants Christ is seen." Sermon 174 (PL 38:944).

27. "Sicut personale transit ad naturam, ita naturale ad personam. . . ." DCV 23 (S II, 165:7–8).

ual act. Anselm still needs to make clear the sense in which this sin is conveyed through the seed.

Existence in Adam. Throughout his discussion Anselm is mindful of both Romans 5:12 ("Sin entered the world through one man") and Romans 5:19 ("By one man many were made sinners").[28] He interprets these verses to mean that when Adam sinned, every man sinned in him.[29] But "sinning in Adam," continues the interpretation, does not mean that individuals sinned before their own births. It is simply a manner of speaking based upon the following consideration: at the time Adam sinned it became necessary that his descendants would be going to sin when they existed.[30] (Similarly, God admonished Adam that on the day he partook of the forbidden fruit, he would die, i.e., he would contract on that day the necessity of dying.)

Yet Anselm wants to claim a second sense in which all men existed in Adam when he sinned. They existed in him in the same way that what comes from a seed exists in the seed — viz., causally or materially (DCV 23). "In Adam they were the seed itself, while in themselves they are individual and different persons. Insofar as they existed in Adam, they were not different from Adam; but insofar as they exist in themselves, they are different from him. In Adam they were Adam, but in themselves they are themselves. Therefore, all infants existed in Adam, but they themselves did not exist in Adam — since they themselves did not yet exist [i.e., exist personally]" (S II, 163:4–6). Anselm thus agrees with Augustine that the human race was seminally present in Adam.[31] For this reason, had Eve alone sinned it would not have been necessary for the whole human race to perish, but only for Eve to perish (DCV 9).[32] For although Eve was made from Adam, she was not made through Adam's seed. Therefore, since the human race was not in her, it did not sin in her; hence God could have created another woman through whom the

28. Surprisingly, he never refers to Heb. 7:5–10.

29. "Sic in ADAM omnes peccavimus quando ille peccavit. . . ." DCV 7 (S II, 148:26).

30. DCV 7. Here Anselm's paradox of freedom comes to bear. Because the will lacks uprightness, it is unable to avoid sinning; because it can retain uprightness were uprightness restored to it, the will is free. See Ch. V, pp. 153–156.

31. Note Augustine, *Incomplete Work Against Julian* 5.12 (PL 45:1442): "By reason of the seed all men were in the loins of Adam when he was condemned; and so he was not condemned apart from them. . . ." N.B. *Merits and the Remission of Sins* 1.55.28.

32. Thomas adopts the same view. ST, 1st of 2nd, 81, 5.

race could have been propagated. Anselm is saying, then, that even though Eve was truly human, she was not of the race of Adam. Therefore, her fall alone could not affect the Adamic race. Correspondingly, we have seen how Anselm has argued in the *Cur Deus Homo* that another man besides Adam — created miraculously from the earth as was Adam — could not admissibly atone for Adam's race, of which he would not be a member. For in that case, mankind would be servant to someone in addition to God.[33]

Jesus, by comparison, comes from Adam's race; for He derives His humanity from Mary, who is of Adam's lineage. But He is propagated not by the power of human nature but by the will and power of God. As Adam was able to keep justice only for those persons who were able to be propagated from him by the power of his will and nature, so he was able to lose justice only for these same persons. Since Jesus was not propagated by the power of the Adamic reproductive nature, Adam could not have lost justice for Him. Therefore, Jesus was born without original sin (DCV 12). He was nonetheless truly human. "Just as any man or woman who exists from the union of a man and a woman is truly man — so Adam, who existed from no other man, is truly man, and so Jesus, who existed from a woman alone, is truly man, and so Eve, who existed from a man alone, is truly man" (DCV 11). Since Jesus comes from Adam, He may be said to have been in Adam, even though He was not in Adam causally: Adamic reproductive nature had no power to beget Him. Yet as Adam existed in the clay from which he was taken, and as Eve existed in Adam but not through Adam, so Jesus existed in Adam, i.e., materially from Adam (according to His humanity), but not through Adam efficiently.[34]

Transmission of original sin. The human seed is not sinful, inasmuch as sin can properly be attributed only to a rational will (DCV 8). In accordance with this tenet Anselm contends that infants are not sinful from the moment of their conception. For at the moment of conception, the new being does not yet have a rational will.[35] But with conception, this being contracts the necessity of sinning at the time he receives a rational

33. CDH I, 5. See p. 191 above.

34. DCV 23 (S II, 164:22–23): "[Christum] vero non nisi deus fecit quamvis de ADAM, quia non per ADAM, sed per se velut de suo."

35. This being does not even resemble a human form (*humana figura*), much less have a will. DCV 7 and 8. Especially S II, 148:7.

will. He contracts this necessity not because the seed itself is sinful but because through the seed he comes to receive a human nature which, in being corrupted by sin, renders his person sinful. Anselm does not specify at what time the fetus becomes a person; however, he does maintain that infants are *born with* original sin, thereby indicating that at birth they already possess rational souls. Original sin, therefore, is transmitted instrumentally through the seed, without the seed itself being unclean.

Although Adam's sin caused his descendants to become sinful, the sins of other ancestors do not affect their children's state of soul. For only someone who can pass on justice to his offspring can also pass on injustice. Since no one except Adam had the power to do the former, no one but Adam could do the latter (DCV 24). Scripture declares that the iniquities of fathers shall be visited upon their sons unto the third and fourth generation (Ex. 20:5). But Anselm does not interpret this verse to refer to the inheritance of sin but to the divine punishment of sin through the abandonment of men to their wickedness. Furthermore, since infants are born with injustice because of Adam's sin, the sins of intervening ancestors cannot more gravely injure infants; for where there is already no justice, its absence cannot be made greater.[36] Original sin thus pertains to every man equally, irrespective of the lives of his immediate progenitors.

Anselm is concerned to defend the justness of each man's being *guilty* of original sin. We have already seen that he refuses to regard a man as condemned for Adam's sin. For original sin is not *Adam's* sin, even though, originally, Adam sinned. That is, Adam's personal sin caused his descendants to be born with original sin. But their sin (in being an effect) is different from his (which is a cause), so that he is not properly said to have original sin, but only they. Thus, an infant is condemned for his own sin — inasmuch as inherited sin *is* his sin. Yet this line of reasoning needs further development. If Adam's personal sin is really the cause of his offspring's natural sin, then it still seems unjust that infants should be condemned for this sin alone. Anselm's suggestion that infants have sinful persons even before they have sinned personally tends to confuse the problem at hand. For even if the natural in some sense passes over into the personal, still it would seem unjust for God to hold a person guilty

36. In DCV 27 (S II, 170:11–14) Anselm states that an individual's personal sin can make his nature more sinful — presumably without making human nature as such more sinful. Note Thomas, ST, 1st of 2nd, 81, 2.

for what he does not personally do. Aware of this objection, Anselm marshals an example with which to offset the feeling of unfairness: "God's judgment in condemning infants is not much different from the judgment of men. For suppose that some man and his wife who have been elevated to great dignity and wealth by pure favor and not by their own merit were together to commit a serious and unpardonable crime, so that they were justly cast down from their position and given into servitude. In this case, who would say that the children born to them after their condemnation should not also be subjected to servitude, but ought rather to be gratuitously restored to the goods which their parents justly lost?" (DCV 28. S II, 171:9–15).

Yet this example does not support Anselm's point. For at best the comparison indicates that children should incur the positional consequences of their parents' wrongdoing; it affords no reason for supposing that they should bear the guilt of that wrongdoing. However, Anselm has been contending that, apropos of the Fall, every man bears guilt as a result of Adam's sin, in addition to incurring servitude to sin. If we deal with the illustration severely, then even the incurring of servitude seems unjust. Children might rightly lose the wealth and social status to which they would have been heirs had their parents not transgressed. But they ought not to lose their own freedom as well. The feudal conditions against which Anselm's defense is mirrored make it difficult for him to feel discomfort at the thought of serfdom and indenture; on the contrary, in his day these conditions supported the subjective appeal of the comparison.

Anselm might have asserted a weaker thesis, viz., that infants inherit a corrupted human nature without inheriting guilt, so that should they die in infancy and apart from Christ, they would not be condemned. Yet for three reasons he does not condone this weaker thesis. First, he sees that what is at stake is a total viewpoint and not simply this particular thesis. Since he is not prepared to surrender the former, he is hesitant to qualify the latter — knowing that such a qualification will not by itself satisfy his opponents. For those who are offended by the notion of inherited guilt will likewise be offended by the doctrine of inherited defect. If Adam's descendants inherit a corrupted, and therefore imperfect, nature (the opponents will contend) and if the inheritance of this nature makes it impossible for them to avoid personal sin when they develop understanding, how can they be held responsible even for personal sins? Anselm sees that what his adversaries are impugning is not the stronger thesis as such but the articulation of any non-Pelagian doctrine at all. What they demand — and what Anselm is unwilling to concede — is that each individual man be viewed as being born with a nature as faultless as was Adam's before the Fall. According to this theory, none of Adam's descendants is to be thought of as fallen *because of* Adam's evil choice. But rather, each is to be regarded as born with a nature whose state is like Adam's original state. Any corruption of this condition results from the fault of the individual person. Accordingly, each man becomes fallen through his own free choice, instead of being born fallen on account of Adam's prior choice. Anselm rejects this theory on the grounds that it is untrue when seen in the light of both Scripture and experience — as Augustine argued in detailed. Anselm is fully aware of the charge that Augustinianism essentially misrepresents the moral fairness of God's transactions vis-à-vis the human race. But he feels that in the name of moral fairness Pelagianism overlooks the gravity of the human situation, thereby misrepresenting the divine program of salvation and at the same time the meaning of Christ's death.

Secondly, Anselm does not weaken his thesis because he holds a theory of universals which makes the stronger version tenable. If Adamic human nature sinned in Adam, in whom alone it at first existed, then human nature is guilty in all individuals propagated through its own power.[37] And since Anselm regards individual human natures as of one species, "guilty in Adam" does not seem to him an unwarranted doctrine. Should there be reason to dismiss the theory that human nature was universally and really present in Adam, this dismissal would leave Anselm's account of original sin without a philosophical basis. Precisely because Anselm feels no need to change his philosophical commitment, he has no misgivings about his theological anti-Pelagianism.

Thirdly, he finds it intrinsically abhorrent to suppose that, once Adam fell, any of his descendants — infants or not — could ever be saved apart from the sacrificial death of Christ. Even if these infants were *not guilty* of original sin, as the weaker thesis suggests, still they could not be admitted into the Heavenly City without justice. But if they possess an original justice which they have not yet lost, then should they die in in-

37. Anselm does not say that human nature as such is guilty. For then it would have been guilty in the person of Jesus — even though Jesus' human nature came from the seed of Mary and, hence, from Adam, yet not through human power.

fancy, they would enter Heaven apart from the efficacy of Christ's death. With respect to them, then, Christ would have died in vain. Moreover, if infants are not born with original sin, then they ought not to die in infancy or suffer disease and affliction. But the very fact that they do suffer and that some do die signifies either that they do have original sin or that God is unjust. In the light of these consequences, Anselm finds it more acceptable to equate original sin with the absence of justice from the soul of each Adamic descendant, and to conclude that where sin is, there is also guilt.

Anselm regards the divine incarnation as the only possible means whereby God could act both justly and mercifully toward mankind. The incarnation was therefore neither superfluous nor foolish. It was rather the manifestation of divine power and dignity: of power because God was able to assume a sinless human nature from the sinful mass; of dignity because in the person of Jesus the divine nature enhanced the human nature. Anselm interprets the efficacy of Christ's death in terms of the monastic penitential system in which satisfaction is required for every sin, even as every virtue is rewarded. Accordingly, when Jesus voluntarily underwent death for the sake of justice, He honored God and earned merit on man's behalf. Because the penitential system of merits blends with the feudal system of services and honors, Anselm is able consistently to draw examples from the latter.[38] These examples should not be understood as depicting the atonement in a purely calculating way. At no time does Anselm lose sight of the fact that God seeks not only to repair His honor, but also to lift man from the mire of sin in order that he may be truly blessed. Never once does Anselm explain Christ's death as substitutionary. Yet he would never deny that Jesus is the Paschal Lamb, who takes unto Himself the iniquities of the human race (cf. John 1:29). If he does not develop this point, it is because he thinks that the notion of substitution is not by itself really explanatory.[39] The *Cur Deus Homo*, consequently, seeks to discover the reason why

38. Scripture too speaks of the honor of Christ's sacrifice (Heb. 5:4–5) and of sin as a debt (Matt. 6:12). Anselm is influenced by the penitential and feudal systems only in conjunction with the influence of Scripture.

39. McIntyre is right in observing: "It is not just to say that St. Anselm has abandoned vicariousness for some totally different conception of Christ's offering of His Death to God; it is much nearer the truth to hold that St. Anselm, by the more extensive description, is endeavouring to show how 'vicariousness' works, how it is effectual unto the cancelling of the debt of sin." *St. Anselm and His Critics*, p. 181.

Jesus' death could justly be counted by God as vicarious. And it tacitly interprets Jesus' bearing the sins of the world to mean His making repayment for them. In a sense the *Cur Deus Homo* represents the zenith of Anselm's systematic theological achievement, even though it is not the last of his major works. Here Anselm breaks with Augustine by expounding a new theory of atonement while retaining a traditional Christology. Here too he assimilates his earlier conclusions about the triunity of God, the universality of human freedom, the fall of men and angels, and the meaning of *assumere hominem*. The later *De Conceptu* perfects the themes of the *Cur Deus Homo* by relating them to the doctrine of original sin. Although this doctrine is not unexceptionable in Anselm, its deficiencies do not by themselves jeopardize the soteriology of the *Cur Deus Homo*.

Anselm's death in 1109 came before he had begun his treatise on the soul. Perhaps he had intended to deal at length with the controversy between creationists and traducianists — a controversy which underlies the discussion of inherited sin in *De Conceptu*. Yet the absence of this work from his corpus of writings cannot be considered a crucial lacuna. Rather, the topics which he did take up and rigorously work-through suffice to constitute him as the major systematic thinker within the early twelfth-century Latin Church. His youthful hesitancy over going to Bec can in retrospect appear amusing. For he proved himself uneclipsed by the scholarly shadow cast there by Lanfranc, his teacher. Whether in Bec or Canterbury, Capua or Rome, Anselm never abandoned his intellectual pursuits. Philosophical and theological interests combined with his goal to determine the rational considerations undergirding the truths of faith. The joy which overwhelmed him as he formulated the ontological argument was in quality no different from the joy with which he developed conclusions regarding the sacraments of the Church. A driving impulse to understand, together with a keen sense for clarity and consistency, placed him in the role of interpreter to believers and of polemicist against unbelievers. And this purely intellectual task accorded more with his desires than did his disruptive role as an ecclesiastical opponent to the king of England. Anselm's system of thought does not withstand all objections, but the undogmatic method by which it proceeds remains a tribute to medieval genius.

Appendixes

Anselm's Philosophical Fragments

EXORDIUM

23:1 *Student.* There are many notions which for some time now I've been wanting you to discuss. Among these are the notions of ability and inability, possibility and impossibility, freedom and necessity.[1] I ask about these all at once because the knowledge of any one of them seems to be connected with the knowledge of the others as well. I shall disclose in part what disturbs me about these concepts, so that when you have cleared up my thinking on these issues, I may more easily go on to other topics at which I am aiming. We sometimes say that there is ability in something which, in actual fact, has no ability. For everyone acknowledges that whatever *is able*, is able by virtue of some ability or power. Therefore, whenever we assert of what does not exist that it is

NOTE: I am grateful to Father Maurice Savard, O.M.I., for reading through this translation and suggesting corrections and improvements, of which I have made use.

My footnotes are indicated by symbols such as the asterisk; footnotes from the Schmitt edition of the Latin text are cited numerically. Those notes which refer only to manuscript variations are omitted.

Numbers in the margin of the translation indicate the page and line of the Latin text (*Ein neues unvollendetes Werk des hl. Anselm von Canterbury*).

1. Cf. CDH I, 1 (S II, 49:7–10). *Potestas* and *impotentia* are also used as opposites at CDH II, 17 (S II, 123:19–20).

able to exist, we are asserting that there is an ability in a nonexistent thing; for example, we say of a house which does not yet exist that it is able to exist. But I can't understand this, for how can there be an ability in something which does not exist?

23:13   Moreover, there is another problem. That which does not in any respect exist has no ability; and so, it has neither the ability to exist nor the ability not to exist. Therefore, it follows that what does not exist is not able to exist and not able not to exist. Now, from the first alternative — viz., that what does not exist is not able to exist — it follows that what does not exist is not possible to be, is impossible to be, and is necessary not to be. But if we adopt the second alternative — viz., that what does not exist is not able not to exist — it follows that what does not exist is not possible not to be, is impossible not to be, and is necessary to be. [So we reach two opposite conclusions about what does not exist.] Thus, on the one hand, because what does not exist is not able to exist, it is impossible for it to be and necessary for it not to be. On the other hand, because this thing is not able not to exist, it is impossible for it not to be and necessary for it to be.

23:25   In like manner, what is not able to be lacks the ability to be; and if it lacks the ability to be, it is unable to be. So too, what is not able not to be lacks the ability not to be; and if it lacks the ability not to be, then it is unable not to be. For this reason what does not exist is not able to be and is not able not to be: it is unable to be and is unable not to be. Now, what is unable to be has the ability not to be; and likewise what is unable not to be has the ability to be. And so, what does not exist both has the ability to be and is unable to be, and also has the ability not to be. Therefore, it has both an ability to be and an ability not to be, and likewise an inability to be and an inability not to be.

24:8   But these conclusions are quite absurd. For it can never be true of something that at the same time it is impossible to be and impossible not to be. Nor can it be the case that at the same time it is necessary to be and necessary not to be — nor that it has at once both the ability and the inability to be or the ability and the inability not to be. Hence, if these conclusions are impossible, then so is the premise from which they derive, namely: "What in no respect exists is not able to be and is not able not to be, since it has no ability." But I can in no way understand how this premise could be false.

24:16   I am also troubled about the impossibility and the necessity which we assert of God when we say, for example, that it is impossible for God to lie, or that by necessity He is just.[2] For impossibility implies powerlessness, and necessity implies compulsion; but in God there is neither powerlessness nor compulsion. If God keeps to the truth because of a powerlessness to lie or if He is just because of compulsion, then He is not freely truthful and just.[3] If you answer that this impossibility and necessity signify in God an insuperable strength, then I ask, Why should this strength be designated by names signifying weakness?[4]

These and perhaps other questions cast me into a certain quandary about the notions of ability, possibility, and their opposites, and also about freedom and necessity. Although these perplexities are childish, nevertheless I want you to teach me how to reply if someone were to ask me about these puzzles, for I admit that I don't know the solutions.[5]

25:1   *Teacher.* Even though your questions seem to you to be puerile, their solutions are not so simple as to appear to me anile. Indeed, I can foresee that you will ask me about more difficult matters once I begin my reply. Still, I ought not to hold back on the things that I can answer, God granting, even should I not be able to answer all your questions.

PRAENOTANDA

25:7   *Teacher.* In order to answer the questions you've proposed, I think it necessary first to say something about the verb "to do" and about what is properly called one's own possession or prerogative.[6]* Unless we take this matter up now, we may be compelled

2. Cf. CDH II, 10 (S II, 106:17-18); the title of CDH II, 17 (S II, 122:23-24); and DCD 12 (S I, 253:32).

3. Cf. CDH II, 10 (S II, 107:11-13). See also CDH II, 16.

4. Cf. CDH II, 17 (S II, 123:11-12).

5. Cf. CDH II, 18 (S II, 128:4-6). See also CDH II, 16 (S II, 122:20-21) and DV 2 (S I, 178:28-29).

6. Cf. CDH I, 14 (S II, 72:14-15). * Note PF 37:1 where *suum alicuius* recurs.

to make a digression later on when the topic becomes essential to the argument. But keep well in mind the questions you've just asked.

Student. As long as you return to the questions I've raised, nothing you propose displeases me.

FACERE
25:14 to 26:22

*Teacher.** We commonly use the verb "to do" in place of all other verbs, regardless of the signification of these other verbs and regardless of whether they are finite or infinite.† In fact, "to do" may even stand for "not to do." If you think about it carefully, you will see that when we ask about someone, "What (how) is he doing?" here "doing" stands for any verb that can be given in answer. And so too, these other verbs stand for the verb "to do." For in a correct reply to one who asks "What (how) is he doing?" any verb at all will indicate a doing on the part of the person asked about. If someone were to respond, "He is reading" or "He is writing," it is the same as if he were saying, "He is doing this, namely, reading" or "He is doing that, namely, writing."

25:23   So then, any verb can be used in the answer. In many cases this is obvious, as for example when we reply, "He is singing" or "He is composing." In other cases, however, the substitution may seem somewhat problematical, as for example when we reply, "He is," or "He lives," "He is powerful" (*potest*), "He owes" (*debet*), "He is named" (*nominatur*), "He is summoned" (*vocatur*). But no one would reproach us if we were to answer someone who asked "What (how) is so-and-so doing?" by saying, "He is in church" or "He is living as a good man should live," "He is powerful (ruler) over the whole domain in which he lives," "He owes much money," "He is named above his neighbors," "Wherever he is, he is summoned before all others." Therefore, if you know how to do it, every verb can at some time or other be given in

---

* The Latin text contains two insignificantly different versions of the first part of this section: 25:14–26:22 and 26:23–27:26. I have omitted the latter version.

† Note Boethius on infinite terms, PL 64:520. Cf. Aristotle, *On Interpretation* 19ᵇ5ff.

reply to one who asks, "What (how) is so-and-so doing?" So whatever verbs are used in response to the question "What (how) is he doing?" stand for "doing," and "doing" stands for these verbs — since what is asked for is the reply and what is answered is the question.

26:5 Moreover, every subject (*omne*) of which a verb is predicated (*dicitur*) is a "cause" of the state signified by this verb. And in common parlance every cause is said to do that of which it is the cause.[7] For this reason, every subject of which a given verb is predicated (*pronuntiatur*) does, or causes, what is signified by that verb. This is known to be the case, not only with verbs which properly signify a doing, such as "running" (and other verbs of this kind, which I pass over unmentioned), but also with other verbs, though their significations may seem unrelated to "doing" in the proper sense of the word. In this way, whoever is sitting is doing (causing) sitting, and whoever is suffering is doing (causing) suffering — because unless someone were suffering there would be no suffering.[8] And there would not be naming unless something were named. Nor would anything be said in any respect to be unless what is said to be were first thought. We see, then, from this argument that whenever a verb is predicated of a subject, a doing is signified — viz., the doing which is indicated by the verb. Thus with good reason the verb "to do" is sometimes in everyday discourse substituted for every other verb.

26:20 *Student.* To one who is willing to understand, what you say is quite clear. Still, I don't yet see why you are going to all this trouble.

Teacher. You will understand in what follows.

* * *

27:26 For when we say "Man is" or "Man is not," what is signified by the noun "man" is conceived in the mind before it is said to be or not to be. And so, what is conceived is the cause of our being able to say about it that it is. So also, if we say "Man is an animal," *man* is the cause of being, and being called, an animal. I do not mean that *man* is the cause of the existence of *animal* but that be-

7. Cf. M 8 (S I, 22:13–15).
8. Cf. DV 5 (S I, 182:18–19).

ing a man implies being an animal and being called an animal. For by the name *man* we signify and conceive man in his totality (*totus homo*), and in this totality *animal* is contained as a part. So in this way, the part follows from the whole because it is necessary that the part be wherever the whole is. Therefore, because in the name "man" we conceive the whole man, *man as a whole* is the cause of man's being and being called an animal; for the conception of the whole is the cause of the part's being conceived in it and being predicated of it. In this way, then, the conception of whatever thing we say to be — whether said simply (e.g., "Man is") or by adding another word (e.g., "Man is an animal," "Man is rational") — precedes the assertion and is the cause of that thing's being said to be or not to be, and is likewise the cause of the intelligibility of what is said. We see, then, from this argument that whenever a verb is predicated of a subject, a doing is signified — viz., the doing which is indicated by the verb. Thus with good reason the verb "to do" is sometimes in everyday discourse used in place of every other verb, and every verb is called a doing.

28:13   Indeed, the Lord Himself in the Gospel uses *facere* and *agere*, which mean the same thing, viz., "to do," in place of every other verb when He says, "Whoever does evil hates the light" and "Whoever does the truth comes to the light" (John 3:20–21).[9] For he who does what he ought not or does not do what he ought does evil. And any other verb can be substituted for "does" in this sentence. For he who is present at some place he ought not to be or is there at a time when he ought not to be, does evil. So too, whoever sits or stands where or when he ought not, does evil; and whoever is not present, does not sit, or does not stand where or when he should also does evil. But he does the truth who does what he ought and who does not do what he ought not do. Likewise, he does the truth who is present, is sitting, or is standing where and when he ought, and is not present, is not sitting, or is not standing where and when he ought not. In this way the Lord reduces every verb, whether positive or negative, to a form of "to do."[10]

9. Cf. DV 5 (S I, 182:10–12).

10. Cf. *Liber de Voluntate* (Migne, PL 158:488C). Note also DV 5 (S I, 181: 24–25; 182:12–14).

28:26   We must consider another thing about the verb "to do," or "to cause" (*facere*), namely, the different modes in which it has a use in our language. Although these distinctions are very numerous and especially complex, nevertheless I shall say a word about them, which, as I think, shall be of aid to us in our present inquiry; it will also be a help to anyone who wishes to pursue the nature and number of these distinctions further.

Some causes are called efficient; for instance, the man who composes a literary work is the efficient cause of this work. But other causes, by contrast, are not called efficient — for instance, the material from which something is made.[11] Nonetheless, every cause (as I mentioned) is said to do something, and everything which is said to do something is called a cause. Now, whatever is said to do (or to cause) either brings about something's being or else brings about something's not-being. Therefore, every doing can be called either (A) causing something to be or (B) causing something not to be. These are contrary affirmations, whose negations are, (C) not causing something to be, and (D) not causing something not to be. But the affirmation (A) "causing something to be" is sometimes used in place of the negation (D) "not causing something not to be," and vice versa. Likewise (B) "causing something not to be" and (C) "not causing something to be" are sometimes used in place of each other. Thus, someone may on occasion be said to cause evil to be because he does not cause it not to be; or he may be said not to cause evil not to be, because he causes it to be. In the same way, he may be said to cause good not to be, because he does not cause it to be; and he may be said not to cause good to be, because he causes it not to be.

29:20   Let us now arrange the different modes of *doing* (*facere*) under a division. Since *doing* is always either causing (*facere*) something "to be" or causing something "not to be" (as we said), it will be necessary to add these phrases to our different modes in order to make the different divisions clear. We speak in six modes of "causing to be": We say that X causes Y when (A.1) X causes Y itself to be; or when (A.2) X does not cause Y itself not to be; or when (A.3–6) X causes Y to be by causing Z to be, by not causing Z to be, by causing Z not to be, or by not causing Z not

11. Cf. M 6 (S I, 19:1–3).

to be. For we say that one thing causes another to be because it (1) directly causes this other thing to be, or (2) does not directly cause this other thing not to be, or (3) causes an intervening thing to be, or (4) does not cause an intervening thing to be, or (5) causes an intervening thing not to be, or (6) does not cause an intervening thing not to be.*

29:31   In the first mode, a man is said to cause the death of another when he slays him with a sword. In this instance he does by his own agency that which we say he does [viz., he causes to be dead].

In the second mode the only example I have for "causing to be dead" is that of someone who would be able to restore a dead man to life, but who would be unwilling to do so.[12] In this instance the one who is unwilling would be said to cause the other's death by virtue of *not causing* him *not to be dead*. Examples of a different kind abound. We say, for instance, that someone causes the occurrence of the evil which he could have caused not to occur but does not cause not to occur.

30:3   The third mode of "causing to be" is illustrated by our saying that one man has killed another (i.e., has caused his death) because he ordered that the other be killed, or because he gave a sword to the man doing the killing, or because he brought an accusation against the man who was killed.[13] [In another case] the slain man may even be said to have killed himself because he did something on account of which he was killed. Such persons do not do by themselves what they are said to do: they do not directly kill a man or cause him to be dead or slain. But they *cause* a man *to be dead* by doing one of these intermediate things.

The fourth mode of "causing to be" is exemplified by our saying that someone has killed another because he has not given him weapons to defend himself with, or because he has not restrained the killer, or has not done something else which, had he done, the man should not have been killed.[14] Such a person has not slain

* See Diagram I, table A, in the Appendix.

12. Cf. CDH II, 10 (S II, 107:29–31).

13. Cf. CDH I, 9 (S II, 62:9–10).

14. Cf. CDH I, 9 (S II, 64:3–8). For a similar example, though in a different context, see DV 12 (S I, 193:14–15).

with his own hand; still, by *not causing* something else *to be*, he causes what we ascribe to him [viz., another's death].

30:16   In the fifth mode, we say that someone has killed another when he has removed this other man's weapons, thus causing him not to be armed, or when by opening a door he has caused the killer not to be locked in where he was detained. This man is said to have killed the other, though he has not done it by his own hand but rather by *causing* something else *not to be*.

In the sixth mode, someone is accused of causing another's death when, by not disarming the killer, he has not caused him not to be armed, or when by not helping the intended victim to escape, he has not caused him not to be found. Such a man does not kill directly but kills by *not causing* something else *not to be*.

30:26   "To cause not to be" has the same distinctions. For we say that a thing causes something else not to be either because (1) it directly causes this other thing not to be, or (2) it does not directly cause it to be, or (3) it causes an intervening thing to be, or (4) it does not cause an intervening thing to be, or (5) it causes an intervening thing not to be or (6) it does not cause an intervening thing not to be. Examples of these distinctions can be illustrated by reference to killing, just as we have done with "to cause to be." *

Just as in the first mode of "causing to be," a killer is said to cause another to be dead, so in the first mode of "causing not to be" he is said to *cause* another *not to be living*.

31:1   The only example I have of the second mode of "causing not to be living" is the one I've given before about someone who could restore a dead man to life. If he were unwilling to do this, he would be said to "cause someone not to be living," because he *does not cause* him *to live* again. Now, to be dead and not to be living are not the same thing; for only what has been deprived of life is dead, but many things are not living, though they have not been deprived of life — for instance a stone. Nevertheless, just as to kill is nothing other than to cause to be dead, or to cause not

---

* See Diagram I, table B, in the Appendix. N.B. The example of the armed man is also found in Augustine's discussion of Aristotle's categories. *Confessions* 4.16.28. DT 5.7.8.

to be living, so to revive is the same as to cause to be living, or to cause no longer to be dead. There are many examples of the second mode in other cases. For instance, he is said to cause good not to occur who, although able, does not cause it to occur.

31:13 In the four remaining modes (causing or not causing something else either to be or not to be) the examples given for (A) "to cause to be" are sufficient.*

Let us now state the six modes which I mentioned to be contained also in (B) "to cause not to be." These modes are exactly the same as for (A) "to cause to be" since they are merely transferred.

The first mode consists of our saying "to cause not to be" because someone directly causes not to occur that which he is said to cause not to occur. Whoever kills a man is said to *cause* him *not to be living*, because he directly causes what he is said to cause [viz., that the man not be living].

The second mode consists of our saying "to cause not to be" because someone does not directly cause to occur that which he is said to cause not to occur. I am unable to furnish an example of this mode in the case of "to cause a man to be living" or "to cause a man not to be living" unless I posit someone who is able to cause a dead man to be living. For should he not do so, then he would be said to cause the dead man not to be living because he did *not cause* him *to be living*. In other cases there are numerous examples. For instance, if the person who has the task of causing a house to have light at night does not do the task he ought, he is said to cause the house not to have light because he does not cause it to have light.

31:33 In the third mode, we say "to cause not to be" when someone causes something not to be by causing something else to be. For example, we say that the man who has *caused* a killer *to have a sword* has thereby caused the victim not to be living.

In the fourth mode, we say "to cause not to be" when someone causes something not to be by not causing something else *to be*. Thus, we say that a man who has *not caused* another *to be armed* in the face of death has caused him not to be living.

In the fifth mode, we apply this phrase to someone who causes

* The Latin text begins the discussion of *facere non esse* anew.

something not to be by causing something else not to be. Thus, we may say that someone has caused another not to be living because he has *caused* him *not to be armed* in the face of death.

In the sixth mode, we use the phrase "to cause something not to be" of someone who causes something not to be by not causing something else not to be. Such a man, in our example, would be one who does *not cause* a killer *not to be armed*; i.e., he could remove his weapons, but does not. [Thus, he indirectly causes the victim not to be living.]

32:6   Note 1. Now notice that although "to cause to be" and "not to cause not to be" are used for each other, nevertheless they are different from each other. Thus, properly speaking, he causes to be who causes there to be what previously was not. But "not to cause not to be" is said of him who neither causes to be nor causes not to be — as well as of him who causes to be. Likewise, "to cause not to be" and "not to cause to be" differ from each other. Properly speaking, whoever causes there not to be what previously was causes not to be. But "not to cause to be" is said alike of him who causes there not to be what previously was and of him who causes neither to be nor not to be.

Note 2. These examples which I've given about "causing to be" and "causing not to be" all concerned efficient causation. I adopted these examples of efficient causation since what I wished to point out can be seen more clearly in them. But the same six modes are also found in the case of nonefficient causation, as one may discover if he cares to pursue the matter intently.

32:21   *Student.* I see this clearly.

*Teacher.** I adopted these examples of efficient causes since what I wished to point out can be seen more clearly in them. Now, efficient causes in modes 2–6 do not cause what they are said to cause. [But they *are* said to cause:] in the second mode, by "not causing not to be" the thing which the first mode causes to be; in the third mode, by causing something else to be; in the fourth mode, by causing something else not to be; in the fifth mode, by not causing something else to be; in the sixth mode, by not causing

---

* The Latin text repeats "Haec quidem exempla de causis efficientibus assumpsi, quoniam in his clarius apparet, quod volo ostendere," which is found in the text at the beginning of note 2. The teacher's speech reverses modes 4 and 5, as presented in the earlier ordering.

something else not to be. And so, just as the five examples I have given are always said to cause what the first mode causes [viz., the death of a man], so too nonefficient causes are said to cause in accordance with these same modes.

32:31   Now, there are nonefficient proximate causes, which cause what they are said to cause. And there are nonefficient remote causes, which cause what they are said to cause only by causing something else. A window, for instance, which causes a house to be lighted is not an efficient cause but only a way through for light. Nonetheless, it is a proximate cause of that state of affairs which it is said to cause [viz., the lighted house]; for it causes its effect by itself and not through an intermediary cause. This mode of nonefficient causation corresponds to the first mode of efficient causation, since in its own way it causes that to be which our way of speaking says it causes to be. But if the window were not there or if it were shuttered, its absence or its being shuttered might be said to cause the house to be dark. This would be proximate causation of the second mode, for the window is said to cause darkness by virtue of not causing it not to occur. But sometimes we say that the man who has made a window causes a house to be lighted or that the man who has not made a window causes a house to be dark; or a man might say that his own land feeds him. In such cases the causation involved is remote causation, for the subjects do not cause their effects by themselves. The man causes the house to be lighted by making a window, or he causes the house to be darkened by not having made the window which he ought to have made. Or again, the earth feeds a man by means of fruit, which it yields [or causes]. Thus, all the causes which are of the first and second modes are proximate causes, whether in addition they be efficient or nonefficient causes; whereas efficient and nonefficient causes belonging to modes 3–6 are all remote causes.

33:9   The negative tables (C) "not to cause to be" and (D) "not to cause not to be" have just as many modes [as the affirmative tables (A) "to cause to be" and (B) "to cause not to be"]. We can see this from the examples which have already been given for the affirmative tables, if in the affirmative tables we negate the modes so that the negative modes become affirmative and the affirmative modes become negative. [This negation of the modes in the two affirmative tables transforms them into two corresponding negative tables.] But if anyone wishes to keep the same [lexical] order for modes 3–6 of the negative tables, he may state affirmatively as the third mode of the negative tables what I have stated negatively as the fourth mode of the affirmative tables; and he may state negatively as the fourth mode of the negative tables what I have stated affirmatively as the third mode of the affirmative tables. Likewise, he may state affirmatively as the fifth mode of the negative tables what I have stated negatively as the sixth mode of the affirmative tables, and state negatively as the sixth mode of the negative tables what I have stated affirmatively as the fifth mode of the affirmative tables.

33:17   It must be noted that while the first mode of the negative tables simply negates, without implying anything else, each of the five subsequent modes in the negative tables contains statements which can be substituted for those statements which appear in that table which is the contrary of their corresponding affirmative table.* For example, whoever revives someone may be said "not to cause him to be dead" [i.e., ~CB, the second mode in table B] † in the place of "to cause him not to be dead" [i.e., C~B, the second mode in table C]; and we may also substitute "not to cause him not to be living" [i.e., ~C~B, the second mode in table A] for "to cause him to be living" [i.e., CB, the second mode in table D]. In the remaining four modes, we say that someone does not cause another person to be dead when he causes the intended victim to be armed by giving him weapons [i.e., CB, the third mode], or when he does not cause the intended victim not to be armed, even though he is able to disarm him [i.e., ~C~B, the sixth mode], or when he causes the intending killer not to be armed by remov-

---

* See Diagram III in the Appendix. The corresponding affirmative table to table C is table A (the contradictory of table C), and the contrary of table A is table B. Hence, Anselm means that table B can be substituted for table C; and, by like reasoning, table A can be substituted for table D. Therefore, statements in the same mode in tables B and C can be substituted for each other, just as statements in the same mode in tables A and D can be substituted for each other.

† The examples which follow are illustrated in Diagram II in the Appendix. The letters "CB" in combination stand for "to cause to be," and "~" is the sign for negation.

ing his weapons [i.e., C~B, the fifth mode], or when, by denying weapons to the intending killer, he does not cause him to be armed [i.e., ~CB, the fourth mode]. But if, by means of any of these modes, we say that someone does not cause another person to be dead [i.e., ~CB, the primary mode of the table C], we understand that, as best he can, he causes that person not to be dead [i.e., C~B, the primary mode of table B]; or if by means of these modes we say that someone does not cause another person not to be living [i.e., ~C~B, the primary mode of table D], we understand that, as best he can, he causes that other person to be living [i.e., CB, the primary mode of table A]. [From these considerations, we see that the five subsequent modes in the negative tables contain statement-forms which can be substituted, *mutatis mutandis*, for statement-forms in the affirmative tables. Table B can be substituted for table C; table D for table A.]

33:30   The same principle of division which I've said holds true for "causing to be" and "causing not to be" holds true likewise for every verb that "to cause" is joined with — for example, "I cause you to do or to write something" or "I cause something to be done or to be written."

The same modes which I've distinguished in "to cause" (*facere*) can in some respects be found in other verbs as well. Although not every mode is found in every verb, nevertheless one or more are found in each, and especially in verbs such as "ought to" and "is able to," which are transitive to other verbs. When we say "I am able to read or to be read [through my writings]" or "I ought to love or to be loved," then "able to" and "ought to" are used transitively.

33:40   There are also verbs which, though transitive, are not transitive to other verbs but to some noun; for instance we say "to eat bread" or "to cut a piece of wood." And there are certain other verbs which are not transitive to anything, for example "reclining" or "sleeping." However, certain verbs in this last category seem to be transitive to other verbs as, for example, when we say "The people sat eating and drinking, and they rose up to play" (Exodus 32:6). But this is not so, for it is not like saying "The people wish to eat and to drink and to play" [where the verb "wish" is transitive to "to eat," "to drink," and "to play"]; rather it is to be construed as "The people sat down in order to eat and drink, and they rose up in order to play."

The verb "to be" has some of the six modes which we have mentioned.* Indeed, the first two modes are clearly recognized. But the four remaining modes (viz., causing or not causing something else to be or not to be) are more difficult to detect, because there are many ways in which things are caused and not-caused to be and not to be. Nevertheless, from the few cases that I shall mention with regard to the kind of things in Scripture and in everyday discourse, you will be able to find the other cases that I shall not mention.

34:16   The verb "to be" copies the verb *facere*. For we often say that a thing is something or other which it really isn't; and we say this not because this thing itself is what we call it, but because it is something else which is the reason (*causa*) for our calling it what we do. Indeed, someone is said to be "eyes to the blind and feet to the lame" (Job 29:15), not because he is what he is called [viz., eyes, feet] but because he is something else which serves the blind and the lame as eyes and feet. So too, the lives of those just individuals who are enduring many burdens because they desire eternal life are called happy — not because they really are happy, but because their present lives are the cause of their someday being happy.

The verb "to have" is also similar to the verb *facere* in its modes. For someone bereft of eyes is sometimes said to have eyes, not because he actually has them but because he has someone else who does for him what eyes do. Likewise, someone who has no feet is sometimes said to have feet, not because he actually has feet but because he has something else which serves in place of feet.

34:29   We sometimes attribute a noun or a verb improperly to a subject because the improper subject is in one of the following relations to the proper subject of this noun or verb:

It is similar to it, or it is its cause, effect, genus, species, whole, or part.

It is equal in capacity.

* The idea expressed in this paragraph repeats the earlier statements about *facere esse*.

It is its external form [i.e., shape] * or the thing shaped according to that form. (True, every external form is similar to the thing shaped according to it, but not every similarity is a form.)

In some other way than through external form, it signifies or is signified by the proper subject of this noun or verb.

It is its content or container.

It uses it as an instrument or is so used by it.

[Whenever one of these relationships occurs, the improper subject seems to be doing what we say of it.]

34:40   All the modes which I have mentioned for *facere* are sometimes found in other verbs as well, though not all are found in every particular verb. Still, one or more such modes exist for any given verb. For every verb which is properly used with respect to something, so that that thing does what the verb declares, is uttered according to the first mode. Thus we say "He reclines," "He sits," "He runs," "He builds a house" when he himself does this (e.g., he runs with his own feet or builds a house with his own hands); or we say "It is day" or "The sun shines" or some such thing [because it *is* day and the sun *is* shining. All these verbs accord with the first mode]. But we are speaking in accordance with a mode other than the first when we say that someone is doing something which he is not really doing. This is the case, for instance, when we say that someone builds a house, and in reality he gives the orders for its being built rather than doing the actual work himself. Or again, the situation is the same when we say that a horseman runs, although he is not himself running but is making the horse run. Thus, as often as we hear a verb being predicated of some subject which is not really doing what that verb declares, then if we look carefully we shall discover some one of the remaining five modes to be operative.

35:14   Indeed, when someone says to me "I ought to be loved by you," he is speaking improperly.[15] For if he *ought* to,† then he has an obligation to be loved by me. And so it ought to be demanded

---

* *Figura.* Boethius uses *forma* and *figura* to translate Aristotle's fourth kind of quality. See PL 64:250D (Aristotle, *Categories* 10ᵃ11).

15. Cf. CDH II, 18 (S II, 128:27–30). See also DCD 12 (S I, 253:22–27); DV 8 (S I, 188:9–18).

† In this section *debere* is translated as "ought to," "is obliged to," and "is under obligation to."

from *him* that he be loved by *me* because he is under obligation to be loved by me; if he does not discharge this obligation he is sinning. But although this is what he is saying, this is not what he means. So it is said that he ought to be loved by me inasmuch as he causes me to have an obligation to love him. For if he has merited my love, he has caused me to owe him love. But if he has not merited this by virtue of his own actions, then, nonetheless, the very fact that he is a man is a reason (*causa*) within him for my obligation to love him. [Therefore we have a parallel with one of the modes of causing.] For just as someone is said to cause something, though not himself directly causing it but rather causing another to do it (in one of the aforesaid modes), so a man is said to be under obligation, though not himself owing anything, but being (in a certain manner) the cause of someone else's having an obligation. After this same fashion we say that the poor ought to receive from the rich, although the poor have no obligation, but rather the rich.[16] That the poor are in need is the reason (*causa*) for the rich being obliged to expend money.

36:3 We also say that we are "not obliged to sin" (*non debere peccare*) as a substitute for saying that we are "obliged not to sin" (*debere non peccare*). But properly speaking not everyone who does what he is not obliged to do sins. For just as to owe and to be under obligation are the same, so also not to owe and not to be under obligation are the same. A man does not always sin when he does something he is not obliged to do. To be sure, a man is not obliged to marry, for it is permissible for him to keep his virginity.[17] Thus, he is not obliged to marry; but if he does marry, he does not sin. Hence, a man does not always sin by doing what he is not obliged to do, provided we properly understand "is not obliged to." Nevertheless, no one denies that a man ought to marry. So he is under and not under the obligation to marry. Now as you remember, we said earlier that "not to cause to be" may be used in place of "to cause not to be." In the same way, we say "is not obliged to do" for "is obliged not to do," and "is not obliged to sin" for "is obliged not to sin." But our [Latin] usage is such that by "is not obliged to sin" we really mean "is obliged not to

16. Cf. CDH II, 18 (S II, 128:30–129:1).
17. Cf. CDH II, 18 (S II, 128:23–26).

36:18 sin." Now, with regard to "ought," if a man wishes to marry we say "He ought to marry," meaning "He is not obliged not to marry." The parallel here is our using "to cause to be" in place of "not to cause not to be." So then, just as we say "is not obliged to do" for "is obliged not to do," we also say "is obliged to do" for "is not obliged not to do." However, "is obliged to do" can be understood in the sense in which we say that God is under obligation to rule over everything.[18] For God ought to be subject to no one else; rather everyone and everything else ought to be subject to Him. So we say that God is under obligation to be the head over all things because He is the cause that all things are under obligation to be subject to Him. The parallel here is with the poor, who ought to receive from the rich because in them lies the reason (*causa*) why the rich ought to contribute to them. In this sense, then, we can say that a man ought to marry. For everything which is one's possession or prerogative (*suum alicuius*) ought to be subject to one's will. And it is a man's prerogative either to marry or not to marry, so long as he has not taken the vow of chastity. Thus, since marrying or not marrying ought to be in accordance with a man's wishes, we say that if he wishes to marry, then he ought to marry, and if he doesn't wish to marry, then he ought not to marry.[19]

37:6 When we ask God to forgive us our sins, it is not advantageous for us that God should do precisely what our words request. For if He forgives us our sins, He does not blot them out or remove them from us. But when we pray that our sins be forgiven, we are not praying that they themselves be forgiven us, but that the debt which we incur on account of them be forgiven us. Since our sins are the cause of our owing what we have the necessity of being forgiven for, we pray that these sins be forgiven us when we ought to pray that the debt of sin be forgiven us. But in praying as we do, we do not really desire that our sins be forgiven, but that the debt they have incurred be forgiven. This is clear from the Lord's Prayer, where we pray "Forgive us our debts" (Matt. 6:12).[20]

18. Cf. CDH II, 18 (S II, 129:1–2).
19. Cf. CDH II, 18 (S II, 128:13–22).
20. Cf. CDH I, 19 (S II, 86:1–2).

Thus it happens that a man typically says to someone who has burned down his house or has caused him some other injury, "Restore to me the injury you've caused." And the man who has burned the house responds, "Forgive me the injury I've caused you." But it is not the injury as such which must be restored and forgiven; rather what has been destroyed because of the injury must be restored, and what must be paid because of the injury must be forgiven.

For the same reason the Lord says that those whom we mercifully forgive and to whom we mercifully give "will pour into your bowl a good measure, pressed down, shaken together, and running over" (Luke 6:38). For since those to whom mercy is shown are the cause of mercy being returned to men who show it, the former are said to return mercy to the latter.

VELLE, VOLUNTAS

37:29   We say "to will to be" in the same six modes as "to cause to be." [21] Likewise, "to will not to be" has just as many distinctions as "to cause not to be."

Let us note that we sometimes will something in such a way that if we are able, we cause what we will actually to occur. In this way, a sick man wills health; for if he is able, he causes himself to be healthy; and if he is not able, nevertheless he would cause himself to be healthy if he could. We can call this will the *efficient* will, since insofar as it is able it effects what it wills.

But sometimes we will something which we are able to cause to be and yet do not cause to be. Still, if it does occur, we are pleased by it and we approve of it.[22] For if a poor, naked man, whom I am unwilling to clothe, should tell me that he is naked because I want him to be naked or don't want him to be clothed, I answer that I want him to be clothed and not to be naked. Furthermore, I approve of his being clothed rather than his being naked, even though I myself do not cause him to be clothed.* This

21. Cf. *Liber de Voluntate* (Migne, PL 158:487C).
22. Cf. CDH I, 10 (S II, 65:21–25).
  * Cf. DCD 1 (S I, 234:9–14).

will by which I want the man to be clothed can be called the *approving* will.

38:14 We also will in another way. For example, a creditor may, as a concession (*indulgendo*), be willing to accept barley instead of wheat from a debtor, since the debtor is unable to repay the wheat. We can call this will merely a *conceding* will, for the creditor prefers wheat but concedes to a repayment with barley on account of the debtor's poverty.

Moreover, we frequently speak of someone's willing a thing which he neither consents to nor concedes but only *permits*, though he could prevent it.[23] Thus, when a ruler does not will to restrain robbers and plunderers in his dominion, we maintain that he wills the evil which they do, though they displease him; and we maintain this on the basis of his being willing to permit such evil.

38:24 Now, it seems to me that every kind of willing is contained within these four divisions. And with respect to these four different kinds of will, the one which I have called the efficient will causes what it wills insofar as it is able to, and it also approves, concedes, and permits. But the approving will does not cause what it wills; it only approves, concedes, and permits. The conceding will neither causes nor approves what it wills (unless possibly for the sake of something else), but it only concedes and permits. And the permitting will neither causes, approves, nor concedes what it wills, but it only permits this thing — though disapproving it.

Holy Scripture mentions all four kinds of willing. I shall give a few examples of this. For instance, Scripture says that God "has done whatsoever He has willed to do" (Ps. 115:3), and that God "is merciful to whomever He wills to be merciful" (Rom. 9:18). This is the efficient will, and it belongs to the first mode of "willing to be" because it is similar to the first mode of "causing to be" in that it wills the very thing which it is said to will.

But when Scripture says of God that "He hardens whomever He wills to harden" (Rom. 9:18), this is the permissive will and belongs to the second mode of "willing to be," for He is said to will that a man's heart be hard because He does not will efficiently that it not be hard; i.e., He does not will to cause a man's heart not

23. Cf. CDH I, 10 (S II, 65:26–27).

to be hard. On the other hand, if we say that God wills to harden because "He does not will to soften," the sense is the same as before and refers also to the permissive will. But now we are exhibiting the fourth mode of "willing to be," for we are saying that God "wills to harden" because He does not will something else, viz., for a man's heart "to be softened." For whoever softens causes to be softened and not to be hardened.[24]

39:21   Now, when we hear that "God wills every man to be saved" (I Tim. 2:4), this is the approving will. Like "willing to harden" this will belongs to the second mode of "willing to be," because it does not will efficiently for any man not to be saved. And an approving will belongs to the fourth mode as well, because it does not efficiently will a man's condemnation, i.e., it does not will something else to occur through which his condemnation might result. This verse is directed against those who argue that the will of God is the cause of their being unjust instead of just and the cause of their not being saved — although, in fact, the injustice for which men are condemned originates from themselves and does not come from the will of God.

    If we say that God wills for virginity to be kept among those whom He causes to keep it, then we are speaking of efficient will in the first mode of "willing to be." In other men, whom He does not cause to preserve chastity, His will for their virginity is an approving will because He does not efficiently will that their chastity not be kept (second mode), or because He does not will that their chastity be violated (fourth mode).

CAUSAE

40:1   Some causes are called efficient — for instance a craftsman who creates his own work, or wisdom, which causes a man to be wise.[25] * Other causes, by contrast, are not called efficient — for instance, the matter from which something is made, or the time

---

24. Cf. CDH I, 9 (S II, 64:3–5).

25. Cf. M 6 (S I, 19:1–3). Both passages are without doubt inspired by Boethius, *On Cicero's Topics* (PL 64:1145ff).

   * Schmitt has now shown that Anselm did not know this part of Boethius's commentary on Cicero's *Topics*, although he did know the *Topics* itself. See "Anselm und der (Neu-) Platonismus," AA I, 44.

and place in which temporal and spatial things occur. Still, in its own way every cause whatsoever is said to do (*facere*) something, and everything which is said to do something is called a cause.

Every cause does something. One cause actually does what it is said to cause to be or not to be; another does not actually do what it is said to cause to be or not to be, but only causes something else which is the reason for our saying what we do. So both Herod and a guard are said to have killed John the Baptist, because both were causes of the state of affairs which they are said to have brought about. And the fact that the Lord Jesus during infancy and childhood was brought up by Joseph as if He were his son is the semblance which caused not His having been the son of Joseph, but His having been called the son of Joseph.[26] I shall first say a word, God granting, about that kind of cause which actually causes what it is said to, and afterwards I shall say something about the other kind of cause.*

40:18 There are proximate causes which do by themselves what they are said to do, with no other causes intervening between them and their effect. And there are remote causes which do what they are said to do — doing it not by themselves but only through one or more intermediary causes. For the man who orders that a fire be set, and the man who sets the fire, and the fire that he sets all cause burning. A fire, however, causes burning by itself, and immediately. But he who sets on fire causes burning by the intermediary cause of a fire. And he who orders that something be set on fire causes burning by means of two intermediary causes: a fire and the man who actually sets the fire. So we see that proximate causes really themselves do that which they are said to do, whereas remote causes cause some other thing which produces the same effect.

But it sometimes happens that an effect is attributed more to a cause which acts remotely than to a cause which acts proximately. This is the case when we attribute to a magistrate, for instance, something which is done upon his order or by his authority, or

26. For a similar example in a different context, see CDH I, 9 (S II, 63:13–15).

* Anselm does not go on to discuss this "other kind of cause," as Schmitt notes. Cf. 34:29–34:39.

when we say that a man who does something for which he is put to death is killed by himself rather than by another.

41:3   Moreover, just as some efficient causes bring about proximately and through their own agency what they are said to cause, and others bring about by intermediaries what they are said to cause, so too nonefficient causes may be either proximate or remote. Thus, iron is the proximate [material] cause of a sword, and it is such a cause by itself and apart from any intermediate cause. And the earth from which iron comes is a remote [material] cause of the sword by way of an intervening proximate [material] cause, viz., iron. Every cause has other causes of itself. This chain of causation continues until it reaches God, who is the supreme cause of all things which are something, though He Himself has no cause. So too, every effect has several causes of different kinds — except for the first effect [which has only one cause], since only the supreme cause has created everything. Indeed, in the death of a single man several causes may be present: the man who actually does the killing, the man who orders it to be done, the reason for which the victim is killed, and (as necessary conditions) the time and the place of the killing, to mention a few.

Some causes are said to operate by doing something, others by not doing something — or even, in some cases, by not existing. For we say that whoever does not restrain evil causes it to occur and that whoever does not do good causes it not to occur. In the same way, we say that chastisement causes good to be and evil not to be; however, when this is absent, then its very absence is said to cause evil to occur and good not to occur. Causes of this last kind are included among those causes which are said to cause by not doing anything.

41:25   Although causes are quite frequently said to cause *per aliud* (i.e., through an intermediary, and thus are termed remote causes) rather than to cause *per se*, nevertheless every cause has its own proximate effect which it causes *per se* and in relation to which it is a proximate cause. For whoever kindles a flame is the proximate cause of the flame; and he is the remote cause of the fire he sets by means of the flame. Thus, when a cause is proximate, it is properly said to cause since it causes *per se*. But when a cause is remote, it is said to cause since it causes something else.

Every cause is either a being or a not-being. And every effect is likewise either a being or a not-being, since every cause either makes something to be or makes it not to be. Now, I designate as being anything or any state of affairs which may be mentioned without negation in one or more utterances; I designate as not-being anything or any state of affairs which is mentioned by way of denial. So when we utter the word "sun," we mention a certain being (*essentia*) without yet signifying it to be a cause. Likewise, when I utter the verb "shines," I mean something, though without yet signifying it to be an effect. But when I say "The sun shines," I indicate that the sun is a cause and shining is an effect, and that each exists and is something, for the sun has its own existence and causes light to exist. In this example, then, both the cause and the effect are beings. However, if I say "The sun causes night not to be," the cause is a being but the effect is a not-being. (The same holds true for many expressions in which I use the verb "to be.") For the sun's being above the horizon is something and causes day to be and night not to be. Here, then, is an example of being causing both being and not-being. Contrariwise, the sun's not being above the horizon causes night to be and day not to be. In this example not-being causes both being and not-being. Now, just as what is said to do something is obviously a cause, so whatever in some way or other is signified to be a cause does that thing whose cause it is said to be. For example, to say "Because of the sun's presence, it is day and not night" or "Because of the sun's absence, it is night and not day" is the same as saying "The sun's presence causes it to be day and not to be night" or "The sun's absence causes it to be night and not to be day." Thus, he who says "my knees are weak from fasting and my flesh is changed because of oil" (Ps. 109:24) is saying, in effect, "Fasting has weakened my knees; oil has changed my flesh." Fasting changes through its presence, oil through its absence. For often we say that a cause makes something be or not be through its presence, or makes something be or not be through its absence. But we don't always explicitly indicate the notions of presence and absence. We say, for instance, that the sun causes day to exist and night not to exist and that it causes day not to exist and night to exist. But

42:2

here we understand that the sun causes the one through its presence, the other through its absence.

ALIQUID

42:22   We speak of something in four modes.

We properly call something anything which has a name, is a concept in the mind, and exists in reality. Thus, for example, a stone and a piece of wood are something because they have names, are conceived by the mind, and exist in reality.

That is also called something which has a name and is a concept in the mind, but does not exist in reality. A chimera, for instance, is the concept of a kind of animal, which is signified by a name; nevertheless no chimera actually exists.

We also ordinarily say that whatever has only a name is something, even though there is no concept of this name in our minds and no real existence of the thing which is named. Injustice and nothing are examples of this type.[27] For we call injustice something when we assert that someone who is punished on account of injustice is punished on account of something. And we call nothing *something*[28] if we say of something "it is nothing" or "it is not nothing."[29] For since a proposition is true or false, we say that it either affirms something about something or denies something about something. Nevertheless, injustice and nothing are not concepts in our minds, even though they admit of being understood (as do infinite nouns). Indeed, to admit of being understood and to be something in the understanding (mind) are not the same.[30] For "not-man" admits of being understood because it causes the hearer to understand that *man* is not contained in its signification, but is removed. Yet there is not something in the understanding which is the thing signified by the expression "not-man" — unlike the expression "man" which *does* determine and

27. Cf. DCV 5 (S II, 147:1–3).

28. Concerning *iniustitia* and *nihil* as purely negative concepts, see such passages as DCD 9, 11, and 16.

29. Cf. DCD 11 (S I, 248:4–5).

30. We find a formally similar antithesis in *Proslogion* 2: "Aliud enim est rem esse in intellectu, aliud intelligere rem esse." S I, 101:9–10.

signify a concept in the understanding. So too, "injustice" signifies the removal of justice where justice ought to be, and it does
not posit anything in the understanding; likewise, "nothing" signifies the removal of something and does not posit anything in the
understanding.

43:14   We also call something that which does not have a name and is
not a concept and does not have any existence at all — for instance,
when we say that not-being is something or that not-being "is."
For we say that the sun's not being above the earth causes it not
to be day. And if every cause and every effect are said to be something, we will not deny that its not being day and the sun's not
being above the horizon are something, since the one is the cause
and the other the effect. Moreover, we say that not-being is,
when, upon hearing someone maintain that something is not the
case, we say that the state of affairs is as he says it is. But we ought
rather, properly speaking, to say that the state of affairs is not, as
he says it is not.

Although we speak of *something* in the four modes [discussed
above], only the first mode is properly called "something." The
others are not really something, but only "as if something" (*quasi
aliquid*), because we speak about them as if they were something.

DE POTESTATE

44:1   Ability is an "aptitude for doing" (*aptitudo ad faciendum*). I
use "doing" here to stand for every verb, finite or infinite, which
occurs in ordinary discourse. For whoever speaks or sits or stands
when he ought, and whoever wills or suffers what he ought, and
whoever is where he ought to be when he ought to be there does
well. But whoever does not speak or sit or stand when he ought,
and whoever does not will or suffer what he ought, and whoever
is not where he ought to be or is not there when he ought to be
does evilly. And he who does not do what he ought, does evilly;
and he who does not do what he ought not, does well. Therefore,
"to do" may be substituted for every other verb, whether finite
or infinite — even for "not to do."

So then, ability is an aptitude-for-doing, and every aptitude-
for-doing is an ability. But we must be cautious; for aptitude-for-

doing (*aptitudo ad faciendum*) is not precisely the same as apti-tude-to-do (*aptitudo faciendi*). For every aptitude-for-doing is also an aptitude-to-do, but not every aptitude-to-do is an apti-tude-for-doing. For example, the aptitude-to-write (*aptitudo scribendi*) encompasses aptitude-for-writing (*aptitudo ad scribendum*), which is present before anything is written; this aptitude-for-writing is called the ability-to-write. And aptitude-to-write (*aptitudo scribendi*) also encompasses aptitude-at-writing (*aptitudo in scribendo*), in accordance with which we say that some-one writes aptly. This aptitude-at-writing does not precede the act of writing, nor is it an ability-to-write; it is an effect of the ability-to-write. For the act of writing aptly depends upon a prior ability to write aptly; the ability does not depend upon the act.*

44:21   If an aptitude-for-something (e.g., the aptitude of clothing for the body) is not also an aptitude-for-doing, it cannot be an abili-ty. Clothes are said to be apt for the body, but they are not for this reason said to be an ability. Therefore, we have rightly called ability an "aptitude-for-doing." For by calling it an aptitude, we distinguish it from everything which is not an aptitude; by calling it an "aptitude-for-doing," we distinguish it from every other kind of aptitude. That is, we distinguish it from aptitudes which are not aptitudes-for-something (e.g., from an aptitude-at-writing), and from aptitudes which, though aptitudes-for-something, are not aptitudes-for-doing (e.g., from the aptitude of clothing for the body — better expressed as *vestis apta corpori* than as *aptitudo vestis ad corpus*). Hence, the definition of "ability" includes neither more nor less than it should.

    This definition of "ability" is composed in accordance with our way of speaking and not in accordance with the proper significa-tion of the word "ability." So every case of "being able" can be accounted for on the basis of this definition of "ability." For ex-ample, wood is able to be cut, and man is able to cut. Wood is able

---

* *Aptitudo scribendi* encompasses:
  1. *aptitudo ad scribendum*
    a. praecedit ipsam scriptionem
    b. idem est ac potestas scribendi
  2. *aptitudo in scribendo*
    a. non praecedit ipsam scriptionem
    b. effectum aptitudinis ad scribendum
    c. secundum quam dicimus quia "apte scribit"

to be cut because it has an aptitude for cutting [i.e., for being cut], and man is able to cut because he has an aptitude for cutting.

Diagram I: "To Cause Someone to Be Dead"

Affirmative Tables

Table A: "To Cause to Be Dead"

1.	CB*	A directly causes C to be dead.
2.	$\sim$C$\sim$B	A directly causes C to be dead, because A does not cause C not to be dead.
3.	CB	A causes C to be dead, because A causes B to be armed.
4.	$\sim$CB	A causes C to be dead, because A does not cause C to be armed.
5.	C$\sim$B	A causes C to be dead, because A causes C not to be armed.
6.	$\sim$C$\sim$B	A causes C to be dead, because A does not cause B not to be armed.

Table B. "To Cause Not to Be Living"

1.	C$\sim$B	A directly causes C not to be living.
2.	$\sim$CB	A directly causes C not to be living, because A does not cause C to be living.
3.	CB	A causes C not to be living, because A causes B to be armed.
4.	$\sim$CB	A causes C not to be living, because A does not cause C to be armed.
5.	C$\sim$B	A causes C not to be living, because A causes C not to be armed.
6.	$\sim$C$\sim$B	A causes C not to be living, because A does not cause B not to be armed.

Negative Tables

Table C: "Not to Cause to Be Living"

1.	$\sim$CB	A does not directly cause C to be living.
2.	C$\sim$B	A does not directly cause C to be living,

* CB = Causing to Be. When cited separately, A, B, C indicate persons. "$\sim$" is the sign of negation. Parentheses show where Anselm varies the lexical order (See PF 33:9–16).

		because A directly causes C not to be living.
3.	($\sim$CB) CB	A does not cause C to be living, because A causes B to be armed.
4.	(CB) $\sim$CB	A does not cause C to be living, because A does not cause C to be armed.
5.	($\sim$C$\sim$B) C$\sim$B	A does not cause C to be living, because A causes C not to be armed.
6.	(C$\sim$B) $\sim$C$\sim$B	A does not cause C to be living, because A does not cause B not to be armed.

Table D: "Not to Cause Not to Be Dead"

1.	$\sim$C$\sim$B	A does not directly cause C not to be dead.
2.	CB	A does not directly cause C not to be dead, because A directly causes C to be dead.
3.	($\sim$CB) CB	A does not cause C not to be dead, because A causes B to be armed.
4.	(CB) $\sim$CB	A does not cause C not to be dead, because A does not cause C to be armed.
5.	($\sim$C$\sim$B) C$\sim$B	A does not cause C not to be dead, because A causes C not to be armed.
6.	(C$\sim$B) $\sim$C$\sim$B	A does not cause C not to be dead, because A does not cause B not to be armed.

Diagram II: "To Cause Someone to Be Living"

Affirmative Tables

Table A: "To Cause to Be Living"

1.	CB	A directly causes C to be living.
2.	$\sim$C$\sim$B	A directly causes C to be living, because A does not cause C not to be living.
3.	CB	A causes C to be living, because A causes C to be armed.
4.	$\sim$CB	A causes C to be living, because A does not cause B to be armed.
5.	C$\sim$B	A causes C to be living, because A causes B not to be armed.
6.	$\sim$C$\sim$B	A causes C to be living, because A does not cause C not to be armed.

Table B: "To Cause Not to Be Dead"

1.	$C \sim B$	A directly causes C not to be dead.
2.	$\sim CB$	A directly causes C not to be dead, because A does not directly cause C to be dead.
3.	CB	A causes C not to be dead, because A causes C to be armed.
4.	$\sim CB$	A causes C not to be dead, because A does not cause B to be armed.
5.	$C \sim B$	A causes C not to be dead, because A causes B not to be armed.
6.	$\sim C \sim B$	A causes C not to be dead, because A does not cause C not to be armed.

Negative Tables

Table C: "Not to Cause to Be Dead"

1.	$\sim CB$	A does not directly cause C to be dead.
2.	$C \sim B$	A does not directly cause C to be dead, because A directly causes C not to be dead.
3.	CB	A does not cause C to be dead, because A causes C to be armed.
4.	$\sim CB$	A does not cause C to be dead, because A does not cause B to be armed.
5.	$C \sim B$	A does not cause C to be dead, because A causes B not to be armed.
6.	$\sim C \sim B$	A does not cause C to be dead, because A does not cause C not to be armed.

Table D: "Not to Cause Not to Be Living"

1.	$\sim C \sim B$	A does not directly cause C not to be living.
2.	CB	A does not directly cause C not to be living, because A directly causes C to be living.
3.	CB	A does not cause C not to be living, because A causes C to be armed.
4.	$\sim CB$	A does not cause C not to be living, because A does not cause B to be armed.
5.	$C \sim B$	A does not cause C not to be living, because A causes B not to be armed.
6.	$\sim C \sim B$	A does not cause C not to be living, because A does not cause C not to be armed.

Diagram III. Relationship between Tables

A: To cause to be.
B: To cause not to be.
C: Not to cause to be.
D: Not to cause not to be.

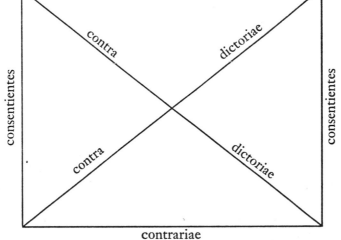

Anselm's Methods
of Arguing

Anselm had at his disposal the basic principles of syllogistic argumentation conveyed generally to the medieval schools from Aristotle and the Stoics through Boethius, including the rules of *modus ponens* and *modus tollens*. His informal logical arguments constantly resort to these two principles. In *De Casu Diaboli* 21 he argues, for instance, that Satan could not have foreknown his fall.

Teacher: Let us suppose that while Satan was persisting in a good will he foreknew that he was going to fall in the future. Then either he would have been willing for it to happen or he would not have been willing for it to happen.

Student: One of these must be true.

T. Now, if together with this foreknowledge of his fall, Satan were ever willing to fall, he would already be fallen because of that evil will itself.

S. What you say is clear.

T. So if we suppose he were willing to fall, it would not be the case that he knew he was going to fall *before* he did fall [since to be willing to fall is to be *already* fallen].

S. There can be no objection to your conclusion.

T. On the other hand, if Satan were not willing to fall, then he would have been wretched with grief to the same degree that he wished to remain upright.

S. It can't be denied.

Anselm's Methods of Arguing

T. But the more he willed to remain upright in justice, the more just he was; and the more just he was, the more he should have been happy because of it.

S. This can't be denied either.

T. Therefore, if he foreknew that he was going to fall and if he were not willing to fall, he would have been as wretched as he should have been happy. But this is not consistent.

In other words, either Satan foreknew or he did not $(F \vee \sim F)$. Assume that he foreknew. Then either he was willing or not willing to fall $[F \supset (W \vee \sim W)]$. From this, Anselm shows that it is logically unacceptable to assert W and theologically unacceptable to assert $\sim W$. But if both W and $\sim W$ are false, then by *modus tollens* F must also be false (assuming that the conditional holds). And if F is false, then $\sim F$ is true. This simple type of alternation argument, which proceeds to deduce implications, typically turns up in Anselm's works. No doubt, Anselm was aware of Augustine's use of the hypothetical syllogism in *Christian Doctrine* 2. There Augustine contends that an *argumentum modus tollens* is valid, whereas an argument of the form $(p \supset q \cdot \sim p) \supset \sim q$ is invalid.[1] Moreover, he explicitly distinguishes the question of an argument's validity from the question of the truth of its premises.

How much logic Anselm knew beyond these and other elementary deductive formulas is not clear. Certainly he was familiar with the modal syllogism and Boethius's limited discussion of it. Thus his treatment of possibility and necessity in the *Philosophical Fragments* (and in the ontological argument itself) relies upon a primitive notion of modal logic. But these notions are for the most part only implicit in his texts. He handles the question of whether the world was possible before it was created by saying that in itself the world was not possible because the world did not yet exist; however for God, the world was possible because He had the power to cause it to be (DCD 12). He goes on without further ado; nowhere does he explicitly distinguish two types of possibility (the contingent and the necessary), though it seems clear that he was aware of such a distinction.[2] As for contrary-to-fact conditionals, we know only of his view that when both antecedent and consequent are "impossible," the consequent may be said to follow from the antecedent. "Therefore, to say 'If God wills to lie' is to say nothing other than 'If

1. 2.32.50–34.52 (PL 34:59–60).
2. See D. P. Henry, *The Logic of Saint Anselm* (Oxford, 1967), especially p. 146.

God's nature be such as to will to lie.' And from this we cannot infer 'A lie is just' — unless in the way we say of two impossible statements 'If the one be the case, then so is the other,' inasmuch as neither is the case. For example, someone might say: 'If water be dry, then fire is wet' — neither of which component statements is true" (CDH I, 12. S II, 70:20–24). Even here, the point is as much linguistic as it is logical. Anselm is stressing that we do sometimes say such things as "If A, then B" where B is known to be contrary to fact and where A is also known, or at least believed, to be contrary to fact. In such cases we are emphasizing the utter preposterousness of asserting A.

Anselm's notion of an impossibility encompasses both logical impossibility (i.e., self-inconsistency and inconsistency with other propositions which are held) and causal impossibility (i.e., what is counter to the laws of nature). He holds that from a logically impossible statement another logically impossible statement is derivable. If, then, there is some contradiction in asserting both God's foreknowledge and man's freedom of will, Anselm's way of discovering this is to posit both foreknowledge and freedom.[3] If he can then validly deduce a proposition which is inconsistent with the system of other propositions known to be true, he will know that foreknowledge and freedom are incompatible; if he cannot make such a deduction, and if there are only a restricted number of deductions possible, then he will have no reason to suppose that an incompatibility exists.

De Processione 14 is another place where Anselm invokes the notion of impossibility. In defending the *filioque* doctrine against the Greeks, he concludes with the summary: "So we have seen with how much truth and necessity it follows that the Holy Spirit proceeds from the Son. But if this doctrine be false, then either something is false in those premises from which we have demonstrated this doctrine or else we have not argued correctly. But to assert that the premises are false is against the Christian faith which we and the Greeks affirm; and it cannot be shown that our argument is faulty. For this reason, if this doctrine of procession is not true then the Christian faith is destroyed. And it is also clear to one who understands, that if the doctrine is asserted to be false, no truth follows from it." Anselm rightly sees that if a proposition (or a

3. "Let us see whether it is impossible for the two to coexist. If it is impossible, then there will arise a further impossibility, since an impossible thing is one which, if posited, is followed by another impossible thing." DC I, 1 (S II, 246:4–7).

set of propositions) is true, then any proposition validly deducible from it is also true. In the passage above he does not go on to suggest the general (and wrong) point that from false premises no true conclusion can validly follow. His method throughout *De Processione* is to start with theological premises which both the Latin and the Greek churches agree are essential to the Christian faith, and from these premises to show that the *filioque* doctrine follows validly. Should the Greeks then continue to maintain that the *filioque* doctrine is false, they will be forced to assert the falsity of the premises from which the doctrine validly follows (assuming that it does follow validly). But since the Greeks cannot ascribe falsity to those premises without surrendering the Christian faith, they must, argues Anselm, concede the truth of the *filioque* doctrine. Thus he is saying that because the Christian faith is true, any denial of its truth is necessarily false. And rejection of the doctrine that the Holy Spirit proceeds also from the Son leads to this very falsehood. In this special sense (rather than in a general sense) no truth follows from asserting that the *filioque* doctrine is false.

In addition to the basic logical rules of inference, Anselm employs a number of a priori principles construed as self-evident. Both the *Monologion* and *De Processione* utilize the principle that the one from whom someone is begotten cannot be the same as the someone who is begotten from him.[4] From this truth Anselm argues that the Son, who is begotten by the Father, cannot be the same person as the Father, and that the Holy Spirit, who proceeds from the Father and the Son, cannot be the same person as the Father or the Son. Again, the definitional principle that God embodies all perfections allows Anselm to deduce the various divine attributes in the *Monologion*; in the *Proslogion* it becomes the pivotal point of the ontological argument.

Where a priori truths are of no service, Anselm appeals to the notion of "appropriateness" to help him carry an inference. He is not misled into thinking that these considerations of what is suitable to believe about God can serve in place of a priori rationalistic principles; rather he views them as supplements which help confirm a point already established, or which bear some but not all of the weight in a chain of reasoning. A vivid example of this type of reasoning is offered in *Cur Deus Homo* I, 3: "As death had entered upon the human race through man's disobedience, so it was fitting that through man's obedience life should be restored to the

4. M 43; DP 1. Cf. Augustine, DT 1.4.7.

human race. As the sin which caused our condemnation had its beginning from a woman, so the Author of our justice and salvation should be born of a woman. And as Satan had conquered man by having persuaded him to taste of the tree, so Satan should be conquered through man's bearing of suffering on a tree." Here, then, is an attempt to minimize the scandal of the incarnation by showing that the notion of divine incarnation is not altogether repugnant to one's sense of the appropriate.[5]

Anselm also uses a method of division which goes back at least as far as Plato, in whose *Sophist* it becomes a way of arriving at a definition. Not new to the Middle Ages, this method stems through Cicero's *Moral Obligation* (*De Officiis*), Porphyry's *Introduction* (*Isagoge*), and Boethius's theological tractates. It is essentially a tool for classifying and distinguishing concepts.[6] Anselm's pronounced version of this method occurs at the end of *De Libertate*, where he summarizes the definition of "free choice" arrived at in the course of the dialogue:

Teacher: [Here are the distinctions appropriate to freedom:]

I. There is an "unoriginated freedom of choice," which is neither created nor received, and this freedom belongs to God alone.

II. There is a "created freedom of choice," which was created by and received from God, and this freedom is characteristic of men and angels. This "created freedom" either (A) *does* have an uprightness which it may keep, or (B) *doesn't* have an uprightness to keep.

II-A. The "created freedom which has uprightness" keeps this uprightness either (1) so as *to be able* to lose it, or (2) so as *not to be able* to lose it.

II-A-1. The "created freedom which has uprightness so as to be able to lose it" was characteristic of all angels before the good ones were confirmed and the evil ones fell; and it characterizes, throughout their earthly lives, all men who have uprightness.

---

5. Note also the difference between the two types of reasons given for why angels cannot be saved: (1) There is no race of angels, since angels do not share a common father, as Adam was the common father of the human race; thus, a God-angel could not atone for all angels in the course of assuming angelic nature. (2) Angels ought to be saved without anyone's aid since they fell without anyone's abetment; but this self-elevation is impossible. The second reason differs from the first in being merely a *fitting* reason, although Anselm does not explicitly call it that. CDH II, 21.

6. E.g., note Boethius, *The Person and the Two Natures* 2 (PL 64:1343): "Some substances are corporeal, others incorporeal. Of the corporeal, some are living, others not. Of the living, some have faculties of sensation, others do not. Of those having faculties of sensation, some are rational, others non-rational." In *Division* Boethius mentions Plato's *Sophist* by name (PL 64:876).

II-A-2. The "created freedom which has uprightness so as not to be able to lose it" is characteristic of elect angels and elect men: it characterized elect angels immediately after the fall of the reprobate angels, and it characterizes elect men immediately after their death.

II-B. The "created freedom which does not have uprightness" either (1) *is able* to regain it, or (2) *is not able* to regain it.

II-B-1. The "created freedom which does not have uprightness and yet is able to regain it" characterizes, throughout their earthly lives, all men who lack it — although many may never regain it.

II-B-2. The "created freedom which does not have uprightness and is not able to regain it" is characteristic of reprobate angels and reprobate men — of the angels after their fall, and of these men after their death.

Aside from this passage and an additional section in *De Veritate* 12 (and possibly *De Processione* 16), Anselm has no occasion to resort to *divisiones*. But his use of this method at all suggests that it had become part of the technical apparatus of the monastic school at Bec, along with the usual studies in grammar and dialectic.

Another equally ancient technique, familiar in Plato's *Republic* and throughout the dialogues, and used pervasively in the Middle Ages, is the argument from elimination. The simplest example of this may be drawn from Boethius:

Allow that the following four statements are not outside the scope of reason: viz., that in Christ there were (1) two natures and two persons (as Nestorius says); (2) one person and one nature (as Eutyches says); (3) two natures but one person (as the Catholic faith affirms); (4) one nature and two persons. Now we have already refuted the doctrine of two natures and two persons in replying to Nestorius — as well as having shown impossible the doctrine of one person and one nature embraced by Eutyches. Moreover, no one has ever been so mad as to believe that in Christ there was one nature but two persons. Therefore, it follows that the affirmation set forth by the Catholic faith is true.[7]

Anselm adopts this very procedure of setting out three or four alternatives, claiming that they are exhaustive, showing that objections can be raised against all but one of them, and then concluding that the remaining alternative must hold true. Hence, in *De Libertate* 3 he queries why Satan and Adam had free choice. "(1) Was it for the purpose of acquiring uprightness, without anyone's giving it, when they didn't yet have it? (2)

7. Boethius, *The Person and the Two Natures* 7 (PL 64:1352).

Or was it for receiving what they didn't yet have, if it were given to them? (3) Or was it for deserting what they had received and for later reclaiming, by their own means, what they had deserted? (4) Or was it for constantly keeping what they originally had received?" By faulting hypotheses 1–3, Anselm is able to assert, straightway, hypothesis 4. And having once established in this way the *purpose* of the gift of uprightness, he is able to begin investigating the *reason* for man's obligation to keep uprightness.[8]

Anselm is quick to embrace whatever procedures he feels will lead justifiably to theological clarity. Where need be, he appeals to experience; where need be, to an intrinsic sense of congruity. Against those who argue that the just or unjust lives of immediate ancestors affect their descendants' states of soul, he insists on a look at the lives of infants: "If it cannot be shown that, as soon as infants have a soul, some will more and others will less what they ought or ought not, then no one can prove that some children are begotten more or less just than others" (DCV 24. S II, 167:21–24). And common experience, he thinks, bears out the fact that infants behave more or less alike. Where experience cannot in principle decide an issue, Anselm often resorts to a *reductio ad absurdum*. On what basis does one decide whether or not a fetus has a rational soul from the very moment of its conception? Because no appeal to experience can ever decide this question, Anselm tries to show that attributing a rational soul at the moment of conception leads to a view which is completely foreign to the mind of the Church. Such an attribution, he notes, would force one to say that "whenever the human seed which has been received perishes before attaining a human form (even should it perish at the moment of its reception), then the [alleged] human soul in that seed would be condemned, since it would not have been reconciled to God through Christ. But such a conclusion is utterly absurd" (DCV 7. S II, 148:5–8).

No one method characterizes Anselm's works, which seem to make

8. On occasion Anselm reverses the process and argues that because, say, there are only four ways to do a thing, and because God has already acted according to the first three, it is appropriate that He act also according to the fourth way. In such cases Anselm is not offering a rigorous argument, but rather is appealing to the notion of fittingness to show that the divine activity in question is not surprising. Cf. CDH II, 8 (S II, 104:3–8): "God can make a man in four ways: (1) from a man and a woman (as normally happens); (2) neither from a man nor from a woman (as He created Adam); (3) from a man without a woman (as He made Eve); (4) from a woman without a man (which He was yet to do). Therefore, in order to prove that this way was also within His power and was reserved for this purpose, nothing

full use of whatever techniques were available in that day. Anselm attempts to do justice to both reason and experience, to both logic and language. In recognizing that a sound deductive argument cannot be given for every point of doctrine, he was not embarrassed about relying upon considerations of suitability and fittingness. By avoiding a merely mechanical and artificial approach to language, he promotes a way of thinking which responds effectively to puzzles arising out of the semantics of that very language. His invoking of experience and common sense tends to balance his reliance upon a priori principles of reason. And those places in his later treatises where a premise for an argument is drawn solely from the authority of Scripture witness to his conviction that reason can never supplant revelation.

is more suitable than for that man whom we seek to have been assumed from a woman without a man."

English Translations
Abbreviations
Bibliography

English Translations
of Anselm's Works

Monologion: S. N. Deane.*
Proslogion: M. J. Charlesworth, S. N. Deane, E. R. Fairweather, J. H. Hick and
 A. C. McGill (selections), J. S. Maginnis, A. C. Pegis, C. C. J. Webb.
De Grammatico: D. P. Henry.
De Veritate: J. Hopkins and H. Richardson,† R. McKeon.
De Libertate Arbitrii: J. Hopkins and H. Richardson.
De Casu Diaboli: J. Hopkins and H. Richardson.
Epistola de Incarnatione Verbi: E. R. Fairweather (excerpt), J. Hopkins and H.
 Richardson.
Cur Deus Homo: Anonymous (1909), J. M. Colleran, S. N. Deane (reprinted from
 J. G. Vose), E. R. Fairweather, E. S. Prout, J. G. Vose.
De Conceptu Virginali: J. M. Colleran, E. R. Fairweather (selections), J. Hopkins
 and H. Richardson.
De Processione Spiritus Sancti: J. Hopkins and H. Richardson.
Epistola de Sacrificio Azimi et Fermentati: J. Hopkins and H. Richardson.
Epistola de Sacramentis Ecclesiae: J. Hopkins and H. Richardson.
De Concordia: J. Hopkins and H. Richardson.
Orationes 1, 2, 3, 4, 18, 19: Anonymous (1952).
Oratio 7: E. R. Fairweather.
Oratio 18: C. C. J. Webb, pp. 126–130.
Oratio 19: C. C. J. Webb, pp. 130–134.
Meditatio ad Concitandum Timorem: G. Stanhope, pp. 305–313; C. C. J. Webb,
 pp. 89–95; Anonymous (1872); Anonymous (1952).
Deploratio Virginitatis Male Amissae: Anonymous (1872).
Meditatio Redemptionis Humanae: G. Stanhope, C. C. J. Webb, Anonymous
 (1872), Anonymous (1952)

---

* For full citation consult the entries in the bibliography under either the transla-
tors' names or "Anselm."

† In the *Companion* the English translations of Anselm are either taken from J.
Hopkins and H. Richardson or else are independently by J. Hopkins.

Epistolae 129, 136: J. Hopkins and H. Richardson.
Epistolae 214, 217: E. R. Fairweather (excerpts)
The following letters have been translated anonymously and appended to a translation of the *Cur Deus Homo* (Edinburgh, 1909). Although the letters in translation are numbered consecutively, their respective ordering in the Schmitt texts would be numbers: 1, 2, 9, 4, 5, 6, 41, 54, 57, 64, 67, 83, 84, 10, 117, 140, 148, 156, 160, 166, 176, 209, 186, 210, 349, 198, 214, 315, 246, 251, 306, 290, 329, 330, 336, 218, 264, 268, 280, 217, 205, 285, 293, 294, 291, 302, 319, 327, 335, 343, 355, 391, 368, 375, 378, 387, 389, 403, 404, 405, 406, 407, 413, 414, 418, 420, 421, 427, 435, 436, 443, 446, 451, 472, 228, 168, 229, 277, 324, 345, 346, 412, 449, 265, 196, 245, 254, 328, 204.
Epistolae 13, 51, 264, 413, 414 appear consecutively in J. J. C. Webb, pp. 136–151.

Abbreviations

AA   *Analecta Anselmiana*, ed. F. S. Schmitt. Frankfurt. Vol. I (1969); Vol. II (1970). (A continuing series.)

HSD *Actes du premier congrès international de philosophie médiévale: L'homme et son destin.* Louvain, 1960.

PL   *Patrologia Latina*, ed. J.-P. Migne.

SB   *Spicilegium Beccense.* Vol. I. Paris, 1959.

SR   *Sola ratione*, ed. H. Kohlenberger. Stuttgart, 1970. (Anselm Studies for F. S. Schmitt on his seventy-fifth birthday.)

Bibliography

CRITICAL EDITION OF LATIN TEXTS

Schmitt, F. S. *Sancti Anselmi Opera Omnia.* Vol. I, Seckau, 1938 (republished in Edinburgh, 1946); Vol. II, Rome, 1940; Vol. III, Edinburgh, 1946; Vol. IV, Edinburgh, 1949; Vol. V, Edinburgh, 1951; Vol. VI, Edinburgh, 1961. All volumes reprinted by F. Frommann Verlag (Stuttgart-Bad Cannstatt), 1968, with an introduction by Schmitt drawing together his articles on Anselm.

SELECTED TRANSLATIONS, ANTHOLOGIES, AND BOOK-LENGTH STUDIES SINCE 1945

Anselm of Canterbury. *Prayers and Meditations.* Trans. anonymously by a Religious of C.S.M.V. London, 1952.
——. *Cur Deus Homo. Warum Gott Mensch Geworden.* Trans. and intro. F. S. Schmitt. Munich, 1956.
——. *Proslogion.* Trans. and intro. F. S. Schmitt. Stuttgart-Bad Cannstatt, 1961.
——. *Pourquoi Dieu s'est fait homme.* Trans. and intro. R. Roques. Paris, 1963.
——. *Monologion.* Trans. and intro. F. S. Schmitt. Stuttgart-Bad Cannstatt, 1964.
——. *De Veritate. Über die Wahrheit.* Trans. and intro. F. S. Schmitt. Stuttgart-Bad Cannstatt, 1966.
——. *Gebete.* Trans. and intro. L. Helbling. Einsiedeln, 1965.
——. *Truth, Freedom, and Evil: Three Philosophical Dialogues.* Trans. and intro. J. Hopkins and H. Richardson. New York, 1967.
——. *Why God Became Man and the Virgin Conception and Original Sin.* Trans. and intro. J. M. Colleran. Albany, 1969.
——. *Trinity, Incarnation, and Redemption: Theological Treatises.* Trans. and intro. J. Hopkins and H. Richardson. New York, 1970.
Bütler, P. *Die Seinslehre des hl. Anselm von Canterbury.* Ingenbohl, 1959.
Cantor, N. *Church, Kingship, and Lay Investiture in England, 1089–1135.* Princeton, N.J., 1958.
Charlesworth, M. *St. Anselm's Proslogion.* London, 1965.
Cicchetti, A. *L'Agostinismo nel pensiero di Anselmo d'Aosta.* Rome, 1951.
Eadmer. *The Life of St. Anselm, Archbishop of Canterbury.* Ed. and trans. R. W. Southern. London, 1962.
——. *History of Recent Events in England.* Trans. G. Bosanquet. London, 1964.
Fairweather, E., ed. *A Scholastic Miscellany: Anselm to Occam.* Philadelphia, 1956.

Bibliography

(Contains translations of *Proslogion, Cur Deus Homo, De Conceptu Virginali,* among others.)

Hammer, F. *Genugtung und Heil: Absicht, Sinn und Grenzen der Erlösungslehre Anselms von Canterbury (Wiener Beiträge zur Theologie 15)*, Vienna, 1967.

Hartshorne, C. *Anselm's Discovery.* LaSalle, Ill., 1965.

Henrich, D. *Der ontologische Gottesbeweis: Sein Problem und seine Geschichte in der Neuzeit.* Tübingen, 1960.

Henry, D. P. *The De Grammatico of Saint Anselm.* South Bend, Ind., 1964.

——. *The Logic of Saint Anselm.* Oxford, 1967.

Hick, J., and A. McGill, eds. *The Many-faced Argument: Recent Studies of the Ontological Argument for the Existence of God.* New York, 1967.

Kohlenberger, H. *Similitudo und Ratio.* Bonn, 1972.

——, ed. *Sola ratione.* (Anselm Studies for F. S. Schmitt on his seventy-fifth birthday.) Stuttgart, 1970.

Kopper, J. *Reflexion und Raisonnement im ontologischen Gottesbeweis.* Cologne, 1962.

La Croix, R. *Proslogion I and II: A Third Interpretation of Anselm's Argument.* Leiden, 1972.

McIntyre, J. *St. Anselm and His Critics: A Reinterpretation of the Cur Deus Homo.* London, 1954.

Mazzarella, P. *Il pensiero speculativo di S. Anselmo d'Aosta.* Padova, 1962.

Pegis, A. C., ed. and trans. *The Wisdom of Catholicism.* New York, 1949. (Contains a translation of the *Proslogion* pp. 203–228.)

Perino, R. *La dottrina trinitaria di S. Anselmo (Studia Anselmiana 29).* Rome, 1952.

Plantinga, A., ed. *The Ontological Argument.* New York, 1965.

Pouchet, J.-R. *Saint Anselme: Un croyant cherche à comprendre.* Paris, 1970.

Pouchet, R. *La rectitudo chez saint Anselme (Etudes augustiniennes series).* Paris, 1964.

Schmitt, F. S., ed. *Analecta Anselmiana.* Frankfurt, 1969 (Vol. 1), 1970 (Vol. 2). A continuing series.

Schurr, A. *Die Begründung der Philosophie durch Anselm von Canterbury.* Stuttgart, 1966.

Southern, R. W. *Saint Anselm and His Biographer.* Cambridge, 1963.

——, and F. S. Schmitt. *Memorials of St. Anselm.* London, 1969.

Spicilegium Beccense I. Paris, 1959. (A collection of articles.)

Vanni Rovighi, S. *S. Anselmo e la Filosofia del Sec. XI.* Milan, 1949.

Williams, G. H. *Anselm: Communion and Atonement.* St. Louis, 1960.

ARTICLES SINCE 1945

Ontological Argument

Abelson, R. "Not Necessarily," *Philosophical Review,* 70 (January 1961), 67–84.

Adams, R. M. "The Logical Structure of Anselm's Arguments," *Philosophical Review,* 80 (January 1971), 28–54.

Allen, R. E. "The Ontological Argument," *Philosophical Review,* 70 (January 1961), 56–66.

Alston, W. P. "The Ontological Argument Revisited," *Philosophical Review,* 69 (October 1960), 452–474.

Anderson, A. "Anselm and the Logic of Religious Belief," *Harvard Theological Review,* 61 (1968), 149–173.

Armour, L. "The Ontological Argument and the Concept of Completeness and Selection," *Review of Metaphysics,* 14 (December 1960), 280–291.

Balz, A. G. "Concerning the Ontological Argument," *Review of Metaphysics,* 7 (December 1953), 207–224.

Baumer, W. H. "Ontological Arguments Still Fail," *Monist*, 50 (January 1966), 130–144.

Beckaert, A. "Une justification platonicienne de l'argument a priori?" SB, pp. 185–190.

Berg, J. "An Examination of the Ontological Proof," *Theoria*, 27 (1961), 99–106.

———. "Über den ontologischen Gottesbeweis," *Kant-Studien*, 62 (1971), 236–242.

Bouillard, H. "La preuve de Dieu dans le 'Proslogion' et son interprétation par Karl Barth," SB, pp. 191–207.

Brown, T. P. "Professor Malcolm on 'Anselm's Ontological Arguments,'" *Analysis*, 22 (October 1961), 13–14.

Brunton, J. A. "The Logic of God's Necessary Existence," *International Philosophical Quarterly*, 10 (June 1970), 276–290.

Chatillon, J. "De Guillaume d'Auxerre à saint Thomas d'Aquin: L'argument de saint Anselme chez les premiers scolastiques du XIIIᵉ siècle," SB, pp. 209–231.

Coburn, R. C. "Professor Malcolm on God," *Australasian Journal of Philosophy*, 41 (August 1963), 143–162.

———. "Animadversions on Plantinga's Kant," *Journal of Philosophy*, 63 (October 13, 1966), 546–548.

Crawford, Patricia. "Existence, Predication, and Anselm," *Monist*, 50 (January 1966), 109–124.

Crittenden, C. "The Argument from Perfection to Existence," *Religious Studies*, 4 (October 1968), 123–132.

Dematteis, P. B. "The Ontological Argument as Wishful Thinking," *Kinesis*, 1 (Fall 1968), 1–14.

Engel, S. M. "Kant's 'Refutation' of the Ontological Argument," *Philosophy and Phenomenological Research*, 24 (September 1963), 20–35.

Evdokimov, P. "L'aspect apophatique de l'argument de saint Anselme," SB, pp. 233–258.

Ewing, A. C. "Further Thoughts on the Ontological Argument," *Religious Studies*, 5 (October 1969), 41–48.

Feuer, L. S. "God, Guilt, and Logic: The Psychological Basis of the Ontological Argument," *Inquiry*, 2 (Autumn 1968), 257–281.

———. "The Autonomy of the Sociology of Ideas: A Rejoinder," *Inquiry*, 12 (Winter 1969), 434–445.

de Finance, J. "Position anselmienne et démarche cartésienne," SB, pp. 259–272.

Findlay, J. N. "Some Reflections on Necessary Existence," in *Process and Divinity*. ed. W. L. Reese and E. Freeman. LaSalle, Ill., 1964, pp. 515–527.

Fitch, F. B. "The Perfection of Perfection," *Monist*, 47 (Spring 1963), 466–471.

———. "The Perfection of Perfection," in *Process and Divinity*. Ed. W. L. Reese and E. Freeman. LaSalle, Ill., 1964, pp. 530–532.

Forest, A. "L'argument de saint Anselme dans la philosophie réflexive," SB, pp. 273–294.

Grave, S. A. "The Ontological Argument of St. Anselm," *Philosophy*, 27 (January 1952), 30–38.

Gunderson, K., and R. Routley. "Mr. Rescher's Reformulation of the Ontological Proof," *Australasian Journal of Philosophy*, 38 (December 1960), 246–252.

Hardin, C. L. "An Empirical Refutation of the Ontological Argument," *Analysis*, 22 (October 1961), 10–12.

Harrison, C. "The Ontological Argument in Modal Logic," *Monist*, 54 (April 1970), 302–313.

Hartmann, R. S. "Prolegomena to a Meta-Anselmian Axiomatic," *Review of Metaphysics*, 14 (June 1961), 637–675.

Hartshorne, C. "The Logic of the Ontological Argument," *Journal of Philosophy*, 58 (August 17, 1961), 471–473.

Bibliography

———. "What Did Anselm Discover?" *Union Seminary Quarterly Review*, 17 (March 1962), 213–222.

———. "How Some Speak and Yet Do Not Speak of God," *Philosophy and Phenomenological Research*, 23 (December 1962), 274–276.

———. "Ten Ontological or Modal Proofs for God's Existence," Ch. 2 of his *Logic of Perfection*. LaSalle, Ill., 1962.

———. "Further Fascination of the Ontological Argument," *Union Seminary Quarterly Review*, 18 (March 1963), 244–255. (Replies to C. C. Richardson by C. Hartshorne, pp. 244–245, J. Brkić, pp. 246–249, W. R. Comstock, pp. 250–255.)

———. "Rationale of the Ontological Proof," *Theology Today*, 20 (July 1963), 278–283.

———. "What the Ontological Proof Does Not Do," *Review of Metaphysics*, 17 (June 1964), 608–609.

———. "Necessity," *Review of Metaphysics*, 21 (December 1967), 290–296.

Henle, P. "Uses of the Ontological Argument," *Philosophical Review*, 70 (January 1961), 102–109.

Henry, D. P. "The Proslogion Proofs," *Philosophical Quarterly*, 5 (1955), 147–151.

———. "Proslogion Chapter III," AA, pp. 101–105.

Henze, D. F. "Language-Games and the Ontological Argument," *Religious Studies*, 4 (October 1968), 147–152.

Hochberg, H. "St. Anselm's Ontological Argument and Russell's Theory of Descriptions," *New Scholasticism*, 33 (1959), 319–330.

Howe, L. T. "Existence as a Perfection: A Reconsideration of the Ontological Argument," *Religious Studies*, 4 (October 1968), 78–101.

———. "One God, One Proof," *Southern Journal of Philosophy*, 6 (Winter 1968), 235–245.

Huggett, W. J. "The 'Proslogion' Proof Re-examined," *Indian Journal of Philosophy*, 2 (1960–61), 193–202.

———. "The Nonexistence of Ontological Arguments," *Philosophical Review*, 71 (July 1962), 377–379.

Johnson, O. A. "God and St. Anelm," *Journal of Religion*, 45 (October 1965), 326–334.

Kiteley, M. "Existence and the Ontological Argument," *Philosophy and Phenomenological Research*, 18 (June 1958), 533–535.

Kuntz, P. "The God We Find: The God of Abraham, the God of Anselm, and the God of Weiss," *Modern Schoolman*, 47 (May 1970), 433–453.

Lewis, D. "Anselm and Actuality," *Nous*, 4 (May 1970), 175–188.

McDonald, H. D. "Monopolar Theism and the Ontological Argument," *Harvard Theological Review*, 58 (October 1965), 387–416.

McGreal, I. P. "Anselm," in his *Analyzing Philosophical Arguments*. Scranton, Pa., 1967, pp. 171–195.

Malcolm, N. "Anselm's Ontological Arguments," *Philosophical Review*, 69 (January 1960), 41–62. Reprinted in *The Ontological Argument*. Ed. A. Plantinga. Garden City, N.Y., 1965, pp. 136–159.

Mann, W. E. "Definite Descriptions and the Ontological Argument," *Theoria*, 33 (1967), 211–229.

———. "The Logic of Saint Anselm's Ontological Argument." Ph.D. dissertation, University of Minnesota, 1971.

Matthews, G. B. "On Conceivability in Anselm and Malcolm," *Philosophical Review*, 70 (January 1961), 110–111.

———. "Aquinas on Saying that God Doesn't Exist," *Monist*, 47 (Spring 1963), 472–477.

Mavrodes, G. I. "Properties, Predicates, and the Ontological Argument," *Journal of Philosophy*, 63 (October 13, 1966), 549–550.

Miller, P. J. "The Ontological Argument for God," *Personalist*, 42 (July 1961), 337–351.

Miller, R. G. "The Ontological Argument in St. Anselm and Descartes," *Modern Schoolman*, 32–33 (May, November 1955), 341–349, 31–38.

Nakhnikian, G. "St. Anselm's Four Ontological Arguments," in *Art, Mind, and Religion*. Ed. W. H. Capitan and D. D. Merrill. Pittsburgh, 1965, pp. 29–36.

———, and W. Salmon. "'Exists' as a Predicate," *Philosophical Review*, 66 (October 1957), 535–542.

Naulin, P. "Réflexions sur la portée de la preuve ontologique chez Anselme de Cantorbéry," *Revue de métaphysique et de morale*, 74 (January 1969), 1–20.

Nelson, J. O. "Modal Logic and the Ontological Proof for God's Existence," *Review of Metaphysics*, 17 (December 1963), 235–242.

O'Connor, M. J. "New Aspects of Omnipotence and Necessity in Anselm," *Religious Studies*, 4 (October 1968), 133–146.

Pailin, D. A. "Some Comments on Hartshorne's Presentation of the Ontological Argument," *Religious Studies*, 4 (October 1968), 103–122.

———. "An Introductory Survey of Charles Hartshorne's Work on the Ontological Argument," AA I, 195–221.

Paliard, J. "Prière et dialectique: Méditation sur le Proslogion de saint Anselme," *Dieu vivant*, 6 (1946), 51–70.

Pegis, A. C. "St. Anselm and the Argument of the 'Proslogion,'" *Mediaeval Studies*, 28 (1966), 228–267.

———. "Four Medieval Ways to God," *Monist*, 54 (July 1970), 317–358.

Penelhum, T. "On the Second Ontological Argument," *Philosophical Review*, 70 (January 1961), 85–92.

Plantinga, A. "A Valid Ontological Argument?" *Philosophical Review*, 70 (January 1961), 93–101. Reprinted in *The Ontological Argument*. Ed. A. Plantinga. Garden City, N.Y., 1965, pp. 160–171.

———. "Kant's Objection to the Ontological Argument," *Journal of Philosophy*, 63 (October 13, 1966), 537–546.

———. "The Ontological Argument," in his *God and Other Minds*. Ithaca, N.Y., 1967, pp. 26–63.

Pollock, J. L. "Proving the Non-Existence of God," *Inquiry*, 9 (Summer 1966), 193–196. Also note D. Föllesdal's "Comments on Dr. Pollock's 'Proving the Non-Existence of God,'" *ibid.*, pp. 197–199.

Potter, V. G. "Karl Barth and the Ontological Argument," *Journal of Religion*, 45 (October 1965), 309–325.

Purtill, R. L. "Hartshorne's Modal Proof," *Journal of Philosophy*, 63 (July 14, 1966), 397–409.

———. "Ontological Modalities," *Review of Metaphysics*, 21 (December 1967), 297–307. Also note C. Hartshorne, "Rejoinder to Purtill," *ibid.*, pp. 308–309.

Rescher, N. "The Ontological Proof Revisited," *Australasian Journal of Philosophy*, 37 (August 1959), 138–148.

Richardson, C. C. "The Strange Fascination of the Ontological Argument," *Union Seminary Quarterly Review*, 18 (November 1962), 1–21.

Ross, J. F. "God and 'Logical Necessity,'" *Philosophical Quarterly*, 11 (January 1961), 22–27.

Roth, M. "A Note on Anselm's Ontological Argument," *Mind*, 79 (April 1970), 270–271.

Ruja, H. "The Definition of God and the Ontological Argument," *Australasian Journal of Philosophy*, 41 (August 1963), 262–263.

Runyan, Mary. "The Relationship between Ontological and Cosmological Arguments," *Journal of Religion*, 43 (January 1963), 56–58.

Rynin, D. "On Deriving Essence from Existence," *Inquiry*, 6 (Summer 1963), 141–156.

Bibliography

Scott, F. "Scotus and Gilson on Anselm's Ontological Argument," *Antonianum*, 40 (1965), 442–448.

———. "Scotus, Malcolm, and Anselm," *Monist*, 49 (October 1965), 634–638.

Scott, G. E. "Quine, God, and Modality," *Monist*, 50 (January 1966), 77–86.

Sessions, W. L. "Feuer, Psychology, and the Ontological Argument," *Inquiry*, 12 (Winter 1969), 431–434.

Shaffer, J. "Existence, Predication, and the Ontological Argument," *Mind*, 71 (July 1962), 307–325.

Smart, H. "Anselm's Ontological Argument: Rationalistic or Apologetic?" *Review of Metaphysics*, 3 (December 1949), 161–166.

Sontag, F. "The Meaning of 'Argument' in Anselm's Ontological 'Proof,' " *Journal of Philosophy*, 64 (August 10, 1967), 459–486.

Stearns, J. B. "Anselm and the Two-Argument Hypothesis," *Monist*, 54 (April 1970), 221–233.

Tooley, M. "Does the Cosmological Argument Entail the Ontological Argument?" *Monist*, 54 (July 1970), 416–426.

Van Steenberghen, F. "Pour ou contre l'insense," *Revue philosophique de Louvain*, 66 (May 1968), 267–281.

Vanni Rovighi, S. "C'è un 'secondo argomento ontologico'?" SR, pp. 79–86.

Watt, E. D. "Feuer on Guilt and Logic," *Inquiry*, 12 (Winter 1969), 427–430.

Werner, C. G. "The Ontological Argument for the Existence of God," *Personalist*, 46 (April 1965), 269–283.

Wolz, H. G. "The Empirical Basis of Anselm's Arguments," *Philosophical Review*, 60 (July 1951), 341–361.

———. "The Function of Faith in the Ontological Argument," *Proceedings of the American Catholic Philosophical Association*, 25 (1951), 151–163.

Yolton, J. "Professor Malcolm on St. Anselm, Belief, and Existence," *Philosophy*, 36 (October 1961), 367–370.

Zabeeh, F. "Ontological Argument and How and Why Some Speak of God," *Philosophy and Phenomenological Research*, 22 (December 1961), 206–215.

———. "Category Mistake," *Philosophy and Phenomenological Research*, 23 (December, 1962), 277–278.

Other Topics

d'Alverny, M. "Achard de St. Victor, Evêque d'Avranches – Disciple de Saint Anselme," AA II, 217–222.

Anstey, C. R. "St. Anselm De-mythologized," *Theology*, 64 (1961), 17–23.

Armstrong, C. "St Anselm and His Critics: Further Reflection on the *Cur Deus Homo*," *Downside Review*, 86 (October 1968), 354–376.

Audet, Th. André. "Une source augustinienne de l'argument de saint Anselme" in *Etienne Gilson: Philosophe de la Chrétienté* (Rencontres 30. Ed. J. Maritain et al.). Paris, 1949, pp. 105–142.

Baron, R. "L'idée de liberté chez S. Anselme et Hugues de Saint-Victor," *Recherches de théologie ancienne et médiévale*, 32 (1965), 117–121.

Bouvier, M. "La pensée du Révérend Père Thomas-André Audet, O. P., sur la théologie du 'Cur Deus homo' de saint Anselme," SB, pp. 313–325.

Chibnall, Marjorie. "The Relations of Saint Anselm with the English Dependencies of the Abbey of Bec," SB, pp. 521–530.

Colish, Marcia. "St. Anselm: The Definition of the Word," Ch. 2 of her *Mirror of Language*. New Haven, Conn., 1968.

Congar, Y. "L'Église chez saint Anselme," SB, pp. 371–399.

Cousin, P. "Les relations de saint Anselme avec Cluny," SB, pp. 439–453.

Crouse, R. "The Augustinian Background of St. Anselm's Concept of *Justitia*," *Canadian Journal of Theology*, 4 (1958), 111–119.

ST. ANSELM

Daoust, J. "Le Janséniste Dom Gerberon, éditeur de saint Anselme (1675)," SB, pp. 531–540.
Delhaye, P. "Quelques aspects de la morale de saint Anselme," SB, pp. 400–422.
Dickinson, J. "Saint Anselm and the First Regular Canons in England," SB, pp. 541–546.
Dickson, Marie-Pascal. "Introduction à l'édition critique du coutumier du Bec," SB, pp. 599–632.
Fairweather, E. " 'Justitia Dei' as the 'Ratio' of the Incarnation," SB, pp. 327–335.
√ ——. "Truth, Justice and Moral Responsibility in the Thought of St. Anselm," HSD, pp. 385–391.
Fiske, A. "Saint Anselm and Friendship," *Studia Monastica*, 3 (1961), 259–290.
Flasch, K. "Zum Begriff der Wahrheit bei Anselm von Canterbury," *Philosophisches Jahrbuch*, 72 (1965), 322–352.
——. "Vernunft und Geschichte. Der Beitrag Johann Adam Möhlers zum philosophischen Verständnis Anselms von Canterbury," AA I, 165–194.
——. "Der philosophische Ansatz des Anselm von Canterbury im Monologion und sein Verhältnis zum augustinischen Neuplatonismus," AA II, 1–43.
Foreville, R. "L'école du Bec et le 'Studium' de Canterbury aux XIᵉ et XIIᵉ siècles," *Comité des travaux historiques et scientifiques* (Paris, 1955–56), pp. 357–374.
——. "L'ultime *ratio* de la morale politique de saint Anselme: *Rectitudo voluntatis propter se servata*," SB, pp. 423–438.
Fröhlich, W. "Die bischöflichen Kollegen des hl. Erzbischofs Anselm von Canterbury. Erster Teil: 1093–1097," AA I, 223–267.
——. "Die bischöflichen Kollegen des hl. Erzbischofs Anselm von Canterbury. Zweiter Teil: 1100–1109," AA II, 117–168.
Gagacz, M. "La 'Ratio Anselmi' en face du Problème des relations entre Métaphysique et Mystique," AA II, 169–185.
Glorieux, P. "Quelques aspects de la christologie de saint Anselme," SB, pp. 337–347.
Gross, J. "Die Natur- und Erbsündenlehre Anselms von Canterbury," *Zeitschrift für Religions- und Geistesgeschichte*, 13 (1961), 25–45.
Haenchen, E. "Anselm, Glaube und Vernunft," *Zeitschrift für Theologie und Kirche*, 48 (1951), 312–342.
Hayen, A. "Saint Anselme et saint Thomas. La vraie nature de la théologie et sa portée apostolique," SB, pp. 45–85.
Heinzmann, R. "Veritas humanae naturae. Ein Beitrag zur Anthropologie Anselms von Canterbury," *Wahrheit und Verkündigung* (M. Schmaus Festschrift). Munich, 1967, pp. 779–798.
Henry, D. P. "Numerically Definite Reasoning in the *Cur Deus Homo*," *Dominican Studies*, 6 (1953), 48–55.
——. "St. Anselm on the Varieties of 'Doing,' " *Theoria*, 19 (1953), 178–183.
——. "Why 'Grammaticus'?" *Archivum Latinitatis Medii Aevi*, 28 (1958), 165–180.
——. "Remarks on Saint Anselm's Treatment of Possibility," SB, pp. 19–22.
——. "The Scope of the Logic of Saint Anselm," HSD, pp. 377–383.
——. "St. Anselm's De 'Grammatico,' " *Philosophical Quarterly*, 10 (1960), 115–126.
——. "An Anselmian Regress," *Notre Dame Journal of Formal Logic*, 3 (1962), 193–198.
——. "St. Anselm on Scriptural Analysis," *Sophia*, 1 (October 1962), 8–15.
——. "St. Anselm and Paulus," *Law Quarterly Review*, 79 (1963), 30–31.
——. "St. Anselm's Nonsense," *Mind*, 72 (1963), 51–61.
——. "Was St. Anselm Really a Realist?" *Ratio*, 5 (1963), 181–189.
——. "St. Anselm and Nothingness," *Philosophical Quarterly*, 15 (1965), 243–246.
——. "Saint Anselm as a Logician," SR, pp. 13–17.

266

Bibliography

Hernandez, M. "Les caractères fondamentaux de la pensée de saint Anselme," SB, pp. 9–18.

Herrera, R. A. "St. Anselm: A Radical Empiricist?" AA II, 45–56.

Hödl, L. "Die ontologische Frage im frühscholastischen Eucharistietraktat Calix benedictionis," SR, pp. 87–110.

Hopkins, J., and H. W. Richardson. "On the Athanasian Creed," *Harvard Theological Review*, 60 (July 1967), 483–484.

Hufnagel, A. "Anselms Wahrheitsverständnis in der Deutung Alberts d. Gr.," SR, pp. 19–33.

Kohlenberger, H. "Zur Metaphorik des Visuellen bei Anselm von Canterbury," AA I, 11–37.

———. "Sola ratione – Teleologie – Rechtsmetaphorik," SR, pp. 35–55.

Lapierre, M. "Aquinas' Interpretation of Anselm's Definition of Truth," *Sciences Ecclésiastiques*, 18 (1966), 413–441.

Laporte, J. "Saint Anselme et l'ordre monastique," SB, pp. 455–476.

Leclercq, J. "Une doctrine de la vie monastique dans l'école du Bec," SB, pp. 477–488.

Lefèvre, Y. "Saint Anselme et l'enseignement systématique de la doctrine," SB, pp. 87–93.

Lewicki, J. "Saint Anselme et les doctrines des Cisterciens du XIIᵉ siècle," AA II, 209–216.

de Lubac, H. "Sur le chapitre XIVᵉ du 'Proslogion,' " SB, pp. 295–312.

McIntyre, J. "Premises and Conclusions in the System of St. Anselm's Theology," SB, pp. 95–101.

———. "Cur Deus-Homo: The Axis of the Argument," SR, pp. 111–118.

Mascall, E. "Faith and Reason: Anselm and Aquinas," *Journal of Theological Studies*, 14 (1963), 67–90.

Mason, J. "Saint Anselm's Relations with Laymen: Selected Letters," SB, pp. 547–560.

Mazzarella, P. "L'Esemplarismo in Anselmo d'Aosta e in Bonaventura de Bagnoregio," AA I, 145–164.

Merton, L. "Reflections on Some Recent Studies of St. Anselm," *Monastic Studies*, 3 (1965), 221–234.

Michaud-Quantin, P. "Notes sur le vocabulaire psychologique de saint Anselme," SB, pp. 23–30.

Nédoncelle, M. "La notion de personne dans l'oeuvre de saint Anselme," SB, pp. 31–43.

Ottaviano, C. "Le basi psichologiche dell'argomento ontologico in un importante brano dei 'Dicta Anselmi,' " SR, pp. 57–70.

Plagnieux, J. "Le binôme *justitia-potentia* dans la sotériologie augustinienne et anselmienne," SB, pp. 141–154.

Porcelloni, E. M. "Le Prolème de la dérivation du Monde à partir de Dieu chez Scot Erigène et chez saint Anselme," AA II, 195–208.

Pouchet, J.-M. "La componction de l'humilité et de la piété chez saint Anselme d'après ses 'orationes sive meditationes,' " SB, pp. 489–508.

Pouchet, J.-R. "Existe't'il une 'Synthese' Anselmienne?" AA I, 3–10.

Pucelle, J. "Note sur Kant et la preuve ontologique," AA II, 187–193.

Rassam, J. "Existence et vérité chez saint Anselme," *Archives de philosophie*, 24 (1961), 330–337.

Rondet, H. "Grace et péché: L'augustinisme de saint Anselme," SB, pp. 155–169.

Roques, R. "*Derisio, Simplicitas, Insipientia*: Remarques mineurs sur la terminologie de saint Anselme," *L'homme devant Dieu* (Mélanges offerts au père H. de Lubac), 57 (1963), 47–61.

———. "Structure et caractères de la prière Anselmienne," SR, pp. 119–187.

Salmon, P. "L'ascèse monastique dans les lettres de saint Anselme de Cantorbéry," SB, pp. 509–519.

Schmaus, M. "Die metaphysisch-psychologische Lehre über den Heiligen Geist im Monologion Anselms von Canterbury," SR, pp. 189–219.

Schmitt, A. "Die Englischen Märtyrer in den Zeiten der Glaubensspaltung. In ökumenischer Beurteilung," SR, pp. 221–230.

Schmitt, F. S. "Zur neuen Ausgabe der Gebete und Betrachtungen des hl. Anselm von Canterbury," *Miscellanea Giovanni Mercati*, 2 (1946), 158–178.

———. "Des hl. Anselm von Canterbury Gebet zum hl. Benedikt," *Studia Anselmiana*, 10, fasc. 18–19 (1947), 295–313.

———. "Die Chronologie der Briefe des hl. Anselm von Canterbury," *Revue Bénédictine*, 64 (1954), 176–207.

———. "Geschichte und Beurteilung der früheren Anselmausgaben," *Studien und Mitteilungen zur Geschichte des Benediktiner-Ordens*, 65 (1953–54), 90–115.

———. "Dante und Anselm von Canterbury. Zum Prolog der Divina Commedia," *Medioevo e Rinascimento*. (Studies in honor of Bruno Nardi.) Vol. 2, 653–666. Florence, 1955.

———. "Die echten und unechten Stücke der Korrespondenz des hl. Anselm von Canterbury," *Revue Bénédictine*, 65 (1955), 218–227.

———. "La *Meditatio redemptionis humanae* di S. Anselmo in relazione al *Cur Deus homo*," *Benedictina*, 9 (1955), 197–213.

———. "Die unter Anselm veranstaltete Ausgabe seiner Werke und Briefe: die Codices Bodley 271 und Lambeth 59," *Scriptorium*, 9 (1955), 64–75.

———. "Neue und alte Hildebrand-Anekdoten aus den Dicta Anselmi," *Studi Gregoriani*, 5 (1956), 1–18.

———. "Anselm von Canterbury," *Lexikon für Theologie und Kirche*, 1 (1957), 592–594.

———. "Anselm von Canterbury," *Religion in Geschichte und Gegenwart*, 1 (1957), 397–398.

———. "Die wissenschaftliche Methode in Anselms 'Cur Deus homo,'" SB, pp. 349–370.

———. "Zur neuen Gesamtausgabe der Werke des hl. Anselm von Canterbury: Erbe und Auftrag," *Benediktinische Monatsschrift*, 37 (1961), 116–128.

———. Review of R. W. Southern's *Saint Anselm and His Biographer*, in *Theologische Literaturzeitung*, 1965, pp. 199–201.

———. "St. Anselm of Canterbury," *New Catholic Encyclopedia*. Vol. I, 580–583. New York, 1967.

———. "Anselm und der (Neu-)Platonismus," AA I, 39–71.

Secret, B. "Saint Anselme, bourguignon d'Aoste," SB, pp. 561–570.

Séjourné, P. "Les trois aspects du péché dans le 'Cur Deus homo,'" *Revue des sciences religieuses*, 24 (1950), 5–27.

Söhngen, G. "Die Einheit der Theologie in Anselms Proslogion," in his *Einheit in der Theologie*. Munich, 1952, pp. 24–62.

———. "Rectitudo bei Anselm von Canterbury als Oberbegriff von Wahrheit und Gerechtigkeit," SR, pp. 71–77.

Southern, R. W. "St. Anselm and Gilbert Crispin, Abbot of Westminster," *Mediaeval and Renaissance Studies*, 3 (1954), 78–115.

———. "The Canterbury Forgeries," *English Historical Review*, 73 (1958), 193–226.

Spedalieri, F. "De intrinseca argumenti S. Anselmi vi et natura," *Gregorianum*, 29 (1948), 204–212.

Steiger, L. "Contexe syllogismos. Über die Kunst und Bedeutung der Topik bei Anselm," AA I, 107–143.

Thonnard, F.-J. "Caractères augustiniens de la méthode philosophique de saint Anselme," SB, pp. 171–183.

Bibliography

————. "La personne humaine dans l'Augustinisme médiéval (Saint Anselme et Saint Bonaventure)," HSD, pp. 163–172.

Tonini, Simone. "La Scrittura nelle Opere sistematiche di S. Anselmo," AA II, 57–116.

Trentman, J. "Extraordinary Language and Medieval Logic," *Dialogue*, 7 (September 1968), 286–291. (A review of D. P. Henry, *The Logic of Saint Anselm*.)

Urry, W. "Saint Anselm and His Cult at Canterbury," SB, pp. 571–593.

Urs von Balthasar, H. "La *concordantia Libertatis* chez saint Anselme," *L'homme devant Dieu*, 57 (1963), 29–45.

Vagaggini, C. "La hantise des rationes necessariae de saint Anselme dans la théologie des processions trinitaires de saint Thomas," SB, pp. 103–139.

Vanni Rovighi, S. "Notes sur l'influence de saint Anselme au XIIᵉ siècle," *Cahiers de civilisation médiévale*, 7–8 (1964–65), 423–437, 43–58.

————. "L'etica di S. Anselmo," AA I, 73–99.

Verweyen, H. "Faith Seeking Understanding: An Atheistic Interpretation," *New Scholasticism*, 44 (Summer 1970), 372–395.

Vignaux, P. "Structure et sens du *Monologion*," *Revue des sciences philosophiques et théologiques*, 31 (1947), 192–212.

————. "La méthode de saint Anselme dans le *Monologion* et le *Proslogion*," *Aquinas*, 8 (1965), 110–129.

Warnach, V. "Wort und Wirklichkeit bei Anselm von Canterbury," *Salzburger Jahrbuch für Philosophie*, 5–6 (1961–62), 157–176.

Widmer, G. "L'incognito de Dieu," *Archives de philosophie*, 32 (October–December 1969), 577–608.

Williams, C. "Saint Anselm and His Biographers," *Downside Review*, 82 (1964), 124–140. (Review of R. W. Southern, *St. Anselm and His Biographer*).

Zathey, J. "Gallus l'Anonyme, auteur de la Chronique de Pologne. Tentatives pour définir son milieu," SB, pp. 595–597.

WORKS BEFORE 1945

Books, Translations, and Monographs

Allers, R. *Anselm von Canterbury: Leben, Lehre, Werke*. Vienna, 1936. (Contains translations of the *Monologion* and *Proslogion*, among others. These have been reprinted and reintroduced by Allers under Anselm of Canterbury, *Monologion. Proslogion. Die Vernunft und das Dasein Gottes.* Cologne, 1966.)

Anselm of Canterbury. *St. Anselm's Book of Meditations and Prayers*. Trans. anonymously M. R., with a preface by Henry Edward. London, 1872.

————. *Cur Deus Homo. To Which Is Added a Selection from His Letters*. Trans. anonymously R. C. Edinburgh, 1909. (Ancient and Modern Library of Theological Literature.)

Baeumker, F. *Die Lehre Anselms von Canterbury über den Willen und seine Wahlfreiheit. (Beiträge zur Geschichte der Philosophie des Mittelalters*, 10). Münster, 1912.

Barth, K. *Fides quaerens intellectum*. Munich, 1931 (2nd ed., Zurich, 1958; 3rd ed., Darmstadt, 1966. English trans. I. W. Robertson, *Anselm: Fides Quaerens Intellectum*, London, 1960; reprinted Cleveland, 1962).

Castel, A., trans. *Méditations et prières de saint Anselme*. (Intro. A. Wilmart, "Le recueil des prières de saint Anselme," i–lxii.) Paris, 1923.

Combes, A. *Un inédit de saint Anselme? Le traité 'De unitate divinae essentiae et pluralitate creaturarum' d'après Jean de Ripa. (Études de philosophie médievale*, 34). Paris, 1944.

Daniels, A. *Quellenbeiträge und Untersuchungen zur Geschichte der Gottesbeweise im dreizehnten Jahrhundert, mit besonderer Berücksichtigung des Arguments im Proslogion des hl. Anselm* (*Beiträge zur Geschichte der Philosophie des Mittelalters*, 8/1–2). Münster, 1909.
Deane, S. N., trans. *St. Anselm: Basic Writings.* La Salle, Ill., 1962. (1st. ed., *St. Anselm. Proslogium; Monologium; an Appendix in Behalf of the Fool by Gaunilon; and Cur Deus Homo.* Chicago, 1903.) The translation here of the *Cur Deus Homo* is by J. G. Vose and is reprinted from *Bibliotheca Sacra*, 1854.
Domet de Vorges, E. *Saint Anselme.* Paris, 1901.
Druwé, E. *Libri Sancti Anselmi "Cur Deus Homo" prima forma inedita.* Rome, 1933.
Filliatre, C. *La philosophie de saint Anselme.* Paris, 1920.
Fischer, J. *Die Erkenntnislehre Anselms von Canterbury nach den Quellen dargestellt* (*Beiträge zur Geschichte der Philosophie des Mittelalters*, 10/3). Münster, 1911.
Funke, B. *Grundlagen und Voraussetzungen der Satisfaktionstheorie des hl. Anselm von Canterbury.* Münster, 1903.
Kolping, A. *Anselms Proslogion-Beweis der Existenz Gottes* (*Grenzfragen zwischen Theologie und Philosophie*, vol. 7). Bonn, 1939.
Koyré, A. *L'idée de Dieu dans la philosophie de st. Anselme.* Paris, 1923.
———. *Fides Quaerens Intellectum. Paris*, 1930. (A French translation of the *Proslogion, On Behalf of the Fool,* and *Reply to Gaunilo.*)
Lohmeyer, E. *Die Lehre vom Willen bei Anselm von Canterbury.* Leipzig, 1914.
McKeon, R., ed. *Selections from Medieval Philosophy*, Vol. 1. New York, 1929. (Contains a translation of *De Veritate.*) Reprinted in part in *Classics in Logic.* Ed. D. Runes. New York, 1962, pp. 28–40.
Maginnis, J. S. "Translations from Anselm," *Bibliotheca Sacra*, 8 (July 1851), 529–553. (A translation of the *Proslogion.*)
Prout, E. S., trans. *Cur Deus Homo? Why God Became Man?* London, n.d. (Christian Classics Series 1.)
de Rémusat, C. *Saint Anselme de Cantorbéry.* Paris, 1853.
Rousselot, X. *Études sur la philosophie dans le moyen-âge (première partie).* Paris, 1840.
Schmitt, F. S. *Ein neues unvollendetes Werk des hl. Anselm von Canterbury* (*Beiträge zur Geschichte der Philosophie und Theologie des Mittelalters*, 33/3). Münster, 1936.
Stanhope, G., trans. *Pious Breathings. Being the Meditations of St. Augustine, His Treatise of the Love of God, Soliloquies and Manual. To which Are Added, Select Contemplations from St. Anselm and St. Bernard.* London, 1708. 3rd edition. (Translations of *Meditatio Redemptionis Humanae*, pp. 289–303, *Meditatio ad Concitandum Timorem*, pp. 305–313.)
von den Steinen, W. *Vom Heiligen Geist des Mittelalters: Anselm von Canterbury, Bernhard von Clairvaux.* Breslau, 1926 (2nd ed., Darmstadt, 1968).
Stolz, A. *Anselm von Canterbury.* Munich, 1937. (Contains German translations of M, P, CDH, the three meditations, three prayers.)
Vose, J. G., trans. "Anselm's Doctrine of the Incarnation and Atonement. A Translation of the 'Cur Deus Homo,'" *Bibliotheca Sacra*, 11 (October 1854), 729–776; 12 (January 1855), 52–83. Reprinted in *St. Anselm: Basic Writings.* Ed. S. N. Deane.
Webb, C. C. J., ed. *The Devotions of Saint Anselm.* London, 1903. (Contains a translation of the *Proslogion*, pp. 3–53, the *Meditatio Redemptionis Humanae*, pp. 105–119, the *Meditatio ad Concitandum Timorem*, pp. 89–95.)
Welch, A. C. *Anselm and His Work.* Edinburgh, 1901.
Wilmart, A. *Auteurs spirituels et textes dévots du moyen âge latin.* Paris, 1932. The following chapters are of particular interest: "Une prière au saint patron attribuée

Bibliography

à saint Anselme," pp. 147–161; "Le recueil de prières adressé par saint Anselme à la comtesse Mathilde," pp. 162–172; "Les méditations réunies sous le nom de saint Anselme," pp. 173–201; "Prières à sainte Anne, à saint Michel, à saint Martin, censées de saint Anselme," pp. 202–216.

Articles

Adloch, B. "Rosecelin und Sanct Anselm," *Philosophisches Jahrbuch der Görres-Gesellschaft*, 20 (1907), 442–456.

Antweiler, A. "Anselmus von Canterbury, Monologion und Proslogion," *Scholastik*, 8 (1933), 551–560.

Bainvel, J. "La théologie de saint Anselme. Esprit, méthode et procédés, points de doctrine," *Revue de philosophie*, 15 (1909), 724–746.

———. "Anselme de Cantorbéry," *Dictionnaire de théologie catholique*. Vol. 1, 1327–60. Paris, 1923.

Balthasar, N. "La méthode en théodicée. Idéalisme anselmien et réalisme thomiste," *Annales de l'Institut Supérieur de Philosophie*. Vol. 1, 421–467. Louvain, 1912.

Baudry, L. "La prescience chez saint Anselme," *Archives d'histoire doctrinale et littéraire du moyen âge*, 15–17 (1940–42), 223–237.

Bayart, J. "The Concept of Mystery According to St. Anselm of Canterbury," *Recherches de théologie ancienne et médiévale*, 9 (1937), 125–166.

Becker, J. "Der Satz des hl. Anselm: *Credo, ut intelligam* in seiner Bedeutung und Tragweite," *Philosophisches Jahrbuch*, 19 (1906), 115–127, 312–326.

Betzendoerfer, W. "Glauben und Wissen bei Anselm von Canterbury," *Zeitschrift für Kirchengeschichte*, 48 (1929), 354–370.

Braga, G. "Il problema della libertà in S. Anselmo," *Sophia*, 3 (1935), 334–345.

Broad, C. D. "Arguments for the Existence of God," *Journal of Theological Studies*, 40 (1939), 16–30, 156–157.

Cappuyns, M. "L'argument de saint Anselme," *Recherches de théologie ancienne et médiévale*, 6 (1934), 313–330.

Choquette, Imelda. "Voluntas, Affectio and Potestas in the Liber De Voluntate of St. Anselm," *Mediaeval Studies*, 4 (1942), 61–81.

Davies, A. "The Problem of Truth and Existence as Treated by Anselm," *Proceedings of the Aristotelian Society*, 20 (1920), 167–190.

Domet de Vorges, E. "Le milieu philosophique à l'époque de st. Anselme," *Revue de philosophie*, 15 (1909), 605–617.

Dräseke, J. "Zur Frage nach dem Einfluss des Johannes Scottus Erigena," *Zeitschrift für wissenschaftliche Theologie*, 50 (1908), 323–347.

———. "Zu Anselms 'Monologion' und 'Proslogion,' " *Neue kirchliche Zeitschrift*, 11 (1900), 243–257.

———. "Sur la question des sources d'Anselme," *Revue de philosophie*, 15 (1909), 639–654.

Druwé, E. "La première rédaction du 'Cur Deus homo' de saint Anselme," *Revue d'histoire ecclésiastique*, 31 (1935), 501–540.

Dufourcq, A. "Saint Anselme: Son temps, son rôle," *Revue de philosophie*, 15 (1909), 593–604.

Dyroff, A. "Der ontologische Gottesbeweis des hl. Anselmus in der Scholastik," in *Probleme der Gotteserkenntnis (Veröffentlichungen des katholischen Institutes für Philosophie, Köln)*. Münster, 1928, pp. 79–115.

Folghera, J.-D. "La vérité définie par saint Anselme," *Revue Thomiste* 8 (1900), 414–426.

Geyer, B. "Zur Deutung von Anselms Cur deus homo," *Theologie und Glaube*, 34 (1942), 203–210.

Gilson, E. "Sens et nature de l'argument de saint Anselme," *Archives d'histoire doctrinale et littéraire du moyen âge*, 9 (1934), 5–51.

Haenchen, E. "Anselm und Barth," in *Wort und Geist* (Festgabe für Karl Heim). Berlin, 1934, pp. 181–205.

Hartshorne, C. "The Necessarily Existent," Ch. 9 of his *Man's Vision of God and the Logic of Theism.* Chicago, 1941.

———. "Formal Validity and Real Significance of the Ontological Argument," *Philosophical Review*, 53 (May 1944), 225–245.

Jacquin, A. "Les *rationes necessariae* de saint Anselme," in *Mélanges Mandonnet.* Vol. 2, 67–78. Paris, 1930.

Janssens, H. "Saint Thomas et saint Anselme," *Xenia Thomistica*, 3 (1925), 289–296.

Jelke, R. *"Fides Quaerens Intellectum," Theologisches Literaturblatt*, 60 (1939), 1–8.

Landgraf, A. "Der Gerechtigkeitsbegriff des hl. Anselm von Canterbury und seine Bedeutung für die Theologie der Frühscholastik," *Divus Thomas*, 5 (1927), 155–177.

Losacco, M. "La dialettica in Anselmo d'Aosta," *Sophia*, 1 (1933), 188–193.

Lottin, O. "Baptême et péché originel, de saint Anselme à saint Thomas d'Aquin," *Ephemerides Theologicae Lovanienses*, 19 (1942), 225–245.

Porée, A. "L'Ecole du Bec et saint Anselme," *Revue de philosophie*, 15 (1909), 618–638.

Rivière, J. "Contribution au 'Cur Deus homo' de saint Augustin," in *Miscellanea Agostiniana.* Vol. 2, 837–851. Rome, 1931.

———. "Un premier jet du 'Cur Deus homo'?" *Revue des sciences religieuses*, 14 (July 1934), 1–41.

———. "La question du 'Cur Deus homo,'" *Revue des sciences religieuses*, 16 (1936), 1–32.

———. "D'un singulier emprunt à saint Anselme chez Raoul de Laon," *Revue des sciences religieuses*, 16 (1936), 344–346.

———. "Saint Anselme logicien," *Revue des sciences religieuses*, 17 (1937), 306–315.

Ryle, G. "Mr. Collingwood and the Ontological Argument," *Mind*, 44 (April 1935), 137–151.

Schmitt, F. S. "Zur Ueberlieferung der Korrespondenz Anselms von Canterbury. Neue Briefe," *Revue Bénédictine*, 43 (1931), 224–238.

———. "Zur Chronologie der Werke des hl. Anselm von Canterbury," *Revue Bénédictine*, 44 (1932), 322–350.

———. "Der ontologische Gottesbeweis Anselms," *Theologische Revue*, 32 (1933), 217–223.

———. "Eine dreifache Gestalt der 'Epistola de Sacrificio azimi et fermentati' des hl. Anselm von Canterbury," *Revue Bénédictine*, 47 (1935), 216–225.

———. "Zur Entstehungsgeschichte von Anselms 'Cur Deus homo,'" *Theologische Revue*, 34 (1935), 217–224.

———. "Eine frühe Rezension des Werkes *de Concordia* des hl. Anselm von Canterbury," *Revue Bénédictine*, 48 (1936), 41–70.

———. "La lettre de saint Anselme au Pape Urbain II à l'occasion de la remise de son 'Cur Deus homo' (1098)," *Revue des sciences religieuses*, 16 (1936), 129–144.

———. "Ein weiterer Textzeuge für die I. Rezension von *de Concordia* des hl. Anselm," *Revue Bénédictine*, 48 (1936), 318–320.

———. "Zur Entstehungsgeschichte der handschriftlichen Sammlungen der Briefe des hl. Anselm von Canterbury," *Revue Bénédictine*, 48 (1936), 300–317.

———. "Les corrections de S. Anselme à son *Monologion*," *Revue Bénédictine*, 50 (1938), 194–205.

———. "Cinq recensions de l'*Epistola de Incarnatione Verbi* de S. Anselme de Cantorbéry," *Revue Bénédictine*, 51 (1939), 275–287.

Southern, R. W. "St. Anselm and His English Pupils," *Mediaeval and Renaissance Studies*, 1 (1941–43), 3–34.

Bibliography

Stolz, A. "Zur Theologie Anselms im Proslogion," *Catholica*, 2 (January 1933), 1–24.
———. " 'Vere esse' im Proslogion des hl. Anselm," *Scholastik*, 9 (1934), 400–409.
———. "Das *Proslogion* des hl. Anselm," *Revue Bénédictine*, 47 (1935), 331–347.
Thieme, K. "*Fides Quaerens Intellectum*," *Divus Thomas*, 22 (1944), 452–459.
Van der Plaas, P. "Des hl. Anselm 'Cur Deus Homo' auf dem Boden der jüdisch-christlichen Polemik des Mittelalters," *Divus Thomas*, 7–8 (1929–30), 446–467, 18–32.
Vergnes, J. "Les sources de l'argument de saint Anselme," *Revue des sciences religieuses*, 4 (1924), 576–579.
Weisweiler, H. "Das erste systematische Kompendium aus den Werken Anselms von Canterbury," *Revue Bénédictine*, 50 (1938), 206–221.
———. A review of *Ein neues unvollendetes Werk des hl. Anselm von Canterbury*. Ed. F. S. Schmitt, in *Scholastik*, 13 (1938), 103–105.
Wilmart, A. "Les éditions anciennes et modernes des prières de saint Anselme: Pages présentées à l'Académie des Inscriptions et Belles-Lettres," *Comptes rendus des séances de l'année 1923*, pp. 152–162.
———. "La prière à Notre-Dame et à saint Jean publiée sous le nom de saint Anselme," *La Vie spirituelle*, Supplément, 18 (1923), 165–192.
———. "Une prière inédite attribuée à saint Anselme," *Revue Bénédictine*, 35 (1923), 143–156.
———. "Le recueil des prières de saint Anselme," in *Méditations et prières de saint Anselme*. Trans. A. Castel. Paris, 1923, pp. i–lxii.
———. "Une prière ancienne à sainte Anne," *La Vie spirituelle*, Supplément, 11 (1924), 18–26.
———. "La tradition des prières de saint Anselme," *Revue Bénédictine*, 36 (1924), 52–71.
———. "La destinataire de la lettre de S. Anselme sur l'état et les voeux de religion," *Revue Bénédictine*, 38 (1926), 331–334.
———. "Les homélies attribuées à saint Anselme," *Archives d'histoire doctrinale et littéraire du moyen âge*, 2 (1927), 5–29.
———. "Les méditations VII et VIII attribuées à saint Anselme," *Revue d'ascétique et mystique*, 8 (1927), 249–282.
———. "Une lettre inédite de S. Anselme à une moniale inconstante," *Revue Bénédictine*, 40 (1928), 319–332.
———. "Prières à saint Michel et à saint Martin sous le nom de saint Anselme," *La Vie spirituelle*, Supplément, 21 (1929), 1–14.
———. "Les prières envoyées par saint Anselme à la comtesse Mathilde en 1104," *Revue Bénédictine*, 41 (1929), 35–45.
———. "Les propres corrections de saint Anselme dans sa grande prière à la Vierge Marie," *Recherches de théologie ancienne et médiévale*, 2 (1930), 189–204.
———. "Le premier ouvrage de saint Anselme contre le trithéisme de Roscelin," *Recherches de théologie ancienne et médiévale*, 3 (1931), 20–36.
———. "La tradition des lettres de S. Anselme: Lettres inédites de S. Anselme de ses correspondants," *Revue Bénédictine*, 43 (1931), 38–58.
———. "Textes attribués à saint Anselme et récemment édités," *Revue Bénédictine*, 48 (1936), 71–79.

OTHER RELEVANT WORKS

Altaner, B. "Augustinus und Athanasius," *Revue Bénédictine*, 59 (1949), 82–90.
Becker, G. *Catalogi Bibliothecarum Antiqui*. Bonn, 1885.
de Blic, J. "Le péché originel selon saint Augustin," *Recherches de science religieuse*, 16 (1926), 97–119.

Blumenkranz, B. "La *Disputatio Judei cum Christiano* de Gilbert Crispin, Abbé de Westminster," *Revue du moyen âge latin*, 4 (1948), 237–252.

Bourke, V. J. "Human Tendencies, Will and Freedom," HSD, pp. 71–84.

Chenu, M.-D. "Grammaire et théologie aux XIIe et XIIIe siècles," *Archives d'histoire doctrinale et littéraire du moyen âge* (1935), 7–28.

———. *La théologie au douzième siècle* (*Etudes de philosophie médiévale*, vol. 45). Paris, 1957.

Crouse, R. "Honorius Augustodunensis: *De Neocosmo*," Ph.D. dissertation. Harvard Divinity School, 1970.

Dodwell, C. R. *The Canterbury School of Illumination 1066–1200*. Cambridge, 1954.

Endres, J. "Lanfranks Verhältnis zur Dialektik," *Der Katholik*, 25 (1902), 215–231.

———. "Die Dialektiker und ihre Gegner im 11. Jahrhundert," *Philosophisches Jahrbuch*, 19 (1906), 20–33.

———. *Petrus Damiani und die weltliche Wissenschaft* (*Beiträge zur Geschichte der Philosophie des Mittelalters*, 8/3). Münster, 1910.

Geyer, B. "Die Stellung Abaelards in der Universalenfrage nach neuen handschriftlichen Texten," *Beiträge zur Geschichte der Philosophie des Mittelalters*. Münster, 1913, pp. 101–127.

de Ghellinck, J. "Dialectique et dogme aux Xe–XIIe siècles," *Beiträge zur Geschichte der Philosophie des Mittelalters*. Münster, 1913, pp. 79–99.

———. "Les bibliothèques médiévales," *Nouvelle Revue theologique* (January 1938), 1–20.

———. *Le mouvement théologique du XIIe siècle*. 2nd ed. Paris, 1948.

Gilson, E. "Descartes et saint Anselme," Ch. 4 of his *Etudes sur le rôle de la pensée médiévale dans la formation du système cartésien*. Paris, 1930.

Grabmann, M. *Die Geschichte der scholastischen Methode*. Freiburg, 1909.

Grunwald, G. *Geschichte der Gottesbeweise im Mittelalter bis zum Ausgang der Hochscholastik* (*Beiträge zur Geschichte der Philosophie des Mittelalters* 6/3). Münster, 1907.

Hayen, A. "Le Concil de Reims et l'erreur théologique de Gilbert de la Porrée," *Archives d'histoire doctrinale et littéraire du moyen âge*, 10–11 (1935–36), 32–102.

Hunt, R. "Studies on Priscian in the Eleventh and Twelfth Centuries," *Mediaeval and Renaissance Studies*, 1 (1941–43), 194–231; 2 (1950–54), 1–56.

Jalbert, G. *Nécessité et contingence chez s. Thomas d'Aquin*. Ottawa, 1961.

James, M. *The Ancient Libraries of Canterbury and Dover*. Cambridge, 1903.

Kneale, W. "Is Existence a Predicate?" *Proceedings of the Aristotelian Society*, Supplementary vol. 15 (1936), 154–174. Reprinted in *Readings in Philosophical Analysis*. Ed. H. Feigl and W. Sellars. New York, 1949, 29–43.

Knowles, D. *The Monastic Order in England*. Cambridge, 1949.

———. *The Evolution of Medieval Thought*. London, 1962.

Landgraf, A. *Einführung in die Geschichte der theologischen Literatur der Frühscholastik*. Regensburg, 1948.

Leff, G. *Medieval Thought: St. Augustine to Ockham*. Baltimore, 1958.

Liebeschütz, H. "Western Christian Thought from Boethius to Anselm," in *The Cambridge History of Later Greek and Early Medieval Philosophy*. Cambridge, 1967.

Lottin, O. "Les définitions du libre arbitre au douzième siècle," *Revue Thomiste*, 32 (1927), 104–120, 214–230.

———. "Le concept de justice chez les théologiens du moyen âge avant l'introduction d'Aristote," *Revue Thomiste*, 44 (1938), 511–521.

Maître, L. *Les écoles épiscopales et monastiques avant les universités (768–1180)*. Paris, 1924.

Manitius, M. *Philologisches aus alten Bibliothekskatalogen (bis 1300)*. Frankfurt am Main, 1892.

Bibliography

———. *Handschriften antiker Autoren in mittelalterlichen Bibliothekskatalogen.* Leipzig, 1935.

Mathon, G. "Jean Scot Érigène, Chalcidius et le problème de l'âme universelle," HSD, pp. 361–375.

Macdonald, A. *Lanfranc. A Study of His Life, Work and Writing.* Oxford, 1926.

Migne, J., ed. "Catalogus librorum Abbatiae Beccensis circa Saeculum Duodecimum," PL 150:770–782.

Moore, G. E. "Is Existence a Predicate?" *Proceedings of the Aristotelian Society,* Supplementary vol. 15 (1936), 175–188. Reprinted in *Logic and Language.* Ed. A. Flew. Oxford, 1959, pp. 82–94. 2nd series.

Muckle, J. "Greek Works Translated Directly into Latin before 1350," *Medieval Studies,* 4–5 (1942–43), 33–42, 102–114.

Nortier, Geneviève. *Les bibliothèques médiévales des abbayes bénédictines de Normandie.* Caen, 1966.

O'Donoghue, D. "The *Tertia Via* of St. Thomas," *Irish Theological Quarterly,* 20 (1953), 129–151.

Reiners, J. *Der Nominalismus in der Frühscholastik (Beiträge zur Geschichte der Philosophie des Mittelalters,* 8/5). Münster, 1910.

Rivière, J. " 'Justice' et 'droit' dans la langue de saint Augustin," *Bulletin de littérature ecclésiastique,* 33 (1932), 5–15.

Rohmer, J. *La finalité morale chez les théologiens de saint Augustin à Duns Scot.* Paris, 1939.

Schmitz, P. "Un manuscrit retrouvé de la 'Vita Anselmi' par Eadmer," *Revue Bénédictine,* 40 (1928), 225–234.

Schrimpf, G. *Die Axiomenschrift des Boethius (De Hebdomadibus) als philosophisches Lehrbuch des Mittelalters.* Leiden, 1966.

Southern, R. W. *The Making of the Middle Ages.* New Haven, 1953.

Sulowski, J. "Studies on Chalcidius. Anthropology, Influence and Importance," HSD, pp. 153–161.

Thompson, J. *The Medieval Library.* Chicago, 1939.

Van de Vyver, A. "Les étapes du développement philosophique du Haut Moyen Âge," *Revue belge de philologie et d'histoire,* 8 (1929), 425–452.

Waszink, J., ed. *Timaeus a Calcidio translatus commentarioque instructus* (vol. 4 of *Plato Latinus,* ed. R. Klibansky). London, 1962.

Index

Index

Abbey of St. Edmund's, 11

Abbo, 31n60

Ability: and uprightness, 23, 153, 154; and freedom, 27, 143–146, 149, 151, 153, 166–167; and use of will, 145–149, 149n51, 151, 157, 167; and inability, 154–155, 164, 215–217, 228, 240–241; as related to Christ, 164–165; of action, 165–166; of choice, 165–166; and possibility, 178–179; as aptitude for doing, 240–242

Adam: and God's gift of perseverance, 23, 166, 169, 182; creation of, 49, 122, 123, 125, 127, 139, 190; relation to world of nature, 122; relation to Divine Nature, 122; Fall of, 123, 124, 125, 140–141, 153, 155, 156, 167, 168, 185, 186; and freedom of will, 139, 140–141, 152; as rational and moral, 140; and freedom of choice, 144, 156–157, 167, 251; misused freedom, 168; sin of, 170, 172–173, 192, 204–205, 208–209; imperfect will of, 171; salvation of, 187, 191; and original sin, 192, 196, 201, 204–210 *passim*; as universal man, 201; mankind exists in seed of, 206–207, 210

Against a Sermon of the Arians, 198

Against Two Letters of the Pelagians: quoted, on Adam's freedom, 157n63

Alcuin, 34

Alexander, 37

Analytics, 28

Anselm of Canterbury: consistency of views, 3–5, 16, 56, 66; method and style of, 5–8, 16, 212, 246–253 *passim*; arguments *remoto Christo*, 6, 55, 63, 64, 69; use of Scripture, 6–7, 61, 66, 105, 111n34, 113–115, 211n38, 253; postulates truth of propositions, 7, 135–137; use of "ought," 7, 195–197; lack of reference to authorities, 8; in exile, 9, 11; as archbishop, 9, 11, 37; chronological orderings of works, 9–12; letters of, 10, 10n10; revision in works, 13–16; Augustine's influence on, 16, 17, 20, 21, 26, 29–30, 32, 35, 36, 95, 116, 159; in Augustinian tradition, 18, 64n59, 91, 120; and degrees-of-reality principle, 18, 59; theory of vision, 21, 31, 137–138; doctrine of exemplarism, 21, 132; extends Augustine's theology, 24; independence from Augustine, 28, 212; influenced by Aristotle, 28–29, 136, 159; influenced by Boethius, 29, 29n55, 30, 159; availability of Platonic translations to, 30–31, 32n63; not directly influenced by Plato, 31–32; and Pope Gregory I, 32–33; and Lanfranc, 33–34, 212; interest in Aristotelian logic, 34; and Fredegisus, 34, 175n97; possibly influenced by Cicero, 34, 34n74; not influenced by pseudo-Dionysius or Erigena, 35–36; influence on others, 36–37; as scholar, 37; recognizes noetic consequences of Fall, 52, 55; "rationalism" of, 52–53, 55, 66; and Damian, 53–54, 54n35; discerns man's need for grace, 60–61; and doctrine of universals, 68, 128–129, 210; and Aquinas, 87–89; distinguishes between Christian faith and Catholic faith, 102n23; and Western orthodoxy, 120; praises monastic virtues, 126; deals only minimally with question of immortality, 127; argues for unity and independent existence of Truth, 135–137; explanation of perceptual errors, 137–138; view of language, 138–139; views on necessity of Christ's death, 162–164, 167; notion of causation, 171, 173–174, 178–180, 183–185; uses *potestas* to express capability and possibility, 178; Christology and theory of atonement intersect in theology of, 202, 212; argues for virgin birth of Christ, 202, 204; death of, 212; as major systematic thinker, 212; informal logical arguments of, 246–253 *passim*; notion of impossibility, 248; use of a priori principles, 249; notion of "appropriateness," 249–250; method of division, 250–252, 252n8; argument from elimination, 251–252; use of *reductio ad absurdum*, 252. *See also titles of individual works*

Doctrine of Incarnation: ahistorical approach to, 6; argues *remoto Christo*, 6, 63; rational justification of, 40, 63, 190–192, 197–198; examination of, 65, 104–107; articulates necessity of, 65, 190–198, 202, 207, 211; rejects devil-ransom theory of atonement, 188–190, 212; notion of rendering satisfaction, 193; use of *assumptus homo*, 198–201, 212; rejects Nestorianism, 199; follows Quicumque, 200n18; notion of "appropriateness," 250

Doctrine of Original Sin: sustained argument regarding, 6; defines original sin as lack of justice, 7, 203, 204, 205, 211; question of salvation through good works, 205; transmission of through Adam's seed, 205–208, 210; defends justice of each man's guilt for, 208–211

Ontological Argument, 7, 19, 42n14, 62, 212: *reductio ad impossible* structure of, 71, 77; proves God's existence in understanding and in reality, 71–74, 76, 78, 81–82; problem of conceivability, 72, 77, 81–82, 89; use of *cogitare* and *intelligere*, 73–75, 75n10, 76; attempts to prove God as necessary being, 78–85; distinction between necessity and contingency, 78–80, 80n22, 81, 82, 89; problem of necessity and possibility, 82–88, 247

Doctrine of Freedom, 7: upholds freedom of fallen man, 141, 157; distinguishes deliberative choice from appetitive inclinations, 141; distinguishes actual from dispositional notions of willing, 142–143, 146; views freedom as ability to keep uprightness of will, 143–146, 149, 151, 167; difference between ability and use of will, 145–149, 149n51, 151, 157, 167; relation between motivation and free choice, 148–149, 149n51, 150; argues that no power can deprive human will of freedom, 151–152; paradox of freedom, 153–156, 167, 206n30; distinguishes will's ability-to-keep from inability-to-regain, 154–155; tendency to hypostatize uprightness, 155–156; views freedom as absence of necessity, 156n60; reconciles freedom with divine foreknowledge, 159–161, 167, 248; distinguishes between ability of action and ability of choice, 165–166; and condition of sin, 168; distinguishes between object and rule of will, 170–171

Doctrine of Evil, 7: denies God is cause of not-being, 173–174, 178, 182, 185; view of creation from nothingness, 175–182; equates "nothing" with "not something," 176–177, 179–181; examines meaning of "nothingness," 179–181, 182; notion of evil as nothing, 181–182; distinguishes between absolute and relative evil, 182–183

Compared with Augustine: on theory of truth, 20, 127; on theory of vision, 21; on doctrine of exemplarism, 21; on perceptual sense, 22; on God's gift of perseverance, 23; on divine foreknowledge and free will, 24–25; on begottenness, 25; on *filioque* doctrine, 26; on faith and reason, 26, 43n16; on devil-ransom theory, 27, 188–190; on freedom, 27; on goodness, 27, 133–135; on evil, 45, 172n94; on believing and understanding, 64n59; on God's trinity, 94, 95, 96–97, 120; on body-soul relationship, 124–126, 127; on participation, 129–133; on free choice, 156–158, 167; on cause of creation, 175–176; on what constitutes a nature, 201; on original sin, 203, 206

Doctrine of Trinity: and *filioque* doctrine, 26, 108, 111–120, 248–249; distinguishes between relational and substantial aspects of Godhead, 26,

Index

95–96, 101, 106, 120; attempts to show God's nature as triune, 90–91, 120; use of patterns of similarity, 91, 99, 107; use of *substantia* and *persona*, 92–93; deduction from purely a priori principles, 94; describes Father, Son, Holy Spirit as memory, understanding, love, 95; reconciles God's plurality and singularity, 95, 97; argues for eternal begottenness, 99; construal of "three persons in God," 100–108; demonstrates procession of Holy Spirit from Father and Son, 108–120, 248, 249; distinction between procession and begottenness, 110–111, 116, 118

Faith and Reason: relationship between, 26, 38–39, 55, 99; and imperative *crede ut intelligas*, 26, 43, 63, 64; method of arguing by reason alone, 38, 53, 60, 65, 69, 104–105; distinguishes between partial and full understanding, 39; discusses why Christian faith is true, 40; notion of *credo*, 42, 43, 58; presupposition that reason and revelation never conflict, 44–48; distinguishes necessary reasons from considerations of appropriateness, 48–49; use of *ratio*, 49–50, 57–58, 104; distinguishes between necessary and fitting reasons, 50n28, 52–53, 64, 65, 202–203, 250n5; against antidialecticians, 53–55; pursues rationale of revelation, 54, 58; acknowledges limitations of reason, 55, 61; use of reason interpreted by Barth and Stolz, 57–59, 61; envisions common ground between believer and nonbeliever, 61, 61n52

Doctrine of Man: argues God not responsible for man's depravity, 122, 167–169, 170–172, 182–184, 185; account of body-soul relationship, 123–126, 127; idea of soul's participation in God, 129–130; concern with truth dominates philosophy of man, 139; discusses man's Fall, 167–168, 170–172, 183–185; attack on "nominalism," 201

Anselm of Laon, 36
Anti-Pelagianism, 157, 167, 210
Antidialecticians, 53
Antirationalists, 54
Apollinarianism, 200n18

Appetites: of fallen man, 140; subordinate to man's will, 141

Aquinas, St. Thomas, 8, 52, 80: intellectual influence of, 37; Third Way of, 81, 81n23, 85, 88; problem of necessity and possibility, 85–87, 87n29, 87n31, 88–89; and Anselm, 87–89; and doctrine of Trinity, 120; view of source of being and not-being, 178–179

Arianism, 103n25, 200n18
Arians, 129
Aristotle, 30, 34, 75: influence of on Anselm, 28–29, 136, 159; and definition of necessary, 79, 81n23; notion of possibility, 86, 87n29; categories of, 98, 130–131, 223n; notion of contingent propositions, 136, 159; and syllogistic argumentation, 246
Athanasian Creed, 102n23, 104, 120. *See also* Quicumque
Atonement, 197, 211: devil-ransom theory of, 27, 188–190, 193n10, 212; and God's mercy, 198; intersects with Christology, 202, 212. *See also* Incarnation, Redemption, Salvation
Augustine, 5, 52, 62, 72n6, 174: compared with Anselm, 3, 4, 17–27, 43n16, 64n59, 94–97 *passim*, 120, 124–135 *passim*, 156–158, 167, 172n94, 175–176, 188–190, 201, 203, 206; Anselm's indebtedness to, 8, 29, 95; influence on Anselm, 16, 20, 21, 26, 29, 30, 32, 35, 36, 81, 159; as Anselm's major source, 16–20 *passim*, 32, 35, 36, 116; considered greatest of Church Fathers, 17; theory of vision, 21, 31; views on free will, 24–25, 27, 143, 156–157; and *filioque* doctrine, 26, 116, 116n41; devil-ransom theory of, 27, 188–190, 193n10; and Platonism, 30, 124, 171, 175; theory of contemplation, 32; intellectual influence of, 37; rendering of *credere*, 39; formulates imperative *crede ut intelligas*, 41n13; experience with Manicheism, 53; views on sin, 53n34, 126, 170; notion of degrees of reality, 59; and doctrine of Trinity, 91–93 *passim*, 95, 98, 101n22, 115n38, 120; compares Word of God with concepts in human mind, 94n9; substance and accidents in objects, 95–96, 97; and Aristotelian categories, 98, 130–131, 223n; attacks Sabellianism,

281

103n25; distinguishes original immortality from future immortality, 123; view of man, 124-126; use of *anima* to signify *homo*, 125n13; identifies truth with God, 128, 129; doctrine of universals, 129; idea of participation, 130-134; question of proving God's existence, 135; interpretation of man's Fall, 140, 171, 172; calls evil form of not-being, 172n94; distinguishes *ex ipso* from *de ipso*, 175-176; necessity of God-man, 195n13; use of *assumpsit hominem*, 198; theory of original sin, 203, 206, 206n31; use of hypothetical syllogism, 247. *See also* Anselm of Canterbury

Quoted: on degrees of reality, 17; on God as supreme good, 19; on God's existence, 19; on perceptual sense, 22; on faith and reason, 38n1, 43n16, 52n-31; on authority and reason, 39; on reason and revelation, 46n22; on unbelievers and understanding, 60n50; on necessity of God's existence, 78n19; on soul's functions, 93; on substance and relationships in God, 96; on ineffable nature of God, 107n29; on man as body and soul, 124-125; on original sin, 125n13; on immortality, 126n17; on essence of God, 131, 132; on loss of free choice through sin, 140; on free will, 151n54; on freedom and necessity, 156n61; on freedom and servitude, 156n62; on natural free choice, 157n65; on perseverence, 169; on deficient and efficient cause, 171; on evil as nothingness, 171n93

Baptism, infant, 4: and original sin, 7, 205n26; and grace, 158
Bari, Council of, 11, 120
Barth, Karl, 65: views on *Proslogion*, 57, 61; views on *Monologion*, 57, 67; interpretation of Anselm's use of reason, 57-58, 59; criticism of, 59, 60, 61; sees meditation as theology, 62n54; treatment of ontological argument, 70

Quoted: on Anselm's Christian audience, 56; on *Monologion*, 56-57; on Christology, 57n40; on *Cur Deus Homo*, 58n46
Bec, 8, 11n12, 36, 251: Anselm at, 4, 7, 9, 11, 12, 16, 36, 100, 212; library of, 30, 34n74, 36

Becker, J., 31, 31n62
Believing: precedes understanding, 38, 40, 41-42, 43, 44, 60, 64n59, 99-100, 107. *See also* Faith
Berenger, 33
Boethius, 32n63, 75, 169: tractates of, 8, 250; Anselm's acquaintance with works of, 8, 28; deals with freedom and divine foreknowledge, 25n46; mediates Aristotelian tradition, 28, 28n53, 159; influence of on Anselm, 29, 29n-55, 30, 159; and Plato, 30; criticizes Cicero, 34; distinguishes between two types of necessity, 79; and doctrine of Trinity, 91-92; definition of "person," 92; idea of participation, 132; remarks on divine foreknowledge, 159; and syllogistic argumentation, 246, 247; use of argument from elimination, 251

Quoted: on substance and relation, 97n15; on participation, 132n29; on substance, 250n6; on Christ as two natures in one person, 251
Books of Sentences, 17
Boso, 5, 6, 49: as Anselm's interlocutor in *Cur Deus Homo*, 40, 43, 54, 65, 165-166, 188; syllogistic objections to necessity of Christ's death, 162-163, 164; poses questions on necessity of incarnation, 190-195 *passim*, 198

Quoted: on necessity and fittingness, 50; on understanding God's mysteries, 51, 121; on believing and understanding, 63-64; on *sola ratione*, 65

Canterbury, 10, 37, 132, 212
Capua, 14, 16, 212
Catalogi Bibliothecarum Antiqui, 31
Categories, 28, 29
Catholic and Manichean Ways of Life, 19, 124-125
Causation, notion of, 168, 221-238 *passim*, 242-245, 247: deficient and efficient, 171-172; of not-being, 172-174, 178-180; of Satan's sinning, 183-185
Chalcedon, Council of, 200n18
Chalcidius, 30, 30n59, 31, 32n63
Charlesworth, M.: quoted, on Anselm's "world view," 35
Chartres, 30, 31
Christian Doctrine, 247
Christology, 188, 200n18: intersects with theory of atonement, 202, 212

Index

Church. *See* Greek Church, Latin (Roman) Church

Cicero, 32n63, 250: translation of *Timaeus*, 30; influences Anselm, 34, 34n74; criticized by Boethius, 34

City of God, 156n61, 171

Combes, A., 16n38: quoted, on Anselm's *De Unitate*, 36n80

Commentary on the Timaeus, 30n59

Confessions, 5, 19, 62

Consolation of Philosophy, 29, 30, 159

Council of Bari, 11, 120

Council of Chalcedon, 200n18

Council of Soissons, 100, 120

Crede ut intelligas, imperative of, 26, 41: formulated by Augustine, 41n13; addressed to Christians, 43, 64; spiritual nature of, 43; not hermeneutical rule, 43; compatibility of with *Christo remoto* principle, 63–64

Crispin, Gilbert, 36

Critique of Pure Reason, 70n4

Cur Deus Homo, 3, 9, 10, 11, 13, 40, 163, 164: and *De Conceptu*, 4, 12; in dialogue form, 5; subject of, 7–8, 14, 123; compared with *Libellus*, 14, 15–16; idea of men replacing fallen angels, 24, 33, 212; theory of atonement, 27; influences Crispin, 36; definitions from borrowed by Honorius, 37; method of arguing by reason alone used in, 38; discusses God's provision for salvation, 43; methodology of, 48; *Christo remoto* approach of, 55, 63, 64, 69; formula articulated in, 59; proceeds by necessary reasons, 63, 65; deals with incarnation, 63, 65, 187, 190–198 *passim*, 206; compared with *Proslogion*, 63, 64, 64n58; compared with *Monologion*, 63, 64, 64n58; *assumpsit hominem* standard phrase in, 198; interpretation of title of, 201; virgin birth discussed in, 202, 203; represents zenith of Anselm's theological achievement, 212

Quoted: on ability, 13n14; on possibility and necessity, 13n14; on reason and revelation, 47; on sin and salvation, 48–49; on necessary reasons, 49, 50; on understanding God's mysteries, 51; on God's will as rational, 54; on understanding, 60n50; on preceding and subsequent necessity, 79–80; on body-soul relationship, 124; on Christ

as two natures in one person, 187–188; on man's conquering Satan, 189; on devil-ransom theory, 189n6; on making satisfaction for sin, 191, 193; on forgiveness of sin, 194; on sin and salvation, 196, 249–250; on Christ as divine and human, 202n21; on contrary-to-fact conditions, 248

Damian, Peter, 53–54, 54n35

Darkness and Nothing, 34, 34n73

De beatitudine caelestis patriae, 37

De Caelo, 86

De Casu Diaboli, 4, 5, 8, 9, 10, 11, 12, 13, 14, 22, 24, 171: in dialogue form, 5; and Scriptural interpretation, 6; and *Darkness and Nothing*, 34; focus of, 170; treats meaning of "nothingness," 179; as attempt to defend perfection of creation, 185

Quoted: on good and evil, 19; on evil as not-being, 20; on gift of perseverance, 23, 168–169; on language and truth, 138; on Satan's free will, 149n51, 246–247; on Satan's evil will, 172; on God and not-being, 173, 174; on creation from nothingness, 177–178; on blindness as "not something," 181; on privation, 181n108; on relative and absolute evil, 182, 183

De Conceptu, 9, 10, 11, 14, 15: and *Cur Deus Homo*, 4, 12; makes use of biblical teaching, 7; *assumpsit hominem* standard phrase in, 198; argues for virgin birth, 202, 203, 204; discussion of original sin, 204–209 *passim*

Quoted: on original sin, 7, 125n12, 209, 252; on fallen condition of body and soul, 125; on virgin birth as sinless, 204; on human race as seminally present in Adam, 206; on Christ as truly man, 207

De Concordia, 3, 4, 10, 11, 14, 15, 160, 163, 170: subject of, 8; evidence of revisions in, 13; explicates definitions of will, 142

Quoted: on free will and divine foreknowledge, 25, 46; on faith, 39; on understanding as a grace, 44n17; on evil caused by God, 45; on Scripture and reason, 47; on baptism, 52n32; on eternal present, 98–99, 160; on willing, 142; on free choice and divine rewards, 149n51; on free choice without justice, 155; on uprightness of will, 156n59, 158, 158n69

De Grammatico, 11: in dialogue form, 5; exhibits interest in dialectic, 12; draws on *Categories*, 29; notion of participation, 132, 133; formal considerations of grammatical rules, 138, 139

De Incarnatione Verbi, 10, 118: overlaps with *De Conceptu*, 4; deals with doctrine of Trinity, 4, 90, 91, 99, 100–101, 101n22, 102–105; addressed to Pope Urban II, 9, 11, 100; differences in versions of, 13; first recension of, 15; compared with *Monologion*, 90, 99–100; theological nature of, 100; as extensive apology, 100; as refutation of Roscelin, 100, 120; no mention of Quicumque in, 104; concerned with substance/relation distinction, 106, 120; use of patterns of similarity, 107; deals with procession of Holy Spirit, 109; notion of eternity, 115; *assumpsit hominem* standard phrase in, 198; "nominalism" attacked in, 201

Quoted: on believing preceding understanding, 42, 44; on proof by necessary reasons, 63; on substances and persons in Trinity, 93; on incarnation of Christ, 106–107; on universals, 128; on *homo assumptus*, 199, 200–201, 200n19

De Libertate Arbitrii, 3, 8, 9, 11, 12, 13: in dialogue form, 5; and Scriptural interpretation, 6; argues man's freedom of will, 46, 143, 148, 250–251; describes fallen man, 157; use of method of division, 250

Quoted: on vision, 21; on difference between ability and use of will, 145; on free choice, 251–252

De morum qualitate per exemplorum coaptationem, 37

De Processione, 9, 10, 11, 251: overlaps with *De Incarnatione*, 4; deals with doctrine of Trinity, 4, 90, 95, 99, 108; makes use of biblical teaching, 6; compared with *Monologion*, 7, 90, 99–100; defense of *filioque* doctrine, 26, 110–118 *passim*, 120; theological nature of, 100; as extensive apology, 100; no mention of Quicumque in, 104; substance/relation distinction in, 106, 120; concerned with procession of Holy Spirit from Father and Son, 108;

110; notion of impossibility, 248; method of, 249

Quoted: on Holy Spirit's procession, 6–7, 7n6, 112, 113, 114–115, 118, 119, 248; on reason and Scripture, 48

De Sacrificio Azimi, 13, 14

De Unitate, 16n23, 36n80

De Veritate, 3, 9, 11, 12, 13, 130: in dialogue form, 5; and Scriptural interpretation, 6; influenced by *On Interpretation*, 29; Platonic influence in, 32n63; use of *oratio*, *enuntiatio*, and *propositio* in, 75, 135, 135n31; idea of participation, 133; use of method of division, 251

Quoted: on eternal nature of truth, 17; on perceptual sense, 21; on natural rightness of all things, 136; on truth as rightness, 137n33; on truth as eternal, 137n34; on theory of vision, 137–138

Death: as penalty of sin, 123, 125, 126, 127, 200n18, 206, 249; of Christ, 141, 161–164, 167, 185, 194–196, 211

Debate between Christian and Jew, 36

Degrees-of-reality principle: Anselm's adherence to, 18, 59; and good and evil, 19

Descartes, René, 89

Devil-ransom theory of atonement, 27, 193n10: rejected by Anselm, 188–190, 212

Dialectic, 33

Dialecticians, 41, 54

Dicta Anselmi, 37

Dionysius the Areopagite. *See* Pseudo-Dionysius

Divine Omnipotence, 53

Divine Predestination, 35–36

Draeseke, J.: quoted, on Anselm's knowledge of *Timaeus*, 32n63

Druwé, E., 14, 15

Eadmer: Anselm's biographer, 9, 11n12, 78; and chronological ordering of Anselm's works, 11–12; quoted, on Anselm's zest for conversation, 37

Eighty-Three Different Questions, 20, 128

Ein neues unvollendetes Werk des hl. Anselm von Canterbury, 12

Elucidarium, 37

Enchiridion, 20, 24, 25, 124

Erigena, John Scotus, 30: translates pseudo-Dionysius, 34; pantheistic

Index

metaphysics of, 35; no influence on Anselm, 35–36

Eternity, 29: identical with God's essence, 129; different from time, 160; and temporal distinctions, 161

Eutyches, 251

Eutychianism (Monophysitism), 202

Eve: taken from man, 49, 206; not of Adamic race, 207

Evil: nature of, 7; as form of not-being, 19–20, 172n94, 182; as injustice, 45, 182, 183; as disadvantage, 45, 46, 183; as nothingness, 53, 168, 171, 180, 181–182; and fallen man, 140; and man's freedom of choice, 143, 149, 157; as lesser good, 149; as privation, 181; source of, 184–185; antithesis of God, 186; Christ not subjected to, 204. See also Anselm of Canterbury

"Example of Meditating about the Rational Basis of Faith, An": original title of *Monologion*, 5, 38

Exemplarism, doctrine of, 20, 35, 178: and Anselm's theory of truth, 21; adopted by Augustine from Plotinus, 21; and idea of participation, 132

Expositions of the Psalms, 18

Faith: relationship with reason, 26, 38–39, 40–41, 55, 99, 212; Scripture's rendering of, 39; cannot exist without some conception, 39; distinction between act of and content of, 41n11; real meaning of lies in its contrast to knowledge, 43; as necessary condition for understanding, 44; understanding as reward of, 44; "necessities" of, 52; involves deliberate choice of will, 60; rational consistency of, 100; comes through grace, 158; uprightness of will restored through, 170. See also Anselm of Canterbury, Believing

"Faith Seeking Understanding": original title of *Proslogion*, 26

Fall of man: noetic consequences of, 52, 55; affected man's intellect, 66; God not responsible for, 122, 167–168, 170–172, 182–184, 185; resulted in bodily death, 123, 125, 127, 185, 186; distorted true human nature, 123, 125, 126, 127, 155, 168, 205; away from morality into immorality, 140; destroyed original harmony between reason, will, and appetites, 140; and freedom, 140–141,

156–157, 167, 210; affected man's will, 143, 153, 154–156, 186; and salvation, 153; result of evil willing, 171–172, 192; in relation to God's justice, 185; and bondage in sin, 188, 189, 209; dishonored God, 189

Filioque doctrine: defended by Anselm, 26, 108, 111–118, 248–249; raises controversy in Christian Church, 108, 115, 118–119, 120; and Scripture, 113–115, 118–119; history of, 120

Filliatre, C.: quoted, on Plato's influence on Anselm, 32n63

Flasch, K., 130n25

Fleury, 31n60, 31n62

Foreknowledge: and Satan's Fall, 24, 161n75, 246–247; of God, 24–25, 30, 141, 159–161; and freedom, 25, 46, 141, 159–161, 167, 248; and necessity, 158–161; and death of Christ, 162

Fredegisus, 34, 175n97

Free Choice, 21–22, 24, 26, 133, 135, 188

Free choice: and grace, 3, 156, 157–158; of fallen man, 140, 156, 156n62, 157, 167; and man's reason, 140; used interchangeably with free will, 141; as ability to keep uprightness of will, 143–146, 149, 151, 153; and sin, 144, 156, 158; and necessity, 148, 158–161; relation to motivation, 148–149, 149n51, 150; and divine rewards, 149; and preference of a lesser good, 150; useless without justice, 155; and divine foreknowledge, 158–161, 167; and death of Christ, 162; and Fall of man, 210; definition of, 250–251. See also Free will, Freedom

Free will: compatibility of with divine foreknowledge, 24–25, 159; and sin, 25, 140, 152–153, 166n86, 206n30; and fatalism, 46; truth in, 139; used interchangeably with free choice, 141; and man's will to consent and to desire, 141–142, 152; cannot be overcome by any power, 151–152; cannot will unwillingly, 151–152, 157; of unredeemed fallen man, 154–156; justice necessary to, 155; and death of Christ, 162–164. See also Free choice, Freedom, Will

Freedom, 3, 7: and God's foreknowledge, 25, 46, 141, 159–161, 167, 248; and ability, 27, 143–146, 149, 151, 153, 166–167; and uprightness of will, 27, 141, 143–146, 148, 149, 151–153, 156, 167,

250–251; threatened by man's Fall, 140–141; and justice, 140–141, 155; and will as instrument of, 143; and choice of lesser goods, 149–150; and salvation, 153; paradox of, 153–156, 167, 206n30; of fallen man, 156–157, 167; and necessity, 156n60, 159, 215–217, 247; and ability to sin, 157; of Jesus Christ, 162–166, 167; and condition of sin, 168, 184; universality of, 212. *See also* Free choice, Free will

Fulbert, 31: quoted, on library at Chartres, 31n61

Fulco, bishop of Beauvais, 100n21, 104

Gaunilo, 17, 62, 70, 78: Anselm's appeal to faith of, 57, 59–60; objections of, 72, 75, 76; dissatisfaction with soundness of ontological argument, 77; notion of "possibility," 83–85

Gilson, E.: quoted, on *Proslogion*, 62n54

God: proof of existence of, 7, 19, 52, 58–59, 62, 67, 69–79, 81–83, 88, 134; and truth, 17, 20, 128, 129, 130, 135; nature of, 18, 40, 51, 52, 53, 67, 76, 93, 98, 99, 102, 105, 108, 131, 132, 133, 134, 165n83, 168, 176, 185, 187, 192; as source of being, 19, 116–117, 128, 134, 168, 174–179, 181, 185, 186; and gift of perseverance, 23, 166, 168–170, 172, 182; foreknowledge of, 24–25, 30, 141, 159–161; and atonement, 27, 198, 211; conception of precedes belief in existence of, 39; belief in precedes knowledge of, 42, 43; understanding as gift from, 44; and creation of evil, 45–46, 167, 168, 171, 173–174, 178, 183–185; and man's free will, 46, 141, 143, 149, 151–152, 159–161; creation of Adam, 49, 122, 123, 125, 127, 139, 190; and history, 54; will of, 54–55, 162–163, 170; as necessary being, 78–81; as Trinity, 90–91, 95–97, 101–120 *passim*, 129, 199, 212; Christ begotten of, 99, 109, 111, 115, 116; Holy Spirit proceeds from, 108–114, 116–119, 248, 249; not responsible for man's Fall, 122, 167–168, 170–172, 182–184, 185; all universals within mind of, 128; soul's participation in, 129–130; freedom of, 143, 144, 157, 161, 164, 165n83, 166, 217; grace as gift from, 158, 167; as antithesis of nothing, 186; freed man from captivity, 188, 211; dishonored by man's disobedience, 190, 192–194,

196; honored through Christ's death, 194–195, 197, 211; *assumpsit hominem* in Christ, 199–201; and Christ's virgin birth, 202–204; moral fairness of, 210

Goodness: and existence, 19–20, 133–134; identical with God's essence 129, 131; mind's conceiving of, 130, 133–135; as universal source of all good, 133–134

Grace: relevance of to free choice, 3, 156, 157–158; and uprightness of will, 44n17, 158, 167; fallen man unaided by, 52; as precondition for theological understanding, 52–53, 60–61; as gift from God, 158, 167; as precondition for act of faith, 158; required for salvation, 167; necessary for Adam's meriting perseverance, 169–170

Greatness: identical with God's essence, 129, 131

Greek Church: and doctrine of Trinity, 91, 93; and *filioque* doctrine, 108–119, 120

Gregory of Nyssa, 120, 120n43

Gundulf, bishop of Rochester, 10

Happiness: coincides with justice, 122

Henry I of England, 37

Henry, D. P., 29n55, 34n74

Hildebert, bishop of Le Mans, 10, 10n10

Hilduin of Saint-Denis, 34

Historia Novorum, 11

Holy Spirit: proceeds from Father and Son, 26, 99, 107–120, 176, 248, 249; as love in Trinity, 95; relation to God in Trinity, 102, 107, 108–110; and Christ's incarnation, 106

Honorius Augustodunensis, 37

Hugh, archbishop of Lyons, 10

Human nature. *See* Man

Immortality: of soul, 52, 122, 123, 126–127; of body, 123, 126; original, 123; future, 123

Incarnation, 65, 121, 163, 250: and man's salvation, 3, 164, 186, 187, 189–194 *passim*, 211; seen by Christian as precious, 43; necessity of, 48, 63, 190–198 *passim*, 202, 207, 211; and question of God's will, 54; and doctrine of Trinity, 102–103, 104–105; only of Christ, 103, 106–107, 187, 190, 197–198, 200, 211; nature of man exalted in, 188; and devil-ransom theory, 189–190; and *assumpsit hominem*, 198–201; and virgin birth of

Index

Christ, 204. *See also* Anselm of Canterbury

Infant baptism, 4: and original sin, 7, 205n26; and grace, 158

Injustice: as absence of uprightness of will, 172, 181; as nothing, 172, 180, 182

Introduction, 250

Jesus Christ: begottenness of, 25, 99, 109, 111, 115, 116, 120, 176, 249; virgin birth of, 49, 53, 202–203, 204, 206; as two natures in one, 51, 124, 187, 199, 200–201, 202; as understanding in Trinity, 95; relation to God in Trinity, 96, 101–103, 106–110, 114; incarnation of, 103–107, 187, 190, 197–198, 200, 211; Holy Spirit proceeds from, 109–110, 112, 114–119, 248, 249; as God-man, 124, 194, 200–201; of same essence as God, 129; death of, 141, 161–164, 167, 185, 194–196, 211; and free will, 141, 162–166, 167; inability to sin, 165–166, 195; does not possess original sin, 192, 202, 203, 206; as man's salvation, 194–197, 198, 202, 210–211; not subjected to evil, 204

John the Monk, 116, 116n40

John of Ripa, 16n23

John Scotus Erigena. *See* Erigena, John Scotus

Joy: associated with understanding, 40, 57

Justice, 3: as uprightness of will, 32, 140n39, 155n58; and fallen man, 52, 140, 155, 167; coincides with happiness, 122; identical with God's essence, 129, 131; as a quality, 129, 130; as a priori concept, 133; and freedom, 140–141, 155; and redemption, 141; of Christ's death, 195, 211; deprivation of through original sin, 203, 204, 205; cannot be regained through good works, 205. *See also* Righteousness

Kant, Immanuel, 70, 70n4, 89

Koyré, A.: quoted, on Plato and Anselm, 32n63; on Lanfranc and Anselm, 33n67

Lanfranc, 4, 17, 33n67, 34n74: correspondence with Anselm, 10, 32, 132; suggests corrections in *Monologion*, 13; controversy with Berenger, 33; not profound influence on Anselm, 33n67; teacher of Anselm, 34, 212

Latin Church (Roman), 39, 212, 252:

creeds of, 47–48, 100, 106, 108, 120; and doctrine of Trinity, 91–93; and *filioque* doctrine, 108, 111, 113, 115, 118–119; efforts to crystallize theological doctrines, 117; and doctrine of salvation, 141

Leibniz, Gottfried Wilhelm, 70n4, 89

Libellus, 14–16

Literal Commentary on Genesis, 21

Lombard, Peter, 17

Lyons, 11

McIntyre, J., 55, 63: quoted, on necessity and fittingness, 49n52; on necessity of salvation, 191n9; on Anselm's view of atonement, 211n39

Malcolm, N.: quoted, on ontological argument, 42n14, 82; and ontological argument, 70, 81, 82; quoted, on necessity and possibility, 82–83; criticism of, 82–84; as thoroughly Anselmian, 83

Man (human nature): creation of, 122, 167, 168; reflects image of God, 122, 128, 139–140, 167, 168; effect of Fall on, 123, 125, 126, 127, 140, 143, 153, 154–156, 167–168, 185, 186, 188, 205; as soul and body, 123–127 *passim*, 185–186, 200n18; freedom of, 140–147, 149, 153–154, 157, 166, 210, 212; and irrational choice of lesser good, 150; cannot will unwillingly, 151–152; and salvation, 153, 167, 187, 190–198; as both servant and free, 153–155, 167, 189; inability of perfection without divine assistance, 158; ability to sin, 166; dishonored God through sin, 190, 192–194, 196; must make satisfaction for sin, 191–194, 196–197; in Christ, 200, 201–202; corrupted by original sin, 203, 204–206, 208–209; in seed of Adam, 206–207; as guilty in Adam, 210, 211. *See also* Anselm of Canterbury

Manicheism, 53, 172n94

Manitius, 31, 31n62

Mathilde, queen of England, 34n74

Meditation on Human Redemption (*Meditatio Redemptionis Humanae*), 11, 190: quoted, on redemption and repayment, 196

Memory: as part of soul's triad along with understanding and will, 93; as God, 95

Middle Ages, 20, 27, 28, 30n59, 32, 34, 250, 251

287

Monologion: deals with doctrine of Trinity, 4, 90–91, 92, 101, 106, 107, 108, 120; original title of, 5, 38; method of arguing by reason alone used in, 7, 38, 56, 62, 64n58; compared with *De Processione*, 7, 90, 99–100; evidence of revisions in, 13; indebtedness to Augustine apparent in, 17; "eternity" defined in, 29; doctrine of being, 31, 35, 176, 177; compared with *Proslogion*, 56, 62–63, 69; Barth's views on, 57, 67; Stolz's interpretation of, 58–59; compared with *Cur Deus Homo*, 63, 64, 64n58; Anselm's purpose in, 67–68, 99–100; compared with *De Incarnatione Verbi*, 90, 99–100; apologetical nature of, 100; concept of participation, 130, 132; compared with *On the Trinity*, 133; compared with *Reply to Gaunilo*, 133; proofs for existence of supremely excellent Nature, 134, 249; mentioned, *passim*

Quoted: on degrees of reality, 18, 77n16; on begottenness, 25–26; on the creating Essence, 35; on faith's certainty, 50n27; on God's ineffability, 51; on necessity and fittingness, 64–65; on developing proof of God's existence, 69; on relational and substantial aspects of Godhead, 95; on nature of man, 123; on soul's immortality, 126–127; on universals, 129n23; on creation, 176, 177

Monophysitism (Eutychianism), 202
Moral Obligation (De Officiis), 250
Moralia, 32, 33

Nature of the Good, 20, 175
Necessity: of incarnation, 48, 63, 190–198, 202, 207, 211; and fittingness, 48–51 *passim*, 53, 202–203; distinction beteen preceding and subsequent, 79, 162; and contingency, 79–80, 80n22, 81; and possibility, 83–89, 247; and free choice, 148, 158–161; and freedom, 156n60, 159, 215–217, 247; and God's foreknowledge, 158–161
Neo-Platonism, 30, 30n59, 36, 124, 171. *See also* Platonism
Nestorianism, 199
Nestorius, 199, 251
Nicene Creed, 48
Nicene-Constantinople Creed: and *fili-oque* doctrine, 108, 111, 112, 113, 118–119, 120
Nominalism, 201

Obedience: fosters experience of joy, 40; and understanding, 40, 44; owed to God by every human being, 192; and salvation, 249
Ockham, William of, 37
Omnipotence: identical with God's essence, 129
Omniscience: identical with God's essence, 129; unique to God, 161. *See also* Foreknowledge
On Cicero's Topics, 34
On the Gospel of John, 130
On Interpretation, 28, 159: influenced *De Veritate*, 29
On Old Age, 34n74
On the Trinity (Augustine's), 26, 27, 91, 95, 120, 129, 130, 188, 198: theory of vision advanced in, 31; compared with *Monologion*, 133; existence of Supreme Good taken for granted in, 134
On the Trinity (Richard of St. Victor's), 37
Ontological argument, 2, 171, 249: tribute to Anselm's brilliance, 19; shows belief in God's existence rationally justified, 42n14; subtlety of, 62, 77, 89; and God's nature, 67, 102; different versions of, 70, 71–78 *passim*; questions regarding, 70; and Kant, 70n4; *reductio ad impossible* structure of, 71, 77; proof of God's existence in the understanding and in reality, 71–74, 76, 78, 81–82; essential plausibility of, 76; distinction between necessity and contingency, 78–81, 82; notion of inconceivability, 81–82, 89; problem of necessity and possibility, 82–88, 247; and Aquinas's Third Way, 89; vigorous controversy over, 89. *See also* Anselm of Canterbury
Original sin, 4, 6, 191–192, 212: as unconditional, 7; as injustice, 7, 203, 204, 205, 211; of infants, 7, 205, 205n26, 206, 207–211; Christ free of, 192, 202, 203, 206; and Adam, 192, 196, 201, 204–210 *passim*; transmission of, 203, 204, 205–208, 210; associated with concupiscence of sexual act, 203, 205–206; corrupt human nature as effect of, 203, 204–206, 208–209; contrasted with personal sin,

Index

204–205; pertains equally to every man, 208–210. *See also* Anselm of Canterbury, Sin

Pantheism, 35, 130
Parmenides, 128
Paronymy, theory of, 7, 29
Paulus, 34, 34n74
Pelagianism, 210
Pelagians, 123, 141
Perseverance: gift of God, 23, 166, 168–170, 172, 182; and Adam, 23, 166, 169, 182; and Satan, 23, 168–169, 172, 182; and redeemed fallen man, 169–170
Person and the Two Natures, The, 91
Peter Lombard, 17
Philosophical Fragments, 12, 71n5: dialogue format of, 12n14; distinguishes meanings of causation, 173, 221–238, 242–245; distinguishes four different roles of "something," 179, 239–240; notion of ability and inability, 215–217, 228, 240–241; notion of possibility and impossibility, 215–217, 247; notion of freedom and necessity, 215–217, 247; use of "to do," 217–221, 229–230; distinguishes six modes of *velle*, 233–235
Plato, 126, 128: theory of Forms, 5; and Anselm, 6, 31–32; theory of vision, 21; availability of works in Middle Ages, 30–31, 32n63; and doctrine of being, 31, 175, 179; method of division, 250; argument from elimination, 251
Platonism, 31, 125n12, 126, 175. *See also* Neo-Platonism
Plotinus, 20, 21, 128, 175
Pope Gregory I, 32–33
Pope Urban II, 9, 10, 11, 100
Porphyry, 30n59, 250
Predestination and Free Choice, 37
Propositions: truth of, 7, 135–137; and contingency, 136, 159; natural rightness of, 136–137
Proslogion, 9, 10–11, 17, 58, 81: as meditation, 5, 62; argument of God's existence, 18, 19, 43, 59–62, 67, 70–75 *passim*, 76, 78, 89, 108, 134, 249; original title of, 26; *credo ut intelligam* perspective of, 26, 40, 42n14, 43, 55–56, 63; Stolz's interpretation of, 32–33, 33n65, 58–59; compared with *Monologion*, 56, 62–63, 69; Barth's views on, 57, 61; apologetical nature of, 59; compared with *Cur Deus Homo*, 63, 64, 64n58;

use of *cogitatur* and *intelligitur* in, 73–76; problem of incarnation, 198

Quoted: on believing and understanding, 38, 60; on reason's limitations, 51; on two senses of "thinking," 73; on God as only necessary being, 80; on Goodness as source of all good, 134

Pseudo-Dionysius: neo-Platonic treatises of, 34; no influence on Anselm, 35–36; listed at Chartres, 36n79

Questions, 33
Quicumque, 104, 106, 200n18. *See also* Athanasian Creed

Reason: and Scripture, 6, 7, 8, 38, 44–47, 99: relationship with faith, 26, 38–39, 40–41, 55, 99, 212; cannot comprehend full mystery of God, 45, 51, 53, 99, 120, 121; proves man's free will, 46; limited scope of, 48, 55; of natural man, 52, 140; limitations of in relation to revelation, 54, 61, 253; and question of God's will, 55; and man's freedom, 140; will subordinate to, 141; as faculty of soul, 142. *See also* Anselm of Canterbury, Understanding
Redemption: and notion of uprightness, 28; cannot be understood by unbeliever, 43; and justice, 141; and grace, 158; only through Christ, 187; through incarnation, 189–190; belongs only to man, 198. *See also* Atonement, Incarnation, Salvation
Rémusat, C. de, 32, 36: quoted, on doctrine of being, 31
Reply to Gaunilo: quoted, on believers and unbelievers, 41; on God's existence, 78, 87; compared with *Monologion*, 133
Reproof and Grace, 23, 32, 170
Republic, 251
Revelation: reason never conflicts with, 45; fallen man unaided by, 52; reason's limitation in relation to, 54, 61, 253; Anselm's deep commitment to, 55. *See also* Scripture
Rhetorica ad Herennium, 34n74
Richard of St. Victor's, 37
Righteousness: and fallen man, 52, 141, 153; and free choice, 149; salvation contingent on, 153; of God, 170. *See also* Justice

Rightness: and truth, 135, 137n33; in essence of all things, 136
Rivière, J., 15
Roman Catholic Church. See Latin Church
Rome, 212
Roscelin: Anselm's quarrel with over how to construe "three persons in God," 100–107; and tritheism, 102, 103, 108, 120; and Sabellianism, 103, 108
Rufus, William, 37

Sabellianism, 103, 103n25, 108
Sabellius, 103n25
St. Anselm. See Anselm of Canterbury
St. Augustine. See Augustine
St. Martin's, 34
St. Thomas Aquinas. See Aquinas, St. Thomas
Salvation: and divine incarnation, 3, 164, 186, 187, 189–190, 211; divine plan of as revealed in Scripture, 39, 210; through Christ, 43, 52, 164, 185, 190–198 passim, 202, 205, 206, 210–211, 250; cause of, 48–49; and question of man's freedom, 141, 153, 163; contingent upon restoration of original righteousness, 153; grace required for, 167; man's need for, 167; not through good works, 193, 205; and obedience, 249
Satan: and God's gift of perseverance, 23, 168–169, 172, 182; Fall of, 23, 167, 168, 171, 185, 186, 256; question of foreknowledge of Fall, 24, 161n75, 246–247; and freedom of choice, 144, 150, 152, 184, 251–252; sought to set will above God's, 170–171, 192; evil will of, 171–172, 182–184, 185; nature corrupted through sin, 172–173; dominion over fallen man, 188–189, 190, 250
Satisfaction: only rendered by Christ, 187, 194, 196–197; must be made for forgiveness of sins, 190–194, 196–197, 211; as repayment plus reparation, 193–194
Schmitt, F. S., 34, 36, 67, 130n25: chronological ordering of Anselm's works, 5n5, 9n9, 10, 12; quoted, on revisions in De Incarnatione Verbi, 13n15
Scripture, 93, 104, 164: and reason, 6, 7, 8, 38, 44–47, 55, 99; Anselm's use of, 6–7, 61, 66, 105, 111n34, 113–115, 211n38, 253; some truths impossible to understand, 39; supplemented by ra-

tional arguments, 41, 47; primary vehicle of divine revelation, 45; elucidated by philosophical distinctions, 46; as norm of truth, 47; as norm of reason, 54, 66; describes God in spatio-temporal categories, 98; and filioque doctrine, 113–115, 118–119; and theological language, 139. See also Revelation
Simultaneous incarnation, 103n25, 108. See also Sabellianism
Sin: and free will, 25, 140, 152–153, 166, 166n86, 206n30; woman as origin of, 48–49, 250; and conjugal act, 49; and fallen man, 52, 123, 125, 140, 153, 156, 188, 189; relationship with intellect, 53; death as consequence of, 123, 125, 126, 127, 200n18, 206, 249; punishment for, 126, 141; and free choice, 144, 156, 158; and Christ, 165–166; result of defection from uprightness, 168, 189; of Adam, 170, 172–173, 192, 204–205, 208–209; of Satan, 170–171, 172–173, 182–183, 185; resulted in corrupted nature, 172; as dishonor to God, 190, 192–193; making satisfaction for, 190–194, 196–197, 211; debt of canceled by Christ's death, 195–196; attributed only to rational will, 207–208. See also Original sin
Soissons, Council of, 100, 120
Soliloquies, 17
Sophist, 21, 250, 250n6
Soteriology, 212
Soul: immortality of, 52, 122, 123, 126–127; reflects Trinity, 93; relationship to body, 123–127, 185–186, 200n18; infected with carnal feelings as a result of Fall, 125; superior nature of, 125–126; participation of in God, 129–130; and perception, 137–138; will and reason as faculties of, 142, 143; and uprightness, 156; existence of sustained by God, 186
Southern, R. W., 8, 33: quoted, on recensions of De Incarnatione, 13n15; on reason in Anselm's theology, 47n23; on Anselm's doctrine of Trinity, 95n11
Spinoza, Baruch, 89
Spirit and the Letter, The, 23
Stoics, 246
Stolz, A.: quoted, on Pope Gregory I's influence on Anselm, 32, 33n65; interpretation of Proslogion, 32–33, 33n65, 58–59; views on Monologion, 58–59;

Index

criticism of, 61–62; sees contemplation as mystical, 62n54

Sulowski, J., 30, 31: quoted, on Chalcidius's commentary, 30n59

Summa Theologica, 8, 85–86

Supreme Being. *See* God

Systematic Theology, 9n8

Thompson, J., 31

Tillich, Paul, 9n8

Timaeus: theory of vision, 21, 31; Latin versions of, 30–31, 32n63; doctrine of being, 31, 175

Topics, 34

Trinity, doctrine of, 7: as put forth in *Monologion*, 4, 90–91, 92, 101, 106–108 *passim*, 120; of Latin Church, 91–93; of Greeks, 91, 93; notion of plurality in, 92, 95; and God's image of man, 93; reconciliation of unity and plurality in, 95, 97, 108; relational and substantial aspects of, 95–96; unchanging and nonaccidental relations in, 97; eternal indivisibility of, 97–99, 102, 115n38; cannot be fully comprehended by reason, 99, 120, 121; problem of "three persons in God," 100–108; and Christ's incarnation, 102–103, 104–105; and Holy Spirit's procession, 107, 108–120 *passim*; orthodoxy of, 120, 200n18. *See also* Anselm of Canterbury

Tritheism, 102, 103, 104, 108, 120

Truth, 3: eternal nature of, 17, 127–128, 135–137; in essence of all things, 20, 128, 136–137; theory of, 28; Aristotelian notion of as correspondence, 29; often transcends human reason, 51; Adam created in likeness of, 127; identical with God's essence, 129–130, 135; as rightness, 135, 137n33; of propositions, 135–137; man's relation to, 139

Understanding: follows believing, 38, 40, 41–42, 43, 44, 60, 64n59, 99–100, 107; partial and full, 39; associated with joy, 40, 57; pursuit of constitutes act of obedience, 40; and experience, 42–43; as a grace, 44, 44n17; as reward of faith, 44; through grace, 52–53, 60–61; regulated by Scripture, 55; God's existence in, 72–74, 76; as part of soul's

triad along with memory and will, 93; as Christ, 95. *See also* Reason

Universals, 68, 210: within mind of God, 128; accord with Supreme Truth, 128; and particulars, 129; and idea of participation, 129–134; example of Goodness as source of all good, 133–134

Uprightness: as gift of God, 23, 154, 158, 166, 167, 252; and Fall, 23, 168, 171–172, 183, 189; and freedom, 27, 141, 143–146, 148, 149, 151, 152–154, 167, 206n30, 250–251; justice as, 32, 140n39, 155n58; and grace, 44n17, 158, 167; both object and rule of will, 155, 167; lack of, 155–156; of Christ, 166; and perseverance, 169; restored through faith, 170; injustice as absence of, 172, 181

Virgin conception, 49, 163: and incarnation, 106, 204; and original sin, 202, 203, 204; necessary and fitting reasons for, 203

Vision, theory of, 7, 21, 31, 137–138

Vita Anselmi, 11, 37

Voluntarists, 55

Westminster, 36

Will: and commitment to faith, 60; in fallen man, 60, 140, 153, 154–156, 183; as part of soul's triad along with understanding and memory, 93; and truth, 139; appetites subordinate to, 141; subordinate to man's reason, 141; faculty of consent, 141–143; instrument of desire, 141–143; use of, 142–143, 145–149, 151, 157, 167; freedom of, 143–145, 149, 151–155; uprightness of, 143–146, 148, 149, 151, 152, 153–157, 167, 169, 170; and ability, 145–149, 149n51, 151, 157, 167; acts of not unwilling, 151–152, 157; not free without justice, 155; object and rule of, 155, 167, 170–171; and perseverance, 169; as evil, 171–172, 182–185. *See also* Anselm of Canterbury, Free will

Wilmart, A., 36

Wisdom, 130

Wolff, Christian, 70n4

Zeno of Elea, 89